ARTFUL HISTORY

NEW DIRECTIONS IN NARRATIVE HISTORY

JOHN DEMOS AND AARON SACHS, SERIES EDITORS

The New Directions in Narrative History series includes original works of creative nonfiction across the many fields of history and related disciplines. Based on new research, the books in this series offer significant scholarly contributions while also embracing stylistic innovation as well as the classic techniques of storytelling. The works of the New Directions in Narrative History series, intended for the broadest general readership, speak to deeply human concerns about the past, present, and future of our world and its people.

ARTFUL HISTORY

A PRACTICAL ANTHOLOGY

EDITED AND INTRODUCED BY

Aaron Sachs and John Demos

Yale UNIVERSITY PRESS   NEW HAVEN AND LONDON

Yale University Press books may be purchased in quantity
for educational, business, or promotional use.
For information, please e-mail sales.press@yale.edu
(U.S. office) or sales@yaleup.co.uk (U.K. office).

Set in Scala type by Newgen North America.
Printed in the United States of America.

ISBN 978-0-300-23990-4 (paperback : alk. paper)
Library of Congress Control Number: 2019941032
A catalogue record for this book is available from the
British Library.

This paper meets the requirements of
ANSI/NISO Z39.48-1992 (Permanence of Paper).

10 9 8 7 6 5 4 3 2 1

For our teachers and our students

CONTENTS

ACKNOWLEDGMENTS

It's been a rare pleasure to work on this book together over the last several years. What could be better than editorial meetings at Fenway Park? We've often shaken our heads at how long this project was taking, but perhaps we're guilty of not wanting to let it go.

We're grateful, first, to Chris Rogers, now retired from Yale University Press, for helping us launch the New Directions in Narrative History series, and for pushing us to pursue this anthology. It's a shame that he's a Yankees fan, but we eventually got over that. His replacement at the Press, Adina Berk, is the person who ultimately made it possible for us to publish this book in our series, and she'll always have our deepest appreciation.

The authors of the selections also deserve our thanks: they've provided us with the most sustaining kind of intellectual and artistic inspiration.

And many other people inspired and helped us along the way. Thank you all. A couple of dozen colleagues offered suggestions on which selections to include. Several graduate students and faculty members collaborated with us to create a vibrant community in the Writing History and Historians Are Writers workshops, at Yale and Cornell respectively. A few people invited us to their home universities or other institutions to give talks and engage in lively, challenging conversations about the art of scholarly writing. And numerous friends have traveled with us down the circuitous paths toward artfulness, serving as boon companions, reading their work out loud to us, recommending books, and generally bolstering our determination to insist on history as literature.

In gratitude,
A.S. & J.D.
First-base Line
Fenway Park

INTRODUCTION

Can history be literature? The question comes up frequently in our circles. As historians, we tend to answer empirically: the evidence (work through the ages by Herodotus, Edward Gibbon, Francis Parkman, W.E.B. Du Bois) points to "yes." We can even propose the long nineteenth century in Europe and the United States as a time when almost everyone considered history a literary pursuit.

But maybe you'll think we're dodging the broader question: *should* history be literature? When we came of age professionally (John is eighty-one, Aaron forty-nine), that wasn't a germane question for the majority of our teachers and peers. It seemed that many of them, though certainly not all, were invested in a more scientific conception of modern scholarship; they probably would have described the nineteenth century as overly "romantic."

In the past few years, many more historians have been embracing the goal of literary elegance, even as they retain their commitment to rigorous scholarship. At the same time, though, the profession is still focused far more on research than on writing, and students pursuing a Ph.D. in history are almost guaranteed not to encounter a writing course during their time in the trenches. Which means that we can simultaneously assert the clear need for this anthology and claim that it is arriving on a new wave of enthusiasm for seeing history as the branch of literature that it deserves to be.

We think of artfulness as literature's basic requirement. This anthology, then, aims to demonstrate what artful history might look like, as concretely as possible, though not definitively. Perhaps our deepest conviction about artfulness is that it embodies indirection, suggestion, and illumination, rather than didactic, schematic, authoritative explanation. Careful scholars can certainly claim some sort of authority based on their research, but why would authority or any of the other goals of scholarship require any particular style or discourse? Nonfiction writers should have access to just as many literary techniques as fiction writers; some of the tricks of our trade should arise from a sense of *craft*. We shouldn't be stuck with the now-classic academic templates emphasizing straightforward, declarative argumentation. Those templates tend to lull readers into passivity. The magic of artfulness is that it activates the senses and the imagination: artful writing can be not only instructive but also moving. And it also tends to nudge readers away from reductive conclusions and toward complexity and contradiction, toward what the historian John Clive once called the "spell that lingers in the memory and is conducive not just to reading, but to rereading."

Added together, the components of this book, pieces published in the past forty years, should create a snapshot of how artful historians have responded to the solidifying of history as a social science in the 1970s. Quantification was all the rage back then, and young historians were encouraged to think of themselves not as artists or writers or even humanists but primarily as researchers who simply needed to find the most effective way of presenting their data and findings. Importantly, when the cultural or "linguistic" turn occurred in historical scholarship in the late 1980s and early '90s, the dominant mode of historical writing still shied away from any kind of artfulness. Tables and graphs were sometimes replaced by philosophical jargon and postmodernist theory, but young historians were still being trained to think of themselves as having more in common with scientists and other technical experts than with novelists or poets or painters.

Throughout our careers, though, both of us have been grateful for voices in the historical profession that sought to keep history in the humanities and arts. Many of these critics couched their alternative vision in terms of narrative, in contrast to the social scientists who favored data analysis and the cultural historians who suspected all storytelling of certain kinds of elision and distortion. Yet it was also in this same period that "creative nonfiction" was born, and so scholars interested in the writing of history did not limit themselves to straight narratives but rather explored a full range of formal possibilities, drawing inspiration from all kinds of artistic and imaginative work. The bulk of our selections come from the twenty-first century, when creative nonfiction could be said to be flourishing in the American market. Most of our authors are academic historians, but a few have pursued history writing outside the academy, or via other scholarly disciplines.

What we have always returned to are attempts to make history writing eloquent, moving, and memorable in the mode of ambitious essayists. *Artful History* compiles some of the most compelling efforts along these lines, in the realms of both practice and theory. It does not attempt to track any clear change over the past four decades, or claim to be comprehensive. (We wouldn't complain if the words "definitive" and "comprehensive" were banned from scholarly writing.) Our book merely argues that in this era some scholars and writers have consistently asserted the possibility of writing artful history, and they (and others) have practiced what they preached. Sometimes their efforts were judged exceptional; sometimes they were hardly noticed; and sometimes they were dismissed as not sufficiently scholarly or rigorous. Regardless, for us, they prove the great potential of approaching the writing of history as a literary art.

That potential is not *just* about making history compelling to an audience broader than those with an inherent interest in the subject matter, but the audience question is a big one for us. A good writer should be able to make any historical treatise seem like it's raising the most important questions in the world. Certainly, more people would love and follow scholarly history if it were written more artfully. Academic historians sometimes claim that "popular" history is popular because it is "dumbed down" and because it tends to offer comforting, self-congratulatory narratives, and that is true in some cases. But complex and challenging books have also achieved acclaim among nonexperts—in large part through artfulness. Reading a work whose form matches and enriches its substance is a deeply satisfying experience, no matter what it's about. This volume does not argue that historians ought to shape their works according to their idea of what a broad commercial audience desires; rather, we're suggesting that our colleagues might usefully spend as much time thinking about what will make their work seem significant on a deep, human level as they spend thinking about what will make it seem acceptable to the foremost experts in their field. Artfulness is a great enhancer of relevance.

Different selections in the book suggest the power of different aspects of artfulness. Some pieces make subtle use of dramatic tension; some develop a metaphor over several paragraphs; some veer between close-ups and contextual step-backs. In many cases, the storytelling is exquisite, and the voice full of resonance. A couple of our selections are overtly experimental or even strange. Some authors we've included make a point of using the first person much more intensely and extensively than most historians. Others use modulations of rhythm and tone to allow us suddenly to enter a scene or see inside a character or understand a key argument. These writers know what works.

Most historians haven't studied these kinds of techniques, but we believe that they will recognize the potential of artful history when they read it. We've tried to put this book together in a spirit of collective effort and encouragement, hoping that it will intrigue all writers of history, from professors and students to genealogists and essayists. Through our own personal and professional contacts, we know of groups of historians banding together to discuss creative writing in New York City, Chicago, Los Angeles, and Boston, not to mention on college campuses from Providence, Rhode Island, to Athens, Georgia, to Eugene, Oregon. This book is for all of you, and we hope that it will help you expand the conversation. With luck, it will be published by May 2020, when a radical underground organization in Ithaca, New York, called Historians Are Writers (or HAW!) will be holding its 11th Annual History Slam—like a poetry slam, but with history, and no actual slamming, just pieces of creative writing that the authors read out loud. Why not hold one in your community?

This book has two straightforward sections. First comes "Practice: Examples of Artful History"; and then "Theory: Making the Case for Artful History." The first section contains twelve pieces—the kinds of eloquent essays we would hope to encounter at a History Slam. The second section contains five short manifestos, including one by Aaron (previously published) and a brand-new one by John (a "minifesto," he insists). Though our priority was to offer practical examples of artfulness, we also wanted to acknowledge the need for each generation to make the argument that artfulness remains worthwhile. All of the selections have been arranged in chronological order in each section. Each one is introduced by a headnote—a form of writing that you've probably never associated with artfulness. Indeed, burdened by memories of all the hopelessly clunky and didactic headnotes that were foisted on us starting in about seventh grade, we came very close to demurring and letting our selected essays stand on their own. We did not want to risk over-explaining. In the end, though, we took on the headnotes as a writing challenge, and drew inspiration from the quirky, terse, almost oracular examples penned by John D'Agata in the three essay anthologies he has edited over the past several years. We hope you'll find ours stimulating.

Our overriding criterion for inclusion in this anthology was, unsurprisingly, artfulness. At the same time, we're keenly aware that there is only *some* accounting for taste; recognizing artfulness is by no means a science. Moreover, there is a politics to writing artfully, especially within the academy, where creative prose tends to make the research seem more suspect. Without doubt, the two of us both had an easier path in choosing to aim for artfulness, being white and male and having the backing of certain kinds of institutions.

Accordingly, some readers might like to have seen exactly half of our selections written by women, or a higher percentage written by people of color. We weren't comfortable instituting specific quotas, but we did take gender and race into consideration. To claim a race-blind or gender-blind selection process would be merely an expression of privilege. Anyway, maybe the key point is that we would like to see the goal of artfulness become equally available to absolutely everyone who takes an interest in it, and we concluded that being as true as possible to our own conception of artfulness was the best way of nurturing an inclusive conversation.

In parallel fashion, we took note of what parts of the world our selections studied, and we aimed for a wide range, but geography, like race and gender, was never going to be our primary consideration. So rather than make sure we had something about Oceania, we insisted on including a couple of pieces that feature humor. Rather than reach for an example from ancient Greece, we chose a piece that shifts dramatically between seventeenth-century Holland and the United States in the twentieth century. And while we also considered and included a range of historical sub-fields (social, cultural, religious), we did not think it worthwhile to sample all of them in equal measure. We apologize if, for instance, you came to this volume specifically seeking an artful bit of labor history. In our minds, any kind of history can be artfully executed, but it may also be true that some sub-fields are a tougher sell than others.

Of course, many other pieces of historical writing came very close to being included. (One of them had to be cut at the last minute because we were not granted permission to reprint it.) We considered dozens of worthy possibilities, many of them generously suggested by our friends and colleagues. We're grateful to have gotten to read all those compelling histories, and we're sorry that we had to leave so many on the editing room floor. And we're also sorry if we've bored some of you with all of these apologies and caveats.

Just one last observation. Though we want desperately to help historians think of themselves as writers, the real urgency of this project arose from our experience as teachers. In our graduate seminars on the writing of history, we've met many young academics who *already* think of themselves as writers but become frustrated by the professional pressures that tend to transform their characters and themes into data and arguments. Our hope is to create more space for those kinds of scholars, who see artfulness as an integral part of their practice—at least potentially. They need the support of their advisers, and they need evidence that, in our era, history can be literature. We know that some graduate mentors focus almost exclusively on passing along a mastery of the relevant scholarship and methodology. For us, though, the more funda-mental goal has always been to help students find a voice—sometimes just by getting out of their way, and sometimes by offering them the best models of artfulness we can find.

And for one of us—the one sneaking this sentence into the Introduction—the other has himself been the best model, and mentor, imaginable.

ARTFUL HISTORY

PART I
PRACTICE: EXAMPLES OF ARTFUL HISTORY

Jonathan Spence

From *The Death of Woman Wang* (1978)

How often have you encountered a dream sequence in a work of history? One could argue that the whole of *The Death of Woman Wang* is a kind of projection, a series of speculations about the dim contours of life in a remote region of seventeenth-century China, based on scanty evidence. But at least a historian like Spence can know that the woman at the center of his book did in fact commit adultery, whereas he could not possibly know what she was dreaming about just before her husband strangled her. Still: couldn't it be worthwhile to explore her inner life rather than leaving it utterly blank? Wouldn't it make sense to examine fiction and poetry and other cultural texts of the right time and place to see what ideas and images and anxieties seemed to be haunting the local people? Doesn't it take acts of imagination to try to understand anything about what it felt like to live at a different time? It is not enough to know that adultery was illegal and that an adulterous woman and her lover could be punished with death. It is not enough to know that women had very little power within the institution of marriage. It would not be enough even if we had documents in which individuals explained explicitly why they had committed adultery, despite the risk. There is always something more to try to understand, behind the documents, behind the words. The artfulness of speculation involves a graceful acknowledgment of uncertainty and a bold willingness to imagine.

～

But what of the women of T'an-ch'eng with no recourse to magic or to money? What of the woman called Wang who married a man called Jen?

We do not know exactly when they married, though it must have been some time in the late 1660s, nor do we know their personal names. We do not even know how Jen could afford a wife, since there were many fewer women than men available in T'an-ch'eng due to a combination of factors: female infanticide, the lower levels of food supplied to girls, the presence always of several women in the homes of wealthier men. Jen might not have had to pay any cash, or even furnish the customary presents to get woman Wang as his wife, for she seems to have been an orphan—or at least to have had no surviving relatives living nearby—and since Jen's own father was a widower of seventy, she might have been brought in as a young girl to help with the household chores and married to Jen when she was old enough, as was often done with young girls in the country.

What we do know about the couple is this: By early 1671 they were married and living in a small village outside the market town of Kuei-ch'ang, eight miles southwest of T'an-ch'eng city. They were poor, and Jen made his living as a hired laborer on other people's land. They had a one-room house that contained a cooking pot, a lamp, a woven sleeping mat, and a straw mattress. We know too that for six months after the marriage woman Wang had lived with her husband and her seventy-year-old father-in-law, but that the old man finally moved to another house a mile away because he got on so badly with her. And we know that woman Wang was left alone much of the day; that she had bound feet; that she had no children, though there was a little girl living in a house next door who called her "Auntie"; that her house fronted onto a small wood; and that at some time, for some reason, as the year 1671 advanced, she ran away.

She ran away with another man, though we do not know his name, nor where the two of them intended to go. We can see from the map that they had three initial choices: they could move southwest and cross the border into P'ei; they could walk eight miles northeast to the county city of T'an-ch'eng and from there follow the post road, either south to Hung-hua fou and into Kiangsu, or north to I-chou and on into central Shantung; or they could walk eight miles northwest to Ma-t'ou, and from Ma-t'ou head west on the road that led to Chang-ch'eng market and on into T'eng and Tsou counties. Whichever route they chose, unless they could afford carriers or a cart, they would have to move slowly on account of woman Wang's bound feet.

P'ei would not have been a bad choice if they wanted to avoid pursuit. The way there was hilly, but the countryside had for years supported bandits and fugitives who had played the change of provincial jurisdiction to their advantage. One could even travel part of the way by light boat down the River I in summer and autumn when the water level was high and the authorities in P'ei were unlikely to worry about one more fugitive couple. P'ei had been struck by catastrophes as serious as those in T'an-ch'eng—famine, locusts, and war, cycles of drought and flood. P'ei had also suffered from the earthquake of 1668, though less than T'an-ch'eng, but since P'ei was on the Yellow River, flood was a potential catastrophe, which it never was in T'an-ch'eng, with its smaller tributary rivers; and a month after the earthquake high winds and swollen water levels tearing at the banks had broken the land, and much of the city of P'ei fell beneath the waves. Only one or two hundred families escaped, and in the period when T'an-ch'eng slowly began to recover, in P'ei the population dropped by another third.

T'an-ch'eng city was in some ways an obvious goal, but the disadvantages were also obvious. As the site of the magistrate's yamen and the center of county administration, security was tighter than anywhere else. Regulations that remained only on paper elsewhere in the county were enforced here: there were regular patrols outside the city and checkpoints on the roads nearby. Travelers could be stopped for questioning and made to explain their reasons for wanting to enter the city, even refused entrance unless they had relatives living there. The inns were notorious for their dishonesty: many were run by dishonest owners who lured the unwary with displays of cheap food and wine; but once the country folk had registered, the bills began to climb, and outsiders and hangers-on charged items on their accounts. If the guests tried to move to other lodgings they found it impossible, since the innkeepers hired goons to threaten the owners of other places to which they might go. Even if the innkeepers were honest, those within the city walls were expected to keep a daily register of all travelers who lodged there, whether individuals or groups; they also had to note their origins and destinations, the goods they might have for sale, their mules or carts, their weapons if they had them. Armed horsemen without luggage or goods were forbidden to hire grooms or to stay in town overnight. Even lone foot travelers, whether armed or not, could be moved on if they had no baggage and no one in the city to vouch for them. No walking around in the city was permitted after nightfall, though during the hottest summer months the people whose homes had no halls or courtyards were allowed to have their doors ajar and sit on the stoops to enjoy the evening coolness. But the wooden gates that led from the alleys out to the main streets were closed and guarded at nightfall, and only those seeking emergency help from a doctor or midwife were allowed to pass—and then only if they had a regulation "night travel permit," duly authenticated, and if their residence and identity had been checked.

Certainly Ma-t'ou market would seem a more attractive choice for a couple seeking to hide out. Despite its size it had few garrison troops and no senior officials in residence. It had been attacked twice by bandits, in 1641 and 1648, but regained prosperity rapidly—as we can tell by a number of indices. Its major market days on the third and eighth day of every ten-day cycle, and the lesser market days on the fifth and tenth, dictated the market cycle of the surrounding areas. It was the only town with significant trade being moved by both road and water, trade that was worth taxing. It had a sizable urban working population, strong trade guilds, more temples than the other towns, more gardens, larger religious festivals. It was the only town in the county that supported a family of well-known physicians.

The couple needed somewhere to hide, for by the mere act of running away from her husband, woman Wang had become a criminal in the eyes of the law. Only if a wife was severely hurt or mutilated by her husband, or if she was forced by him to commit sexual acts with others, was she free to leave him. An example of a husband who by his actions put himself beyond the pale of the married relationship was furnished in Ning-yang, northwest of T'an-ch'eng (and also in Yen prefecture), in a case that was cited by jurists in the K'ang-hsi reign: a husband who sold his wife off as a prostitute and subsequently, having been forced by the magistrate to take her back, connived at her adultery with their lodging-house keeper, was considered to have "severed the bonds of marriage." But barring acts of this nature by the husband, the woman who ran away was classified as a fugitive and subject to a punishment of one hundred blows. All those who helped her or sheltered her—unless they could prove total ignorance of her fugitive status—could be subject to punishment in the same way as those who harbored fugitives or the wives and daughters of military deserters.

The act of adultery, furthermore, made both woman Wang and her paramour liable to serious punishment. The *Legal Code* stipulated that those having illegal intercourse by mutual consent were to be punished with eighty blows; if the woman was married, with ninety blows; if they intrigued to meet away from the woman's house, with one hundred blows, whether the woman was married or not. The man and the woman who had illegal intercourse, by mutual consent or after intriguing to meet away from the woman's house, received identical punishment. If the woman gave birth to a child after the illegal intercourse, the natural father met the expenses of raising it. The husband could sell off his adulterous wife or keep her, as he chose; but if he sold her in marriage to the adulterer, then both the husband and the adulterer were punished with eighty blows, the woman had to be divorced and returned to her family, and the price originally paid for her was forfeited to the government.

The punishment could be more serious than this, however, since the husband was considered justified in killing either his wife or the adulterer or both if he caught them in the act and slew them while in his initial rage. As in the case of killing to revenge a parent, the husband had to act swiftly, and in 1646 a rider had been added to the law, presumably to prevent vendettas or extended pursuit in the desire for revenge, stating that the husband was not justified in killing either of the adulterers if they merely were dallying before committing the sexual act, or if they had committed adultery but surrendered to him on their own, or "if he caught them in a place other than that where the adultery was committed." Thus by leaving Jen's house without being caught, woman Wang and her lover became legally more secure.

Not that life on the road can have been particularly secure, even if it was lively. The list of people technically under the supervision of the "Inspector of Humble Professions"—whose office like so much else in T'an-ch'eng had been burned down in the 1640s and not yet rebuilt—included such wandering specialists as fortunetellers, diviners, physiognomists and graphologists, jugglers, conjurers, actors, jesters and street wrestlers, storytellers and itinerant Buddhist and Taoist priests, woman dentists and midwives, the chiefs of the beggar groups, pipers, drummers, flute players, firecracker makers, tea sellers, and chair bearers. Huang Liu-hung's own reports often mentioned grooms, yamen runners, couriers and clerks from the post stations, the staffs of the state-managed hostels, and crowds of peddlers so poor and so numerous— their stalls under matting sheds in rows on the streets—that Huang gave up all attempts to tax them. Besides these there were refugees, fugitives from justice, and army deserters. Despite the regulations, such people could often find work, since farmers valued them as a source of cheap labor and asked no questions, while restaurant and lodging-house keepers would give them food and shelter if they could pay; making a living was more important than following the exact letter of the registration laws.

Indeed, there seems to have been a virtual fugitive subculture with its own rules and its own exploitations, inevitably involving the law-abiding civilian population because of the strict laws against harboring fugitives and the rigors of mutual responsibility under the *pao-chia* registration system. We see something of the fugitives' world from a case reported in T'an-ch'eng where a fugitive was used to harass an enemy in a private commercial feud. The police clerk Wei accused the innkeeper Shih Wen-yü of hiring a fugitive for three hundred cash a month to work at his inn on the very steps of the T'an-ch'eng magistrate's yamen. Wei attempted to have Shih imprisoned on this charge; investigation showed, however, that the story was a trumped-up one (though the fugitive was real enough), fabricated by Wei so that he would not have to pay for the hundred or more cups of wine he had drunk on credit in Shih's inn over the previous year. Wei had blackmailed the fugitive into making the false charge. In such cases it was not so much that the fugitive's testimony had to be believed, but rather that his presence had to be disproved, which was not always easy; on this occasion Shih was luckily proved innocent, since the magistrate held an informal police line-up at which the fugitive could not distinguish Shih from a neighboring bean-curd seller. Other cases show that soldiers also harassed the innocent through a fairly subtle confidence game: Soldier A, pretending to be a fugitive, would go into a moored boat or some isolated village; other soldiers would then come and "arrest" him, pretending to be police runners, harassing the locals for harboring a fugitive, and robbing them as they left. Or perhaps they would briefly build up an identity in some village as hired hands and then, when all were drunk together one evening, cut themselves up, tear their own clothes, and claim they had been "robbed" in order to get hush money from the local villagers; if suspicions began to be aroused, one of their friends would come claiming to be a superior officer from the fugitive unit, and would reclaim them. At times it might be the ferrymen themselves running the rackets and claiming far more than the stipulated rate of one copper coin a person and two coppers per mule: demanding extra money in rain or snow or late at night, extra to allow a coffin on their boat, or holding passengers to ransom when out in the middle of the stream. While ashore the ferry guard might levy his own "taxes" and confiscate the goods of those who refused to pay, or fondle the women and make them pay to be released.

If it was hard for the two of them on the run, it must have been a nightmare for woman Wang after her lover abandoned her a short time later and left her alone on the road. The society of T'an-ch'eng did not supply many jobs for women, even if they were regarded as reputable: a few became midwives or diviners; some who were trusted and well known locally served as marriage go-betweens and as guarantors who would take responsibility for the women prisoners in the local jail. A few jobs were available in the orphanages and the homes for the totally indigent and the old, where women were employed as nurses, as children's companions, or as watchmen, as well as houseworkers to clean up and do laundry. For such work they would get their keep and an allowance of three hundred copper cash a month, or else a flat wage of six taels a year—roughly equivalent to the wages of men in the poorer positions in the local yamen. Those women who had the resources for a loom could spin and sell the product, but that was usually work done in one's own home, and woman Wang now had no home. If they were at the right place at the right time, they might get a job as a maid in one of the larger households. There was a slight chance of becoming a worker in a Taoist or Buddhist convent. Otherwise the main employment must have been in the gambling houses, teahouses, and brothels of T'an-ch'eng, of Ma-t'ou market, of Hung-hua post station, even—according to Huang Liu-hung—in quite isolated rural villages, where local gentry set up brothels just as in the urban centers, giving protection to the women and taking a percentage of their money in return.

Woman Wang chose none of these alternatives, nor did she continue her flight alone. What she did was head back to her original home in Kuei-ch'ang; but when she got near the house she was too frightened to confront her husband Jen.

Near her village stood a Taoist temple to the Three Forces—the heavens, the waters, and the earth—forces that could bring happiness (heaven), remission of sins (water), and protection from evil (earth). Here she was given shelter by the sole resident of the temple, a Taoist priest; and here a former neighbor of hers, Kao, came to offer incense one day in November 1671 and caught a glimpse of her in one of the side rooms of the temple.

"You are in charge of a temple to the gods," he shouted to the priest. "What do you mean by keeping women in here?"

"She's the wife of a man called Jen in the village," the priest replied. "I heard that she ran off with someone, and Jen went out looking for her to get her back. But she didn't dare return home and took shelter here. Because she is one of our villagers, it would not have been good to just send her away."

While they were still talking about her, Jen himself came into the temple, having learned that woman Wang had returned and was hiding there. "A fine kind of priest you are," he shouted angrily. "My wife hides out in your temple and you don't even tell me about it."

"She's the wife from your house," countered Kao. "Why should she end up at the temple? You don't even know that, and now you want the priest to explain it to you?"

Even angrier, Jen shouted, "Oh, so in that case it must be you who hid her out here in the temple," and at this insult Kao hit him twice in the face. Jen swore at him and left, leaving his wife where she was.

This sudden outburst of rage between the two men may have been because of some long pent-up grievance—they were neighbors, Kao was comparatively well off, with a covered porch to his house and a wife named Ts'ao whom Jen also seems to have disliked. But Kao should not have hit Jen, however severe the insult; the *Legal Code* was strict about this and drew distinctions about fights of this kind with such minute attention to detail that they were clearly regarded as a major problem. Any person striking another with a hand or foot was to be punished with twenty blows if he caused no wound, with thirty blows if he caused a wound; any person striking another with an object of any kind would receive thirty blows if no wound was caused, forty if there was a wound—a wound being defined by discoloration or swelling in the place struck, as well as by bleeding. Tearing out more than one inch of hair was punished with fifty blows, striking another so as to cause internal bleeding with eighty blows; eighty blows too for throwing ordure at the head of another, and a hundred blows for stuffing ordure into his mouth or nose, for breaking a tooth or bone, or injuring the eyes. (In cases where permanent injury was caused, the offender forfeited half his property to pay the support of the injured party.)

Jen now had a real grievance against Kao, one that would fester for months, but he did not press any charges against him—presumably the situation was too humiliating to air any more publicly. Yet the incident had been awkward enough for both Kao and the priest, and they decided it would be wiser to make woman Wang leave the temple, though they hesitated to send her back to her husband right away. Instead they took her to her father-in-law and explained what had taken place. The father-in-law gave the two men tea. "There's nothing at all that I can do about this bitch," said he, and called a fellow to take woman Wang back to his son's house.

The priest said that Jen had been "out looking" for woman Wang; but however strong Jen's desire might have been to have his wife back—whether because he missed her or because he was planning vengeance against her—he was not in fact entitled to keep her, because of the crime of flight and adultery she had committed. The law was complicated on this point. It did state clearly that a husband could divorce a wife on one of seven grounds: inability to bear sons, lascivious behavior, failure to serve her in-laws properly, talking too much, having a thievish nature, being overjealous, and suffering from serious illness. (Divorce by mutual consent was also permitted under the law.) If the wife did not want the divorce, the husband was not allowed to divorce her if one of these three factors applied: the wife had mourned her husband's parents for three years; the husband had risen from poverty to riches during the time of his marriage; the wife had no family of her own to go to. Since woman Wang did not have a family living that she could return to, the law seemed at first glance to show that she should stay with Jen despite her infidelity; but a substatute added in the Ming stated specifically that the three exemptions from divorce did not apply if the woman had been adulterous. Since another clause of the *Legal Code* also stipulated that a husband would be beaten with eighty blows if he refused to send away his wife after she had committed an act for which she should have been divorced, it appears that technically Jen could have been punished for taking her back. But in fact nobody in the county administration took any action, nor did Jen follow any of the legal channels open to him. He did not start divorce proceedings. He did not arrange to sell woman Wang. He did not report her bad conduct to the local headman, so that her shame would be aired publicly, as he was entitled to do. Instead, he bought a new woven sleeping mat to lay upon the straw that served as their bed.

The two of them lived together again, in their house outside Kuei-ch'ang market, through the last months of 1671 and into January 1672. They would have been cold, for the mean temperature in Shantung during January was in the twenties, and the houses of the poor were frail: the walls were of beaten earth, mud bricks, or kaoliang stalks; the few wooden supports were unshaped branches, often thin and crooked; roofs were thatched thinly with straw and reeds and were not true proof against either wind or rain. If there was fuel available, it was used primarily for cooking, and the warmth from the cooking fire was fed under the raised brick sleeping platform through a system of flues; this sleeping platform was covered with a layer of straw. In Jen's house it was here that he placed the new mat he bought for woman Wang's return.

On an evening toward the end of January 1672, the two of them sat at home. Jen had told woman Wang to mend his jacket, and she was darning it by the light of a lamp. Outside it was snowing. The neighbors could see the light of the lamp shining from their house, and later they heard the two of them quarreling. The neighbors could hear the anger in the voices, though they could not make out the words. They were still listening when the lamp went out.

Woman Wang took off her outer jacket and trousers and her heavy shoes. She drew, over her bound feet, a pair of worn bed shoes, with soft soles of red cotton. Her jacket was blue, her thinner under-trousers were white. She lay in these clothes on the mat in the straw, and Jen waited while she fell asleep.

~

In the world it is winter, but it is warm here. There are lotuses in bloom on the green waters of the winter lake, their scent reaches her on the wind, there are people trying to pick them, but the plants drift away as the boats approach. She sees the winter mountains covered in flowers. The room is dazzlingly bright, a path of white stones leads to the door, red petals are scattered over the white stones, a single branch of blossom pokes through the window.

The branch stretches out over the table, the leaves are far apart, but the blossoms are pressed thickly together, they are not yet opened, they are like the wings of a butterfly, like the wings of a damp butterfly, moistened and hanging down; the stems that hold them to the branch are fine as hairs.

She can see how beautiful she is, the lines are gone from her face, her hands are smooth as a girl's, not rough from work. Her brows are dark and perfectly arched, her teeth are white and perfectly spaced, she practices her smile and the teeth just appear, she checks the corners of the lips and the corners of the eyes.

The sleeping place is covered with furs thick as palm fronds, they are deep and soft, the coverlet is filled with shreds of cotton and powdered incense, the chamber is filled with its fragrance. The man is handsome but he looks ill, his face is bathed with tears. She rubs his temples, she brushes the dust from his clothes, she wipes the tears from his eyes; she can feel on his body the weals from his beatings and she rubs them gently with her fingers.

She unfastens the belt of his robe and slips her hand inside, she massages him lightly with her fists, but he cannot move from pain, there is a tumor growing out of his chest, it is as big as a bowl and gnarled like the growth at the foot of a tree. She slips a golden bracelet off her wrist and presses it down upon the tumor, the flesh rises around the outside of the bracelet, but the center of the tumor rises up through the metal, she draws a knife with a fine blade from her robe and slices it gently around the bracelet's edge. The dark blood gushes out onto the bed and matting, she takes a red pill from her mouth and presses it into the wound, as she presses into the wound it slowly closes.

She is tired. Her limbs feel delicate and heavy, her legs straighten and bend as if she has no force, but the beautiful women admire her, they cluster around her, their foreheads bound in red silk bands, their robes violet with sashes of green. They carry bows and quivers on their backs, they have been out hunting.

She passes through door after door until they reach the courtyard. The trees are tall enough to reach the red eaves of the buildings, the court is full of flowers, and the seed pods are drifting down off the trees in the light breeze, a swing is hanging down on slack cords. They are helping her up into the swing, she stands erect on the swing and reaches up her arms to hold the ropes, she is wearing a short-sleeved dress and her arms are shining, the ropes of the swing are hanging from the clouds, her dark hair swirls around her neck, she stretches up with her bright arms and light as a swallow swings up into the clouds.

There is a boat of many colors drifting toward her in the sky, it is draped with fine clouds. People are climbing aboard. There is only one oarsman, he holds a short wooden oar. The oar has no blade at the end, the end is thickly clustered with feathers like a giant fan; as the oarsman waves the feathers a light wind blows and they move ever faster through the clouds. There is no sound but the throbbing of the light wind. The clouds are all around, they press in on her like cotton wool, they are soft under her feet, and she is slightly dizzy as though still traveling on the boat. She looks up and sees the stars close to her eyes, they range in size from great jars down to tiny cups, they are neatly arranged like the seeds within a lotus flower; below is an infinite silver sea, through gaps in the clouds she sees whole cities big as beans.

In front of her is a flight of steps, the steps are shining like rock crystal, she is reflected in each step as in a mirror. Clear water is running over white sand. There are little pavilions with red windows, there are beautiful women moving in the pavilions, and young men in embroidered coats and red shoes. People are eating fruit from jade bowls, they are drinking wine from goblets a foot around the rim. The peonies are ten feet high, the camellias twice as high again. A girl with white fingers plays an instrument she has never seen before, another plucks a lute with an ivory plectrum and sings of women who weep. As the music sounds a light breeze blows, birds crowd into the courtyard and settle quietly in the trees.

She sits down at the foot of a high tree. The trunk of the tree is wide and smooth, a single thread of yellow sap courses through its center, the leaves grow thickly on its delicate branches. It casts a deep shade. Red blossoms shimmer among the leaves and tinkle like precious stones as they fall. A bird is singing in the tree. Its feathers are gold and green. It is a strange bird, its tail is as long as its body, and the song it sings is a sad song that makes her think of home.

She moves away on high, scented shoes with hurried steps through the morning dew, the dew makes her shoes and stockings glossy with moisture. The trees are growing thickly, but through the trees she can see the tower, the walls are of copper, there are tall pillars of iron supporting a shimmering roof. There are no doors or windows in the walls but there are deep indentations, placed close together, and she climbs up by placing her feet in these. Inside she is quiet, she is safe.

He kneels beside her. He is trembling and hugs his own body with his arms. "Eat this," she says, and with her bare feet she treads the delicacies into the ground. "Over *here," she says, and he offers her the night-soil bucket, holding it out for her in his hands. "Clean these," she says, and gives him her tiny embroidered shoes, caked with mud.*

She places a woman's cap on his head, with her make-up she paints his face, she paints his face like a warrior's. There is a light cotton football, she kicks it into the air and he scampers after it, the sweat is pouring off him. The ball is transparent and filled with a glittering substance, he kicks it up in a shining arc through the air, it whistles through the air like a comet, it falls into the water, its light goes out in the water with a gurgle. And she sees that there is no tower, there are no round walls supporting a shimmering roof, there is no forest; there is only a cheap ring lying on the ground, needles thrust through it on which the lid of a make-up box is resting, all lying abandoned among the briers.

He stands before her in his ragged clothes, the snot is dribbling down his face, he smiles at her. "Does the pretty lady love me?" he asks. He hits her. The crowd presses closer to watch. He rolls a ball from his snot and gives it to her. "Eat it," he says. She puts it in her mouth and tries to swallow, he laughs aloud, "The pretty lady loves me," he cries. She wants to answer but her mouth is full of earth; she is pinned, she is pinned by the snake's coils that enfold her, she struggles harder, her body is thrashing in the water, she can smell the filth in the water, the people are crowded along the river bank, they are watching and laughing, they must help her, she must cry out, they will not help her

As Jen's hands drove deeply into her neck, woman Wang reared her body up from the bed, but she could not break free. His hands stayed tight around her throat and he forced his knee down onto her belly to hold her still. Her legs thrashed with such force that she shredded the sleeping mat, her bowels opened, her feet tore through the mat to the straw beneath, but his grip never slackened and none of the neighbors heard a sound as woman Wang died.

It was still snowing in T'an-ch'eng. Jen picked up his wife's body and drew her blue outer jacket around her shoulders. He opened the door and began to carry her through the woods, toward the house of his neighbor Kao. This was how he had planned it: when she was dead he would take her body to Kao's house and leave it in the gateway; he would say she had been having an adulterous affair with Kao and that Kao had killed her. The story would be plausible: she had already run away once, and Kao was a violent and quick-tempered man. The two of them could have been carrying on every day while Jen was away at work.

But Jen never reached Kao's house with woman Wang. As he walked through the dark wood a dog barked. Watchmen, sheltering in the porch, banged a warning gong. A light shone. Jen dropped the body in the snow and waited. No one came to investigate. The light went out and there was silence again. He left woman Wang lying where she was and returned to his empty house, locked the door, and went to sleep.

The body of woman Wang lay out in the snow all night. When she was found she looked almost alive: for the intense cold had preserved, in her dead cheeks, a living hue.

Robert Rosenstone

From *Mirror in the Shrine:*
American Encounters with Meiji Japan (1988)

Few historians—maybe none—have pursued the goal of artful writing
with as much energy, focus, and flat-out imagination as Robert Rosenstone. His book *Mirror in the Shrine* remains a landmark thirty years on.
Rosenstone brought to this project not only a long engagement with
the worlds of fiction and film but also a year of personal experience as a
Fulbright-sponsored lecturer at a Japanese university. His willingness to
compare and contrast his own "encounter" with that of three American
writers from a century before was groundbreaking. Most historians, even
today, are conditioned from an early stage to hold a firm line of separation
between self and subject. Rosenstone's whole tendency went the opposite
way: a self-reflective pose informs his thinking (and writing) at virtually
every point. This strategy is joined with a host of innovative prose techniques: multivocal intonation; shifting points of view; injunctions to the
reader ("Picture this," "Imagine that"); sentence fragments; quotations
rendered in italics (i.e., no quotation marks ever); and the effort to use images so as to create the sense of a "moving camera." (Powerful visual effects are central to Rosenstone's purpose.) Though frequently categorized
as postmodern, *Mirror in the Shrine* harks back to a much earlier time
when history belonged squarely within the domain of literature.

Before

It is because the Far-East holds up the mirror to our civilization,—a mirror that
like all mirrors gives us back left for right,—because by her very oddities, as they
strike us at first, we truly learn to criticize, examine, and realize our own way

of doing things, that she is so interesting. It is in this that her great attraction
lies. It is for this that men have gone to Japan intending to stay weeks, and
have tarried years.
PERCIVAL LOWELL, *Choson*

How and where to begin? With the personal or the historical? The history
or the historian? With Townsend Harris standing in front of the temple of
Gyokuzenji in the fishing village of Kakisaki late on the afternoon of Thursday,
September 4, 1856? Or with the author at the rail of the S.S. *Philippine Mail*
in Yokohama Harbor on the rainy morning of September 16, 1974? Harris
looks at Shimoda Bay, circled by pointed hills that resemble breasts (and are
called just that in Japanese), watches the steam frigate *San Jacinto* dip its flag
in salute and then steam away towards the open sea. The author gazes at a
misty world of gray docks, trucks, forklifts, and giant cranes, and laments (to
himself) the quick destruction of that cherished travel-poster image of Mount
Fuji, snow-covered cone against a blue sky, framed by branches shimmering
with cherry blossoms. Harris goes inside the temple—his new home—and
turns to the journal where just a few days before he noted in triumph: *I shall
be the first agent from a civilized power to reside in Japan.* Now his mood is more
sober: *Grim reflections—ominous of change—Undoubted beginning of the end.
Query,—if for the real good of Japan?*

I do not encounter these words until sometime in late 1975, after returning
home from a year of teaching at two Japanese universities. Reading Harris's
journal was part of a larger undertaking. From the very first day back in the
United States, a sense of discontent, uneasiness, and dislocation had gripped
me. Home did not look or feel the same as it did before this sojourn in Asia.
Nor were my feelings the same as when I had returned from earlier years spent
abroad in Western Europe. Something strange had happened to me in Japan,
and in an attempt to understand what it was, to learn why my eyes and mind
had apparently been altered and my own culture made to feel more than a bit
alien, I turned (like a good academic) to my own discipline, history, and began
to delve into writings by and about other Americans who had lived there before me. Harris seemed particularly important because he was the first American to reside in Japan legally. Those who preceded him—some shipwrecked
sailors, a group who jumped ship from a whaler, and Ranald Macdonald, the
half-Chinook who got himself to Hokkaido in 1848 in the belief that American
Indians had originated in Japan—were not exactly residents. All were taken
prisoner by government authorities, sent off to Nagasaki, and held until they

could be shipped out on Dutch vessels from Deshima, the sole Western trading post in the land during Japan's 250 years of self-imposed seclusion.

Working in lonely and difficult conditions, Harris negotiated an agreement
on trade that made access to Japan easier for all who followed him. And follow
they did. During the remainder of the nineteenth century, some two thousand Americans came to live in this newly opened ancient land: merchants
looking for profits; missionaries wanting to convert the heathen; and *o-yatoi*,
foreign helpers—teachers of English, engineers, scientists, doctors, attorneys,
military advisers, agricultural and business specialists—hired by the Japanese
government to help with the process of acquiring Western civilization. All, or
all who left significant records of their stay, were quite certain that the science,
technology, government institutions, and morals of their own tradition were
far superior to those of any Asian land.

To read the articles and books, diaries, journals and letters of these men and
women was to enter a land in which the physical landscape, especially of urban
areas, was vastly different, but the human landscape—the social, religious,
and aesthetic attitudes and behavior patterns of the people—surprisingly similar to the Japan in which I had resided. The discoveries, the wonders, the joys,
the difficulties, the beauties, and the misunderstandings I had experienced
as a teacher and traveler had been experienced in much the same way by my
predecessors a century ago. Despite their persistent feelings of cultural superiority, a goodly number of these early sojourners had—though this was usually phrased indirectly—been disturbed by the same questions that troubled
Harris: Were their skills, values, or ideas really good for this ancient culture?
Might they not be destroying something of value by introducing modern ideas
and practices? The reverse question, the one which interested me more, the
question not of what we do to another culture but of what it does to us, did not
seem to be part of their consciousness. At least none of them ever rendered it
into words.

No wonder. This kind of question is likely to arise only in a self-conscious
age, among self-reflective (and reflexive) people, and nineteenth-century
Americans—especially the kind who sought careers in Japan—were anything
but that. Obviously my question was both a modern and a personal one; but
after several years back in America, and after much reading by and about
my predecessors, it began to seem a social question as well. Was there not,
I wondered, some challenge—one that, by living there, I had obviously
internalized—which Japan (and perhaps Asia at large) was issuing to American (and Western) culture? Would it not be possible to launch a powerful cri-

tique of the West from the perspective and premises of Japanese culture? And might not such a critique address the many issues that our own modern critical tradition seemed to me to fumble or ignore?—the importance in human life of aesthetics, faith, morals, manners, harmony; the possibility of finding human fulfillment, even happiness, within the confines of a hierarchical, even repressive, social order.

Somewhere between my questions and wishes, my continuing view of America in part through the eyes of another culture, and my ongoing research into the lives of Americans who had lived and worked in Japan, this book was born. Because I am a historian, it is set in the past, among the first generation of Western sojourners in Japan, when the cultural contrasts were most stark and clear. Because I am no theoretician, but someone who likes to tell stories set in the past, and who believes that the openness and ambiguity of a story is the best method for attempting to represent the complexity of human experience, this work is a narrative. Because I wished to deal with the most subtle shifts in perceptions, attitudes, and world views, the book takes the form of biography, or, to be more accurate, three biographical tales that highlight the Japanese experience of their protagonists.

These three men—the missionary William Elliot Griffis, the scientist Edward S. Morse, and the writer Lafcadio Hearn—were hardly chosen at random. I selected them to represent different parts of the American sensibility, and their stories to highlight different aspects of the American encounter with Japan. Though all three were well-known Japan experts in the latter half of the nineteenth and the first decades of the twentieth century, and though they read each other's books, they never met in person. Their relationship within the covers of this book—indeed, their very lives as recounted here—may be seen as beginning in the mind and words of the historian.

This book itself—where does it begin? At so many times and places: with the author sitting at his desk, green Fulbright Fellowship forms before him, deciding to write *Japan* rather than *Italy* in the space that says *Country of First Choice*. In Kyoto at the historic Tawaraya Inn, with its wooden tubs, dark corridors, serving-women in kimono, and exquisite flower arrangements, all out of a historical film by Kurosawa. At the famed rock garden of Ryoanji, where attempts at contemplation are interrupted by a shrill, amplified voice, explaining in detail that the garden is inexplicable. During a delicious dinner prepared with great delicacy by three huge and bashful sumo wrestlers. On visits to dozens (hundreds! thousands!) of temples, shrines, castles, cemeteries, pottery villages, and sushi bars—where, even though I was obviously relishing

the food, someone always asks "Do you like raw fish?" At a performance of
Noh, when boredom at the slow pace turns suddenly into a powerful feeling of
love for an entire culture. On a midwinter day in a coffee shop when two bulky,
hairy creatures push through the door and I draw back in momentary horror
before realizing that they are nothing but bearded fellow Americans. While
standing on a railway platform, shivering with memories of World War II
movies as a hundred voices join to shout *Banzai! Banzai! Banzai!* Or looking
from the window of a bullet train as it rockets away from a platform and seeing
students, colleagues, and friends vanish in a blur of tears. Or at that instant
five years later when, after so many worries, fears, and doubts, and after more
than a few false starts, I finally sit down at the desk and type the name of the
sacred mountain that I still have never seen.

Seductive Temptations

Mount Fuji. There it is. So pure, so startling, so white with snow. Just the
way it looks in all the pictures. Surely it demands a response from William Elliot Griffis as he stands at the rail of the S.S. *Great Republic* on that chill morning of December 29, 1870, his eyes full of things both familiar and alien—
fishing boats with odd-shaped sails; thatched huts sagging along beaches;
a rolling countryside quilted with rice paddies; ranges of hills; and soaring
above everything else that splendid cone, that image of perfection glowing in
the rosy light of dawn. Such a powerful vision must be named, described, rendered into Christian terms. Japanese deity the mountain may be, but then (or
later) it becomes a *fitting temple of the Creator's architecture,* a mighty signpost
for His children to admire *while their hearts pour out in gratitude for kindly guidance through the perils of the deep.*

On placid waters the ship steams past inlets, and outcroppings of rock,
and jutting green headlands named, with casual Western arrogance, Webster
Isle, Cape Saratoga, Treaty Point, Reception Bay. In Yokohama Harbor the
sky bristles with the masts of junks and sampans, and the water is thronged
with steamers from the ports of Shanghai, Hong Kong, Marseilles, Southamp-
ton, and Rotterdam, and warships flying the flags of Great Britain, France,
Holland, Prussia, and the United States. The shoreline shows no impressive
docks, imposing warehouses, or tall structures. Only small breakwaters, and
behind them a spread of low buildings framed by hills thick with greenery.

Excitement. Wonder. Disbelief. Those must be the feelings, but words can
hardly capture the sensations that belong to Griffis as the engines fall silent,

the great side paddle wheels stop churning, and—after four weeks of shuddering, rolling, and creaking—the ship lies still in the water. Small boats sur-
round the *Great Republic,* and well-dressed Europeans swarm onto the decks
and into plush salons, looking for friends and business associates, giving advice on hotels, asking for news. Are the Germans and French still at war? Are
the British and Russians about to declare one? Among the visitors, no females
are in evidence, save for those few *fancy creatures in velvet and diamonds, with
gold on their fingers and brass in their faces* . . . *on board to see if any of their guild
had arrived from San Francisco.*

The descent to the gangplank leads through steerage, a realm of close-
packed Chinese passengers where local merchants do a brisk business in fish,
mandarin oranges, dried persimmons, and huge brown bottles of *sake*. From
the lower deck, Westerners get a first good look at the native workers, standing
in punts—small, muscular men clad in the *clothing mother Nature provides for
her children,* with only a tiny loincloth for protection. Like Venetian gondoliers,
two of them work a scull in the stern of the shallow craft that skims across the
harbor to shore, where a short flight of stone steps leads up into a customs
shed. Forty-four days after saying goodbye to friends and family in Philadelphia, Griffis sets foot on the soil of what for the next half century he will call
The Mikado's Empire.

Yokohama is not quite that. To land there in 1870 is to enter a place in but
not wholly of Japan, a little bit of the Western world grafted onto the edge
of Asia. Hastily constructed in 1859 as the first of the nation's ports open to
world trade, Yokohama is a boom town, the scene of solid investment and
high-risk enterprise, of major European trading agencies and shady firms
that spring up one week and vanish the next. Fifteen hundred Westerners,
three thousand Chinese, and twenty-five thousand natives call it home, and
the population continues to grow. The original plan—a two-square-mile rect-
angle bounded by rivers and canals meant to isolate the foreigners from the
rest of the nation—has already been abandoned. No longer do Japanese soldiers guard the bridges over the waterways, and many people, both foreign
and native, reside in valleys and hills beyond them. Now the only troops to be
seen are from British and French battalions, here to ensure the extraterritorial
rights of all Europeans.

Like any treaty port in Asia, Yokohama is a meeting place for merchants,
sailors, missionaries, drifters, adventurers, and globe-trotters from a score of

nations. The city boasts four newspapers; two hospitals (British and American); three churches (Episcopal, French Catholic, and Union Protestant); a Public Garden; a Men's Club; a race course; a cricket field; and a theater, the Gaiety, used more for charity bazaars and boxing matches than for stage productions. In the lively streets, Westerners mingle with a variety of natives: vendors, jugglers, samurai, farmers, girls in bright kimono, many of them drawn from Tokyo or even farther points to do business, shop, and observe the odd behavior of the foreigners who have torn their nation from seclusion.

Business, pleasure, and curiosity may bring a cosmopolitan population together in Yokohama, but only in public. Private life, like the arrangement of the city quarters, remains largely segregated. To the left of the customs building lies the Settlement. Facing the harbor across a stone Bund (embankment) are the rambling structures of important Western commercial companies, along with two fine hotels, the International and the Grand. Behind them, on streets plotted at right angles, stand homes set behind iron fences, stone-fronted banks, restaurants, barber shops, livery stables, warehouses, and auction rooms. The best stores, clustered along—what else?—Main Street, reveal through glass windows a variety of products: watches, dresses, suits, shoes, and sewing machines. Farther back, on a patch of land reclaimed from swamp, are the lanes of Chinatown, jammed with stalls selling fruit, vegetables, and herbs.

To the right of the customs shed lies the native town. No stone or brick here, no fenced yards, or plate glass windows, but two-story wooden structures with sliding panels that open the lower floors to the world. On broad Honcho-dori (*Curio Street* in the guidebooks), bargains in silk, painted scrolls, lacquer-ware, porcelain, baskets, carved dolls, paper fans, bronzes, and ivory-inlaid cabinets are displayed on platforms covered with soft white mats. Nearby is the most famous and infamous of institutions: the licensed pleasure quarter, Miyosaki. In the tea shops and restaurants of this district, young women can be hired to play the *koto* or *samisen,* to dance and sing and entertain men in more intimate ways. Most celebrated of all Yokohama's establishments is the Gankiro, an elegant house complete with fish pond, red lacquer bridges, wide balconies, and large banquet halls. Its aim is the foreign trade; its prices are three times those of similar places catering to Japanese.

~

Twenty-seven-year-old Willie Griffis—part missionary, part teacher, part opportunist—is not the sort either to ignore or to sample such fleshly pleasures. A just-completed year of study at Rutgers Theological Seminary has strengthened his moral and religious convictions without either banishing a taste for attractive women or blinding an eye always open to economic opportunity. Griffis is on the way to a teaching position in Fukui, capital of the feudal domain of Echizen, at a salary so large that he expects to save a good deal of money. Brimming with literary ambition, he is already full of plans for articles and books on the oddities of this little-known empire. Cautious, too, and well aware that conservative samurai occasionally use their swords on foreign *barbarians*, Willie has a small Smith and Wesson revolver tucked into a pocket of his coat.

Intruding barbarians have good and rational reasons for being here: Japan needs the commerce, the science, the Western languages, the true religion of a tradition with *treasures of knowledge and wisdom higher* than Asia can provide. This last point is a bit sticky, for the government has yet to repeal a 250-year-old ban on the preaching and practice of Christianity. So Griffis must be prepared to be subversive, not just to teach but also to show—surreptitiously—how progress in industry, commerce, technology, medicine, and government are intimately connected to the spiritual values of Western civilization. That is the way to soften up the natives, to help Christianity spread among them like a *silent conquering force.*

That the need is great cannot be doubted. A *land of seductive temptations of the most fearful sort,* Japan has thirty million souls who desperately need to be educated and saved. That this is no simple task begins to become apparent to Griffis shortly after he leaves the customs office. For the next four days he sleeps in the homes of missionaries; dines, prays, and strolls the streets with them; tags along to New Year's receptions at four Western consulates; and delivers a Sunday sermon in the Union Church. From breakfast until bedtime each day, he listens to the small triumphs and large complaints of these men and women who seem hungry for a sympathetic audience.

The situation of Protestantism in Japan is not at all what Griffis imagined. The view from America made missionaries appear to be exalted beings, but here in Yokohama they seem, at least in their own eyes, more like a *neglected set of peculiar people.* Leaders of local society, Griffis is told, those prosperous merchants and professionals who live in large, elegant homes up on the hilly area known as the Bluff, scorn the missionary endeavor. Far too few Westerners attend church; far too many take economic advantage of the locals; and some act with a most un-Christian brutality, beating, kicking, and blaspheming the native servants. Worse yet is the behavior of the soldiers, sailors, and drifters who carouse, gamble, and brawl in the grog shops and taverns of Blood Town. Add to this the number of tourists who flock to the Miyosaki district, and the foreigners who live openly with native concubines, and you have disturbing hints that the presence of the West here is tinged with ambiguity, and the light of progressive social change shadowed with darkness.

~

January 3, 1871. The Yankee ready to invade the *Land of the Gods*. A frosty day, the air keen as a razor—Willie's pocket thermometer reads twenty-eight degrees Fahrenheit. The colors of the morning are sharp, painful: *Blue sky, blue water, blue mountains, white Fuji.* On the Bund waits a stagecoach, two restless ponies in harness. Cost to the capital city: two Mexican silver dollars. Estimated travel time: two and a half hours. The huge Australian on the driver's bench cracks his whip and off they rattle along the waterfront, turning right at the British Consulate and then heading along Benten-dori into the native quarter. Shop-boys raise curtains on storefronts. Bathhouses overflow with people. And there, nonchalant as if on a Sunday stroll, goes a man *naked as when he stepped out into the world. His copper hue, like a lobster's, is intensified by the boiling he has just undergone. He walks in a self-exhaling cloud of auroral vapors, like a god in ambrosia. He deigns not to make his toilet while in sight, but proceeds homeward, clothes in hand.*

Rumbling over the nation's first iron bridge, the coach speeds toward the Tokaido, the high road that joins Kyoto and Tokyo. Europe lies behind them now—ahead is the *real Japan.* How much it seems like *a wonderful picture book*; how it makes him want *to be a poet to express it, and an artist to paint all I see*—the tiny villages strung along the road; the weathered houses, shutters open, where families devour bowls of rice; the groups of youngsters at play; the women with rosy-cheeked babies strapped to their backs; the priests with shaved heads; the laborers with bare legs; the samurai, hair in lacquered top-knots; the pilgrims, clad entirely in white; the beggars, young and old, dirty, ragged, and covered with sores.

Kanagawa slows the coach to a walk. Where in this *flourishing* town are the *splendid stores,* where the wealth that Griffis expects to find in the Orient? Not here, in these poor streets full of fish and vegetable stalls and shops displaying umbrellas, straw hats, grass cloaks, knives, and tools. Better to forget such preconceptions. Better to enjoy the scenery as the vehicle climbs into hills, then dashes along a *splendid road beneath an arch of pines* to a stop at a teahouse for refreshments. For the horses, water; for the driver, brandy from a flask; for the travelers, tea and sweetmeats carried by pretty girls who come forward with downcast glances and softly voice a word of greeting: *Ohayo*. Stunned by a pair of dark eyes, Willie places a tip on the tray *for beauty's sake*. This brief encounter is memorable, worthy of description, of generalization. Three years later he will write: *The maid is about seventeen, graceful in figure, and her neat dress is bound with a wide girdle and tied into a huge bow behind. Her neck is powdered. Her laugh displays a row of superb white teeth, and her jet-black hair is rolled in a maidenly style. The fairest sight in Japan are Japan's fair daughters.*

Deep bows and cries of *Sayonara* send the coach onward, past thatched villages where iris blazes purple along the ridgepoles. Instead of neat Pennsylvania fields of winter wheat, the eye encounters an endless series of muddy rice fields, vast ditches edged by dark stands of pine and the bright green of bamboo. At Kawasaki, where they stop to await a flat-bottomed boat, a yet unused railway bridge spans a shallow river. Griffis goes into a warming hut and a dozen ill-clad *coolies* step back to allow him access to the fire. How considerate they are, how polite for men who lack schooling, political freedom, or the true faith. Yet never forget a fundamental fact: here in Asia a man is no more than *a wheelbarrow, a beast of burden, a political cipher, a being who exists for the sake of his masters or the government*. At home *A man is a man*.

Beyond the river, paddies give way to villages and more villages, the far-flung suburbs of the capital. Just before the Shinagawa barrier, the coach passes an execution ground where, from a six-foot pole, the severed heads of two executed samurai stare coldly back at travelers. This ghastly welcome seems a fitting example of this despotic nation's *bloody code of edicts, misnamed laws, by which she terrifies her people into obedience*. Inside the great gates, a right view of the vast spread of the city, its leafy hills and distant castle walls. There is Fuji once again, and the blue bay of Tokyo with its chain of tiny forts. And there, at anchor, the half dozen vessels of Japan's navy. Each floats the new national flag, a rising red sun on a white field, the symbol of a reborn nation whose growth Griffis hopes to speed.

～

For six weeks Willie lives at the home of Guido Verbeck, head of Daigaku Nanko, Japan's first Western-style college. Like all of the school's twelve foreign teachers, this Dutch Reformed minister has a bungalow in a compound hidden behind *high and hideous* walls, just across a bridge from the old castle. So powerful is the initial impact of the city that for the entire first week the single word *Rambles* marks the pages of Griffis's journal. Not until January 13 does he begin to describe his activities—the mornings in Verbeck's library, where he studies Japanese; the hours given to tutoring students in English; the two weeks he substitutes at the college for a teacher who is ill; the afternoons he explores the crowded streets of this *wilderness of a million souls,* or lingers in the *monotonous and gloomy* grounds of the old castle. Griffis is an avid tourist. He rides on horseback into the suburbs to see temples, shrines, and gardens; visits Tokyo's first hospital and the Western school run by Fukuzawa Yukichi; watches the Emperor review his troops; attends a sumo wrestling match; and begins to turn what he has seen, done, and learned into articles for the *Christian Intelligencer.*

Even in this short period, the fresh can edge toward the routine, the unusual toward the common. If most of his daily moments quickly vanish, or blend too easily into that smooth narrative called memory, some images from those early days will retain their sharp edge of meaning for years. Picture Griffis as he later will see himself. At Nihonbashi, the humpbacked bridge from which all distances in the empire are measured, he shrinks away from *loathsome beggars* and mendicant priests who chant *doleful prayers,* and gazes at the *kosatsu,* the signboard of edicts whose mysterious (to him) characters proclaim, among other things, *The evil sect called Christian is strictly prohibited. Suspicious persons should be reported to the proper officers, and rewards will be given.* On a street lined with shops, he glimpses a girl sitting in an open window, washing her hair, and thinks, *the human form divine, bare to the waist.* At the end of a day at Daigaku Nanko he watches hundreds of young men thrust swords into sashes and stalk off carrying slates and copybooks in ink-stained hands. At the great temple of Kannon at Asakusa, he finds the atmosphere of a country fair—rows of curio shops, and refreshment booths, and hordes of people eating and drinking. *Religion and innocent pleasure join hands in Japan. Are the Japanese wrong in this?*

The pleasures of Tokyo do not keep Griffis from successfully bargaining with Echizen officials for a 50 percent increase in the salary so recently agreed to in America. A bilingual contract names him teacher of chemistry and natural philosophy at the Meishinken, or College at Fukui, for a three-year term at an annual salary of $3,600, and specifies that he will be provided a house *built in European style* and allowed to keep Sunday as a day of rest. To celebrate this agreement, Prince Matsudaira Shungaku, former ruler of the domain, hosts a banquet for Griffis and Verbeck in the feudal splendor of his Tokyo palace. In a room where the sliding screens are papered in silver and gold and covered with delicate paintings of cherry blossoms and graceful birds, they feast on a ten-course European meal complete with ale, sherry, claret, and champagne.

The single jarring note is provided by two Japanese, who loudly slurp their soup and take occasional refreshing swallows from finger bowls.

Not all of Willie's daily moments are tasty, pleasant, or joyous. Fear hovers over horseback rides to suburban shrines, rambles through streets where no European faces are to be seen, formal dinners in the Western compound. It is impossible to forget that fifty foreigners have in the last decade fallen beneath the sword, or to ignore the rumors of plots, threats, and plans for uprisings that speed through the nervous capital of a government only two years in power. When encountered in the streets, bands of retainers for the *daimyo*, the great provincial lords, appear haughty, swaggering, insolent, and threatening enough to make Griffis feel for his pistol.

Fear becomes reality at 4 a.m. on Saturday, January 14, when a knock on the door rouses the household and brings a messenger with word that two English teachers have been cut down. Behind Verbeck and a servant carrying a lantern, Griffis hurries through a maze of dark streets and enters for the first time into a native house, its dim rooms hung with *emblems and tokens of Japanese religion, enjoyment, and superstition.* In the following days, he plays nurse to the wounded men and talks over the meaning of the assault with Verbeck until the older man's opinion becomes his own. Certainly it is a sad affair, but not much different from what regularly happens in the Five Points area of New York City. Besides, the victims are not entirely blameless. They were out past the curfew; they had dismissed their native guards; they were with prostitutes when the attack occurred. Their actions must be seen as a kind of provocation, an instance of the sort of injustice foreigners regularly perpetrate here, part of a sad story that includes insolence, insult, and exploitation.

Such an insight—achieved or adopted—may hint at a new perspective on Japan, but does not touch Willie's belief system. Yet at the end of his stay in the capital, his usual judgments have become a bit confused, and some of them point in an unexpected direction. In six short weeks he has experienced *paganism, feudalism, earthquakes;* has seen *how long contact with heathen life and circumstances slowly disintegrates the granite principles of eternal right, once held by men raised in a more bracing moral atmosphere;* has met *scores of white men* who have *long since forgotten the difference between right and wrong.* Before leaving for the interior in mid-February, Griffis confesses that the foreign worker in Japan faces a serious problem: *For a man's own salvation of morals and as a surety of duty, it is almost absolutely necessary that he must be either a Christian or a married man.* Although he can take comfort in being one of these, there is little doubt Willie would prefer to be both.

Simon Schama

From *Dead Certainties: Unwarranted Speculations* (1991)

'Twas the first sentence that did the trick: the voice, the sense of wonder, the immediacy of the action. We had to read on. In several long works of historical narrative, Simon Schama has demonstrated a mastery of evocative language and momentum-filled storytelling. But in *Dead Certainties,* the book from which this piece is taken, he is at his most experimental, and so this is perhaps his most generative work for artful historians. It begins with a brief account of the impossible attack on Quebec in 1759, offered by an ordinary soldier in the British Army, in his own voice but not his own words. The ventriloquism is astounding. And toward the end of these unpolished musings—ultra-realistic in their hewing to a line of commentary *on* the events rather than a retelling *of* the events, since the soldier already knew what happened, having lived through it—a portrait of General James Wolfe starts to emerge as the central figure in the battle's drama. Then the soldier's voice abruptly cuts out, to be replaced by the seemingly omniscient and authoritative voice of a biographer, who tells us that for Wolfe, "it had come to this, at last." The soldier gives us glimpses, based on his own experience: the general was humorless, pessimistic, melancholic, but also fearless and trustworthy, willing to "walk before the men under fire, pointing his cane like Old Gideon's staff, and we followed sure enough." The biographer uses various kinds of documents to put Wolfe in his imperialist context, to examine his straining ambition, his struggles with health and relationships, his brilliance and his uncertainty. This surprise assault on the French, launched in the night, requiring a silent climb up sheer cliffs to the Heights of Abraham, might determine the fate of North America. So: was this a grand strategy, the culmination of Wolfe's years of training and service? Or was he just impatient, tired of being bled by his surgeon, propelled by his "endless sense of impotence and

28

rage"? Did the British take Quebec because James Wolfe wanted to die as a hero in battle rather than expiring gradually of kidney failure in his tent by the St. Lawrence River? In Schama's carefully constructed anti-narrative, the soldier's guess is as good as the biographer's.

At the Face of the Cliff

Anse du Foulon, Quebec,
four a.m., September 13, 1759

'Twas the darkness that did the trick, black as tar, that and the silence, though how the men contriv'd to clamber their way up the cliff with their musket and seventy rounds on their backs, I'm sure I don't know even though I saw it with my own eyes and did it myself before very long. We stood hushed on the muddy shore of the river, peering up at the volunteers. They looked like a pack of lizards unloosd on the rocks, though not so nimble, bellies hugging the cliff and their rumps wiggling with the effort. We couldn't see much of 'em for they disappeared now and then into the clumps of witherd cedar and spruce that hung on the side of the hill. But we could feel the squirming, pulling labour of it all. And by God they were quiet alright. Now and then a man's boot would find a foothold he thought secure and away would come a shower of soft dirt, near taking the fellow with him down the cliff. Curses come to a soldier as easy as breathing, but we heard none that night, not at the start of it all. Some scoundrel later put it about that the General himself had struck off the head of a man who curs'd too loud when he dropped his pack to still any who should think to do the same. But that was never the General's way. Though he had the temper in him of a red-hair'd man, he was an orderly commander who lik'd things done by the Regulations and it would go damnd hard on any poor infantryman who thought to help himself to the spoils of war, be it just a goat or a pig, when all the killing and running were done.

I suppose the silence told Wolfe the game was in earnest. For had bodies come tumbling down or firing started from the top he would have stopped it right there and then. For all his soldierly zeal he was rattled by the cliff when he had jumpd from the landing boat and come to its face, and could see the height of it, near enough two hundred feet and the sheerness of it. "I dont think we can by any possible means get up here," we heard him say, "but we must use our best endeavour." And so it fell to the turn of the Twenty-Eighth and we started to haul ourselves over the black limestone, reaching for stumps and scrubby patches of chokecherries and hawthorn that covered the nether part of the hill. By such cumbersome means we lugged ourselves up a bit at a time, skinning our hands, dirtying our breeches and praying the next bit of scrawny stick and leaf was deep enough rooted to hold us up. One thing was sure, our coats and leggings weren't made for such work, for they flapped and pinchd as we dragged ourselves up; and I could swear the Rangers who were fitter dress'd for it sniggerd as they saw us struggling with our tackle. Indeed the whole business seemd perilous, vertical folly and nothing the King of Prussia would have commended. We all feard it might yet go badly as it had done in July at the Montmorency Falls where the French had peppered us with grapeshot and the drenching rain had turned the hill into a filthy slide. Men had come tumbling down in a mess of blood and mud and fear, and those that couldn't run were left to face the Savages as best they could, poor beggars.

But our fortunes were fairer that night for when the sentries challengd our boats as we saild upriver, Mr. Fraser he answered them in French good enough to pass and even threw in an oath or two against the English *bougres* for good measure. And we were all glad of the Scotchmen this time, even the Highlanders, for of Delaune's first men up the rocks they were all Macphersons and Macdougals and Camerons and the like. A good crew for a general who had fought on Culloden Field! And here too they did the King good service for I had no sooner got to the very top and was rejoicing and taking good care not to look down behind me when our men gathered together amidst the tamaracks and the spruce. Before us were a group of tents, white in the first thin light of the coming dawn, and of a sudden a commotion and shouting broke forth. A Frenchy officer came flying out in his nightshirt as we loosd off our first rounds and sent them running across the open fields towards the town leaving a few of their company shot or stuck with our bayonets wearing that surprisd look on their face as they lay there amidst the pine needles and brown grass.

Once the peace was broken and we were masters of the place and the French guns, we set up a huzzaing and men down below threw themselves at the hill, Wolfe first of all, they said, and suddenly the rocks were alive with soldiers, Rangers and Highlanders and Grenadiers groping their way to the top. Monckton even managed to find a zig-zag path, two men wide, to lug our field-pieces up. The boats that had dischargd the first men went back to fetch some more from the ships, and after an hour or two we stood in the dawn light, a cool spraying rain coming down, maybe four thousand of us, more than we had dar'd hope but not so many I still thought as would come to a prize fight at Bartholomews Fair, too few for the business.

Monckton and Barré formd us up again in our lines, smartly enough. The Grenadiers formed to our right and the Forty-Third, Forty-Seventh and the Highlanders to our left, Mr. Burton's Forty-Eighth behind us in reserve and Townshend and the Fifteenth at right angles. Better though our situation was than we might have expected, there was not a man jack of us but didnt feel the scare of the battle crawling through his uniform and was glad of the two days rum we had got issued. The General put some heart in us, coming to our lines to talk of duty and the King and what our country expected of us and all of Canada at our mercy if we but prevaild this once. After he died they made him look like a Roman, even on the penny prints I have seen, but he lookd no Roman to us. For though he was six foot, he carried that height queerly, in a loping gait, with his bony frame and sloping shoulders ending in a poke-up neck. What was on top of it bore little resemblance to the Antiques either, what with his pop eyes and his little chins wobbling under his jaw, his skin the colour of cheese and a snout on him like a ferret. Nor was he much a humorous man, more in the melancholy way. Brigadier Townshend did some scribbles of him peering at the latrines or measuring the height of his reputation which got passed around the camp and gave us some mirth in the midst of all our adversities, but they pleasd their subject not at all. Yet he was a good general to trust, even if it was his fancy to call us "brother soldiers," for he was fearless and would walk before the men under fire, pointing his cane like Old Gideon's staff, and we followed sure enough.

THE LIFE OF GENERAL WOLFE

By seven o'clock the low clouds and drizzle that hung over the Heights of Abraham had given way to a gentle sunshine. Wolfe and his three brigadiers—Murray, the dependable Monckton and the erratic Townshend—had placed their lines in battle order. For the first time in the whole campaign, it was the British who waited, the French who had to react. A stillness descended on the grassy plain, broken only by the occasional crack of musket fire coming from Indian and Canadian shooters hidden in the woods to the left of the British lines.

For James Wolfe it had come to this, at last. Months of misery and frustration, of failing to winkle out Montcalm's troops from their citadel of Quebec, much less dislodging the batteries on the north shore of the St. Lawrence, had finally found some resolution. The humiliation of his position had galled him, and he was not eased by the embarrassing recollection of drunken, swaggering boasts made to William Pitt on the eve of his departure. Once up the river he had realized how daunting his mission was; how idle the hope of dividing Montcalm's army or provoking it to come down from its fortified heights and engage. Nor had his proclamation, written, he thought, in the most sententious French at his command, been effective even though it had exuded magnanimity and had spoken honourably of the protection of the Canadians' religion and their property, and given an assurance that he had come not "to destroy and depopulate" but merely to "subdue" and "bring them into subjection to the King his master." In vexation he had begun to bombard Quebec from the positions set up by the fleet, so that a steady deafening rain of mortars and shells fell on the town, day and night.

But what good had this done except to assuage the endless sense of impotence and rage that swelled inside him as spring turned into a scorching, dripping, foul-smelling summer? His troops were falling sick from putrid fevers and were tormented by blackfly that with their stinging bites could cover a man's face or arms with gobs of blood. When it became apparent that so far from joining themselves to the protection of His Majesty the Canadian trappers and farmers had sent their women and children to the town, while the men had formed irregular companies to harass the troops, a second proclamation, angrier than the first, announced the coming of "violent" measures both to punish and deter. Farm cabins and whole villages had been destroyed, corn burned in the fields. But in return they had the Indians—Abenakis and Iroquois—to contend with, lying in wait for their raiding parties. And of what the Savages were said and known to do, their scalping and tomahawking, the troops were in shuddering terror. Men returned to camp unmanned, with stories of slivers of wood pushed up the penis and behind their nails and more than ever they came to feel they were being sacrificed to some vanity of the General and his thirst for reputation.

So the landing at the Montmorency Falls had been determined as much by the need to do *something* to force the issue, as by any calculated hope of success. Wolfe was agonized by the possibility of returning to England not in a chorus of Handelian Hosannas but in a cloud of ignominy. How would he dare face Amherst, the commander of the expedition, or Pitt, who had been so criticized for putting his faith in a stripling major-general still in his thirties? He dreaded the jeering of the merciless coffee-house press; the caricaturists for whom his peculiar physiognomy must have seemed heaven-sent; the howling catcalls of the theatre as some half-drunk actor bawled a profane air at his expense. How could he greet his betrothed, who overlooked his curious phiz and figure and his graceless manner as the eccentricities of one born for a heroic fate? How could he look his father, the General, in the eye, and worst of all what would he say to his exacting, adamant mother?

But the landing had been horribly botched. The French had prudently refused to descend to engage the British force and had been content to inflict a murderous fire from their batteries on the haplessly climbing soldiers, defenceless and falling over each other in rain-sodden confusion. Painfully aware that he was losing the authority of his command, each day watching his force being eaten up by sickness, boredom and desertion, Wolfe increasingly kept his own counsel and brooded sourly on the disappointment of his hopes. The chivalrous major-general who had exchanged cases of wine with his adversary, the Marquis de Montcalm, who had promised peace and conciliation, now displayed fits of vindictive petulance. Orders were given sending raids deeper into the country to exterminate Canadian settlements at the same time as British guns were obliterating the timbered houses of Old Quebec itself.

Wolfe was running two races, and in both, time seemed to be against him. Unless he found some way to pry the French army from its lair, the swift icing of the St. Lawrence would close his fleet in and cut its supply line from the Louisbourg peninsula at the river's mouth. But there was a greater enemy than the river and the season; greater yet than the damnably canny Montcalm, and that was his own body. He had always been preoccupied by his physical frailty and had even been capable of dark banter on the subject. "If I Say I am thinner," he had written to his friend Rickson, "you will imagine me a shadow or a skeleton in motion. In short I am everything but what the surgeons call a subject for anatomy. As far as muscles, bones and the larger vessels conserve their purpose they have a clear view of them in me, distinct from fat or fleshy impediment. . . ."

But now, he thought, he was dying, withering away of gravel and consumption; a raging, scalding venom that ate at his guts. His bladder was a failing vessel; his kidneys, demons that racked him day and night. It was torture to piss and worse not to piss and periodically he suffered the indignities of dysentery, too. Somehow, though, he grimly preserved his composure, for the sake of his men and for the duty he had taken on. The surgeon bled him profusely, and together with his want of sleep, there arose in his naturally wan features a ghostly mouldy pallor from which big eyes glittered in their darkened sockets.

An escape from this death by degrees—of both the expedition itself and its commander—finally presented itself (as escapes so often do) by way of a response to a secondary problem. Thinking of how to intercept Quebec's supply lines from Montreal to the west, Wolfe's officers and Admiral Saunders, the commander of the fleet, conceived the plan of sailing up-river, past Quebec itself, to a point where a force might interpose itself between the city and its rear. Wolfe himself needed persuading, all the more so since he increasingly mistrusted one of his three brigadiers, the overtly disaffected George Townshend whose natural irreverence and sardonic manner were, Wolfe thought, coming damnably close to insubordination. Once convinced of the idea of an attack from behind, Wolfe converted it from a tactical element in the campaign to the strategy on which victory or defeat would necessarily turn. The risks were alarming since the known landing-sites were heavily fortified with batteries, and wherever the guns were less in evidence, the escarpment seemed too sheer to allow any kind of ascent. The only chance of success lay with careful subterfuge and surprise. A flotilla was to go up-river with the flood tide, beyond its apparent landing, and then allow the ebb, calculated for four in the morning, to drift landing-craft back to the shore. But such was Wolfe's mounting mistrust and anxiety that he refused to divulge to his own senior officers the exact location of this landing, forcing them to write to him for an answer so the plan would not be put in jeopardy.

Wolfe was painfully conscious that the moment that beckoned him was one to which his whole life had been pointing. Since he was a child he had known nothing, nor expected anything, other than the army career in which his father had achieved some rank and modest renown. James had left for camp when he was fourteen, had been an adjutant at Dettingen at sixteen where two horses had been shot from under him and at nineteen had eagerly joined the slaughter of Jacobites at Culloden and Falkirk. Yet nothing much had come of these youthful exertions. He had ended up quartered in Ireland, grumbling in a prematurely bilious way about the corruption, debauchery and insolence of the natives. The coming of another war with France in 1756 seemed to offer liberation from boredom and hypochondria, but instead it enfolded him in fiasco. The amphibious expedition to the Atlantic port of Rochefort had ended up bobbing indeterminately in the roadstead while the naval commander bickered with the army commander about what to do and when to do it. Wolfe was one of the few officers exonerated in the subsequent investigation and was promoted to brigadier for the siege of Louisbourg at the mouth of the

St. Lawrence, French Canada's lifeline to its homeland. While that stronghold eventually fell in 1758, Wolfe regarded the siege as wasteful, prolonged and incompetent and lost no opportunity in letting this be known when he returned on leave at the end of that year.

His reputation had remained unsullied, indeed had even blossomed, as the British imperial war effort staggered from mishap to mishap. When William Pitt, the gouty, bloody-minded genius of global strategy, designed one for America of crushing simplicity, Wolfe was given a commission of crucial significance. There would be a two-pronged onslaught on French America that would be decisive: one to the fort of Ticonderoga in the Appalachians, and an amphibious expedition up the St. Lawrence to Quebec and Montreal. If successful, the two attacks would join at the upper Ohio and sever the line of containment France had constructed from Canada to the Mississippi basin against the westward expansion of the British colonies.

Wolfe had always hungered for such a responsibility, but now that it had come, it seemed more a burden than an opportunity. Perhaps Pitt had recognised in him a fellow neurotic, driven by the volatile mixture of monomania, dejection and elation that fired all the most formidable military imperialists. Exactly to type, Wolfe alternated between undignified self-congratulation and self-reproach. He was, he thought, riddled with shortcomings that would be his undoing. His physique deteriorated sympathetically with this onset of mercurial energy and sent him to Bath to take the waters. It was there that he met Katherine Lowther, handsome, articulate and rich, the daughter of the Governor of Barbados (where one became very rich indeed), who was abominated almost everywhere else.

Wolfe had been in love once before, at twenty-one when he had paid court to Elizabeth Lawson (as plain as Katherine Lowther was good-looking). Though "sweet-tempered," she was seriously disabled in the eyes of General and Mrs. Wolfe by her modest fortune. They had made their own selection for their son, which he in turn rejected. Parents and son then compromised by forgetting about marriage altogether. Once hot with passion, Wolfe cooled rapidly as he distanced himself from his love and got on with war and advancement. He was ten years older when he met Katherine; she commanded a rank and fortune that Wolfe must have presumed would sweep aside any parental reservations. He was sadly disabused of this unwarranted optimism. Henrietta Wolfe remained implacable in her displeasure, unmoveable in her objections. A frosty hostility descended on a relationship which until recently had been suffocatingly close. Wolfe visited the family house at Blackheath just once during his three-month winter leave and instead of bidding his parents farewell sent a letter of bleak severity to his mother:

> DEAR MADAM,—The formality of taking leave should be as much as possible avoided; therefore I prefer this method of offering my good wishes and duty to my father and you. I shall carry this business through with the best of my abilities. The rest you know, is in the hands of Providence, to whose care I hope your good life and conduct will recommend your son. . . . I heartily wish you health and enjoyment of the many good things that have fallen to your share. My best duty to the General.
>
> I am, dear Madam,
>
> Your obedient and affectionate son,
>
> JAM; WOLFE

He took with him on *The Neptune* a miniature portrait of Katherine, whom in his correspondence he greets as his lover and implies a betrothal that was none the less left unannounced and unofficial. To his Uncle Walter in Dublin (yet another military Wolfe) he confided his plan both to marry Katherine and to leave the service if the weakness of his constitution allowed him to see his commission through to a victorious conclusion. He also had with him Katherine's copy of Gray's "Elegy in a Country Churchyard," which he annotated heavily during the long, miserable, nauseating voyage. It was this poem, lugubriously beautiful in its meter and metaphor, and universally admired by Wolfe's generation, that gave rise to the most famous piece of Wolfiana: that on the eve of battle the General recited it to his soldiers. If in fact he did (and the sources are strong enough to resist the automatic modern assumption of apocrypha), it could hardly have raised their spirits even if it moved their souls, concluding as it did with the prophecy that *"the paths of glory lead but to the grave."* "I can only say, Gentlemen," he is reported to have declared at its end, "that if the choice were mine I would rather be the author of those verses than win the battle which we are to fight tomorrow morning."

But Wolfe was always more than a waver of flags and a rattler of sabres. His driven, febrile personality, swinging between tender compassion and angry vanity, was haunted by Night Thoughts, by ravens perched on tombstones. If he was an empire-builder he knew he was also a grave-digger, perhaps his own. When he was feeling most embattled on the St. Lawrence, the news came to him of his father's death. This was not a shock since, as he had written to Uncle Walter, "I left him in so weak a condition that it was not probable we should meet again." But Wolfe's foreknowledge makes the chilling circumstances of his departure from England even more depressing. The "general tenor" of his father's life, he wrote, "has been extremely upright [so that] benevolent and little feelings of imperfections were overbalanced by his many good qualities." Having delivered himself of this overly judicious obituary, Wolfe betrayed a pathetic solitude; he was increasingly convinced that, whether by fire or fever, he would not survive to become a husband. "I know you cannot cure my complaint," he told his surgeon, "but patch me up so I may be able to do my duty for the next few days and I shall be content." His will, dictated to his aides-de-camp shortly before the decisive battle, asked for Katherine's portrait to be set with five hundred guineas' worth of jewels and then returned to her.

To the elegiac resignation of Gray, Wolfe may have added his own Augustan conception of the Hero. For he also transcribed lines from Pope's translation of the *Iliad* together with his own inelegant but telling alterations:

> But since, alas! ignoble age must come
> Disease and death's inexorable doom,
> The life which others pay, let us bestow,
> And give to Fame what we to Nature owe
> Brave let us fall or honoured if we live
> Or let us glory gain or glory give . . .

The night came; the flotilla set off. Challenged with a *"Qui vive?"* the French-speaking Scot obliged with *"La France,"* and persuaded the guards stationed above the river that they were a provisions fleet. *"Laissez les passer,"* came the reassuring response. A gentle September breeze got up, rippling the water as the boats drifted along the high banks lined with walls of fir trees pointing at the stars. In the early hours, at their station, men were dropped into the landing boats which drifted back on the ebb; Wolfe sat bolt upright in one of them, anxious lest they overshoot their mark, which they duly did. So be it. It had to be this or nothing. He held in his hands the design of his posterity. By making Britain's history he could at last make his own. He was at the cliff face.

Stella Tillyard

From *Aristocrats: Caroline, Emily, Louisa, and
Sarah Lennox, 1740–1832* (1994)

In a book that is, first and last, about class difference in early modern
England, Stella Tillyard opens with a small story to introduce the larger one.
"A bleak spring evening" discloses a scene of maternal sorrow, followed
by another several days later in which privilege asserts itself with terrible
force. In barely two pages, Tillyard sets a haunting tableau. The details are
so vivid, so tangible, so tactile even, that readers may cringe in response.
There is, as well, a tempo starkly calibrated to the events described. Tone
and pitch are perfect; irony seals the effect. If artful history is "novelistic" in
some of its contours, this passage suggests how such an approach might
offer readers a more visceral investment in arguments about the past.

~

Prologue

On a bleak spring evening in 1741 a crowd gathered in a dark, narrow
London street. At its edge well-to-do City merchants on their way westward
through Hatton Garden mingled with the wretched and curious poor, washed
up from tenements to the north, east, and south, looking for a handout or a
meal. In the middle, dozens of women in their best clothes jostled and flowed
towards the door of a large double-fronted house like filings drawn to a mag-
net. The light filtering out of the house windows sent dim rays over the crowd,
illuminating their bundles tied in rags and wrapped in flannel blankets. They
were babies, some sleeping, some gazing about, some sick and crying.

For an hour the crowd ebbed and surged and waited. Then at eight o'clock,
in imitation of the mothers' misery and sin, the light in the house's entryway

went out. The door opened. The crowd fell silent and a bell rang. A woman sprang forward and plunged with her child into the darkness. The door closed behind her.

Inside the house the woman was ushered into a room on the right of the hall. She gave her name, but it was not written down. Then she watched as her child, a boy, was stripped layer by layer of the stain of her folly and poverty. First his clothes were taken off and cast away. Then a little memento she had hoped would stay longer with him than she could was catalogued and set aside. Then Dr. Nesbitt, donating his services for the occasion, inspected the child and pronounced him sound. Finally he was given a number, One, as the first child in the hospital. Distraught and relieved, the mother looked on in silence. A few minutes later she was dismissed, came out of the house, and lost herself in the darkness of the crowd. The door closed behind her.

Soon the bell rang again. Another woman darted up with her bundle, entered the house, and returned empty-handed. The bell rang, again and again, until thirty women had taken in their children and come out without them and the Foundling Hospital was full.

For four days the house was quiet. The infants slept and sucked, motherless and nameless. Then, on the evening of 29 March, Hatton Garden was crowded and noisy once again. Heavy four-wheeled carriages, with lamps burning and footmen aloft, lumbered across the cobbles. On their sides were tiny emblems with mottoes curling underneath that dignified those inside. By the lighted entrance of Number 61, the footmen jumped down and opened the heavy leather-covered doors. Noblemen and noblewomen, physicians, merchants, doctors, and Members of Parliament were handed out. Taking care to avoid the mud, they went inside and up the stairs. The state room on the first floor was alive with light. Light twinkled and sparkled from belts and buckles, from necklaces and ornaments. It lay puddled like mercury in the folds of silk gowns and in silver bowls and cups. Servants carrying candles went up and down the stairs and announced the new arrivals: the Duke of Bedford, president of the hospital; the Earl and Countess of Pembroke; the Duke and Duchess of Richmond with their eldest daughter; William and Anne Hogarth; Lord and Lady Albemarle; Captain Robert Hudson; Mr. Lewis Way. Their names rang out over the rustle of gowns, the clink of shoe buckles, and the murmur of greetings.

The company sat and the Reverend Samuel Smith read evening prayers. Then the infants, numbered One to Thirty, were brought in for christening. Beyond the impromptu font sat not their mothers and fathers but surrogate families of the finest, wealthiest, and worthiest in the land. The Reverend Mr. Smith took the first child from his nurse, approached the font, and dabbed the baby's forehead with holy water. The little child, newly clothed in lace and cotton, with a cap jammed tightly on his hairless head, was baptised Thomas Coram, after the hospital's founder. Eunice Coram followed. The aristocracy lent the children their family names. Charlotte Finch was named for the Duchess of Somerset, John Russell for the Duke of Bedford, Charles Lennox for the Duke of Richmond, Sarah Cadogan for his wife. Caroline Lennox was named for the Duke's daughter, an anxious, intelligent girl of eighteen sitting with her parents. Secure in their names, the rich and the mighty bestowed them on little children, sending them forth watered with greatness. Their impoverished, orphaned little doubles would, as long as they lived, reflect the importance of their patrons.

After the baptismal ceremony the company departed, clattering westward in their carriages out of their namesakes' lives. Lady Caroline Lennox, trundling back to Richmond House in Whitehall, left little Caroline to a life in the shadow. Darkness descends over her as it did over the house in Hatton Garden that night. Perhaps she became a servant, perhaps even a milliner or a mantua maker. But it was just as likely that, like one of Lady Caroline's own children, she would die of a fever before she could understand that she had been orphaned into a life of misery.

Saidiya Hartman

"Lose Your Mother":

From *Lose Your Mother: A Journey Along the Atlantic Slave Route* (2007)

"Lose Your Mother" is history as challenge. It darts back and forth between past and present, asking readers to join a communal effort to work through the traumas of both remembering and forgetting. There is no straightforward historical narrative here. Hartman travels from the United States to Ghana and invites us along as she digs into the archives, experiences the slavery-tourism industry, and asks: what is an appropriate relationship to the history of the slave trade? It depends on who you are, of course. But the charge to all of us is to recognize that we are still implicated, and then to commit ourselves not to mere commemoration but rather to "the reconstruction of society."

Hartman is a full-voiced presence in her prose. She is disgusted by the commodification of slavery tourism (including McRoots tours sponsored by McDonald's), frustrated by the erasure of black African slave traders from popular accounts, and ambivalent about pursuing reparations: "there is something innately servile about making an appeal to a deaf ear."

Perhaps the most bitter lines in the chapter are inspired by Hartman's recognition that memorializing the slave trade in Ghana had become "a potent means of silencing the past in the very guise of preserving it, since it effectively curbed all discussion of African slavery and its entailments." The form and style of "Lose Your Mother" seem to suggest that we might apply that judgment to the writing of history as well: there must be no smooth narratives, no pat conventions, no confident assertions that the problem of our relationship to the past has been resolved through painstaking empirical research. Writing the history of the slave trade might entail narrating your search for a lost mother, but it should also entail the acknowledgment that you're never going to get her back.

As I traveled through Ghana, no one failed to recognize me as the daughter of slaves, so the few stories people shared were kinder and less severe than they would be otherwise. No one said things like slaves were a bunch of stupid and backward people, or confided they were fit only for manual labor that required strong arms, or called them barbarians or criminals. If you believed that slavery was a relatively benign institution in Africa, then you certainly would not expect to hear such things, but in fact, masters and traders spoke about their slaves in exactly these terms and people continue to do so today. In my company, the polite refrained from such remarks and instead made jokes about how I had found my way back home or teased me about searching for my roots. They were used to Americans with identity problems. None openly expressed surprise or amazement that nearly two centuries after the abolition of the Atlantic slave trade, I was still hoping to find a hint or sign of the captives. If they experienced a twinge of remorse, no one let on. And even if I was indiscreet enough to mention my slave origins, most refused to follow me down this dangerous path and responded with studied indifference to all my talk of slavery. But silence and withholding were not the same as forgetting. Despite the dictates of law and masters, which prohibited the discussion of a person's origins, everyone remembered the stranger in the village, everyone recalled who had been a slave and with a discerning glance just as easily identified their descendants.

As it turned out, the slave was the only one expected to discount her past. It surprised me at first. Why would those who had lost the most be inclined or likely to forget? Clearly even someone like me, who was three generations away from slavery and who had neither a country nor a clan to reclaim, hadn't been deterred from searching. But as I traveled along the slave route, I soon found out about all the elaborate methods that had been employed to make slaves forget their country.

In every slave society, slave owners attempted to eradicate the slave's memory, that is, to erase all the evidence of an existence before slavery. This was as true in Africa as in the Americas. A slave without a past had no life to avenge. No time was wasted yearning for home, no recollections of a distant country slowed her down as she tilled the soil, no image of her mother came to mind when she looked into the face of her child. The pain of all she had lost did not rattle in her chest and make it feel tight. The absentminded posed no menace.

Yet more than guns, shackles, and whips were required to obliterate the past. Lordship and bondage required sorcery too.

Everyone told me a different story about how the slaves began to forget their past. Words like "zombie," "sorcerer," "witch," "succubus," and "vampire" were whispered to explain it. In these stories, which circulated throughout West Africa, the particulars varied, but all of them ended the same—the slave loses mother. Never did the captive choose to forget; she was always tricked or bewitched or coerced into forgetting. Amnesia, like an accident or a stroke of bad fortune, was never an act of volition.

When I asked, "What happened to the ones taken across the waters?" people passed on twice-told tales in which herbs, baths, talismans, and incantations transformed slaves into blank and passive automatons. In Ouidah, a town that had been a significant port on the Slave Coast, a university student told me that slaves were marched through a grove that induced forgetting, or that they encircled a tree of forgetfulness. Women had to circle the tree seven times, and men had to circle it nine times in order to forget their origins and accept their slave status.

The student joked, "The tree didn't work because now you are back." He pointed out the tree of return on the slave route.

"It doesn't make sense," I replied. "Why did they want the ones who had forgotten to return?"

He just smiled.

"Well, how do you say tree of return in the Fon language?" I asked.

"There's no word for it in our language because it's just something we tell foreigners."

Every part of West Africa that trafficked in slaves possessed its own Lethe, rivers and streams whose water made slaves forget their pasts, dense groves that trapped old memories in the web of leaves, rocks that obstructed entrance to the past, amulets that deafened a man to his mother tongue, and shrines that pared and pruned time so that only today was left. Traditional healers devised herbal concoctions that could make the most devoted husband forget his wife in the blink of an eye, marabouts applied potions and dispensed talismans that erased the trail home, priests forced captives to vow oaths of allegiance to their captors, sorcerers tamed recalcitrants with the powers of the left hand. European traders, too, employed occultists to pacify and entrance slaves with medicinal plants.

A famous slave trader on the Rio Pongo subdued his captives with the aid of an enchanted rock. He lined them up and forced each in turn to take a seat on the rock, which drained away all will. After this treatment, the prisoners no longer resisted their bonds, recalled their pasts, or attempted to flee the trader. After being washed with a brew distilled from plant roots, the slave was integrated into a group of the newly pacified.

In Ghana, captives were given ceremonial baths before sale to wash them clean of old identities. Medicine men, fetish priests, and slave traders recited songs and incantations that lulled the captive into embracing servitude and that eradicated all visions of home. In Ewe country, on the eastern coast, people still told stories of a brew or tonic that prevented slaves from retracing the path back to their country.

In the north, they possessed medicine so powerful that it transformed able-bodied men and women into vacuous and tractable slaves. The plant *Crotalaria arenaria,* a leguminous undershrub found in the savanna, was called *manta uwa,* which means "forget mother" in Hausa. Traders boasted that slaves ingesting the plant soon forgot their origins and no longer attempted to run away.

Manta uwa made you forget your kin, lose sight of your country, and cease to think of freedom. It expunged all memories of a natal land, and it robbed the slave of spiritual protection. Ignorant of her lineage, to whom could the slave appeal? No longer able to recall the shrines or sacred groves or water deities or ancestor spirits or fetishes that could exact revenge on her behalf, she was defenseless. No longer anyone's child, the slave had no choice but to bear the visible marks of servitude and accept a new identity in the household of the owner.

It was one thing to be a stranger in a strange land, and an entirely worse state to be a stranger to yourself.

This was the fate from which the boys in Elmina were trying to rescue me. Through their letters, they were trying to call me back from *donkorland,* not the territory raided for slaves but the land of oblivion. But what, if anything, could I remember after hundreds of years of forgetting?

The paths leading from the hinterland to the coast, to listen to slave traders tell it, swarmed with amnesiacs, soulless men, and walking corpses. As early as the fifteenth century, European traders had described their black captives as absentminded and innately servile. "In time," one traveler observed, "they soon forgot all about their own country." And by the eighteenth century these accounts had been repeated so often that they were accepted as truth. These people of no country were called "negroes" and "donkors." In the end these names were just another way of identifying them as the living dead. Race, Hannah Arendt observed, "is, politically speaking, not the beginning of humanity but its end . . . not the natural birth of man but his unnatural death."

Like the term "Negro," *donkor* was a badge of servitude, a stamp of those who had been uprooted, an earmark of dead men. It did not refer to any home or country or history but only to a dishonored condition. Like the term "nigger," *donkor* implied that "the human pulse stops at the gate of the barracoon."

Donkor was used as an epithet in Asante, the powerful inland state that controlled the traffic in slaves to the coast. It was "synonymous with the barbarian of the Greeks and Romans," a European factor explained, "which they [the Asante] apply to all people of the interior but themselves, and implies an ignorant fellow." A tome on Asante law and custom held that *donkor* was "applied strictly to any man or woman, other than an Asante, who had been purchased with the express purpose of making him or her a slave."

With the knowledge gained from ten slaving voyages to Africa, in which he traversed the territory from Cape Palmas to the Congo River, Captain John Adams judged "the Dunco" to be the most passive of all the people he encountered north of the equator. He first noted their appearance—"they were middle size and the color of their skin is not of so deep a black as those of the Fantee or Asshantee"—and then provided an assessment of their character: mild, tractable, and inoffensive. "They may be called a simple people, who never exhibit any sullenness of manner, but a uniform willingness to do to the best of their ability whatever they are desired; and the term Dunco, which in the Fante language signifies stupid fellow, or ignorant man, from the back country, is invariably given to them by the Fantees, as a term of derision, in consequence. To the Fantees, as well as to the Asshantees, they have a strong aversion, because they consider these people as the authors of their misfortunes."

In the opinion of Ludewig Roemer, a trader at Fort Christiansborg, a Danish settlement, "One could hardly call them human . . . The farther up in the land the slaves come from, the more stupid they are." But contrary to the prevailing view of northerners as a "well-mannered nation," Roemer insisted they were wilder and more savage than other slaves. To his eyes, they possessed a physiognomy like that of a tiger with comparable teeth in their mouths. Notwithstanding their wild nature and feral appearance, Roemer conceded that the fear of men like him hid behind their truculence. "The slaves who come from far north in the land think we Europeans have bought them to be fattened like swine, and that we eat them when they become fat. I cannot describe to what degree of desperation this fear drives them, so they seek to kill us."

Roemer was not the only trader fearful of slaves set upon destruction and revenge. The occult practices to induce forgetting were attempts to avert rebellion and forestall retribution. It wasn't only the memory of their kin and country that royals and merchants wanted the captives to forget but, as well, those responsible for their wretched circumstances.

An elderly Akan man ruminated about the cost of enrichment while conducting business with Roemer.

> "It is you, you Whites," they say, "who have brought all the evil among us. Indeed, would we have sold one another if you, as purchasers, had not come to us? The desire we have for your fascinating goods and your brandy, bring it to pass that one brother cannot trust the other, nor one friend another. Indeed, a father hardly his own son! We know from our forefathers that only those malefactors who had thrice committed murder were stoned or drowned. Otherwise the normal punishment was that anyone who had committed a misdeed had to carry to the injured party a large piece of firewood for his house or hut, and ask on his knees for forgiveness, for one, two, or three days in a row. In our youth, we knew many thousands of families here and at the coast, and now not a hundred individuals can be counted. And what is worse, you have remained among us as a necessary evil, since if you left, the Negroes up-country would not let us live for half a year, but would come and kill us, our wives and our children. That they bear this hatred for us is your fault."

This man was not alone in fearing the punishment to be meted out by slaves. Others shared his apprehension. By the middle of the eighteenth century, African merchants had begun to ponder the consequences of the Atlantic trade. While many weren't aware of the population decline occurring in West Africa as a result of the slave trade, which has been likened by scholars to the demographic impact of centuries of war, they had started to experience the social disruptions of the trade. The state of emergency caused by predatory greed was becoming slowly apparent and fears of social collapse or personal affliction haunted the ruling class. Royals, big men, and merchants feared the revenge of slave spirits, the envy of their inferiors, and the indictment of their riches. Like ruling men everywhere, they dreaded the hewers of wood, the rabble, the multitudes. They fretted about the course of events that might place the bottom rail on top. They nervously anticipated the retribution of slaves. The lives sacrificed for cloth, guns, rum, and cowries left their traces in the anxieties of the ruling class.

In the Congo, a group of traders formed an association called Lemba, which was a therapeutic cult for those afflicted with the disease of wealth. Lemba, which means "to calm," contained the disruptions caused by the slave trade with ritual and medicine. Like Keynesian economists, Lemba priests tried to cure capitalism by regulating the violence of the market and redistributing wealth to their kin and community. The members of the Lemba cult were the elite: healers, chiefs, judges, and the affluent. They were the ones vulnerable to the envy of the less fortunate and blamed for the social ills associated with the trade. Infirmity, sterility, and witchcraft tainted those allied with merchant capital. Gifts offered to high-ranking priests and riches shared with subordinates provided the remedy.

In Senegambia, the Diola built altars to their captives. Shrines adorned with wooden fetters (*hudjenk*) and consecrated with palm wine and the blood of animal sacrifice protected raiders and their captives and also determined who could and could not be seized as a captive. The priests who tended these shrines were required to have captured at least one slave with their own hands. A shrine was named after the first slave taken so that his or her name would perdure and the songs performed at the altar invoked the name of the man or woman responsible for the family's prosperity. The Diola traders recognized that slaves produced their wealth and for this reason they committed the names of their captives to memory. (In Antwerp or Lisbon, Nantes or Bristol, Charleston or Providence, no one invoked the names of the persons responsible for their riches.)

The spirit shrines of the Diola protected the communities involved in slave raiding from internal disruption. If the rules governing raiding were violated, traders were afflicted with a disease called *hupila*, which "made one feel like all one's limbs were bound in a rope." The disease replicated the bonds and immobility of the captive.

On the Slave Coast, the Ewe incorporated the *donkor* into their pantheon of spirits. In the Gorovodu religious practice, the spirits are *amefeflewo*—bought-and-sold people. This practice of spirit possession by slaves, explains an anthropologist, was a form of sacred debt payment by which the stolen lives of captives were redressed. The Ewe host offered her body as a vessel for *donkor* spirits. Possession, as a form of spiritual expenditure or loss, reversed the theft and accumulation of slave trading. By honoring slave spirits, the Ewe endeavored to amend the past and to make a place for strangers.

Even if the captives had managed to forget the acts of violence that made them slaves, ironically the traders could not. They remembered the riches and debts they had incurred by their participation in the trade. Apprehension regarding what they had done and how it might come back to them motivated these rituals of atonement. Royals and merchants could not afford to forget, at least not without risking all they had gained and being engulfed by the chaos and disorder of the slave trade.

Few of the enslaved forgot the royals, merchants, and thieves responsible for their captivity, even when they had forgotten their country. Each generation passed on tales of men who bled dry the lives of other men, who stank from the smell of corpses, and who gorged themselves on human flesh. The ones made property didn't take pleasure in the great wealth of ruling men, so their stories recounted the gruesome means by which the big men had acquired coffers of gold and cowries. In a volume of folktales titled *Nigger to Nigger*, collected in South Carolina by a white amateur folklorist, E.C.L. Adams, there is a portrait of a slave-trading king. The storytellers called him a "big nigger."

Way back in slavery time and way back in Africa, there had been a chief who betrayed his own tribe by helping white folks catch and entrap slaves. White folks used to give him money and trinkets, and, for this the king sent thousands into bondage. He would trick them onto the boat where the white men trapped and chained them. The last time the white men came to the coast, they "knocked dat nigger down an' put chain on him an' brung him to dis country."

When the king died, he was not desired in heaven and was barred from hell. God, the Greatest Master, condemned the king to roam the earth for all times. As retribution for having killed the spirits of men and women as well as their bodies, he would never be permitted any resting place. He would forever wander with the other marauding spirits of the bush. Banished to the dismal swamp, he was forbidden from ever touching a living thing and allowed to feed only off the dead. As he had sucked away the life of men, so he would spend the rest of his days as a buzzard with carrion as his only food.

Sometimes he would appear before those wandering or lost in the swamp, but his doom had been settled. He wouldn't ever hurt another person again. His evil beak and claw would never poke, scratch, or wound any creature still alive. Known all over the spirit world as the King Buzzard, he would travel forever alone.

If in the era of the trade the enslaved had been forced to *forget mother*, now their descendants were being encouraged to do the impossible and reclaim her. In the 1990s, Ghana discovered that remembering the suffering of slaves might not be such a bad thing after all, if for no other reason than it was profitable. So contrary to the legal precedents and prohibitions of three centuries, the state was now trying to create a public memory of slavery. Under the stewardship of Shell Oil, USAID, and a consortium of North American universities, the Ghanaian Ministry of Tourism and the Museum and Monuments Board crafted a story for the ten thousand black tourists who visited the country every year hungering for knowledge of slave ancestors. Tourism provided a ready response with a tale of the Atlantic slave trade as a distinctly African American story, with no mention of the expansion and increasing severity of African slavery in response to the Atlantic trade or of destitute commoners.

Local cottage industries in slave route tourism began sprouting up all over Ghana. In 1998, the Ministry of Tourism encouraged every district to form a Tourism Development Committee. Every town or village had an atrocity to promote—a mass grave, an auction block, a slave river, a massacre. It was Ghana's equivalent to a fried chicken franchise. McDonald's had already organized McRoots tours to Senegal and Gambia. No one knew for sure, but Ghana might be next. Few of the tour operators, docents, and guides put any stock in the potted history of the "white man's barbarism" and the "crimes against humanity" that they marketed to black tourists or believed the Atlantic trade had anything to do with them. They only hoped that slavery would help make them prosperous.

For Ghana, the slave route was a desperate measure to generate needed revenue and to develop a viable economy. For towns and villages scattered throughout the countryside, it was the possibility of digging new wells, building a school, or buying a vehicle to transport the sick to the small hospital one hundred miles away. For the jobless, it was the opportunity for employment in the tourism industry. For petty traders, it was an expanded market for their goods. For dreamers, it was the chance of a ticket to America.

Door of No Return rituals, reenactments of captivity, certificates of pilgrimage, and African naming ceremonies framed slavery primarily as an American issue and as one of Africa's relation to her "lost children." The biennial Panafest Historical Theatre Festival (Panafest), which began in 1992, attracted participants from all over the African diaspora. The reunification of the African family and the return of its children to the homeland were the animating themes of the festival. On the ground, this often translated into a comedy of errors, as in 1994 when the Ghanaian Concert Party Union decided to welcome black Americans to Ghana and pay homage to their culture with an old-style blackface performance. (A bureaucratic obstacle prevented the show from being performed.) A "take their heads" crusade was the response of taxi drivers, peddlers, and merchants.

Most recently, the Ministry of Tourism launched an advertising campaign to change the common perception of African Americans from one of rich tourists to one of brothers and sisters. This effort to make Ghana feel more like Jerusalem and less like Disneyland required Ghanaians to strike *obruni* from their vocabulary and welcome their African American kin back home.

"Remembering slavery" became a potent means of silencing the past in the very guise of preserving it, since it effectively curbed all discussion of African slavery and its entailments—class exploitation, gender inequality, ethnic clashes, and regional conflict. The sorcery of the state, like the sorcery of marabouts and herbalists, was also intended to wash away the past (at least those aspects that might create conflict) and to pacify the heirs of slaves, except that now this process was described as memorializing rather than forgetting. The arrival of "the ones who had been taken away" did not encourage a working through of this history but a bittersweet celebration of return, reunion, and progress.

So the descendants of slaves were welcomed with the red carpet treatment. They mourned their ancestors in great public ceremonies where chiefs assembled to atone for the past and to collect alms. And the brothers and sisters gave generous donations and shopped vigorously, perhaps hoping that the breach of the Atlantic would be bridged by their new roles as consumers. It was to everyone's advantage to believe this.

The heirs of slaves wanted a past of which they could be proud, so they conveniently forgot the distinctions between the rulers and the ruled and closed their eyes to slavery in Africa. They pretended that their ancestors had once worn the king's vestments and assumed the grand civilization of Asante as their own. They preferred to overlook the fact that the Asantehene (king of Asante) had helped to shove their ancestors onto slave ships and refused to admit royal power emanated from "the abuse of human beings and things." It was comic and tragic at the same time. The children of slaves were as reluctant to assume their place among toilers, laborers, and peasants as the elites. The irony of this was suggested by Aime Césaire: "We've never been Amazons of the King of Dahomey, nor princes of Ghana with eight hundred camels, nor wise men in Timbucktu under Askia the Great, nor the architects of Djenné, nor Madhis, nor warriors . . . I may as well confess that we were at all times pretty mediocre dishwashers, shoeblacks without ambition, at best conscientious sorcerers and the only unquestionable record that we broke was that of endurance under the chicote [whip]."

And even if African Americans were seduced by tourism's promise of an African home and willing to dance joyfully around trees of return and eager to experience solidarity with their newfound kin through freshly minted memories of slavery, most Ghanaians weren't fooled by the mirage, even when their survival necessitated that they indulge the delusion. The story of slavery fabricated for African Americans had nothing to do with the present struggles of most Ghanaians. What each community made of slavery and how they understood it provided little ground for solidarity. African Americans wanted to regain their African patrimony and to escape racism in the United States. Ghanaians wanted an escape from the impoverishment of the present, and the road to freedom, which they most often imagined, was migration to the United States. African Americans entertained fantasies of return and Ghanaians of departure. From where we each were standing, we did not see the same past, nor did we share a common vision of the Promised Land. The ghost of slavery was being conjured to very different ends.

In the United States, black people's insistence on reckoning with slavery in the face of national indifference, if not downright hostility, has been an effort to illuminate the crushing effects of racism in our lives. It is less a historical exercise than an ethical and political mandate. Simply put, the "legacy of slavery" is a way of saying that we had been treated badly for a very long time and that the nation owes us. Martin Luther King, Jr., employed the language of creditor and debtor races to underscore the elusive quest for racial justice. In the speech delivered at the March on Washington, he said, "America has given the Negro people a bad check, a check which has come back marked with insufficient funds." The promissory note to which King referred was the Constitution and the Declaration of Independence. As he saw it, the civil rights movement was an effort to "cash this check, a check that will give us upon demand the riches of freedom and the security of justice."

No one has ever been able to make the case persuasively enough to convince the government that this was true or even to be granted a day in court, despite the recent flurry of lawsuits for reparations. In overturning the use of affirmative action in granting city contracts, Justice Antonin Scalia wrote, "Under our Constitution there can be no such thing as either a creditor or a debtor race . . . We are just one race here. It is American." In the eyes of the court, no enduring harm had been passed across generations. And, even if it had been, we had slumbered on our rights for too long. Too much time had passed between the injury and the claim for redress. But for us the opposite was true. The time passed had only intensified the injury. History was an open wound, as Jamaica Kincaid writes, that "began in 1492 and has come to no end yet."

Who could deny that the United States had been founded on slavery or disregard the wealth created by enslaved laborers? Or brush aside three centuries of legal subjection? Yet I remain agnostic about reparations. I fear that petitions for redress are forms of political appeal that have outlived their usefulness. Did the bid to make a legal or political claim in an officially "post-racist" society require us to make arguments in a moral language that appeals to the abolitionist consciousness of white folks, who accept that slavery was wrong *and* believe that racism has ended? Are reparations a way of cloaking the disasters of the present in the guise of the past because even our opponents can't defend slavery now? Did we want a Federal Bureau of African American Affairs to decide and manage what we were owed? Or did we hope that the civil suits could accomplish what a social movement had failed to do, that is, to eradicate racism and poverty?

I had grown weary of pleading our case and repeating our complaint. It seems to me that there is something innately servile about making an appeal to a deaf ear or praying for relief to an indifferent and hostile court or expecting remedy from a government unwilling even to acknowledge that slavery was a crime against humanity.

In 1817, the black abolitionist Robert Wedderburn had warned of the dangers of appeal. In an address to the slaves of Jamaica, he encouraged them to stage a general strike to win their liberty. "Union among you, will strike tremendous terror to the receivers of stolen persons. But do not petition, for it is degrading to human nature to petition your oppressors." In 1845, Frederick Douglass echoed this sentiment when he described the slave's appeal as "a privilege so dangerous" that anyone exercising it "runs a fearful hazard" of inviting even greater violence.

I couldn't help but think of Josiah Wedgwood's famous antislavery medallion of the chained slave on bended knee, begging in supplication, "Am I not a man and a brother?" The medallion had enjoyed such popularity that it became the favored icon of the abolition movement and was worn as a brooch or hairpin by women of fashion in the 1780s and '90s. But the bid for emancipation reproduced the abject position of the slave. And the pleading and praying for relief before the bar struck me in exactly the same way—it was as an act of state worship. I didn't want to get down on my knees as a precondition to arriving at freedom. I didn't want to plead my case, "Yes, I have suffered too." I didn't want to display my scars.

When I envisioned the slave I didn't think of this fellow on bended knee, trying to maintain his dignity as he made the case for his humanity. His clasped hands were folded as if he were praying and his head was upturned slightly as if he were looking for God, but I understood that it wasn't God to whom he was looking and praying but to the people of England or France, who might as well have been God. And anyone looking down upon his naked figure could see that this man was helpless and needed their assistance despite his rippling muscles and broad chest and mighty shoulders. His humiliation moved them and made them feel guilty and excited their sympathy.

Of course, once you have assumed the position of supplicant and find yourself genuflecting before the court or the bar of public opinion, then, like the strapping man on the medallion, you have conceded the battle. It is hard to demand anything when you are on bended knee or even to keep your head raised. And you can forget trying to counter the violence that had landed you on your knee in the first place. Being so low to the ground, it is difficult not to grovel or to think of freedom as a gift dispensed by a kind benefactor or to imagine that your fate rests in the hands of a higher authority, a great emancipator, the state, or to implore that you are human too. "Am I not a man and a brother?" Having to ask such a question, no doubt, would have made the petitioner's nostrils flare with anger and perspiration bead on his forehead and the bile rise to the back of his throat.

Needing to make the case that we have suffered and that slavery, segregation, and racism have had a devastating effect on black life is the contemporary analogue to the defeated posture of Wedgwood's pet Negro. The apologetic density of the plea for recognition is staggering. It assumes both the ignorance and the innocence of the white world. If only they knew the truth, they would act otherwise. I am reminded of the letter that James Baldwin wrote his nephew on the centennial anniversary of the Emancipation Proclamation. "This is the crime of which I accuse my country and my countrymen," he wrote, "and for which neither I nor time nor history will ever forgive them, that they have destroyed and are destroying hundreds of thousands of lives and do not know it and do not want to know it . . . It is not permissible that the authors of devastation should also be innocent. It is the innocence which constitutes the crime."

To believe, as I do, that the enslaved are our contemporaries is to understand that we share their aspirations and defeats, which isn't to say that we are owed what they were due but rather to acknowledge that they accompany our every effort to fight against domination, to abolish the color line, and to imagine a free territory, a new commons. It is to take to heart their knowledge of freedom. The enslaved knew that freedom had to be taken; it was not the kind of thing that could ever be given to you. The kind of freedom that could be given to you could just as easily be taken back. Freedom is the kind of thing that required you to leave your bones on the hills at Brimsbay, or to burn the cane fields, or to live in a garret for seven years, or to stage a general strike, or to create a new republic. It is won and lost, again and again. It is a glimpse of possibility, an opening, a solicitation without any guarantee of duration before it flickers and then is extinguished.

The demands of the slave on the present have everything to do with making good the promise of abolition, and this entails much more than the end of property in slaves. It requires the reconstruction of society, which is the only way to honor our debt to the dead. This is the intimacy of our age with theirs—an unfinished struggle. To what end does one conjure the ghost of slavery, if not to incite the hopes of transforming the present? Given this, I refuse to believe that the slave's most capacious political claims or wildest imaginings are for back wages or debt relief. There are too many lives at peril to recycle the forms of appeal that, at best, have delivered the limited emancipation against which we now struggle.

In Ghana, they joked that if a slave ship bound for America docked off the coast today so many Ghanaians would volunteer for the passage that they would stampede one another trying to get on board.

But who would ever envy slaves or view a cargo hold as an opportunity or risk death to arrive in the Americas? Every year Ghanaians stowed away in packing crates, cargo holds, and ship containers trying to make their way to the United States or Europe. Twenty-three men arrived in New York in 2003 hidden in a cargo ship. The year before, two Ghanaian boys were found dead in the baggage compartment of a plane at Heathrow Airport. The subzero temperatures and lack of oxygen killed them. Each year young men and boys risked deadly voyages to escape poverty and joblessness, while girls fled to Abidjan and other cities and were trafficked internationally as prostitutes. It was the dire circumstances of the present that caused Ghanaians to make wisecracks about volunteering for the Middle Passage and to view black tourists as the fortunate heirs of Kunta Kinte.

What they didn't discern were the two decades of political setbacks and economic decline that had inspired these trips to the dungeon; what they didn't understand was that many of us also lived in poverty. (It didn't look the same, but the assault of poverty was life threatening in the United States too.) A growing sense of despair and an exhausted political imagination incapable of dreaming of radical change had everything to do with the busloads of black strangers looking to shed tears in a slave fort. There were no obvious signs of this diminished hope for the future. The grief of African Americans was opaque here. We were encouraged to mourn because it generated revenue, but our grief struck no common chord of memory, no bedrock of shared sentiment.

To most Ghanaians the government's efforts to commemorate the Atlantic slave trade were irrelevant. Besides, what had Jamaicans and Americans to do with their lives? When President Rawlings declared that on August 1, 1998, Ghana would celebrate Emancipation Day to commemorate the abolition of slavery in the British Caribbean, Ghanaians retorted, "Has slavery ended in Africa?" The British had also abolished slavery in Ghana, but President Rawlings had not planned any public celebrations of the colonial ordinances that ended slavery in the Gold Coast in 1874 and in the Northern Territories in 1897. Had Rawlings asked, "Are we yet free?" most Ghanaians would have answered with a resounding, "No."

This "no" resonated on both sides of the Atlantic. It was the reminder of what abolition and decolonization had failed to deliver. This "no" was the language we shared, and within it resided a promise of affiliation better than that of brothers and sisters.

Wendy Warren

"'The Cause of Her Grief': The Rape of a Slave in Early New England"

From the *Journal of American History* (2007)

Questions. Speculation. Imagination. Necessary parts of any historian's toolkit. But rarely are they as vividly and effectively deployed as in Wendy Warren's essay on a rape of a slave. Warren starts with just a few lines from a traveler's journal, and then builds out, and out, and out, into the surrounding world. These lines, and that world, codify and amplify each other astonishingly. Without the world—all the contingent social, cultural, political, economic circumstances—the rape would seem opaque, indecipherable. Without the rape the world would remain incomplete, at least in one particular sense—a sense with deep political implications. To perform her double-sided feat of illumination, Warren repeatedly confronts us with leading questions. She asks us, as well, to stand in the shoes of the victim. Only thus can we take a small, but significant, step back into her time and place.

... the Second of *October,* about 9 of the clock in the morning, Mr. *Mavericks* Negro woman came to my chamber window, and in her own Countrey language and tune sang very loud and shrill, going out to her, she used a great deal of respect toward me, and willingly would have expressed her grief in *English;* but I apprehended it by her countenance and deportment, whereupon I repaired to my host, to learn of him the cause, and resolved to intreat him in her behalf, for that I understood before, that she had been a Queen in her own Countrey, and observed a very humble and dutiful garb used towards her by another Negro who was her maid. Mr. *Maverick* was desirous to have a breed of Negroes, and

therefore seeing she would not yield by perswasions to company with a
Negro young man he had in his house; he commanded him will'd she
nill'd she to go to bed to her, which was no sooner done but she kickt
him out again, this she took in high disdain beyond her slavery, and this
was the cause of her grief.

John Josselyn, *Two Voyages to New England*, 1674

This is a story of a rape of a woman.

Indefinite articles saturate that last sentence deliberately. They mean to say:
this is not *the* story, not the *only* story—not the only story of rape, not the only
story of this woman. This is a story of a person whose sole appearance in historical documentation occurs in one paragraph of a seventeenth-century colonial travelogue. Given such paltry evidence, perhaps only indefinite articles
capture the indefinite nature of this narrative.

The facts are few. The approximate date and location of the assault seem
fairly certain: early fall 1638, not far from Boston, in the Massachusetts Bay
Colony. The central characters are equally clear: the slave owner, Samuel Maverick, an English merchant; John Josselyn, an English traveler; two enslaved
African women; and an enslaved African man. About the first two, at least,
some evidence exists. Their sex, race, class, and literacy combined to ensure
that some record of their lives survived their times. As for the other three, no
written document other than the paragraph above mentions their existence.
We know only what John Josselyn related: when he was a guest in Samuel
Maverick's house, he encountered a slave woman anguished because another
slave had raped her upon their owner's orders.[1]

But fortuitous timing, if anything about this story can be called fortuitous,
helps. In 1638 very few African slaves lived in the Massachusetts Bay Colony,
and a general scholarly consensus holds that they had all probably arrived
that same year aboard the same ship, the Salem-based *Desire*.[2] The arrival of
those first Africans in 1638 was unusual enough to warrant a brief mention in
Governor John Winthrop's journal; he noted that a trading voyage to the West
Indies had brought back "some cotton and tobacco, and negroes, etc., from
thence, and salt from Tertugos," thus describing the first known slaving voyage to New England.[3] Had the woman arrived even ten years later, her journey
would have been impossible to trace with any certainty at all, since the *Desire*
was only the first ship to engage in what became a prolific New England slave
trade. Instead, the woman's presence among the first Africans in New England makes possible a reconstruction of at least some of her life.

It is a life in need of reconstruction. More than one thousand African slaves lived in New England by the end of the seventeenth century, and slave trading was a crucial part of the early modern market that joined Africa, the West Indies, and England (colonies and metropole) to make early New England prosper as the century progressed. But those captured Africans who lived and labored in the region during the seventeenth century have been, as one historian recently noted, "too often overlooked." A change is certainly afoot: scholars of the colonial North have certainly given attention to the region's African inhabitants, but they have tended to focus on the eighteenth century. The enslaved Africans of seventeenth-century New England have received almost no sustained attention; the last book to focus exclusively on the subject of Africans in colonial New England was published in 1942 and is now out of print.[4]

Certainly one reason for the relative lack of attention to Africans in early New England is the problematic state of surviving evidence. Recorded references to African slaves in seventeenth-century New England are often little more than a line or two, and multiple entries concerning the same slave are almost entirely lacking. Nameless Africans appear and then disappear in court testimonies, in deeds, in wills, in letters, in inventories, and in diaries; their anonymity makes it very difficult to trace their lives with any certainty. That means stories such as the one Josselyn related have gone largely unexplored; an insistence on quantifiable evidence and on demonstrable change over time, combined with an inherent distrust of sources that report otherwise unrecorded events, has limited what scholars can do with documents about slavery in early New England.

Fortunately, many historians have demonstrated how to read documents against the grain, how to excavate "at the margins of monumental history in order that the ruins of the dismembered past be retrieved."[5] In this case, at the margins of colonial New England's monumental history lies the life of an African woman whose presence there can be understood only by envisioning all the region's earliest inhabitants as active participants in the rollicking seventeenth-century Atlantic world. Telling the story of "Mr. *Mavericks* Negro woman" draws attention to the fact that African slaves and sexual abuse existed alongside Puritan fathers, Indian wars, and town meetings in colonial New England. It also deepens the narrative of early African American history, too long located almost exclusively in the South; this enslaved woman first set foot on North American soil, not in Charleston nor in Jamestown, but in the northern port of Boston.[6] And race relations in early New England become tripartite—red, white, and black—when her story is included, complicating our understanding of early New England's racial categories. No matter how brutally Native Americans were treated in New England, we have no evidence that any Englishman ever considered forcibly *breeding* an Indian woman.

One story of one rape opens a view into a larger world of Anglican-Puritan rivalries, of gritty colonial aspirations, of settlement and conquest in the early modern Atlantic world, of race and sexuality and how those two constructs combined to determine the shape of many lives. But there are more compelling and more human reasons to tell this story. This woman's life deserves to be reconstructed simply because too many factors have conspired to make that reconstruction nearly impossible. Brought against her will to a foreign continent populated by peoples speaking unfamiliar languages, sold as property, raped, and then ignored in the public record, her story mirrors that of millions. Still, her individual resistance touches me; violated but not beaten, she "in her own Countrey language and tune sang very loud and shrill" to a passing stranger and thus ensured her life would be remembered.

That passing stranger was John Josselyn, an Anglican who came to New England in 1638 with two purposes: to visit his recently emigrated brother and to complete a fact-finding mission for potential investors and emigrants interested in the new colonies. His early presence reminds us that the synonymization of "Puritan" and "New England" did not occur in the minds of early modern settlers until much later—despite his arrival at the height of the famed great migration of Puritans, this was a young Anglican man, seeing what a still up-for-grabs New England had to offer. The son of an impoverished gentleman, Josselyn (like many other Englishmen of his class) may have seen North America as a place where he could regain the status his father, through lack of business acumen, had lost.[7]

His brother Henry Josselyn was already in the region, trying to do just that. Henry had allied himself early in the seventeenth century with Sir Ferdinando Gorges, one of the earliest speculators in New England and an early supporter of the Virginia Company. The wealthy, Anglican Gorges had hoped to establish a quasi-feudal colony in New England, and he had obtained the rights to the entire region—from Philadelphia to Quebec—as early as 1622. But his inability to lure workers willing to labor in a feudal system, combined with the steady success of the Puritan-run Massachusetts Bay Colony, stymied his colonial ambitions. The latter obstacle earned most of Gorges's wrath; as his venture failed, he became an ardent and lifelong enemy of the Puritans. Henry Josselyn came to New England under Gorges's protection sometime around

1630, serving first as an agent and then as a commissioner, suffering through all of Gorges's defeats and sharing his disappointments. This Josselyn eventually gave up hope of claiming land in southern New England, deciding to avoid conflicts with Puritan authorities by moving north. He settled in Maine, but he had not gone far enough—soon after settling, the beleaguered Henry found himself fighting Massachusetts Bay Colony attempts to annex the region. Perhaps understandably, Henry Josselyn's stance toward Puritans soon mirrored that of his benefactor.[8]

John Josselyn came to share his brother's antipathy to Puritans. Fraternal loyalty aside, Josselyn embarked on his voyage to America keenly aware that Puritans were gaining power and confidence in England and that the rank and privileges his father had once taken for granted were threatened. New England turned out to be no better. Puritans dominated the new settlements, and Josselyn found them less than cordial. He was undoubtedly relieved to stay with Samuel Maverick, a fellow Anglican and a staunch thorn in the side of Massachusetts Bay Colony leaders. Landing in Boston, July 20, 1638, Josselyn went immediately "ashore upon *Noddles Island* to Mr. *Samuel Maverick* . . . the only hospitable man in all the Country, giving entertainment to all Comers gratis." The "only hospitable man"? Witness the words of a disgruntled Anglican wandering the wilds of the city on a hill.[9]

John Josselyn was thirty years old when he met Maverick and the enslaved woman. He apparently spent the first part of his life attaining the education appropriate for an impoverished gentleman's son, which clearly included some scientific training. Such training may have led Josselyn to believe he approached Africans with a more objective eye than most. Certainly, Josselyn's dedication of his *Two Voyages to New England* to "the Right Honourable, and most Illustrious . . . Fellows of the Royal Society" suggests he hoped to interest readers espousing the new scientific world view. The work is filled with asides regarding Josselyn's accumulated scientific knowledge. He noted, for example, that though "many men" believed "that the blackness of the Negroes proceeded from the curse upon Cham's posterity," he knew that Africans simply had an extra layer of skin, "like that of a snake." Josselyn had discovered this extra layer, before coming to New England, while conducting an experiment on a "Barbarie-moor" whose finger became infected from a puncture wound. Josselyn, in attempting to cure the man, lanced the finger, probed the wound, and discovered that "the Moor had one skin more than Englishmen." The fate of the patient's multiskinned finger remains unknown. Still, the story helps clarify what Jossleyn thought of the woman when she came crying to his window, visibly upset even within her snakelike skin.[10]

Josselyn made his transatlantic voyage on the well-armed *"New Supply, alias,* the *Nicholas* of *London,* a ship of good force, of 300 tuns . . . man'd with 48 sailers, [carrying] 164 Passengers men, women, and children." The young traveler enjoyed his trip. Two days out of Gravesend, passengers dined on fresh flounder; Josselyn noted that he had "never tasted of a delicater Fish in all [his] life before." Six days later, the gastronome tasted "Porpice, called also a *Marsovious* or Sea-hogg," which sailors cut into pieces and fried. Josselyn thought it tasted "like rusty Bacon, or hung Beef, if not worse; but the Liver boiled and soused sometime in Vinegar is more grateful to the pallat." An innocent abroad, this Josselyn, delighted at the novelty of food and travel.[11]

But delighted innocence is only part of his story, a part that masks Josselyn's origins in a class and a society deeply invested in the maintenance of a strictly stratified social order. When Martin Ivy, servant to one of Josselyn's companions and only a child, a "stripling," was "whipt naked at the Cap-stern, with a Cat with Nine tails, for filching 9 great lemons out of the Chirurgeons Cabin," Josselyn expressed no sympathy, only amazement that the boy had managed to eat the nine lemons, "rinds and all in less than an hours time." Similar indifference swathes his description of the violent ducking of another servant "for being drunk with his Masters strong waters which he stole." Josselyn was interested enough to note these occurrences, and gentleman enough to consider them normal. This same attitude greeted the enslaved woman when she chose to complain. His journal notes her complaint but then quickly moves on—the very next sentence describes his first encounter with North American wasps. Although at first "resolved to intreat [Maverick] on her behalf," Josselyn ultimately did nothing to help the woman.[12]

Samuel Maverick found his visitor an enjoyable guest. When Josselyn's ship suffered delays before embarking on a trip up the coast, Maverick refused to let his guest sleep on the boat: "when I was come to Mr. Mavericks," Josselyn noted, "he would not let me go aboard no more, until the Ship was ready to set sail." Perhaps Maverick enjoyed having a sympathetic soul around, someone who shared his religion and background. After all, the troubles Josselyn felt in touring New England were experienced daily by his host.[13]

Samuel Maverick, also the son of an English gentleman (and clergyman), had settled in New England sometime around 1623, loosely attached to the Gorges colonization plan; like Josselyn's brother, Maverick had title to lands in Maine. He and another Englishman, David Thompson, settled further south and built fortified houses around what would become Boston. They were the first Europeans to settle in the area, but their settlement was neither peaceful nor secure; Maverick's house was "fortified with a Pillizado [palisade] and fflankers and gunnes both belowe and above in them which awed the Indians who at that time had a mind to Cutt off the English." Indians did attack the fort, "but receiving a repulse never attempted it more although (as they now confesse) they repented it when about 2 yeares after they saw so many English come over." Thompson and Maverick were men determined to make money while perched on the edge of an unfriendly continent. We might admire their grit, were it not for the ruthlessness it engendered.[14]

Maverick had acquired a wife, more land, and a new house—probably equally fortified—by the time the enslaved woman arrived, for the death of David Thompson offered him opportunities he could ill afford to miss. Maverick's marriage to Thompson's widow sometime around 1628, when he would have been twenty-six, gained him control of Thompson's tracts of land, including the "very fruitful" Noddle's Island, more than one thousand acres in the middle of Boston Harbor and the site of the rape. The island was easier to defend than mainland settlements, since reaching it required crossing a long expanse of water in an exposed boat. Maverick built himself a fine house on the island he inherited from Thompson, even playing host to John Winthrop when the soon-to-be governor arrived in Boston to establish the Massachusetts Bay Colony.[15]

European women, a scarce commodity, seldom stayed single long in early New England, so Amias Cole Thompson's quick remarriage was far from exceptional. She was a good match for Maverick; the English-born daughter of a shipwright, she brought to the marriage at least two children and a fair amount of pragmatism. A surviving letter, sent in 1635 from "Nottells Island" details an attempt to obtain an inheritance her father had promised to her children with Thompson, showing both determination and literacy. Both those attributes would have served her well. Life on Noddle's Island, or anywhere else in colonial New England, even given her husband's relative wealth, was labor-intensive. Perhaps this explains the felt need for slaves. With a sparse nearby population pool from which Maverick could hire servants to help his wife with household duties and their children (in addition to adopting Thompson's children, he fathered three of his own), chattel labor might have seemed an ideal solution.[16]

Even if there had been nearby families, it seems unlikely any of them would have sent their daughters to work in the Maverick household. Though the man was an early settler and wealthy, Massachusetts Bay Colony officials found him more annoying than respectful. From the beginning of the colony, Maverick insisted on being admitted as a freeman and having voting rights while he maintained ties to factions back in England who sought to overthrow the Puritan settlement and claim the colony's territory for less religious purposes. Although his wealth earned him admittance in the early years—before laws were passed limiting voting rights to church members—Massachusetts Bay Colony authorities grew increasingly impatient with Maverick's staunch Anglican and royalist leanings, occasionally banning him and more often censuring him. The treatment rankled. He later described the Puritan government as ruling "without the Knowledge or Consent of them that then lived there or of those which came with them."[17]

But the restrictive measures had little effect on Maverick, an ambitious man used to going his own way. Born in 1602, he was only twenty-two years old when he came to North America, willing to settle in a part of New England where no European had settled before, willing to live in a house that required a fortified fence and cannons. He was a merchant through and through—he traded furs with Indians and seems to have chosen to live in Boston because it lay at the mouth of both the Mystic and the Charles rivers, making it an excellent trade post. Living in such an isolated post was no easy feat—he reminisced some years later that the "place in which Boston (the Metropolis) is [now] seated, I knew then for some years to be a Swamp and Pond." As for his wife, her courage and fortitude matched his. In 1635, the same year she wrote the letter mentioned above, Samuel Maverick was away in Virginia, buying corn and supplies for his land. Amias Maverick stayed without her husband for twelve months with her children and servants, running the household on an island three thousand miles away from her birthplace.[18]

One wonders what Samuel Maverick saw and did in Virginia that year. Clearly, it was a business trip—he returned to Boston with "14: heifers & about 80 goates (havinge loste aboue 20: goates by the waye)." And we know he did some sight-seeing in the southern colony. He observed to an interested John Winthrop that eighteen hundred Virginians had died while he was there and that "he sawe the bone of a whale taken out of the earthe (where they digged for a well) 18: foote deepe." Ever the merchant with an eye for a deal, Maverick also bought two boats, one a forty-ton cedar pinnace "built in Barbathes" and "brought to Virginia by Capt. Powell, who there dyinge, she was sold for a small matter."[19]

His trip also seems to have been educational. Virginia may have been one of the first places, if not the first, where Samuel Maverick saw African slavery in practice. Unlike New England, the southern colony had been settled by masses of single men determined to profit from the region's resources by growing the most profitable crop they could. That they found their solution in tobacco, a terribly labor-intensive crop, only meant that they needed to find cheap and plentiful labor. The first slave arrived in that colony in 1619, present from the beginning of the colonial experiment. They would have been scarce when Maverick visited, but it seems possible he saw African slaves, at least some of whom were legally enslaved for life, along with their children. Was all that in his mind when he returned to New England with his ships and cows and goats and corn?[20]

Or did other encounters give him the idea of breeding slaves? Perhaps we should wonder what Maverick might have talked about with the ship's crew from Barbados. That island already had some connections to New England; Henry Winthrop, John Winthrop's son, was one of the first colonizers of Barbados—he hoped to make his fortune by growing tobacco, the island's specialty during the 1630s. Though the elder Winthrop was unenthusiastic about his son's interest in acquiring a fortune (and about the poor quality of the tobacco young Henry grew, which his father considered "verye ill conditioned, fowle, full of stalkes and evil coloured"), they maintained a steady correspondence throughout Henry's stay on the island. Other writers shared similar news with friends and family in New England—through connections like those, Maverick might have already heard about the potential fertility of the soil, the economy, or the climate. We know that his beloved son Nathaniel settled early in Barbados, perhaps demonstrating by actions more than words what his father thought of the island's prospects.[21]

They would not have been alone in believing Barbados an incipient boomtown. Others heard the same news and had the same ideas. The 1630s were a time of trial and error and burgeoning success for English planters determined to profit from the island. African slaves were along from the beginning, though they became essential only after the 1640s, when the planters switched definitively from tobacco to sugar. Still, the first planter on Barbados brought with him ten black slaves, a trend that grew during the next decades.[22] During the seventeenth century, most slaves taken from Africa on English ships went to Barbados, though some found their way to other places in North America and the West Indies. So perhaps the West Indian crew told Maverick about the slowly increasing numbers of African slaves that were just arriving in Barbados, or how cheap they were to purchase, or that any offspring they produced were included in the original purchase price. Perhaps there were slaves on the ship; perhaps Maverick saw some.

Or perhaps Maverick had already intended to use African slaves. He certainly knew about slavery before going to Virginia. Consider the relationship he had with Sir Ferdinando Gorges. Gorges had rights to Maine, but he was also a founding member of the Virginia Company and an investor in both the Bermuda and Guinea companies, organizations that showed no distaste for African slavery. Indeed, the Guinea Company was an early version of the Royal African Company, a slave-trading concern, and Bermuda had slaves long before Virginia did (interestingly, a "Captain Powells" was an active trader in Bermuda during the seventeenth century). Gorges's grandson, another Ferdinando Gorges, became a successful sugar planter in Barbados and also an active shareholder in the Royal African Company. Maverick knew at least one of these men—the first Gorges—and was probably acquainted with others of that ilk. He aspired to join their ranks, and he may have seen slaveholding as his means of doing so.[23]

Last, but far from least, we should also consider the influence of other European powers on a young man such as Samuel Maverick. Spain and Portugal had extensive and well-documented experience in the African slave trade by 1638; by one estimate, each of those empires had already transported 150,000 African slaves to their Atlantic colonies by the mid-seventeenth century.[24] Maverick, as a savvy merchant, would have known this. He would also have known Dutch merchants active in the early seventeenth-century Atlantic world, including the early slave trade. In 1637, one year before the rape, they captured Elmina from the Portuguese, thus solidifying control of one of the most prominent slave forts in West Africa. They were also prominent actors in early New England, due to the proximity of the colony of New Netherlands. Samuel Maverick certainly encountered Dutch merchants while he lived in Boston, and certainly some of them would have had slaves on board their vessels. Slavery was everywhere in the early modern world, even in New England; just three years after the rape, Massachusetts wrote slavery into its Body of Liberties, ordering that "there shall never be any Bond-slavery, Villenage or Captivity amongst us, unless it be lawful Captives taken in just wars, [and such strangers] as willingly sell themselves or are sold to us." Far from exciting repugnance, Maverick's purchases and actions seem to have inspired codification.[25]

Still, Maverick's specific motivations and inspirations for buying slaves remain murky. We know only that by 1638, two years after his return to Boston from Virginia, he owned at least three Africans: two women and a man, of unknown age or ethnicity. Almost certainly the rape victim came from Africa, as her age (she was still young enough to reproduce, perhaps an adolescent) and her linguistic abilities (she could not speak English) combined to suggest a limited time in the Americas. The other female slave seems to have come from the same area, since the two women spoke the same language and apparently shared understandings of their relative status. Their exact point of origin is impossible to identify. In the early seventeenth century the majority of slaves left land from ports in West Africa's Slave Coast, Gold Coast, or the Bight of Biafra, but a point of departure was no indication of birthplace; forts served as points of consolidation for caravans that came from all over the continent.[26]

When speaking of the origins of captured Africans, we are too often reduced to generalities. Slaves left the continent after spending, on average, about three months in the coastal forts. Their mortality rates were extremely high even while they were in Africa; one in five died either on the march or while waiting in the prisons, long before ever setting foot on a ship.[27] Some scholars have posited this experience and the voyage that followed as the key factor creating a new cultural identity: African American. But to assume an automatic sense of community at this stage of captivity is perhaps premature; remember the words of Richard Ligon, an early visitor to Barbados, explaining why slaves did not revolt: "They are fetched from severall parts of Africa, who speake severall languages, and by that means, one of them understand not another." Shared experiences, but not shared histories.[28]

Solidarity of a sort was forced on slaves during the next stage of their trip. Mortality rates for the middle passage in the seventeenth century ranged from 10 to 30 percent during the seven- to eight-week journey across the open Atlantic Ocean, crammed into the holds of wooden ships, trapped in excrement, vomit, and sweat.[29] Stuffed into the ship's steerage in temperatures sometimes rising to about 120 degrees, the slaves jostled for room and steeled themselves for the nightmarish weeks or months to come.[30] Rather than face the unknown horrors ahead and the known terrors at hand, some opted for the only escape they could manage. Weighted by chains, unable to swim, they threw themselves into the swells—a last grim display of human independence. John Josselyn sampled flounder and porpoise during his transatlantic trip; Samuel Maverick's slave woman was almost certainly not so lucky.

Her voyage must have ended in the Caribbean islands, the first stop for most seventeenth-century slave ships headed anywhere in the Americas except Brazil. Dehydrated, weakened, possibly abused, most slaves needed sprucing before going ashore. Brought on deck in the bright tropical sun, they saw their sores masked with a mixture of iron rust and gunpowder. We know that slavers hid the omnipresent diarrhea by inserting oakum—hemp treated with tar and used for caulking seams in wooden ships—far into an afflicted slave's anus, far enough to avoid detection during the invasive bodily inspections potential buyers inflicted on the human goods. Samuel Maverick's slave woman may have sat on the deck and experienced these practices, may have watched sailors throw over-board those too sick to be disguised. Did she consider herself lucky to have survived so long? Did she care? Did she know where she was? Did the Caribbean setting feel strange and new, or did the relief of seeing dry land, any dry land, make these unknown islands feel welcoming?[31]

Someone bought her from the slave ship, and probably at a bargain price; we know that slightly later in the century, a young woman brought only 80 to 85 percent of the price a young man might command in the Caribbean slave market. Ten years after the rape, Richard Ligon described sales of slaves in Barbados this way: "When they are come to us, the Planters buy them out of the Ship, where they find them stark naked, and therefore cannot be deceived in any outward infirmity. They choose them as they do Horses in a Market; the strongest, youthfullest, and most beautifull, yield the greatest prices. Thirty pound sterling is a price for the best man Negro; and twenty five, twenty six, or twenty seven pound for a Woman." This is an early version of a "scramble," a sales method in which prospective buyers rushed on board a ship, seizing and laying claim to all slaves they could reach. A terrifying experience, certainly, to be inspected and purchased by strangers. And for some it must have been emotionally draining to see shipmates carted off in different directions without any hope of seeing them again. And yet, the sale of "Mr. *Mavericks* Negro woman" may have involved at least one person from her ship: her companion, the woman Josselyn called "her maid," who used a "very humble and dutiful garb . . . towards her," was apparently sold with her. Were they marketed as friends? Sisters? Or as a queen and her servant? Was it luck that they were grabbed together? Josselyn does not say. We do know that somehow, at some point, they were both bought and brought to isolated Providence Island. And it was from that small volcanic island located one hundred miles off the east coast of Nicaragua that the first group of African slaves embarked for New England aboard the *Desire*.[32]

A surprising group controlled Providence Island: English Puritans. The colony was founded in 1630, the same year as the Massachusetts Bay Colony, by many of the same people. Although we too often forget that Puritans went to the West Indies, they did so, and with lofty ambitions; the Caribbean colony was expected to be the premier example of Puritan society, a city on a hill with good weather and fertile soil. In the valleys between the volcanic ridges that descended from the towering peak to the Caribbean shores, island proprietors hoped to use slave labor to grow goods destined for a European market. The two Puritan regions maintained frequent contact, comparing growth and progress. The biggest difference, of course, was slavery, a labor system for which these Puritans showed little distaste.[33]

From the colony's inception, slaves were crucial, as the founders decided to grow cotton and tobacco on large plantations. Accordingly, Providence Island colonists—Puritans, remember—imported slaves in relatively large numbers; by the time "Mr. *Mavericks* Negro woman" left in 1638, captured Africans made up almost half the colony's population. That racial balance only exacerbated the insecurity felt by the English planters over their precarious position, alone in the western Caribbean, surrounded by Spanish territorial claims. As it happens, they were insecure for good reason. Slaves first took advantage of their numbers to flee into the island's hilly interior, a steady stream of black fugitives populating the hills above Providence Island's white settlements. And then they got bolder. On May 1, 1638, Providence Island slaves carried out the first slave rebellion in any English colony. Soon after, frightened colony authorities began selling slaves off the island. Despite the sales, when the Spanish conquered the island in 1641, they found 381 slaves and 350 English colonists; the previous year the governor of the colony had warned that the island's slaves threatened to "over-breed us," a phrasing that finds echoes in Josselyn's account.[34]

But Samuel Maverick's slave woman had left long before that. She arrived in Boston in 1638, probably part of that cargo of "some negroes" aboard the *Desire,* commanded by Salem's William Pierce, also eventually a slaveholder; he later died on a return trip to Providence Island, shot dead by the Spanish soldiers who had recently captured the place. The *Desire* was large, one hundred and twenty tons of merchant ship, built and armed in Marblehead, Massachusetts. And it was fast: it once made the trip from Massachusetts to England in just twenty-three days.[35] We do not know how fast it traveled to New England from the Caribbean—but we might imagine the dread the slave woman felt on reboarding a ship, and the memories it must have brought back of the horrendous Atlantic passage she had already endured. A reluctant world traveler. Did she believe she was going home, having paid her dues in sweat and blood? Did she board the ship believing she was about to repeat the middle passage? Can we imagine the courage it would take to believe that and yet keep moving forward?

The trip to New England, on a far less crowded boat and for a far shorter time, may have alleviated some of her anxiety. But think how strange she must have found Boston, a marginal outpost of wooden homes, peripheral not only to the slave trade but also to most of the world. Noddle's Island, when she arrived, was a woodsy and isolated place—a 660-acre coastal island, hilly and marshy and so overgrown with trees that inhabitants of Boston went there to cut firewood. Boston in 1638 was scarcely more; growing rapidly (two years after the founding of Harvard College), as yet it was "rather a Village, than a Town," Josselyn noted, "there being not above Twenty or Thirty houses." But it seems safe to assume that the vegetation would have startled the woman less than the fact that other Africans (aside from the two in her household) were nonexistent, probably for the first time in her life. In the West Indies, she would probably have engaged in agricultural labor alongside other Africans. She had likely lived far enough from the overseers to understand that slaves were one group, the whites another. She might have felt some ease in the nights, sleeping among people who had shared the same horrible experiences. But in New England she probably slept near her owners, probably inside their house. And during the day she labored with them on domestic duties, perhaps side by side with Amias Maverick, certainly alongside white servants.[36]

Not that this common space bespoke familiarity or friendliness. Race set her apart in seventeenth-century Boston, where hers was one of only a handful (if that) of black faces. As she walked among the pale English, perhaps she heard comments in a language she could not understand and felt stares whose meaning was only too clear. Children might have thrown stones at her and laughed at her color. They would have done so in England, and this was, after all, only a new England.[37] How can one assess the emotional toll of such isolation or the pain of that most debilitating of feelings: loneliness? In a world where kinship and connections meant everything, what did such solitude feel like?

Race was not the only factor that could earn ostracism, but it mattered immensely. English children throwing stones in Boston would have had reason to fear people of a different hue, for New England in 1638 had just recently emerged from the violent and bloody Pequot War. The same colonization process that spurred wars and raids in Africa brought similar effects to North America, as Native Americans were threatened and dislocated by the arrival of English settlers—a reminder that Samuel Maverick's fortified house was a necessity, not a whim. The Pequot War began with a now-infamous surprise English attack on a native settlement near the Mystic River in present-day

Connecticut, which saw between three hundred and seven hundred Indians shot or burned to death. As the fighting progressed, some of the Pequots were taken captive and sent into servitude among English settlers, while "fifteen boys and two women" were sent into Caribbean slavery on board the *Desire*. Captained by William Pierce, the *Desire* somehow missed its intended destination of Bermuda and headed instead to Providence Isle. Samuel Maverick's slave woman boarded the ship on the return leg of that same journey. She thus arrived less than a year after the war ended, with the conflict only barely muted, one-half of New England's first slave swap.[38]

Those Pequot captives who remained in New England might have viewed her arrival with some interest. A lack of female servants had plagued New England colonies since their settlement, and female captives were considered an ideal solution to the problem. Racial stereotypes characterized Indian women as submissive and industrious, making them seem ideal domestic labor in Puritan households, and many were placed into a labor situation something like slavery, even if it differed from the experience of Africans. But Indian women did not share English enthusiasm for the project. Many of the women had lost their families to English violence during the war, and they were understandably unwilling to provide their enemies with domestic labor; flight was common. English violence toward female servants did little to encourage Indian women. The rape of an Indian servant by a colonist named John Dawe was well known; one woman subsequently captured during the war asked John Winthrop to ensure that "the English would not abuse her body."[39]

Maverick's slave came to know rape and captivity; perhaps she felt some solidarity with the Native Americans she certainly encountered on Noddle's Island, a key trade post. In the eighteenth century, Africans and Indians in New England did indeed forge bonds—even marriage bonds—as they found themselves simultaneously pushed to the peripheries of Puritan culture.[40] But the connections they forged in the seventeenth century are less clear. Native peoples held far more power during the initial years of encounter than they would after King Philip's War in the 1670s, and so they may not have seen any similarity between their own situation and the plight of the first African slaves in New England. It is equally unclear how a captured African would have viewed Native Americans. Would an African eye, for example, have immediately distinguished them from English colonists? Or would all the foreign garb and the language and the customs—English and Indian—have been equally strange to "Mr. *Mavericks* Negro woman"? A delicious irony if, despite the English settlers' obsession with differentiating themselves from Native American peoples, African eyes could not tell them apart.

But eventually an English sense of superiority and aloofness must have been apparent to the woman. Race and religion were keys to this colonial experiment, and native New Englanders were neither white nor Christian. Surely, English attitudes toward them highlighted this fact. Consider the messages John Winthrop received concerning captive Pequots. A Captain Stoughton, who fought against the Pequots, sent some captives to Boston along with the following note:

> By this pinnace, you shall receive forty-eight or fifty women and children . . . Concerning which, there is one, I formerly mentioned, that is the fairest and largest that I saw amongst them, to whom I have given a coate to cloathe her. It is my desire to have her for a servant, if it may stand with your good liking, else not. There is a little squaw that Steward Culacut desireth, to whom he hath given a coate. Lieut. Davenport also desireth one, to wit, a small one, that hath three strokes upon her stomach, thus: --|||+. He desireth her, if it will stand with your liking. Solomon, the Indian, desireth a young little squaw, which I know not.[41]

Intimate rhetoric, to be sure. Lieutenant Davenport knew the stomach markings of his desired servant so well, he drew them from memory. Steward Culacut gave his coat to another "little squaw" that he "desireth," a proprietary gesture. Even the most benign reading of these lines cannot avoid noting the obvious sense of ownership these men felt, while a less benign reading finds sexual overtones throughout. It seems impossible to imagine the men writing in the same way about European women. Samuel Maverick's sense of ownership was the same, only heightened by the fact that he did legally own the African woman, all of her, including her reproductive capabilities. And like any man on the move, he hoped to make quick use of his purchase.

His actions underscore his hurry. He bought the first slaves off the first slave ship to arrive in New England, thinking like so many others that owning human property would help him on his path to riches. "Desirous to have a breed of Negroes," Maverick compelled his male slave to have sex with the female "will'd she nill'd she"—whether she wanted to or not. And the story is clear: Maverick knew she did not want to. He gave the orders to the slave man only after first "seeing she would not yield by perswasions." Clearly he felt no shame about forcing a woman to submit to rape, since he himself told the story to Josselyn, a man he knew to be writing a report of his trip. Anyway, even if she protested, she was his property—property that, if forced to breed, could make him money.

Consider Samuel Maverick writing to John Winthrop only two years after the rape, concerned that a white, female servant of his had acted inappropriately.

> Worshipfull Sir,—My service beinge remembered, you may be pleased to understand that there is a difference betwene one Ralfe Greene and Jonathan Peirse, each challinginge a promise of mariage from a maide servant left with me by Mr. Babb, beinge daughter unto a friend of his. Either of them desired my consent within a weeke one of the other, but hearinge of the difference, I gave consent to neither of them, desiringe there might be an agreement first amongst themselves, or by order from your worship. The maide hath long tyme denied any promise made to Greene, neither can I learne that there was ever any contract made betwene them, yett I once herd her say shee would have the said Greene, and desired my consent thereunto; but it rather seems shee first promised Peirse, and still resolves to have him for her husband. For the better clearinge of it, I have sent all such of my peopell as can say any thinge to the premises, and leave it to your wise determination, conceivinge they all deserue a checke for theire manner of proceedinge, I take leave and rest
>
> Your Worships Servant at Commaund,
> Samuel Mavericke

This is a different Samuel Maverick, concerned about the propriety of a servant's engagement, reluctant to let her commit to either man without a clearing of the matter. Such attention to details! Such obedience to custom! Did race make the difference in his consideration of sexual mores? Of course it did. If ever there was a reminder of the inextricable linkage of gender and race, here it is. The seeming illogic of his varying degrees of concern becomes utterly rational when Maverick's ideological assumptions replace our own.[42]

His wife must have shared those beliefs. Responsible, like most New England women, for all domestic concerns, it seems likely that Mrs. Maverick would have had more contact than her husband with the slaves in their household. Had she ordered that the woman be raped? Had she suggested it? Did she know? Is it fair of me to wonder if she felt any sisterly bond with the woman under her roof? Her own quick, second marriage to Maverick suggests she may have seen relationships in practical terms. On a frontier, after all, relatively few have time for romance. That pragmatism may have expanded to include her slaves. She must have understood her own marriage and her own status in the world at least partly in contrast to the position held by her slave women. Amias Maverick could not be ordered to have sex with a man; she was something different, and so were her daughters, and everyone on the island knew it. Thus is race, a social construction, made real.[43]

That reality was ugly. Imagine the first time the man came to "perswade" the woman to have sex with him. Perhaps he came under duress. Maverick, after all, held both their lives in his hands. Did the enslaved man understand his own safety to be contingent on his agreeing to harm the woman? Did they even speak the same language? We know from Josselyn's account that the woman refused, even as she may have known that refusal was not an option. So perhaps the man suffered, too. Having watched slavers abuse women in the same ways she had witnessed and experienced, the slave man now found himself obligated, perhaps against his conscience, to use his own body to enact the same violence on an acquaintance. Resistance would have been pointless; even had he run away, Maverick could have bought another slave to "breed" with the woman. An impossible situation.

But maybe the man needed no threats and deserves no sympathy. Slavery could make men feel impotent, powerless—if not literally, certainly socially. Perhaps the man saw as irresistible the opportunity to reassert his masculinity. No matter how low his race placed him in New England's power structure, the woman's gender placed her a step lower still. Impregnating her may have seemed an excellent way to reassert the sense of self-worth and autonomy his environment consistently denied him. Or maybe he was simply a violent man, sold out of the West Indies for the very tendencies that made him willing to rape at his owner's request.[44] Or maybe, just maybe, he thought making a child was resistance itself; a thumb in the eye of a system determined to use Africans until they died.

Those questions can never be answered. But even certainty about the man's motives would not change the outcome.

The woman was raped, and she knew it was coming; Josselyn tells us that she had had warning. She waited, perhaps for nights, knowing that a man she lived with had orders to impregnate her, by force. An extra form of torture, the psychological before the physical, enacting the future attack from memory in her mind before living it in reality. Even if she had been lucky enough to escape the experience herself, she had undoubtedly seen and heard rapes of other women. She *knew* what to expect, in graphic detail. Alone, scared, isolated by race, culture, even language from those around her, she had to wait.

The attack itself remains shadowy. No amount of scholarship can uncover that encounter. I can only ask uncomfortable questions, verging on prurience, wondering how to reflect on the details of a rape without becoming what Saidiya Hartman has cautioned us against, a "voyeur" of pain and terror. Speaking of nineteenth-century slave punishments, she reminded us that "only more obscene than the brutality unleashed at the whipping post is the demand that this suffering be materialized and evidenced by the display of the tortured body or endless recitations of the ghastly and terrible." And yet, describing a rape without inquiring into its circumstances seems to draw the same curtain over the act that one historian did in the early twentieth century; he omitted "Josselyn's story of his interview with Maverick's servant girl," finding it "perhaps a little questionable for discussion here, even in this supposedly modern age."[45]

More than a little questionable, this rape. Professional and personal reticence aside, to me it calls out for inquiry; the woman's cries to Josselyn demanded an investigation. And so, four hundred years later, perhaps we should wonder what rape looked like on Noddle's Island. Did it happen at night? Did the man or Maverick feel enough shame about their actions to want it done in the dark, hidden? If so, where would he have found enough privacy for the attack? In the abundant woods? Or in the house, where no one could have avoided hearing the screams and cries? Eighteen years later, a bill of sale listed the following structures on the island: "the mansion howse. Mill howse and mill bake howses and all the other . . . howses outhowses barnes [and] stables."[46] Signs of prosperity for Maverick, and of multiple locations for an attack.

How did the attack occur? When? Where? Did Samuel Maverick watch? Why didn't he do it himself? Did his skin crawl at the thought of racial mixing? Or at the thought of fathering children fated to be slaves? Did Amias Maverick refuse to allow another woman's blood to stain her marriage bed? Did the Maverick daughters know what was happening? Were they being raised by the woman now being attacked? Everyone in that house knew her name, a luxury we do not share. Did any of them question what was happening? What did her "maid" do?

Did the woman fight back? Did she scream, this woman who "sang" so "loud and shrill" the next day? She must have struggled; a woman unwilling to "yield by perswasions" would not have given in easily to violence. Maybe the description of her troubled "countenance and deportment" the next morning referred to visible bruises, to blood, to tears. Or maybe she resigned herself to the attack, deciding not to make it worse for herself, terribly aware that no part of her body was safe from invasion. Resigned or not, afterward "she kickt him out," an indication that she was beaten but not conquered.

Did she allow herself the luxury of tears afterward? Or was she too accustomed to life's brutality? Was there water available to clean herself? (Questions of seventeenth-century hygiene suddenly take on new importance.) What was recovery like, in a household shared with other slaves (including her attacker) and servants? Maybe the other female slave offered a shoulder to cry on, one familiar face in a crowd of pale strangers. Or maybe, just maybe, the rape meant little to a woman fully immersed in one of the most violent enterprises the world has ever known. Maybe the woman, a proven survivor, took the rape in stride, just as she had the invasive bodily inspections done at every slave sale, just as she might have handled the oakum forced up her anus by greedy slavers hoping to hide the effects of the starvation regimen they had forced on their transatlantic human cargo.

She had the power to thwart Maverick's goals. She knew that getting pregnant could keep her from repeated attacks, knew that not conceiving essentially guaranteed them. She may have resisted to the end, refusing to conceive, denying Maverick and the slave man mastery over her reproductive labor. Did she conceive and then abort the child? By doing so often enough, she could have convinced her owner of her infertility, a bittersweet victory; abortion and infanticide were known and employed in the early modern world, sharp sticks having always been in abundance. The weapons of the weak are seldom pretty.[47]

No record reports whether or not she conceived. We know the assault grieved her enough to make her cry "loud and shrill" to a stranger, John Josselyn, a visiting white man. Desperate and frightened, but also obviously angry and perhaps hopeful of reprieve, she turned to someone from whom—because of his nationality and skin color—she had reason to expect only more abuse. Interestingly, her response fit exactly what English law called for a rape victim to do. The procedure a woman was supposed to follow in early modern England to report a rape was elaborate and relatively unchanged from medieval times:

> She ought to go straight way . . . and with Hue and Cry complaine to the good men of the next towne, shewing her wrong, her garments torne . . .

and then she ought to go to the chief constable, to the Coroner and to the Viscount and at the next County to enter her appeale and have it enrolled in the Coroners roll: and Justices before whome she was again to reintreat her Appeale.[48]

"Mr. *Mavericks* Negro woman" came with hue and cry to complain, but a language barrier prevented her from explaining the situation, and centuries of ideology apparently prevented Josselyn from caring enough to do anything more than note the story, just one more colorful anecdote in a colorful travelogue. In 1672 he published his first book, *New-Englands Rarities Discovered,* which ends by describing Native American women as having "very good Features; seldome without a *Come to me,* or *Cos Amoris,* in their Countenance, all of them black Eyes, having even short Teeth, and very white, their Hair black, thick and long, broad breasted, handsome straight Bodies, and slender." He ended with a poem containing these lines:

> Whether White or Black be best
> Call your Senses to the quest;
> And your touch shall quickly tell
> The Black in softness doth excel,
> And in smoothness; but the Ear,
> What, can that a Colour hear?
> No, but 'tis your Black ones Wit
> That does catch and captive it.
> And if Slut and Fair be one,
> Sweet and fair, there can be none:
> Nor can ought so please the tast
> As what's brown and lovely drest. . . .

Though the poem was, according to Josselyn, originally written about a "young and handsome gypsie" and then changed to describe "the Indian S Q U A, or Female *Indian,*" the black-versus-white color rhetoric, along with the use of the word "captive," seems curiously relevant to his encounter with the slave woman.[49]

Josselyn lived until 1674. He died in England, having apparently decided New England's pleasures were not for him. He never wrote another word regarding the woman, and he published the account of his voyages, *Two Voyages to New England,* some thirty years after his encounter, leaving unchanged his written opinion of Maverick, "the only hospitable man in all the Country."

Though his official writings are fairly numerous, Samuel Maverick's personal papers have long since disappeared; archives lack letters he wrote to his children, his diary, his personal accounts. We know that he died sometime between 1670 and 1676, probably in his early seventies, after a long and active life. He spent some years in New York, became a royal commissioner, and stayed an enemy to Puritan settlement. He also remained a part of the slave business; in 1652 he entered into an agreement with Adam Winthrop and John Parris (of Barbados) "for the delivery of a Negro in may next."[50]

Noddle's Island also stayed in the business. Samuel Maverick sold the island to George Briggs of Barbados, who sold it to John Burch, also of Barbados, who sold it in 1664 to Sir Thomas Temple. The latter sold it in 1670 to Col. Samuel Shrimpton, a prominent Boston merchant whose portrait, which sometimes hangs in the Massachusetts Historical Society, also depicts, in the background, an African slave. All those men were connected to the slave trade.[51] Lured by its ideal position in the harbor, slave traders and slave owners possessed the island continuously during the seventeenth century, and well into the eighteenth.

In the twentieth century, landfill was added and Noddle's Island became East Boston, a working-class area just west of Logan airport. To get there today, take the blue subway line to the Maverick stop. Go, as I did, on a blustery midweek day in early October—the same time of year as the attack. Follow Maverick Street from Maverick Square right down to the docks, and look across the harbor to Boston's center, just as a scared African woman must once have done. Her story will stick in your mind; despite the omnipresence of her owner's name, it is "Mr. *Mavericks* Negro woman" who haunts the spot.

At some point every historian decides how to frame her argument; I deliberately chose a method that makes visible the gaps in my evidence. As a result, perhaps this story is as much about the writing of history as about a rape. Researching in 2006, I am a beneficiary of historical schools that have called into question the validity of histories based on documents written by, and produced for, a minority of any given population. I have been taught to note that early New England's sources are largely written by and for white men, while remembering that before 1800, four-fifths of the females who crossed the Atlantic were African.[52] Some of those women ended up in early New England, and their stories should be told.

In *The Return of Martin Guerre,* Natalie Zemon Davis explained that when documents relating to her characters ran dry, she "did [her] best through other sources from the period and place to discover the world they would have seen and the reactions they might have had." Davis described the finished project as part "invention, but held tightly in check by the voices of the past." Davis had more evidence than I do, to be sure, but her comment seems relevant to my narrative. Without imagination, how can we tell such stories? We are not scientists; we cannot test our hypotheses; we cannot recall our subjects to life and ask them to verify our claims or to provide more information on the topics they fail to discuss. We make our way among flawed sources, overreliant on written texts, hopelessly entangled in our own biases and beliefs, doing the best we can with blurry evidence, sometimes forced to speculate despite our specialized knowledge. The very beauty of history lies in that messiness, the fact that "unless two versions of the same set of events can be imagined, there is no reason for the historian to take upon himself the authority of giving the true account of what really happened."[53]

I don't *know* anything about the woman who ended up on Noddle's Island in 1638—indeed, I suppose it is possible that Josselyn made up the whole story for reasons we cannot fathom, or that he misunderstood the situation, or that I have misunderstood the situation myself. But I have chosen to believe Josselyn's version. Someone else, infuriated by my methods, can tell a different story; I embrace that possibility. In the meantime, I offer this: We have known, for a long time, a story of New England's settlement in which "Mr. *Mavericks* Negro woman" does not appear; here is one in which she does.

NOTES

1. Paul J. Lindholdt, ed., *John Josselyn, Colonial Traveler: A Critical Edition of* Two Voyages to New England (Hanover, 1988), 24.

2. See, for example, Lorenzo Greene, *The Negro in Colonial New England* (New York, 1942), 17–18; George F. Dow, *Slave Ships and Slaving* (Salem, 1927), 268; and Winthrop D. Jordan, *White over Black: American Attitudes Toward the Negro, 1550–1812* (Chapel Hill, 1968), 66–68.

3. John Winthrop, *The Journal of John Winthrop, 1630–1649*, ed. Richard Dunn, James Savage, and Laetitia Yeandle (Cambridge, Mass., 1996), 246.

4. Ann Marie Plane, *Colonial Intimacies: Indian Marriage in Early New England* (Ithaca, 2000), 119. On African Americans in the colonial North, see William D. Piersen, *Black Yankees: The Development of an Afro-American Subculture in Eighteenth-Century New England* (Amherst, 1988); and George Henry Moore, *Notes on the History of Slavery in Massachusetts* (New York, 1866). This article joins a surge of interest in slavery in the North. Examples include John Wood Sweet, *Bodies Politic: Negotiating Race in*

the American North, 1730–1830 (Baltimore, 2003); Thelma Wills Foote, *Black and White Manhattan: The History of Racial Formation in New York City* (New York, 2004); and Jill Lepore, *New York Burning: Liberty, Slavery, and Conspiracy in Eighteenth-Century Manhattan* (New York, 2005). For helpful articles, see Robert C. Twombley and Robert H. Moore, "Black Puritan: The Negro in Seventeenth-Century Massachusetts," *William and Mary Quarterly*, 24 (April 1967), 224–42; Albert J. Von Frank, "John Saffin: Slavery and Racism in Colonial Massachusetts," *Early American Literature*, 29 (Dec. 1994), 254–72; and Melinde Lutz Sanborn, "Angola and Elizabeth: An African Family in the Massachusetts Bay Colony," *New England Quarterly*, 72 (March 1999), 119–29. See also the recent collection formed from the 2003 Dublin Seminar for New England Folklife: Peter Benes and Jane Montague Benes, eds., *Slavery/Antislavery in New England* (Boston, 2005). The 1942 book is Greene, *Negro in Colonial New England*.

5. Saidiya V. Hartman, *Scenes of Subjection: Terror, Slavery, and Self-Making in Nineteenth-Century America* (New York, 1997), 11. See also Emma Perez, *The Decolonial Imaginary: Writing Chicanas into History* (Bloomington, 1999), xii–xvii.

6. Rhode Island merchants dominated the African slave trade to North America for most of the eighteenth century. Jay Coughtry, *The Notorious Triangle: Rhode Island and the African Slave Trade, 1700–1807* (Philadelphia, 1981), 25.

7. Lindholdt, ed., *John Josselyn, Colonial Traveler*, xiv–xv.

8. Miller Christy, "Attempts Toward Colonization: The Council for New England and the Merchant Venturers of Bristol, 1621–1623," *American Historical Review*, 4 (July 1899), 683–85; Bernard Bailyn, *The New England Merchants in the Seventeenth Century* (Cambridge, Mass., 1955), 5–9; Lindholdt, ed., *John Josselyn, Colonial Traveler*, xviii.

9. Lindholdt, ed., *John Josselyn, Colonial Traveler*, 12.

10. Ibid., 5, 3, 129–30.

11. Ibid., 5–7.

12. Ibid., 7–8.

13. Ibid., 23.

14. William Sumner, *A History of East Boston: With Biographical Sketches of Its Early Proprietors* (Boston, 1858), 69–75; Samuel Maverick, *A Briefe Discription of New England and the Severall Townes Therein together with the Present Government Thereof* (1660; Boston, 1885), 13.

15. Mellen Chamberlain, *A Documentary History of Chelsea, Including the Boston Precincts of Winnisimmett, Rumney Marsh, and Pullen Point, 1624–1824*, vol. I (Boston, 1908), 16; Sumner, *History of East Boston*, 9; Winthrop, *Journal of John Winthrop*, ed. Dunn, Savage, and Yeandle, 36.

16. Elizabeth French, "Genealogical Research in England: Maverick," *New England Historical and Genealogical Register*, 69 (1915), 157–59; "Mrs. Amias Maverick to Trelawny," in *Documentary History of the State of Maine*, vol. III: *The Trelawny Papers*, ed. James P. Baxter (Portland, 1884), 76–78.

17. Thomas Prince, *A Chronological History of New England in the Form of Annals* (Boston, 1826), 321; Thomas Hutchinson, *The History of the Colony and Province of Massachusetts-Bay* (Cambridge, Mass., 1936), 124–25; Maverick, *Briefe Description of New England,* 17.

18. Chamberlain, *Documentary History of Chelsea,* 21; Prince, *Chronological History of New England,* 323; Maverick, *Briefe Description of New England,* 26. Samuel Maverick's brother Moses helped his sister-in-law; he is listed in colonial records as having paid taxes on Noddle's Island to the General Court in 1636. See French, "Genealogical Research in England."

19. Winthrop, *Journal of John Winthrop,* ed. Dunn, Savage, and Yeandle, 182. The identity of Captain Powell remains elusive. He may have been John or Henry Powell, ship captains who worked for an influential Barbadian merchant. See Richard S. Dunn, *Sugar and Slaves: The Rise of the Planter Class in the English West Indies, 1624–1713* (Chapel Hill, 1972), 49–50, 58.

20. Edmund Morgan, *American Slavery, American Freedom: The Ordeal of Colonial Virginia* (New York, 1975), 297.

21. A. B. Forbes, ed., *Winthrop Papers, 1498–1628* (5 vols., Boston, 1929–1947), I, 356–57, 361–62, and esp. II, 66–67; French, "Genealogical Research in England," 158–59.

22. Dunn, *Sugar and Slaves,* 71.

23. Madge Dresser, *Slavery Obscured: The Social History of the Slave Trade in an English Provincial Port* (New York, 2001), 10–20; Virginia Bernhard, "Beyond the Chesapeake: The Contrasting Status of Blacks in Bermuda, 1616–1663," *Journal of Southern History,* 54 (Nov. 1988), 546–49.

24. Dunn, *Sugar and Slaves,* 71.

25. Johannes M. Postma, *The Dutch in the Atlantic Slave Trade, 1600–1815* (New York, 1990), 13–19; Pieter Emmer, *The Dutch in the Atlantic Economy, 1580–1880* (Brookfield, 1998), 17–20; "Body of Liberties, 1641," in *Documents Illustrative of the History of the Slave Trade to America,* vol. III, ed. Elizabeth Donnan (New York, 1969), 4.

26. David Eltis, *The Rise of African Slavery in the Americas* (New York, 2000), 246–50.

27. Herbert Klein, *The Atlantic Slave Trade* (Cambridge, Eng., 1999), 130; Paul E. Lovejoy, *Transformations in Slavery: A History of Slavery in Africa* (New York, 2000), 62–64.

28. See Sidney Mintz and Richard Price, *The Birth of African-American Culture: An Anthropological Perspective* (Boston, 1976), 42–43; Richard Ligon, *A True and Exact History of the Island of Barbados* (London, 1673), 46.

29. It is difficult to estimate slaves' shipboard mortality in the early seventeenth century, since the slave trade was not professionalized until the later decades of the century. For a one-in-three estimate for 1663–1713, see Eltis, *Rise of African Slavery in the Americas,* 185. Other scholars suggest that earlier trips were less deadly, as market needs did not yet force maximum efficiency from each trip. A 5 to 10 percent mortal-

ity rate was more typical for early seventeenth-century slaving trips across the Atlantic Ocean, when the Dutch still controlled the trade, according to Carl Bridenbaugh and Roberta Bridenbaugh, *No Peace Beyond the Line: The English in the Caribbean, 1624–1690* (New York, 1972), 245. A 20 percent mortality rate for the early seventeenth century is posited by Klein, *Atlantic Slave Trade*, 136–37.

30. Kenneth F. Kiple and Brian T. Higgins, "Mortality Caused by Dehydration During the Middle Passage" in *The Atlantic Slave Trade: Effects on Economies, Societies, and Peoples in Africa, the Americas, and Europe*, ed. Joseph E. Inikori and Stanley L. Engerman (Durham, 1992), 321–25.

31. Daniel Mannix, *Black Cargoes: A History of the Atlantic Slave Trade, 1518–1865* (New York, 1962), 128–29.

32. Eltis, *Rise of African Slavery in the Americas*, 111; Ligon, *True and Exact History of the Island of Barbados*, 46; Winthrop, *Journal of John Winthrop*, ed. Dunn, Savage, and Yeandle, 246.

33. Karen O. Kupperman, *Providence Island, 1630–1641: The Other Puritan Colony* (New York, 1993), 26, 325–35. Kupperman notes that Providence Island colonists overcame Puritan unease over slavery through hubristic reasoning: an "inward turned logic allowed the company dedicated to Providence to assume that God had provided perfectly acclimated heathens to work in tropical fields. If God had not intended their use, why did he make Europeans ill-suited to such labor conditions, while Africans worked so well under the hot sun?" Ibid., 178.

34. Karen O. Kupperman, "Errand to the Indies: Puritan Colonization from Providence Island Through the Western Design," *William and Mary Quarterly*, 45 (Jan. 1988), 75–81; Kupperman, *Providence Island*, 170–72. For the quotation from Gov. Nathaniel Butler of Providence Island, see ibid., 172.

35. Winthrop, *Journal of John Winthrop*, ed. Dunn, Savage, and Yeandle, 352–57. Pierce's slave, a woman, apparently attempted to burn down his house while he was away on a trip. See James Duncan Phillips, *Salem in the Seventeenth Century* (New York, 1933), 96–97.

36. Nancy Seasholes, *Gaining Ground: A History of Landmaking in Boston* (Cambridge, Mass., 2003), 355; Chamberlain, *Documentary History of Chelsea*, 16; grant of Noddle's Island to Samuel Maverick, in records of a court held at Boston, April 1, 1633, oversize box 1, David S. Greenough Papers, 1631–1859 (Massachusetts Historical Society, Boston); Lindholdt, ed., *John Josselyn, Colonial Traveler*, 18.

37. Jordan, *White over Black*, 6–15.

38. Winthrop, *Journal of John Winthrop*, ed. Dunn, Savage, and Yeandle, 227; Michael L. Fickes, "'They Could Not Endure That Yoke': The Captivity of Pequot Women and Children After the War of 1637," *New England Quarterly*, 73 (March 2000), 58–61.

39. See Margaret Ellen Newell, "The Changing Nature of Indian Slavery in New England, 1670–1720," in *Reinterpreting New England Indians and the Colonial Experience*,

ed. Colin G. Calloway and Neal Salisbury (Boston, 2003), 106–36. Fickes, "'They Could Not Endure That Yoke,'" 67–70.

40. Daniel Mandell, "Shifting Boundaries of Race and Ethnicity: Indian-Black Intermarriage in Southern New England, 1760–1880," *Journal of American History*, 85 (Sept. 1998), 468.

41. George Henry Moore, *Notes on the History of Slavery in Massachusetts* (New York, 1866), 7.

42. Samuel Maverick, "Letters to John Winthrop," *Collections of the Massachusetts Historical Society*, 7 (1865), 307. I am reminded of Elsa Barkley Brown's admonition to recognize that differences in class and race mean "that all women do not have the same gender." Elsa Barkley Brown, "'What Has Happened Here': The Politics of Difference in Women's History," *Feminist Studies*, 18 (Summer 1992), 300.

43. A long-standing and well-developed European discourse on non-European sexuality was employed constantly in encounters with other peoples. See Jennifer Morgan, *Laboring Women: Reproduction and Gender in New World Slavery* (Philadelphia, 2004), esp. 12–49.

44. On African men's reactions to their feminization in the New World, see Edward Pearson, "'A Countryside Full of Flames': A Reconsideration of the Stono Rebellion and Slave Rebelliousness in the Early Eighteenth-Century South Carolina Lowcountry," *Slavery and Abolition*, 17 (Aug. 1996), 22–50.

45. Hartman, *Scenes of Subjection*, 3–4; Edward Rowe Snow, *The Islands of Boston Harbor: Their History and Romance, 1626–1935* (Andover, 1935), 237.

46. "Indenture Between Samuell Mavericke and John Burch," in *Suffolk Deeds*, liber II (Boston, 1883), 325–27.

47. On contraceptive and abortive techniques that may have been used by slave women, including herbs and "pointed sticks," see Barbara Bush, *Slave Women in Caribbean Society, 1650–1838* (Bloomington, 1990), 142. See also Morgan, *Laboring Women*, 114–15.

48. *The Lawes Resolution of Women's Rights; or the Lawes Provision for Woemen: A Methodicall Collection of Such Statutes and Customes, with the Cases, Opinions, Arguments and Points of Learning in the Law, as doe properly concerne Women* (London, 1632), 392–93.

49. John Josselyn, *New-Englands Rarities Discovered in Birds, Beasts, Fishes, Serpents, and Plants of that Country* (London, 1672), 101–2, 99.

50. French, "Genealogical Research in England," 157; "Bond Between Samuel Maverick and John Parris," in *Suffolk Deeds*, liber I (Boston, 1880), 262.

51. "Notice of Sale from Maverick to Briggs," oversize box 1, Greenough Papers; "Petition of Samuel Shrimpton, 1682," Massachusetts Archives (microfilm), vol. 16, p. 309 (Massachusetts State Archives, Boston); Snow, *Islands of Boston Harbor*, 239–40; Andrew Oliver, Ann Millspaugh Huff, and Edward W. Hanson, *Portraits in the Massachusetts Historical Society: An Illustrated Catalog with Descriptive Matter* (Boston, 1988), 93.

52. Eltis, *Rise of African Slavery in the Americas,* 97.

53. Natalie Zemon Davis, *The Return of Martin Guerre* (Cambridge, Mass., 1983), 5; Hayden White, *The Content of the Form: Narrative Discourse and Historical Representation* (Baltimore, 1987), 20.

Stephen Berry

"The Historian as Death Investigator":
From *Weirding the War: Stories from the Civil War's Ragged Edges* (2011)

You find yourself immersed in a little-known set of documents: nineteenth-century coroners' reports from South Carolina. You become enchanted. The starting point is always the same, because you start with the end: someone has died, and here is the body. But the backstories open windows on all kinds of perverse drama: alcoholism, spousal abuse, the violence of children, master-slave murder, accidental poisoning, infanticide. How do you make sense of it?

Perhaps you start by launching census searches on certain individuals and arranging them into categories: "What we are glimpsing here is predominantly the world of the poor white. Fully a quarter of the witnesses are making their marks with an 'X.'"

You of course offer certain caveats, noting that no society should be evaluated based on only one narrow type of archive, and that people in positions of power and authority surely avoided coroners' investigations even when they were implicated in the most dubious deaths.

Then you look for various kinds of trends: "There are fewer coroners' reports for the war years than there are for any four-year span." You conclude that if "you were a white male who died under suspicious circumstances in Spartanburg County, South Carolina, between 1840 and 1870, you most likely died of a combination of alcohol and stupidity." At times, you try to re-create gruesome scenes of death and its aftermath, fully aware of the limitations on your knowledge but committed to conveying the "wretched sympathy" you feel as you witness, in your imagination, the moments when people tie ropes around their necks and kick chairs from under themselves, or when white children, "bedraggled and panting," pull a black playmate from the river after they themselves have drowned him.

And, if you're Stephen Berry, you develop a haunting, lyrical prose style that gropes toward a humane understanding of the relationship between

the dead (them) and the dying (us). You always go into the archive knowing that your subjects are heading toward death, and so their actions, in
the interim, almost inevitably take on an epic quality. But if your focus
remains on ways of dying—if death itself starts to seem mundane, the obvious end of every storyline—then perhaps, out of the corner of your eyes,
you'll be able to glimpse that much more of ordinary life, the immediacy
and indeterminacy of daily muddling.

I learned the profoundest lesson of Civil War history from a dog-eared
1978 translation of *The Song of Roland.* As the translator Frederick Goldin
explained in his introduction, the past, by its past-ness, has an "urge" to
be epic. Roland, we know, is going to die. We know, when he dons his ar-
mor, that he dons it for the last time. We know he can't *not* go into battle.
He does what he does because he *must,* because history demands it, because
we are watching and know that it has already been done. Betrayed and defeated, Roland must helplessly lift his olifant to his lips, and blow until his
temples burst. Whatever he might have hoped, his death is, from our perspective, foreordained. "Roland is the agent of an accomplished action," Goldin
notes, "and we are privileged to witness [his] graceful conformity to the rule of
necessity."[1]

Longstreet's sad nod, allowing Pickett to step off, has, when read from the
vantage of the present, this same epic necessity. Longstreet *has to* nod; he
can't help himself, not because Lee has ordered it, but because, again, history
demands it. (Longstreet may *suspect* the enormity of what's about to happen,
but we *know* it, and his helplessness before providence seems that much more
profound as a result.)

This is why it is almost impossible for the Civil War *not* to turn into an
American *Iliad.* I can perfectly see what Pickett and his boys are up to: they're
about to take canister in the face to protect one of the most repugnant institutions imaginable. And yet, by Goldin's rule, their deaths are epic, because
fore-doomed, and man-boy that I am, and perverse besides, I can't help but
wonder what it would be like to take a faceful of grape for something I believe
in. Staring over Faulkner's "roaring rim," I am constantly in danger of being
captured by the epic past, by epic Death.

And I resent it. So, a tilter-at-windmills, and a historian besides, I give myself the nod and step off, determined to find a battlefield on which I can defeat
the epic-ness of Death.

~

Over the last year, more than three hundred Southerners have died, if not in my arms, then in my hands. Three hundred times I have watched as a woman reaches for the wrong medicine bottle and poisons herself or her infant. Three hundred times I have stood by as an act of discipline, or drinking, goes too far. Three hundred times I have done nothing as people reach the end of their rope and kick the stools out from beneath their feet. Admittedly, these are not people dying for the first time; they are people re-dying for me as I read the reports of their coroners. But historical documents have a way of telescoping the past and present because, though written in the past, they exist in the present. Thus, deaths that are old news to them, who once were, are new news to me, who still is. It is, after all, the me of the present who unfolds the next report to discover that a group of white children has purposely drowned their playmate, a slave boy, not so much out of malice, but because he is different, and a weak swimmer, and obedient, and because they have decided, without speech, to drown their own innocence. And it is equally the me of the present who watches with a kind of rage and wretched sympathy as, bedraggled and panting, they haul the body ashore and look at each other with an unspoken admission that on this day, in this creek, dark deeds, half-understood, have been committed and witnessed too early. And finally it is me who must refold this document and set it aside. I am a professional, after all, and I have an agenda, and a deadline.[2]

I want to return to this subject of the dead (them) and the dying (us) in a moment, but for now I would simply submit that coroners' inquests are some of the richest untapped records we have of life and death in the nineteenth-century South. To be sure, in some cases, a coroner's inquest is pro forma. A jury is called and concludes that the person lying before them died "at the hands of a person or persons unknown." But in many cases the record is far richer. The antebellum coroner was not a homicide detective or a medical examiner—he was both. As a kind of "Quincy" meets "Columbo," he inspected the body and (possible crime) scene, rounded up witnesses, heard testimony, and made a recommendation. If there was cause, he would seek an arrest warrant. Far more than the sheriff, he was familiar with the strange intimacies inherent in the varied ways people go out of the world.[3]

The history of the office is interesting in itself. The coroner is as old as death and taxes—and related to both. In medieval England, if the sheriff was the king's guard dog, charged with keeping the peace, the coroner was the king's

vulture, charged with scavenging the countryside in search of potential revenue. (The word "coroner" itself is derived from "corona," Latin for "crown.")
Wherever disaster loosed property from its legal moorings—whether by ship-
wreck, fire, or act of God—wherever a coin fell from a private pocket into the
public square (as in cases of buried treasure), the circling coroner was apt to
descend. The medieval coroner did, as today, investigate sudden deaths, but
he did so less to establish cause or criminality than to determine if the crown
could turn a profit in the Reaper's wake. Where the coroner suspected suicide,
the crown could claim the estate. Where the coroner found a dead Norman on
the village commons (which evidently happened a lot), the crown could levy a
fine called the "Murdrum," from which the word murder derives.[4]

Gradually coroners became different animals, though they have always
been creatures of the state. The state is not a disinterested observer in our
comings and goings, after all. It has a vested interest in us. We are, as taxpay-
ers, its lifeblood, a fact which may explain why the titles of coroners' reports
imply an almost adversarial relationship with the dead: "The State of South
Carolina vs. the dead body of William Jasper," for instance, or "The State of
South Carolina vs. the dead body of a person unknown." The state, it seems,
resents the passing even of strangers, if not as a financial matter, then at least
as a bureaucratic inconvenience.[5]

But for now let's say I am more interested in the reports themselves than
in the coroners who wrote them or the office that produced them. In the 311 inquests I have examined so far, I have found evidence that would support studies of antebellum abortion, child abuse, spousal abuse, master–slave murder,
and slave-on-slave violence. To be sure, one might get glimpses of these same
things in more traditional court records. But especially in the Old South, cases
like these had a way of not quite percolating up through the court system.
(And this says nothing of cases in which nothing "actionable" occurred, cases
of suicide, accidental death, or "acts of God.")

To be sure, the view from a Southern coroner's office is unrelentingly bleak.
No society can or should be judged wholly from its morgue, nor indeed from
any single place. But surely there is something significant in knowing that
if, for instance, you were a white male who died under suspicious circumstances in Spartanburg County, South Carolina, between 1840 and 1870, you
most likely died of a combination of alcohol and stupidity. If it was winter,
you passed out and died of exposure. If it was spring or summer, you fell
off your horse and broke your neck. This reality is sad enough. Sadder still
is the price your dependents paid for your right to drink yourself stupid. If

you were a white female in the same county over the same time span, and the coroner came to claim you, you most likely hung yourself. And if you were a black male? Again, you most likely hung yourself. Long before Billie Holiday thought to sing about it, variegated fruit hung from the South's poplar trees. (Although to be candid, these coroners' reports are strangely precise about *what* these people hung themselves from, and it is usually not poplar. In Spartanburg, the preference was for oak or walnut.) The Old South is often remembered as a violent place, but if you asked the coroner before the war, he'd tell you it was more fair to call it a self-destructive place. Looking out his window, what he mostly saw was white men drinking themselves and their dependents to death.[6]

Now, it is possible that the suicides among blacks and white women are unrelated to male abuse and binging. On September 3, 1849, for instance, Sarah Shacleford was laundering some clothes with a friend when she suddenly stopped, excused herself, took a long handkerchief from the pile and walked into the woods where she hung herself from an unspecified tree. We will probably never know why she was doing laundry one minute and hanging from a tree the next. At the coroner's inquest Anderson Rogers volunteered that Sarah's mind had been "deranged for some time," and perhaps it was.[7]

But the word "deranged" covers a lot of territory. At her inquest, jurors used the same word to describe Jane Soseby, who hung herself on January 12, 1859. "I thought she presented some signs of derangement," noted one witness. "I have heard of her being deranged," noted another, or, at least, "[I] think [I have] seen her when she was not altogether alright." And indeed Jane was not all right. Because her husband was beating her with anything handy. "I seen one [wound] on her as if she had been struck with a stick," one witness told the coroner, "and one on her eye as if he had kicked her which she said he had done." Another witness testified that Jane had showed her "some marks or bruises on her body inflicted as she said by her husband. . . . I should suppose they were done by a good heavy hickory." (Again, Southerners grimly know their timber.) Such spousal abuse is hardly surprising; Jane's husband, and men like him, were masters of small worlds. But the indifference of Jane's community *is* a little surprising. Jane showed her wounds to at least five neighbors, admitted to all of them that she wanted to kill herself, and admitted to some that she thought she might "destroy her children [first] as they were suffering and would suffer" worse when she was gone. But the neighbors could not, or did not, intercede. And so, "no satisfaction to herself or any body else," Jane tried to cut her throat but found the knife too dull, tried to find a river in which to drown herself, but could never find it, and finally gathered up her courage with her husband's rope and went to the woods. Jane had found her exit strategy; her children would have to find their own.[8]

Like the fact that they beat their spouses, I was not surprised to learn that men and women occasionally murdered their slaves. I *was* surprised to learn how often the coroner responded. In her WPA interview, Mittie Freeman remembered the coroner as "that fellow that comes running fast when somebody gets killed." The coroner is mentioned in many of the most famous slave narratives, including those by Frederick Douglass and William Wells Brown. The coroner, in fact, is often the only magistrate mentioned because he was the only outside law the slaves ever saw. To be sure, there were undoubtedly countless masters who murdered their slaves and effortlessly covered it up. But if the murderer was someone other than the master, or if the master failed to cover it up, there was usually an investigation, at the very least because property had been destroyed, and someone expected compensation. Reflecting on the South he was forced to flee because of his Unionism, John Aughey noted: "Of course the laws which exist in every state against the murder or torturing of slaves are about as well observed as might be laws enacted by wolves against sheep-murder, and providing that between wolf and sheep no sheep could be witness." He is partly right But there was actually a subtle game of community standards going on. Standing over the body of a slave and surveying the grim damage, a coroner's jury was often perfectly comfortable recommending that a white be indicted. And at coroners' inquests slaves *were* allowed to testify. The actual jury nullification came later, in the courtroom, when the mangled body was not actually present and the murderer was let off. But by then he had been held up to public scrutiny; his judgment and decency had been questioned publicly and legally. It is less than justice, but it is not nothing, a fact which slaves themselves recognized. When the coroner came a-runnin', many slaves thought he might bring justice with him from some far off, saner place. And in his own *Narrative*, Frederick Douglass tells the story of an unnamed slave girl whose mistress "pounded in her skull" with a piece of firewood because she allowed the baby to wake the household. "I will not say that this murder most foul produced no sensation. It *did* produce a sensation. A warrant was issued for the arrest of Mrs. Hicks, but incredible to tell, for some reason or other, that warrant was never served, and she not only escaped condign punishment, but the pain and mortification as well of being arraigned before a court of justice." It is hard to believe that for all he'd seen of the institution of slavery, Douglass still thought it capable of any justice at all.[9]

What does not make it into many of the slave narratives, including Douglass's, is the violence that existed *within* the slave community. To be sure, the building and sustaining of communal and family bonds in the slave quarter were acts of enormous political and psychological courage and resistance. But we must be careful never to overly revere slave life. Ignorance and violence degrade the conscience, even when you are their victim. Thus did the slaves of the Haile plantation turn their children over to Tamer, the slave nurse, on their way out to the fields, little knowing that she liked to punish the children by tying them too close to a fire—a practice that was only discovered when she finally cooked one of them to death.[10]

Life in this Faulknerian world, as you might guess, was especially cheap for children. Catherine Berry, a domestic in the R. C. Poole household, was told that she would be terminated if she was indeed pregnant. In an awful feat of endurance, she continued with her chores until, doubled over with pain, she snuck away to give birth in the potato shed. Reeling from the loss of blood, she still managed to strangle the baby and fling it into the Pacolet River, where it landed at the feet of some fishermen. I could literally multiply such stories a hundredfold. When Peggy Bedenbaugh felt her first contractions, she went out to a corner of the yard, gave birth in a hole, and covered the baby over with dirt. Luly Collins threw her baby down a well. Nancy Owens swept hers under a brush pile. All had denied for months that they were in the "family way"; all had killed the evidence; all were indicted for murder.[11]

Or take the case of Jane Arnold. On September 7, 1857, Brazeal Cox and his wife found sixteen-year-old Jane Arnold stretched out on the ground with a baby beside her, bleeding from its umbilical cord. When Arnold became aware of the couple she called out to Mrs. Cox, who wrapped the dying infant in Arnold's apron and took it into the Arnold home. Mrs. Cox then returned and asked the girl why she hadn't given birth indoors. Because her daddy was "doging" her, she said, and had cast her from the house. "She seemed to be grieving," Cox told the coroner in a model of understatement, "but [I] don't know what for, whether on the part of her dead child or the abuse of her father."[12]

Three years later, at four in the morning, a shivering Jane Arnold knocked at the door of a neighboring farm. She was cold and unkempt, but she couldn't make up her mind to stay. Instead she returned to the abandoned schoolhouse where she had taken her latest baby, born in the middle of the road, to die of exposure.[13]

While I have yet to do census searches on all three hundred of these unfortunates, it is already clear that what we are glimpsing here is predominately the world of the poor white. Fully a quarter of the witnesses are making their marks with an "X." Glimpses of this world are rare, but potent. In 1850, for instance, while traveling the rural rim of Spring Dale, Mississippi, a country doctor named Elijah Walker stopped in for a "fine mess of melons" at a homestead belonging to Thomas Addington. "Here I beheld what I was astonished at," Walker later noted in his diary. "All the little children were allowed a seat along with the adult company, each one (there were about seven) as dirty as the earth could make them and the smallest ones with their dressing tucked up behind, exposing the posteriors, [each] with a swarm of gnats after it." Staring into the face of Southern poverty, Walker was agog. And it wasn't just the Addingtons. On court day and election day, the "strong-lung[ed]" sovereigns poured in from the forests on their broken-backed nags, and Walker's sleepy village became a maelstrom of drunkenness and commerce, camaraderie and pugilism. Who were these people, Walker sometimes wondered. "Thus live thousands," he marveled, "and as happy as queens and Kings."[14]

Of such a world, of such a people, of such stuff too was the Confederate army made; of such stuff, in part, is any army made. An army is not a moral instrument, and sympathy is the long suit of few fighting men. Glancing over a battlefield after victory, an adjutant with the Thirty-Eighth Illinois noted that "it was a sad sight and yet [not an] unpleasant one to see those infernal rebels lying on the field—Kicking like a flock of dead partridges." David Strother, with other members of the Army of the Potomac, actually pitched camp on the Antietam battlefield, right in the midst of the Confederate dead—or, rather, the Confederate mostly dead. "Many were black as Negroes," Strother remembered, their "heads and faces hideously swelled, covered with dust until they looked like clods. Killed during the charge and flight, their attitudes were wild and frightful. One hung upon a fence killed as he was climbing it. One lay with hands wildly clasped as if in prayer. From among these loathsome earth-soiled vestiges of humanity, the soldiers were still picking out some that had life left." Despite this ghoulish scene, Strother and company drank, smoked, and told funny stories, then bedded down amid the disregarded corpses.[15]

It is admittedly difficult to measure the impact of male mobilization on death back home. There are fewer coroners' reports for the war years than there are for any four-year span. It is tempting to chalk this up entirely to bureaucratic realities: given shortages from manpower to paper, county

record-keeping simply got spotty. But the cases that do survive are sugges-
tive: no more self-hangings; no more spousal abuse; no more dead babies.
The situation was undoubtedly different in counties with lower mobilization
rates, earlier occupation dates, and more urban settlement, or in places where
guerrilla violence cheapened life for everyone. But when men left certain sections of the South, they took Death with them, and practiced it in new ways,
primarily on themselves.[16]

As a Civil War historian, this is the Death I am familiar with. I long ago
lost count of how many letter collections and diaries I've read from Civil War
soldiers. In the summer of 1999, I read nothing else, did nothing else. I went
to the library and checked out more than a hundred volumes. I took them
home, dumped them out, and read them cover to cover, one after another after
another. I would never read the introductions. I'd just dig right in: 1861, 1862,
the pages would flit by, and the soldier would get a little tougher, rougher, sadder. Then on page 300 or so, I'd realize we were only at Gettysburg or Chicka-
mauga, and it would dawn on me: this kid isn't going to make it. Sometimes
he would. Sometimes he wouldn't. I thought it was the perfect way to read the
war: unsure, just as they were, what was going to happen to them. But at some
point I began to see and to profoundly feel something I had only sensed fleet-
ingly before: Death gives History its weight, its epic scope; Death is History's
gravity, its physics, its medium, and its math. Death is the essence of history,
the essence of change over time; Death is the great discontinuity, our own
discontinuity, bound up and reflected in the proxies we study.

Anyone who has done work in an archive knows the Zen-like moment
when you forget not merely where you are but when you are, who you are, almost *that* you are. The mood sneaks up on you, like sleep. At some point, half-
bored and half-wishing you were finding something better, you unconsciously
let go. At some point unknown to you, the boredom itself became narcotizing,
trance-inducing, and it has ferried you down a wormhole. This fact you will
only know when the trance is broken, when you snap back to the present with
a feeling of temporal vertigo.

And this, I guess, is what the buffs call "period rush," but in my experience
it is more of a languor, a stupefaction, a dissolution of self into the stream of
time. And it is, like sleep, a little death, a preview of the vast, oceanic purgatory
of nonbeing. And it is in this moment, while pulling yet another inquest from
the stack, that I can feel Death itself, as Poe would have it, looking gigantically
down. These coroners' reports are not like the books I read in 1999. They all
end the same. They are nothing *but* endings. There is no question but the how.

There is no answer to the why. Each death, taken individually, is apt to be sad and stupid. But I am taking them together, and the sheer repetition creates a pass and review of mortality's many faces; it is a great army of the undead, redeemed by its collectivity, redeemed by the momentary notice it has taken of me: "How will you die?" the army asks in unison, and I don't know. I know only that for a moment I feel bound to the infinitude of the past. I have joined the Borg, the great dead collective, and I have to admit it doesn't seem so bad.

But then inevitably the moment's gone, the wormhole closes. The spell is broken, and I don't want to pull another inquest from the stack. I am bored again. And I realize I don't like this kind of death; I don't want this kind of death. I miss the Civil War. I miss being borne irresistibly, with all my chains, back to the battlefield, where death has always made sense. Maybe Drew Faust is right; maybe kicking like a flock of dead partridges isn't a "good" death. But these boys could take it. They volunteered for it. They believed in themselves as men. They watched their regiments get cut to ribbons and fought the next day. They charged death itself.[17]

I can't do that. But I *can* pull another inquest from the stack. Someone new has died. At least it's not (yet) me. And I am the historian, the death investigator, and so I come on the run.

NOTES

1. Frederick Goldin, trans., *The Song of Roland* (New York: W. W. Norton, 1978), 14–18.

2. "The State of South Carolina vs. the dead body of George, a negro child," July 19, 1855, Kershaw County, Coroner's Inquisitions, South Carolina Department of Archives and History (hereafter SCDAH).

3. There is only one history of the coroner's office in America: Jeffrey M. Jentzen, *Death Investigation in America: Coroners, Medical Examiners, and the Pursuit of Medical Certainty* (Cambridge, Mass.: Harvard University Press, 2009). On death in the Civil War specifically, see Drew Gilpin Faust, *This Republic of Suffering: Death and the American Civil War* (New York: Thorndike, 2008); and Mark S. Schantz, *Awaiting the Heavenly Country: The Civil War and America's Culture of Death* (Ithaca, N.Y.: Cornell University Press, 2008). On death in the Civil War era more generally, one might profitably begin with: Gary Laderman, *The Sacred Remains: American Attitudes Toward Death, 1799–1883* (New Haven, Conn.: Yale University Press, 1996); James Farrell, *Inventing the American Way of Death, 1830–1920* (Philadelphia: Temple University Press, 1980); Nancy Isenberg and Andrew Burstein, eds., *Mortal Remains: Death in Early America* (Philadelphia: University of Pennsylvania Press, 2003); *Facing the "King of Terrors": Death and Society*

in an American Community, 1750–1990 (Cambridge, U.K.: Cambridge University Press, 2000); Lewis O. Saum, "Death in the Popular Mind of Pre–Civil War America," in *Death in America,* ed. David Stannard (Philadelphia: University of Pennsylvania Press, 1974); Martha V. Pike and Janice Gray Armstrong, eds., *A Time to Mourn: Expressions of Grief in Nineteenth Century America* (Stony Brook, N.Y.: Museums at Stony Brook, 1980); Russ Castronovo, *Necro Citizenship: Death, Eroticism, and the Public Sphere in the Nineteenth-Century United States* (Durham, N.C.: Duke University Press, 2001).

4. R. F. Hunnisett, *The Medieval Coroner* (Cambridge, U.K.: Cambridge University Press, 2008).

5. There is a rich literature on the state's interest in our bodies that most profitably begins with Michel Foucault's concept of biopower as outlined in *History of Sexuality.* For more applied and less theoretical approaches, see, for instance, Nancy F. Cott, *Public Vows: A History of Marriage and the Nation* (Cambridge, Mass.: Harvard University Press, 2002); or Henrik Hartog, *Man and Wife in America: A History* (Cambridge, Mass.: Harvard University Press, 2002).

6. These results are provocative, but preliminary. Until we know more about how the coroner functioned, we cannot compensate for all the biases present in his reports. The coroner did not investigate all deaths, for instance, only those for which the cause was uncertain. Probably he was more likely to investigate the deaths of the friendless and the poor, and more likely to investigate deaths that occurred in public rather than private spaces. Undoubtedly, elites could do much to deflect and resist a coroner's probe. Granting then that these reports give us a skewed portrait, the question becomes: skewed how? Skewed why? For more on suicide among African Americans, see David Andrew Silkenat, *Moments of Despair: Suicide, Divorce, and Debt in Civil War Era North Carolina* (Chapel Hill: University of North Carolina Press, 2011).

7. "The State of South Carolina vs. the dead body of Sarah Shacleford," September 3, 1849, Spartanburg County, Coroner's Inquisitions, SCDAH.

8. "The State of South Carolina vs. the dead body of Jane Soseby," January 12, 1859, Spartanburg County, Coroner's Inquisitions, SCDAH.

9. Mittie Freeman interview in George E. Lankford, *Bearing Witness: Memories of Arkansas Slavery: Narratives from the 1930s* (Fayetteville: University of Arkansas Press, 2006), 430; John Hill Aughey, *Tupelo* (Chicago: Rhodes & McClure, 1905), 420; Frederick Douglass, *Narrative of the Life of Frederick Douglass* (Boston: Anti-Slavery Office, 1845), 24–25.

10. "The State of South Carolina vs. the dead body of Ann, a slave girl," January 2, 1844, Kershaw County, Coroner's Inquisitions, SCDAH. This case did make it into the legal system via the Magistrates and Freeholder Court where records reveal that Tamer was found guilty of manslaughter and sentenced to be jailed for one month and receive one hundred lashes.

11. "The State of South Carolina vs. the dead body of an infant negro girl," March 7, 1868, Spartanburg County, Coroner's Inquisitions, SCDAH; "The State of South Caro-

lina vs. the dead body of an infant child (colored)," April 14, 1869, Kershaw County, Coroner's Inquisitions, SCDAH; "The State of South Carolina vs. the body of an infant child," July 16, 1868, Kershaw County, Coroner's Inquisitions, SCDAH; "The State of South Carolina vs. the body of an infant child of Nancy Owens," September 24, 1836, Kershaw County, Coroner's Inquisitions, SCDAH. For comparison with Northern incidents of infanticide, see Kenneth H. Wheeler, "Infanticide in Nineteenth Century Ohio," *Journal of Social History* 31, no. 2 (Winter 1997): 407–19.

12. "The State of South Carolina vs. the dead child of Jane Arnold," September 7, 1857, Spartanburg County, Coroner's Inquests, SCDAH.

13. "The State of South Carolina vs. the dead child of Jane Arnold," November 29, 1860, Spartanburg County, Coroner's Inquests, SCDAH.

14. Lynette Boney Wrenn, ed., *A Bachelor's Life in Antebellum Mississippi: The Diary of Dr. Elijah Millington Walker, 1849–1852* (Knoxville: University of Tennessee Press, 2004), 72, 109.

15. Arthur Lee Bailhache to brother, October 22, 1861, Bailhache-Brayman Papers, Illinois State Historical Library, quoted in David W. Rolfs, "'No Nearer Heaven Now but Rather Farther Off': The Religious Conflicts and Compromises of Northern Soldiers," in Aaron Sheehan-Dean, ed., *The View from the Ground: Experiences of Civil War Soldiers* (Lexington: University Press of Kentucky, 2007), 132; David Hunter Strother quoted in Earl J. Hess, *The Union Soldier in Battle: Enduring the Ordeal of Combat* (Lawrence: University Press of Kansas, 1997), 149.

16. Again any claims about the nature of death "back home," as revealed in coroners' reports, must be treated as preliminary and speculative. Pieces of the puzzle are falling into place, however. We are, for instance, beginning to get a clearer picture of public health during the Civil War. See Lisa A. Long, *Rehabilitating Bodies: Health, History, and the American Civil War* (Philadelphia: University of Pennsylvania Press, 2004); Margaret Humphreys, *Intensely Human: The Health of the Black Soldier in the American Civil War* (Baltimore: Johns Hopkins University Press, 2008); and Lisa Marie Herschbach, "Fragmentation and Reunion: Medicine, Memory and Body in the American Civil War," PhD dissertation, Harvard University (1997).

17. Faust, *This Republic of Suffering*.

Paul A. Kramer

"The Importance of Being Turbaned":
From the *Antioch Review* (2011)

Paul Kramer's "The Importance of Being Turbaned" is a compelling story perfectly told. At its center lies a remarkable feat of exposure: we learn the true identity of an African American clergyman traveling in exotic guise (turban and robe) through the South of the 1940s, who succeeded in confounding widely prevalent Jim Crow traditions. He's black, but he's not seen as a "Negro," and that makes all the difference. In Kramer's hands the tale unfolds with extraordinary power and grace. Narrative fuses with interpretive comment—we get first one, then the other, and soon we hardly notice the transitions. The words of the protagonist (and others directly involved) flow into and out of Kramer's own. It's writer's music, this fusing, this flow. Some key notes sound gently, others with great force. In particular, the humor inherent in many of the details both undercuts and underscores the central theme. As readers we may chuckle over sly maneuvers and misunderstandings; we may also weep over the injustices of race in modern America.

It didn't occur to Rev. Jesse Wayman Routté until later that the best way for a colored man to dodge white harassment was to wear a turban.

In September 1943 Routté, the pastor of the Holy Trinity Lutheran Church in the Jamaica section of Queens, New York City, boarded the train to Mobile, Alabama, to officiate at his brother Louis's wedding. In Mobile, Routté, a gifted singer and lecturer, sang spirituals before a "mixed audience," in the words of the *New York Amsterdam News,* and received "many congratulations from both races." He was also greeted with segregationist hospitality. "I was Jim Crowed here, Jim Crowed there, Jim Crowed all over the place," he later told a reporter. "And I didn't like being Jim Crowed." On his way South, Routté had ridden in a luxurious Pullman car and encountered "little if any segregation." But on his return trip, he chose to ride coach, "for educational purposes only." He was consigned to a dirty, airless car directly behind the steam engine; in the dining car, porters partitioned him off from other passengers with a screen. He fasted for the next two days in protest and contemplation. Back home, he told the *New York Amsterdam News* that such outrages called for a "great deal of prayer" and, he added, "an equal amount of planning."

Routté returned to Mobile at his brother's invitation in November 1947 and this time, he planned. Sisters in Mobile's Lutheran missionary societies had told him that when they expected a "visiting Negro of rank" they always suggested traveling in a turban and robes. "They say it makes things easier," Routté said later. A showman not given to halfway measures, he visited a costume shop in Manhattan and rented a towering, spangled, purple turban. On the train to Washington, D.C.'s Union Station, segregation's northern railroad terminus, he kept it packed away and rode in his official clerical collar. But before the train pulled into the station, he slipped into the men's room, removed his collar, donned a velveteen robe that he wore during concerts, and arranged the turban on his head. "I was so scared I didn't know what I was doing," he recounted. "But I was doing it just the same."

Routté wasn't the first black person to trump Jim Crow by conjuring up the "foreign." Author James Weldon Johnson had spoken Spanish with a friend and been allowed to remain in a first-class railway car. Others had acted on what one black writer later called "the chapeau theory of interracial rapprochement." Turban-clad, Dicky Welles, who owned a Harlem nightclub, had traveled with white patrons on cruises to Nassau and Cuba as the "Maharajah of Hattan." Joseph Downing of Edwardsville, Illinois, had thrown on "exotic" headwear and a moniker and emerged as Prince Jovedah de Rajah; he had grown rich advising white bankers and, before going broke, had taken rooms at the most fashionable, otherwise white hotels in Miami and Palm Beach. By 1947, conning the multi-colored race of the gullible was nothing new.

What was it about the mysterious foreigner? Each of these discovered how little headgear or accented speech was required to turn a threat into a guest. Guests were not full social members—their incomplete rights and responsibilities hinged on the sense that they would leave—but if they attracted certain suspicions (they might be spies, subversives, or moral contaminants), they could also achieve the peculiar freedom of strangers. You expected them to try to conform to your rules, but you didn't necessarily expect them to succeed; you realized that compelling them to recognize your norms might be impossible, requiring incivility or even force. You might be titillated when they accidentally tweaked your conventions. You imagined powerful forces behind them—influential families, allied governments, sponsoring institutions—that made their presence in your midst possible. You thought of your society's reputation and the tales they might tell, for better or worse, back home. Your sense of hospitality, however thick or threadbare, was activated without your noticing. And then there were those turbans, still dusted with fading vaudeville magic in the 1940s: who knew what sorcery was coiled in them?

Still, Routté's game was different. Where other turban and language acts leveraged solitary exemptions for private gain, Routté chose to invite the world in. While he insisted on the innocence of his plot ("I wasn't trying to fool anybody," he told reporters, trying to fool them), there was no mistaking its aggression. "I felt like a paratrooper behind enemy lines," he said. And Mobile was no Palm Beach. In June 1946, during a campaign to register black voters, a white Mobile police officer had beaten a retired, seventy-two-year-old black hauling contractor named Napoleon Rivers Sr, who was vouching for black registrants. The officer had fractured Rivers' skull and broken his jaw; five weeks later, Rivers was still recovering from his wounds and waiting to face charges of disorderly conduct and resisting arrest. The assault had happened inside the Mobile courthouse.

I did not set out in search of a Lutheran minister in an odd hat. I had stumbled upon Routté while researching international students from Africa, Asia, and the Middle East who had lived and studied in the United States in the 1950s and 1960s, that peculiar moment when the United States was both a global power and an iron-clad apartheid society. The students had circulated a practical tip among themselves: that they would not be mistaken for "negroes," and could mess with the racial strangeness of their "host" society, by wearing a turban. In my world, the idea of a protective turban was counterintuitive and worth delving into. After a keyword search on "turban" and "negro" in digitized newspaper archives, Routté's grainy portrait—baubles dangling, eyes theatrically aloof—looked out at me from a 1947 issue of the *New York Times*.

What kind of person—what kind of Lutheran minister—pulled a stunt like this? Online archives yielded up the names of his family members, colleges, and churches. Google, and the reverend's unusual last name (pronounced Root-*ay*), brought me to a sermon that quoted him and to the sermon's author, a colleague and former classmate of his. It also led me to the inbox of Routté's daughter Maud Enid, a retired journalist in Puerto Rico, who sent me an article she'd written about what came to be called "the turban trip," based on her mother's recollections. Energetic archivists at Routté's college and seminary, and at his home town's historical society, scoured and scanned microfilmed newspapers for me.

By August 2009, a branch of the trail had carried me to a shady street in Wyomissing, Pennsylvania. I sat in the living room of Jesse's son Luther: black belt, ultra-marathoner, former athletic coach of troubled teenagers, health-food store owner, and Lutheran minister. We sat beside an upright piano topped with a row of family snapshots and beneath a gigantic poster of Barack Obama. Seventy-one years old, Luther Routté is wiry, limber, and growls in a Queens accent. He describes the turban trip as a judo flip, and his arms curl in a slow, precise arc, ending with a muscular snap. His father, he tells me, had hoped to show that "when it came to segregation and the whole *meshugas* about who blacks were, these people did not know what they were doing."

We meander to a nearby coffeeshop and it becomes clear that Jesse Routté's tricks had not ended when he folded up his velveteen cape. Luther tells me his father was born in Canada, which is what Routté had told the *Times*: he was the son of "William Gehena Routté," an economics professor at Yale. Yale archivists poked around and told me they could find no trace of such a person; "Gehenna" is Old Testament for Hell. I traced Routté's path back from college and ministerial records, and online census reports, and found he was born in June 1906, in Macon, Missouri, the eldest of three sons of Lulu and Lewis Routté. Lulu was musical; Lewis had entered the African Methodist Episcopal Church ministry when Jesse was about six years old. The family was poor: Lewis had worked at a local iron and steel plant while serving the small black community of Kewanee, Illinois, and moved his family with him as he ministered to congregations there and in Iowa. Lewis's death in the 1918 influenza epidemic had left Lulu and their children destitute. She'd moved the family to Rock Island, Illinois, and made ends meet by arranging for the boys to sing at public performances. Jesse's brother, Frederick Douglass Routté, died on the road of "inflammatory rheumatism" in 1921. The concerts stopped for a year, then resumed, until Lulu herself fell ill. Jesse attended high school in Rock Island and worked before and after school for a cleaning and dyeing company. He recalled later that they sometimes went hungry. But his faith girded a sturdy optimism. Luther remembers his father speaking of "making ladders out of the crosses that life handed me."

Routté's discovery of Swedish Lutheranism and graduation from Rock Island's Augustana College and Seminary were, by most measures, unlikely. The Augustana Lutheran Church was strongest in the Midwest, New York State, and New England, and while it had expanded beyond an ethnic self-definition by the late 1920s, nearly all of Routté's classmates were of first- or second-generation Swedish descent, and most of his instructors spoke Swedish.

How had Routté made his way into the Augustana world? His parents had raised him in the A.M.E. Church; he had taken "Wayman," the name of Rock Island's A.M.E. church, as his middle name. But according to Luther, his father felt uneasy with the black church's "emotional denominations," as he had called them, preferring more solemn worship. Jesse discovered Augustana—located only a short stroll from his home, on the south shore of the Mississippi River—but insiders opened the door. Conrad Bergendorff, a scholar and pioneer in the Lutheran ecumenical movement, had supported his admission, and Routté's employer, admiring his work ethic and energy, had helped pay his room and board.

Routté was up to the challenge of being the first black person at a mostly Swedish college in 1926, the year after the Ku Klux Klan had taken over the state government of neighboring Indiana. According to a classmate, he was "well-received." But in an interview with the student paper ("Jesse Routté, Colored Student at Augie, Has Life Story of Interest," read the headline), the twenty-two-year-old freshman described the school as "chilly." Routté said he'd feared he would "have a hard time of it and be friendless," but with his professors' backing, he eventually "learned to handle the situation." Routté's humor, music, and what a colleague called his "winsome" personality gathered into a quiet charisma. "The Swedes draw a tight circle around themselves with their *kaffe klatsches,*" he later told his children. "But I drew a larger circle around them, and drew them in." By his final year of college, Routté was a "popular negro senior," active in one-act plays, the oratorio society, and student government. Still, some viewed him with suspicion. Rumors swirled—toxic and typical of the age—that he had a transgressive affinity for white women.

Over his summer breaks, Routté restlessly journeyed, singing and lecturing on vast circuit-riding loops. The shows, arranged and sponsored by church officers in part to recruit for Augustana, were densest in the Midwest, but stretched as far as New England, New York State, and the Middle Atlantic. In the summer of 1931 alone, Routté apparently clocked 6,000 miles in transit between 110 appearances at Augustana churches, black churches, universities, summer schools, and charitable institutions. The concerts supported Routté and his mother and siblings, honed his craft, and lifted his standing and reputation. Anticipating a Fourth of July concert by "a colored friend" in 1930, the *Lafayette Ledger* of Lafayette, Minnesota, announced, "This will be a rare treat."

That same summer, during a swing down the East Coast, Routté's musical odyssey carried him, for the first time, to Harlem. He was fascinated by what he called the "thriving black city." "Harlem is strange," he told the Augustana newspaper, "a mad medley." Routté had been especially drawn to what he called the city's "surprising types": "colored people speaking Jewish, Danish, Swedish, German, Spanish, Italian, and French, as if each language were their native tongue."

As he straddled distant, if neighboring, white and black worlds, Routté boldly equalized Western classical and religious music and what one article called "the best in Negro music and poetry" in his performances. He lectured on "the development of the Negro in America," recited poetry by Paul Laurence Dunbar, sang "sacred songs, including Negro spirituals," and played classical music on piano and violin. (One of Routté's role models appears to have been Marian Anderson: I uncovered in her archived papers an exuberant fan letter he wrote in 1937, asking for her "philosophy of life.")

Routté's far-flung campaign for cultural recognition did not make the question of his placement in a congregation upon graduation in 1933 any less thorny. Here the church's circle proved tight indeed. It may have been possible to admit a black student to the seminary; the idea of a black pastor for a white congregation was, one bishop emeritus recalled, seen as "repugnant." Unlike other Lutherans, the Augustanans had not evangelized among African-Americans; the closest black Augustana churches were missions in Danish-colonial Tanganyika.

Church officials found a place for Routté: race trumped denomination, and in a highly unorthodox move, church officials transferred him to the United Lutheran Church, which in turn assigned him to the Church of the Transfiguration on 126th Street in Harlem. Theologically speaking, the new church was home to the closest thing to black Swedes: black Lutheran immigrants from St. Thomas and St. Croix, whose ancestors had been converted by Danish missionaries and whose religious practices were—via Scandinavia—recognizable to Routté and vice versa. (In the Midwest, Routté's appointment had been inconceivable. It was a near thing among West Indians in Harlem. "They always called for somebody from Denmark to be pastor," Luther tells me.)

Routté moved to New York, ministering to what he later called a "racial mosaic" of congregants. Black Lutheranism trailed West Indians in motion: when they streamed from Harlem to Jamaica, Queens, drawn to new industrial jobs, Routté opened the Holy Trinity Lutheran Church there in May 1933. Spreading Lutheranism beyond its Caribbean base was tough. Apart from West Indians, it was "foreign to a great extent among people of [Routté's] race," as the *News* put it. And Luther told me his father's ministry was neglected by the larger Lutheran church. "It wasn't implacable hatred," he said, "but it felt like it."

Routté reached out to a larger circle. He led Lutheran and inter-denominational associations. In 1947, he was made chaplain of the Army Air Force's Squadron C, an all-black unit, at Camp Santini, Mitchell Field; with the unit under his moral guidance, one report noted, "the AWOL rate has been reduced considerably." He pressed his church to provide social sup-ports like daycare, adult education, and vocational guidance for its working-class congregants. He campaigned against juvenile delinquency and engaged in what Luther calls "intercessory" work between blacks and whites: finding summer jobs for kids, raising funds for camp, gathering Christmas gifts for the poor. Large consequences, he believed, could flow from small, "transfor-mational" acts.

He called down fire from the pulpit. In a June 1941 sermon that I discovered reprinted in a Lutheran magazine, Routté spoke of black peoples' "multitudi-nous contributions" despite their emancipation without capital, land, tools, or training. He called on Lutherans to catechize "this vast nation of dark Ameri-cans" to prepare them "to meet life's exacting demands." His metaphor for his effort—the sermon's opening salvo—was a woman's sacrificial rescue of a child under attack by a ferocious eagle, which then descends upon her with "terrific force." "Every day we come in contact with those who are torn and wounded by the cruel talons of intolerance," he told his congregation. "To go to their rescue, and bare our shoulders to their danger, and conquer their en-emies in Christ's strength, is our blessed privilege." At parable's end the eagle, struggling to escape the woman's grasp, breaks its own neck.

Luther suspects that his father felt some resentment at assignment to New York. "But then he met his wife there, and he thinks, 'Well, there's the fin-ger of God moving.'" Routté found a formidable marriage partner in Harlem. Enid Gómez had been born in St. Thomas to a privileged family; her father was a doctor and her mother, with whom she had migrated to New York in her teens, was a teacher. Sharp, ambitious, and intense, attracted to business and politics, Enid studied social work at Fordham University and journalism at Columbia. She and Routté met in the church and married in June 1938; they eventually had four children. She rose quickly in real estate; initially hired to attract prospective black homeowners to white-owned realty companies, she formed her own real estate company and became a lawyer in order to arrange titles on her own.

Jesse's political style leaned toward uplift; Enid preferred confrontation. A founding member of the Jamaica branch of the NAACP, she combated restrictive real estate covenants in the courts even as she punctured all-white neighborhoods in the real-estate marketplace. As a broker, she sold homes to black families on previously all-white blocks, which triggered panic selling and rapid white-to-black turnover, and brought in brisk sales commissions. A German Lutheran prep school refused to admit Luther; Enid threatened to enroll him in a Catholic school and to take their racism to the newspapers. School authorities relented.

Jesse and Enid assembled a broad social circle. They lived eight blocks from the church in a middle-class black neighborhood known for its respectability—lawyers, teachers, railroad porters—and for its star power, especially in the music world. Jesse presided at the wedding of Pearl Bailey and big-band leader Louie Bellson; Enid socialized with Count Basie's wife, Catherine. "I delivered newspapers to Jackie Robinson and Lena Horne," Luther says. Their annual open-house drew hundreds of friends, parishioners, and notables.

As his ministry grew, Routté prized his ability to connect to New York's riotous multitude of cultures, but he grew particularly close to Jews, brunching with a cluster of rabbis each Friday morning at the Horn and Hardart automat or Bickford's cafeteria on Jamaica Avenue. Norman Newhouse, the Jewish editor of the Long Island *Daily Press,* became a close friend and confidante, and the only person Routté told of the "turban trip" beforehand. Routté's working knowledge of Yiddish helped. He had learned Hebrew at the seminary and, like the Harlemites he had seen speaking "Jewish," he had acquired some Yiddish back in Rock Island while working part-time as a synagogue janitor. "The lingua franca of existence," Luther told me, "is being able to speak to people on their own level."

Up to this point, Routté had chosen dignified, resolute, quiet approaches to the problem of race: why did he suddenly decide to count coup, to reveal the enemy's weakness not by slaying him, but by drawing close enough to touch him, then escaping unharmed to tell the tale? There was, of course, the purely tactical hope that, on a journey he was taking for other reasons, a turban might "make things easier," confusing and temporarily disarming potentially hostile white people uncertain of his "place." And there was personal precedent. In

Harlem, Routté had been enthralled by black people who spoke in unantici-pated tongues; at Augustana, he had always reliably gotten a rise out of fellow students by uttering Swedish expressions no one expected him to have on hand.

But by his own accounting, Routté had at least two other fish to fry. The first was social-scientific: a desire to determine what exactly it was that white people feared and hated in people of color. "One reason why it is so hard to solve the interracial problem," asserted Theophilus Lewis in an *Interracial Review* editorial, "is because it is so hard to discover the basis of race prejudice and nail it down." Routté wanted to nail it down.

His second goal was pedagogical, the propaganda of the mischievous deed. If Routté's goal had been purely experimental, he could, after all, have con-ducted it far more safely in private. Instead, prior to the turban trip, he had enlisted Newhouse and the *Daily Press* to publicize the story, and to intervene if something went wrong. In line with one of his favorite calls-to-arms—"We are fighting an empire of ignorance!"—the trip would hold potent lessons.

There is also, ultimately, something that eludes explanation here. Routté had been attracted to Lutheran restraint. He had been praised by Augustanans for his optimism and lack of bitterness. He had traveled thousands of miles gently persuading white audiences to respect black artistry. He had spent long hours telling teenagers not to misbehave, and soldiers not to desert the Jim Crow Army. One is tempted to read into this strange exploit the satisfying release of a person no longer trying to civilize himself or anyone else. In this respect, the turban trip was the opposite of his oft-performed musical eve-nings. Rather than easing open the circle—lifting spirituals onto a plane of equality with the classical canon, for example—this was a guerrilla assault on the circle's exclusionary edge.

The news arrived first by radio. Enid later recalled having heard an announce-ment over WOR that her husband "had just found freedom from Jim Crow by way of the turban." She feared for his safety and prayed for strength and courage. But she also recalled feeling proud, explaining to her children that their father "had just made an important discovery in human relations." Lu-ther remembers it differently. Do you think she approved? I asked him. "No," he says. "I don't think so." He's sure they had a quarrel about it, one he didn't hear. "But she was supportive. She always thought he was a great man. Crazy, but—" He chuckles.

The story spilled out onto a full spread on the front page of Newhouse's *Long Island Sunday Press* on November 16—"Jamaica Negro Minister Dons a Turban and 'Jim Crow' Dixie Rolls Out a Carpet"—but Routté also interviewed with the *St. Louis Post-Dispatch*, local radio, and the *New York Times*, which placed the story on its front page the following day (and, in turn, introduced me to Routté some sixty years later).

Routté's tale migrated a bit between tellings, but its overall outlines held. Stepping out turbaned onto the platform at Union Station, he had walked among the throngs, returning nervous looks. "The Negroes were more pop-eyed than the whites," he said. When the Southern Railway train for Mobile pulled in, he bypassed the Jim Crow car located behind the engine "that was meant for the likes of me." He entered a coach reserved for whites and sat down and when passengers stared, he stared back, "because Negroes in the South always look down." The conductor took his ticket without comment; he fended off a glower from a suspicious porter.

No one spoke with Routté until the train reached Greenville, North Carolina, around lunchtime. Hungry, Routté walked back four cars to the diner, only to find it packed, the only vacant seat at a table occupied by two white couples. Routté went over and joined them, "my robes flowing, my turban still perched jauntily on my head." One of the men grinned. "Well, what have we got here?"

Routté smiled pleasantly and, in his best Swedish accent, answered, "We have here an Apostle of Good Will and Love."

The man looked baffled. Routté suspected he was being sized up as "an Oriental potentate, probably a delegate to the United Nations." A black porter eyed him fiercely upon taking their order ("He knew what I was," Routté said later) but Routté just glared back. Lunch with the white passengers, featuring courteous, Swedish-accented chitchat about the weather, went smoothly. "It shows what courtesy and politeness can do in human relationships," he told the *Daily Press*. Luther explained his father's strategy to me differently. "He could see and identify a racist, and he knew how to disarm that person by small-talking him," establishing innocent-seeming common ground in order to "find out what the other person will fight for." You "find something that you both like, and then attack."

Routté got off the train in Mobile turbaned and, throughout his week-long stay, wore it whenever he appeared in public (apart from recitals and devotions at his brother's church). The turban took him far. Traveling alone as the "Oriental nabob," he dropped in on police officials, the Chamber of Commerce, merchants, and factory owners, introducing himself as "an apostle of human relations, seeing how other men lived and doing what I could to help all men live in peace and harmony." An officer in the Mobile Police Department took him on a tour of headquarters. Routté asked a desk sergeant about juvenile delinquents, especially black ones, and was told that they gave little trouble, that they knew their place. He asked a captain how police handled the "Negro problem." There was no such problem: "If we have any trouble with a nigger we just knock him down."

Officials treated Routté to a tour of segregated city public schools and told him they were unready for mixed classes; Routté urged teachers and pupils to be more "tolerant." He bluffed his way into meals at Mobile's finest restaurants, staring down any skeptical staff. "What happens if a Negro gentleman comes in here and sits down to eat?" he asked a headwaiter. He would not be served, the man replied, but the question was irrelevant, as "no Negro would dare come in here to eat." Routté "stroked his chin gravely and ordered dessert."

Within days of its initial circulation in New York, the story seized headlines across the country. One columnist observed wryly that the turban trip had managed to elbow itself onto the front pages despite a royal wedding and a special congressional session, a testament to the way it captured "the elements of drama dear to a city editor's heart." (James Thurber sent the clipping to H. L. Mencken.)

The black press was jubilant. For *The Pittsburgh Courier*, Routté had turned the "No. 1 headgear of the Far Eastern countries" into "the big gun in a one-man blitz of jim crow." "Because this whole question of race relations is so full of contradictions," B. F. Phillipps of *The Baltimore Afro-American* wrote, "it always amuses me to hear of incidents where 'we put one over on them.'" Lucius Harper of *The Chicago Defender* imagined Routté, having revealed "What the Power of a Rag Does in a Democracy," "enjoying a hearty laugh—and we join him."

While not downplaying danger (the police captain's off-handed threat of brutality had frightened him), Routté played the story for laughs. His flamboyantly scrambled otherness—where else in the known universe did turbans and Swedishness mingle?—the earnestness with which white Mobilians had fielded his questions about the everyday workings of white supremacy, the resting of social membership on the question of a hat—all this cast Jim Crow in a glaring, absurdist light. "Race prejudice has been denounced for its injustice, cruelty, and stupidity," wrote the editorialist Lewis. "Rev. Routté has proved that it is also silly."

Not everyone was amused. Eleanor Roosevelt expressed her sadness, citing the trip during a lecture to advertising executives on the need to "sell" the United Nations to Americans. Because "every time we allow something to happen that is not democratic it hurts the cause of democracy," she had "grieved" over the turban story. She seemed less concerned about the racism it exposed than the bad impressions it might give off. If the country was appropriately ashamed, she said, stories about it had been "worth writing." If not, "I wish we hadn't written it, because the rest of the world won't be impressed that it could happen."

The Augustana College newspaper congratulated Routté; his superiors in the United Lutheran Church did not. "They thought the trip obfuscated his work and his effectiveness," Luther tells me. Shortly after the trip, a producer offered him the lead in *Lost in the Stars,* a Broadway adaptation of Alan Paton's novel *Cry, the Beloved Country,* and Routté asked church officials for permission; he was told he would have to withdraw from the ministry if he wished to participate. Particularly in Mobile, black Southerners expressed their apprehensions about Routté's ostentatious feat; he had prodded, and then left, the hornets' nest in which they lived. "A lot of folks down there thought it was going to hurt," Luther explains, "that there were going to be repercussions." Enid recalled that her husband had been told by an "old-time preacher" that it would "take one hundred years to see the good you've done, but you'll see the evil soon."

Some observers took away from the turban trip a serious, novel, and durable point: that racial prejudice was, as Marjorie McKenzie put it in a column in *The Pittsburgh Courier,* "a problem of semantics." Whites did not react to black people as such—Routté had never ceased to be black—but to "the Negro" as what McKenzie called "a Word Symbol." "A man in a jeweled turban is not a Negro," she wrote, and so he failed to "evoke the response that is called up in the southern white mind when the word Negro is mentioned or thought to apply to a person or a group."

In this way, Routté's journey represented the inverse of passing: where passing for white involved rigid conformity to a behavioral script in order to render blackness invisible, Routté had projected and confounded blackness by rendering it illegible. The fact that, in the guise of a foreigner, he had been so "well-received" in the South, suggested that conventional wisdom on the root of racism was wrong. It was not that black people were mistreated because they were seen as alien, but because they were American; not because they were unknowable, but because they were presumed to be known. Stripped of meaningful citizenship, they had fewer rights than real—or imaginary—guests. "In such situations," James Weldon Johnson wrote in 1933 of his own, Spanish-purchased ticket to ride, "any kind of Negro will do; provided he is not one who is an American citizen."

Among those on whom this distinction was lost was the Ku Klux Klan. According to Luther, shortly after news of the trip broke, Routté received a phone call at his home from Klan leaders, who threatened to kill him. The Klan burned a cross on the family's front lawn; Jesse and Enid sent the children to live with church members for several months. Luther relates that Enid worked connections with the Truman White House and somehow managed to secure Secret Service protection for her husband. But Jesse found the bodyguards burdensome and frequently slipped away.

Predictably, white Mobile newspapers sent a reporter out to investigate—and debunk—Routté's story. "Eastern Colored Man Claims He Crashed 'Color Line,' Here" read *The Mobile Press* headline on November 17, the day after the story broke in Long Island. Two captains in Mobile's police force "denied having talked with such a turbaned individual." City commissioners and the Chamber of Commerce's general manager similarly "did not recall a visit by such an individual." While the managers of most "leading" restaurants also denied seeing anyone like Routté, the owner of Joe Jefferson House told the reporter that "a dark-skinned person, wearing a turban-like hat" had come in about two weeks earlier and placed an order, but had been told that "he could not be served unless he removed his hat." The man had refused to comply and walked out.

Had he or hadn't he? Under the circumstances, there is no particular reason to trust *The Mobile Press* on this. And in the end, the turban trip's most telling feature may be that, apart from a few angry editors in Mobile, no one seems to have thought to ask. The reason for this, I suspect, is that Routté's story, whether true or not, arrived at precisely the moment when the surrounding culture was willing to help invent it. By late 1947, the NAACP had launched unprecedented campaigns to integrate wartime housing, industry, and the military. Thousands of black veterans had returned to the United States frustrated with the strong resemblance between Nazi Aryanism and the segregated American army sent against it. In December 1946, Truman had appointed a Committee on Civil Rights to investigate American racial politics and to propose reforms; by coincidence, its report was issued within weeks of Routté's train trip South. In March 1948, civil rights activists in Alabama filed a lawsuit against, and succeeded in striking down, the literacy test that disenfranchised most black voters; when white supremacists resurrected it, it was filibustered to defeat.

The electricity of the turban trip, in other words, rushed from a society poised to believe that people engaged each other—for better and for worse— through the "word symbols" they had at hand; that for all its austere trappings of science, law, and religion, race was capricious and arbitrary; that far from commanding terrorized deference from both blacks and whites, Jim Crow could and should be poked in the eye. Routté continued to be known for the episode: civil rights leaders enlisted him to tell the tale in the 1960s. And Luther says that when he traveled to Mobile to officiate at his uncle's funeral, older folks recalled the incident. "You know," they told him, "your daddy changed the whole thing up." Jesse Routté himself didn't place much emphasis on it in the years that followed. He had larger circles to draw.

Craig Harline

From *Conversions: Two Family Stories from the Reformation and Modern America* (2011)

One summer, Craig Harline, a seasoned historian of early modern Europe, discovered the secret diary of a man who converted from the Dutch Reformed religion to Catholicism in the seventeenth century. Harline knew at once that such an unusual document could form the basis of a potentially gripping historical study. But what confused him was that this man's strange and painful story seemed so intensely familiar. Indeed, Harline could not stop thinking about the emotional resonance between the life of Jacob Rolandus in the seventeenth century and that of his own friend, Michael Sunbloom (not his real name), in the late twentieth century—especially in terms of the family strife caused by their respective conversions.

Historians are trained to make distinctions between time periods: we track change. Many of us don't believe that anything should be labeled as timeless or universal. So: what to make of this eerie sense of parallel experience, of continuity through the ages?

In this excerpt from Harline's book, Jacob has just fled to Antwerp from the town in the Dutch Republic where his father Timothy serves as a Reformed preacher. Timothy, furious and righteous, but also guilty and anguished, flies off in pursuit, worried about all the Catholic influences in this borderland where he is trying to earn his own converts to the Reformed Church. There have been hints that Jacob feels more at home outside the confines of his father's congregation—that, inexplicably, a powerful inner voice is leading him away from his family's fundamental assumptions.

And then there's Michael—the entire book alternates between the two stories, dwelling with each for only a few pages at a time—switching religions every time he switches girlfriends (often), drinking too much, struggling to come to grips with his parents' distrust of each other. When he suddenly discovers Mormonism, it's as if he is discovering what he has always been. The only problem—the only thing competing with this newly audible inner voice—is his reluctance to jeopardize his already fraught relationship with his parents.

Emotions are difficult to probe in both historical research and historical writing. But Harline had a secret diary to work with—and a cache of letters, plus a deep contextual knowledge of religious culture in the seventeenth century. And perhaps the emotional complexity of Michael's story pushed Harline even further into the inner life of Jacob and Timothy Rolandus. One of the accomplishments of the book is how Harline strikes a taut balance between what he knows as a scholar and what his own inner voice suggests to him.

~

Take thou thy lord's servants, and pursue after him,
lest he get him fenced cities, and escape us.
2 Samuel 20:6

At about the same time that Jacob reached Antwerp on that early Tuesday morning of May 26, Timothy Rolandus was, just as Jacob feared, making plans to go after his son.

Various family members were, just as Timothy hoped, ready to go too: they would arrive shortly in Boxtel, or meet Timothy on the road. In the meantime, he had started asking questions around town to try and figure out just exactly where Jacob had gone, and just exactly who had enticed him to do so. As one of the prominent figures on the local scene, Timothy would have had little problem convincing the sheriff or a town councilor to help with his inquiries.

Leading a minor astray was at least as serious as stealing a horse. This explains why so many of Jacob's friends were willing to help behind the scenes with his escape, but not actually to be seen riding or walking with him—not the separate-traveling Vlierden, not the promised guide who dropped out at the last minute, not the hiding Ravenskot, not even the achy-footed Faes was eager to be spotted with Jacob on the road, day or night.

It wouldn't have taken Timothy long to learn that Christian Vlierden had headed south just hours before Jacob, and to suspect that there must have been a connection between the two events. It also wouldn't have taken long to learn that Vlierden's servant, Faes, was missing too (though not, as Timothy might have supposed, because he was following his master—rather, Faes was off fetching Jacob's horse).

Then suddenly, on that Tuesday, there was Faes again in Boxtel. Did someone see him with the horse before he could get it to its owner, Secretary Hugens? Did Timothy and, say, the sheriff corner Faes and make him talk?

Perhaps Timothy received intelligence as well from some local Catholic parent, who was worried about Jacob's example of rebellion against his father (even if it was in the name of true religion), and who therefore offered some tidbit of information, some fragment of a rumor someone had heard, about where Jacob was headed.

Whatever the order of events, however information was learned, Ravenskot was soon being arrested, and Timothy, convinced that Jacob was heading south, set out after him, with an entourage of perhaps half a dozen men. Among them was Secretary Hugens, still fuming about his horse.

No one could have blamed Timothy Rolandus if, while moving along the road, he entertained the wish that he had never brought his family to this strange new province called Brabant.

Of course after the debacle in Ouderkerk there had been little choice, but the situation in the family's new home was, unbelievably, even worse than in the old.

The biggest problem, and what made Brabant so strange, was that virtually everyone there was Catholic. No other part of the Dutch Republic could say that.

Timothy knew by heart how it had happened. The 17 provinces that made up the Netherlands (or Low Countries) had once been united under a common ruler, the king of Spain, and a common faith, Catholicism. But in 1566, some Netherlanders started rebelling against their king, and in some cases even against his religion: war was the result, and all unity crumbled.

During the 1580s, the seven northern provinces declared themselves independent from Spain, came to prefer the Reformed religion, and called themselves the United Provinces of the Netherlands, or more simply the Dutch Republic. The ten southern provinces remained loyal to Spain, and to Catholicism, and were called the Spanish Netherlands.

But the struggle was far from over; in fact, it lasted another 60 years. During that time, families were split in two, by politics or religion or both, and then by distance, as massive migrations followed, much of it from south to north. Some provinces were also split in two, especially those that lay in the middle, such as Brabant, where much of the interminable fighting took place.

For most of the war, the Spanish Netherlands managed to hang on to sprawling, wealthy Brabant. But in 1629, the Dutch conquered a big northern chunk of the province, for good, along with some smaller holdings nearby. (The conquered territories together were called the Generality Lands, because they were run by the States General, the foremost centralized institution in the Republic. But Brabant was clearly the main prize.) Dutch rulers were elated, except for one thing: virtually all of their new subjects were Catholic.

Although it had been possible from the start of the Republic to be both Dutch and Catholic, most such people were spread around the land. In Brabant, however, Catholics were as dense as peat, and that made Dutch rulers worry. Could this many Catholics together in one place ever truly be loyal to their new state, especially when that state officially preferred the Reformed religion and outlawed Catholicism?

Perhaps to pacify Brabanders while the war raged on, rulers hinted that once the war was over, maybe an exception would be made in the new province and Catholic worship would be openly allowed. But when the war finally did end, in 1648, all such hints ceased.

Dutch rulers decided to treat Catholicism in Brabant just as it was treated elsewhere: as an outlawed religion. Monks were expelled from monasteries, priests and congregations were thrown out of churches, and churches were refurbished in Reformed style. Only one exceptional gesture was made toward the new province: the introduction of a small army of Reformed preachers and civic officials, whose task was to show locals the bright side of Reformed living, and to convert as many as possible to the true religion.

This was where Timothy Rolandus came into the picture.

Thanks to his troubles in Ouderkerk, and the intervention of Jacob Triglandius, Timothy was among the 56 dominees who wound up in Brabant shortly after the war's end. And oh how optimistic he and his new brethren all were! Surely the preachers' friendly manner and their message of irresistible truth would win over the Catholic populace, who surely remained in their false religion only because they had been blinded for so long by devious pastors and monks. And surely many of these pastors and monks would themselves convert, once they heard the truth.

And how heroic it must have felt, even to the bruised Timothy. After his ignoble departure from Ouderkerk, here was a chance to bring light to those in darkness, and to redeem himself. More mundanely, here was also opportunity at last for a reliable, improved income, which had always eluded him, yet which now was promised to every preacher who braved moving to Brabant.

It didn't take long to see how formidable the task would be. The new motley army of Reformed preachers in Brabant was too small, and pathetic, to win much ground. And the new Reformed communities in Brabant were tiny, even tinier than in Ouderkerk, and were all recently imported from elsewhere.

The Catholic communities, in contrast, were enormous, and angry that their precious churches had been confiscated for the sake of a handful of Reformed while Catholics had to worship nervously in cramped attics and barns, where smuggled-in priests illegally performed services while lookouts guarded the door. In revenge, local Catholics made life difficult for their new Reformed neighbors—interrupting church services, tying up church bells, ruining pulpits, filling in the locks on church doors with molten lead so that entirely new doors had to be made, and refusing to rent or sell housing to anyone who was Reformed.

The Rolandus family never did find a place to live in Timothy's first community in Brabant, called St. Michielsgestel. During Timothy's four years as preacher there, the Rolandus family actually lived some five miles away in Den Bosch, the chief city of Dutch Brabant and home of the newly erected Reformed classis for Brabant. The commute ate up a good chunk of Timothy's time (and perhaps his salary too) and made it difficult for him to know or enlarge his flock.

Then what disappointment when the promised salaries in Brabant turned out to be less reliable than supposed! And when the promised conversions never materialized! It's possible that no Catholic priests in the province ever became Reformed. And laypeople were nearly as stubborn: those very few who wanted to convert faced ostracism from local Catholics if they went through with it.

Within a couple of years after their arrival, the Reformed preachers of Brabant were all sighing from weariness and pleading with Dutch rulers to send more help or they might all just give up.

It never came. More preachers were not sent, despite the pleas. As promised, some of the preachers in Brabant did give up, and left. A few assigned to take their places from elsewhere never bothered to show up once they heard the discouraging stories.

And those who stayed—because they wanted to see it through, or had no prospects elsewhere—lowered their sights. They worried less about converting anyone, and settled for achieving a grudging coexistence with locals. Or they moved to some other town in Brabant where the Catholic population was a bit less aggressive, or the Reformed community a smidgen stronger, or living conditions a little better.

This last was what Timothy Rolandus finally found. After four years of no housing in St. Michielsgestel, Timothy perked up his ears when a position came open in 1653 in the nearby town of Boxtel—because Boxtel had a rectory for its preacher.

Other than that, it wasn't much different from the last place. In fact, in some ways it was worse. Timothy knew, for instance, that cantankerous Catholics in Boxtel had recently shot up the precious rectory, and narrowly missed hitting the last preacher as he sat working in his study. But at least there was a rectory, and a study, and a new office and kitchen too. Timothy hadn't known such things for years.

And so he put himself forward to his classis, in Den Bosch, for the post, and was granted it with little fuss. He moved his family there around July 1653.

He would come to regret it, for Boxtel was where real disaster happened. At least in St. Michielsgestel there had been no sign of dispute between Timothy and his flock. No sign of tension between him and the classis. And no sign of trouble with Young Jacob. But all that changed in Boxtel.

Moreover, the Catholics in Boxtel were highly aggressive, and even angrier than usual about the loss of their church—a surprisingly fine and large church for such a modest town, thanks to centuries of pilgrims leaving donations at the church's miracle-working altar.

Besides shooting up the rectory, and throwing rocks at its windows, Boxtel's Catholics had also recently put up armed resistance to civic authorities who came to shut down secret Masses. The locals didn't beat up those authorities until they were bloody and blue, or sew them in blankets, as believers in nearby Texel did. But they came close.

Catholics in Boxtel also made a point of frequenting the last openly Catholic institution left in town: the convent of Poor Clares. Unlike male convents in Brabant, which were simply closed after the war, female convents were allowed to continue until every sister had died out. Since that could take decades, believers took advantage while they could, and visited often, showing their defiance as well as their devotion.

Timothy did his best to get along with local Catholics. As the missionary guidelines for Brabant suggested, he was to learn their names, interact in friendliness, seek occasion for *affectionate conversation*, and use his Sunday afternoon sermons to preach on subjects meant especially for them. He also urged them to study the Reformed religion with open hearts and minds, for if they did so, he promised, then they would discover that only in this religion could they find the means to salvation.

But for all of his efforts, Timothy saw little fruit among Catholics. In the end he even came to despise many of them, for what they did to his son.

To compound his problems with Catholics in Boxtel, Timothy, just as in Ouderkerk, quickly had problems with some of the local Reformed as well.

In fact he blamed them for Jacob's ruin too—especially that scoundrel the schoolmaster. Any official Dutch schoolmaster, by definition Reformed, should have been the local preacher's closest ally. Yet within weeks, even days, of first arriving in Boxtel, Timothy had picked a fight with his, named Jan Gerard van Santen.

Part of the reason Timothy did so was due to his stubborn sense of right-ness. But much of it was due as well to the difficulties of being a Reformed of-ficial in Brabant: namely, there was never enough income for any of them, and they tended to fight, even among themselves, for every penny they could get.

Timothy and the schoolmaster lived on adjoining lots, just north of the church. But they couldn't agree on the precise boundary between their lots, which appeared to be divided by a small barn and a plot of cultivable land. Timothy argued that both the barn and the plot were his, as his predecessor had used them. He had indeed, admitted the schoolmaster, but the predeces-sor had also paid a fee, because both actually lay on the schoolmaster's prop-erty. Timothy knew nothing of any such fee, and refused to pay it. He needed that barn and land.

But so did the schoolmaster, who received only part of his income from the state, and the rest from student tuition—and here in Brabant tuition was scarce, as few Catholic parents were willing to send their children to any of-ficial (Reformed) school. The schoolmaster was therefore just as willing as Timothy to fight for the property in dispute. He even enlisted in his cause the church custodian, who likewise was convinced that he had a beef against Timothy Rolandus.

With tiny audiences for the preacher, no students for the schoolteacher, and little cleaning for the custodian, these men had a lot of time on their hands, and too often they spent it arguing with one another.

In August 1653, having barely introduced himself to the community, Timothy took his schoolmaster to court. By November the court reached its decision—in favor of the schoolmaster. Timothy was ordered to pay a fee to use the barn and garden, or hand them back.

Although Timothy was disappointed, he remained sure as ever that he was right. He also knew the notorious slowness of Dutch law, and that it might take months, even years, to see the verdict enforced. Thus he didn't pay a penny for using either barn or garden and decided simply to stay put until some officer showed up to remove or fine him.

Seeing Timothy's underhanded tactics, the schoolmaster decided to try some of his own—involving young Jacob Rolandus. Specifically, the schoolmaster began to attack Timothy's reputation by spreading unflattering tales about Jacob, who in the schoolmaster's eyes was just a little too friendly with local Catholics, more than a preacher's son ought to be.

One night in January 1654, someone placed a disturbing note on the door of the rectory. The note didn't survive, but reports said that it repeated rumors already circulating around town about Jacob. That he helped to sing Adoration, or the Sunday afternoon service, in the convent of Poor Clares. That he had asked the schoolmaster from a neighboring town to go along with him to this service. That he had told various *papists* in town he had no intention of becoming a preacher himself, as his father hoped. And more.

An infuriated Timothy immediately brought another lawsuit, this time for libel, against his rival the schoolmaster, whom he suspected of authoring the note. What really infuriated Timothy, in the end, was that the trouble-making schoolmaster turned out to be right. Not in the details, or the specific accusations, but in the essential truth: that something was stirring in the heart of Jacob Rolandus, and it was not, as his father had hoped, the Reformed religion.

In fact Timothy may have been the last to know.

No, Boxtel was at the moment not exactly a place that conjured up warm memories in the soul of Timothy Rolandus.

He hoped that he wasn't too late to catch his son.

He had to find Jacob before the boy did something foolish, such as enter a religious order, where his damnation would be assured. For some reason Timothy remembered that Jacob had once expressed admiration for the Capuchins; was that where he was headed? To the closest Capuchin convent? What a disaster that would be!

Why hadn't Jacob listened to him? Why had he ignored the counsel of Deuteronomy 13:6, which warned against being enticed away to go *and serve other gods, which thou has not known, thou, nor thy fathers?*

Timothy kept moving south.

The truth was refreshened from within me.

Michael stayed with his roommate through college, but he pulled himself together to get his usual good grades and a degree in elementary education.

The autumn after graduation, he started his first teaching job, at a school on the edge of sprawling Valleytown, where the heat waves rising from the pavement were a little less searing than those downtown.

He also cut back on parties—thanks to unhappy experience, his new job, and especially one of his old girlfriends, Joni, with whom he'd stayed friendly. She had recently joined a non-partying religion that Michael hadn't tried yet: Mormonism.

He had heard only some talk of Mormons while growing up, and at All Folks, but none of it was good. In his mind he simply assumed that Mormons were right down there with Catholics, if without as catchy a derogatory nickname as papist. But, said in the right tone, Mormon all by itself could be derogatory enough.

That Joni, a bright and open girl, liked the religion, and that various friends Michael met through her liked it too, surprised him, and made him curious. Around New Year of 1973, a few months into his first job as a sixth-grade teacher, Michael started looking closer.

Once again he was following a girl to church, and this girl for the second time.

Joni suggested that if Michael was serious about learning more then he ought to speak with the Mormon missionaries, who would tell him all he needed to know about the religion.

This was the usual way it went if you wanted to investigate Mormonism, as Mormons called it. Most Mormon missionaries by now were young men between 19 and 21, who ideally spent most of their two years as missionaries looking for and teaching investigators.

Michael had seen the missionaries, everyone had seen them, riding around on bikes, wearing white shirts and dark suits and nametags, and calling themselves Elder so and so. They weren't elderly, of course. It was just an ecclesiastical office they had borrowed, like other churches, from the New Testament.

In fact most missionaries were young on purpose, because their difficult task required zeal, energy, enthusiasm, and a little naïveté.

Certainly youth had its disadvantages too. Such as naïveté, uninformed opinions, rigidity, and know-it-all-ism. But those disadvantages were much less pronounced in the missionaries who came to teach Michael—at least in one of them.

Missionaries always went in twos, for support and safety and to keep each other from straying, but they were hardly clones. Elder Garner, for instance, the senior of the two who visited Michael, was cosmopolitan, while his companion was rigid, and over the weeks and months of their meetings had to be pulled from the room more than once (by Elder Garner) to be told to ease up.

Michael prepared a long list of questions for each meeting, usually held at his apartment. The companion sometimes dismissed those questions, or took them as a sign of inhumility, but Elder Garner understood that they were reasonable, and searching. He also understood quickly that Michael responded to teasing, and Elder Garner was full of that.

It wasn't long before the ear jokes started, but Michael came right back with observations about Elder Garner's *gigantic* nostrils. And it escalated from there. They quickly became great friends.

Michael didn't get satisfactory responses from the missionaries to all of his questions.

In fact, he probably had more questions than any church could answer. But he heard enough, and had enough Mormon friends by now, to realize that many unflattering tales he had heard about the faith were spurious, or sensationalized, or if true troubled him less than he supposed they might.

Mormons didn't have horns on their heads (that one was easy, but it was amazing how long that rumor endured). They didn't practice polygamy any longer (not since around 1900), though some breakaway groups still did. They didn't, it was true, believe in the same sort of Trinity as most Christians (*three in one*); rather, they believed in a Trinity of three separate beings, and omitted the *one* in the traditional formula (Michael Servetus had been executed in Geneva 400 years earlier for omitting the *three*). But that particular doctrine had never mattered much to Michael, and the Mormons' kindly God-the-Father, circumscribed in a glorified body but still omniscient and omnipotent, appealed to him, because it seemed closer to the image he had of his own father.

It was also true, as Michael had heard, that Mormons would not ordain black men to their lay priesthood. All black people could belong to the church, but none could be part of its ministry. This was the hardest teaching of all for Michael, who by this time was known among his friends for his compassion toward any group that suffered prejudice; but because so many American churches were still segregated in practice, if not in theory, and because he liked so much else that he was learning about Mormonism, he put his negative judgment of the *Negro Policy* on hold for the time being.

More pleasing to Michael, and quite unexpected, was that many of the missionaries' teachings were not so drastically different from the Christianity he had learned growing up. Most fundamentally, Mormons too believed that salvation came through an atoning sacrifice by Jesus Christ, even if they disagreed with Protestants and Catholics (who also disagreed with each other) about the details.

Moreover, though Mormons were Restorationists (who claimed that Christ's original church had been lost through centuries of change, and required full restoration rather than merely a little fixing), they were not alone. Restorationist ideals, in one form or another, had roots that extended to the Middle Ages (such as among the English Lollards), the Reformation (elements of Calvin's theology, of Ulrich Zwingli's in Zurich, or of Puritanism and Anabaptism), and to various American churches (including the Disciples of Christ, Churches of Christ, Seventh-Day Adventists, or the sort of Pentecostalism that Michael grew up with).

Certainly these groups differed in their views of what needed restoring: Mormons included the *restoration* of some Old Testament practices not favored by others (most famously polygamy and temple rites). They also added the canonization of scripture besides the Bible (such as the *Book of Mormon*, which gave the church its nickname) and new appearances by heavenly beings (rather than just the biblical appearances). These beliefs, plus others, led many Christians to set Mormons at the edge of Christian respectability, or even beyond—to consider them as a cult rather than as Christians. But none of the beliefs troubled Michael: polygamy had been halted, the idea of the temple appealed to him, the additional scripture contained much that he already believed, and which Christian religion didn't claim supernatural events in its history? None of it really seemed strange to him.

In this Michael followed a common pattern of conversion detected by modern sociologists: namely, people tend to convert to what is mostly familiar. Not entirely familiar, of course, or there'd be no point in changing: rather, the familiarity makes potential converts comfortable enough to study further, and during that process they discover the new and different features that are appealing enough to provoke them to convert.

The two most provocative new features for Michael were not the high theological stuff about the Trinity or additional scripture or other such issues. Rather, they were ideas he had never heard before, and that struck him to the core when he did hear them.

One was the Mormon twist on eternal life, which took eternal to include not only endless life after death, but endless life before birth. For as long as he could remember, Michael had felt that he had always existed and always would. Upon hearing this idea, he thought: *Talk about the truth ringing clearly within your heart, or should I say refreshened from within me.*

Here was a sense of conversion beyond those commonly understood: not merely *turning around,* as suggested by the Latin root *convertere*; not merely undergoing a change, as in conversion's usual sense of changing from one thing to another; not merely a conversion table, as in finding an equivalent form; but rather conversion as discovering what you have always been, or believed.

It wasn't a new phenomenon. The classical thinker Plotinus thought of conversion as *a return to origins.* And the Amsterdam preacher Jacob Triglandius, Old Jacob Rolandus's friend, grew up Catholic but upon reading Reformed theology for the first time immediately felt at home: as he put it, he had *already been reformed, before I knew the doctrine of the Reformers.*

The second provocative idea for Michael was the belief that family bonds could continue after death. Popular Christian culture often held the same belief, though various churches Michael had attended taught officially that family bonds would dissolve at death. He liked the Mormon teaching, for despite his own family's hiccups, Michael had always felt close to them, and he liked the idea of continuing together.

Though the familiar and new ideas mattered to Michael, in the end what moved him most of all were the people he had already begun meeting in the new faith. Here he followed another fairly common pattern of conversion: namely, relationships come before doctrine. You start by meeting some friends in the new religion. You like those friends, and become interested in their beliefs. You then study those beliefs, and if you like them too (and you may be predisposed to like them, given your new friends), your connection to those friends becomes so strong that you want to join them.

How long that connection remained, of course, and on what conditions, were other matters, as Michael would learn. But at least in the early stages of conversion, including his, the promise of new relationships was crucial.

To the missionaries, Michael was ready to convert. In fact while many missionaries spoke of their most promising investigators as *golden,* Elder Garner and his companion wrote melodramatically, in their weekly report to superiors, that Michael was *platinum*.

Whatever precious metal he was, Michael did indeed want to convert. Only one thing made him hesitate, even briefly, and that was another relationship he cared about: that with his parents. What would they think?

Amy Reading

"Benjamin Franklin's Disciples":
From *The Mark Inside: A Perfect Swindle, a Cunning Revenge, and a Small History of the Big Con* (2012)

The movie version of Amy Reading's book would probably keep a tight focus on its charismatic protagonist, a classic rube who first gets taken for all he's worth by a gang of professional con artists and then cons them in return. In other words, the book itself could have taken shape as a straightforward, suspenseful narrative set in the wild, wide-open, Prohibition-era West. But Reading chose instead to interrupt her story periodically and take us on historical tours. And these long asides do far more than simply contextualize confidence games in the relevant time period, or teach us the lingo and secret techniques of the Big Con. Reading's more analytical chapters, like the one you have here, dip back into the past to show that in fact American economic culture was founded on "imposture, speculation, and counterfeiting, because America was, from its inception, a confidence trick."

It's always a risk to interrupt one's story, but Reading's arguments are just as playful and dramatic as her action sequences. This chapter opens with the spotlight on one of the original confidence men, the spiffy Samuel Williams—"or was it Samuel Thomas? or William Thompson?" The uncertainty allows us to get into the spirit of the game. And within each chapter, Reading's structure trains us to be good readers of the book as a whole. Here, she jumps quickly back and forth from character sketches of early con artists like Williams "(as we'll call him)" to brief explanations of things like bankruptcy law, speculation in western lands, counterfeit detection manuals, bond markets, and Alexander Hamilton's national securities scheme. After Williams, we get to meet the charming charlatan Tom Bell, who dressed up in refined clothes and forged letters of introduction to secure business loans, and who once talked his way into Ben Franklin's house by impersonating a learned schoolmaster named William Lloyd. Bell left Franklin's company having lifted a ruffled shirt and a silk handkerchief, thus teaching the young printer a thing or two about what it means to be a self-made man.

When you get to the end of Reading's chapter, you realize that American capitalism is not so much about frugality and steady striving as it is about placing bets, crossing fingers, and looking confident—looking like you're one of the players. In other words, it's kind of fun, and Reading's writing captures that appeal—while also delivering barbed reminders that the game has always been rigged.

Confidence artistry began one day in May 1849 when a well-dressed young man named Samuel Williams—or was it Samuel Thomas? or William Thompson?—walked up to a stranger on the streets of lower Manhattan and engaged him in a few minutes of intimate small talk. The stranger felt that he knew but couldn't place this friendly fellow; certainly he seemed like an old friend who was delighted to see him. Williams (as we'll call him) then asked the stranger, in a disarmingly direct manner, whether or not he had confidence in him. When the man answered yes, the only possible answer in polite conversation, Williams said jovially, "Have you confidence in me to trust me with your watch until to-morrow?" In high humor, his mark handed over his gold watch. And Williams sauntered off into the city, laughing and promising over his shoulder that he'd return the watch the next day. In the span of just a few days in May, he swindled John Deraismes out of a watch valued at $114, John Sturges out of a watch worth $80, and Hugh C. McDonald out of a watch valued at $100.

A few weeks later, Hugh McDonald was walking down Liberty Street when he spotted a familiar figure. He alerted a nearby police officer, and Williams found himself caught by his own mark. He was taken into police custody—though not before he tried to bribe McDonald into dropping the charges. He went before the magistrate, and when it was found that he was "a graduate of the college at Sing Sing," he was committed to prison to await a trial. *The New York Herald* broke the story in its Police Intelligence column the next day, and the newspaper immediately recognized that it was witnessing an entirely new genre of criminal enterprise. It was a reporter at the *Herald* who coined the name "Confidence Man" and who urged New Yorkers to stop by the Tombs for a look at him; then the *New-York Tribune* and *National Police Gazette* also picked up the story. Two days later, the *Herald* reported, "Yesterday, in consequence of the publicity given in the daily journals respecting the arrest of

Samuel Williams, the 'confidence man,' quite a numerous attendance was brought to the police office, who were all anxious to witness a man who could so far humbug any sensible man." He was peered at like an animal in a zoo. One visitor from Philadelphia identified him as Edward Stevens, a petty criminal whose first arrest was for stealing a "firkin of lard" and who was known in the underworld as a spotter, a stool pigeon, or a betrayer of confidences. The *Herald* noted Williams's reactions to his visitors: "The prisoner, yesterday, at being shown to so many persons, asked if he was a wild beast, and appeared to be much vexed and alarmed at the identifications." After all, he was far subtler than a pickpocket or safecracker. He himself described his effect on his marks as "putting them to sleep."

Nonetheless, he met the fate of a common criminal. After sending a lady friend to attempt to bribe Hugh McDonald a second time, and after being duped by his own bondsman and left to rot in jail, the Confidence Man went before a jury, who handed him a guilty verdict without even leaving their seats. He headed back to his alma mater to serve a two-and-a-half-year sentence. By then, though, a second confidence man by the name of Julius Alexander—or was it Byron Alexander?—was on the prowl.

Williams's was a remarkably distilled act of trickery, and it seized the public's imagination. The *National Police Gazette* crowed loudly at the conviction of "Confidence" but ended its coverage of Williams on a worried note: "We trust this word in time will not be thrown away." In fact, the very opposite happened, and the term "confidence man" almost instantly entered popular discourse. Two weeks after Williams's arrest, Burton's Theatre on Chambers Street in New York presented a farce titled *The Confidence Man*. Eight years later, in 1857, Williams's fame was still strong enough that he would have been recognizable as the model for Herman Melville's protagonist in *The Confidence-Man*, about an unnamed swindler who roams the decks of a Mississippi steamboat on April Fools' Day, cheating passengers out of money by disparaging their willingness to trust him. Melville's confidence man taunts a potential dupe, "What are you? What am I? Nobody knows who anybody is. The data which life furnishes, towards forming a true estimate of any being, are as insufficient to that end as in geometry one side given would be to determine the triangle." The *National Police Gazette* formalized the new criminal pastime by defining "confidence man" in its 1859 *Rogue's Lexicon:*

CONFIDENCE MAN. A fellow that by means of extraordinary powers of persuasion gains the confidence of his victims to the extent of drawing upon their treasury, almost to an unlimited extent. To every knave born into the world it has been said that there is a due proportion of fools. Of all the rogue tribe, the Confidence man is, perhaps, the most liberally supplied with subjects; for every man has his soft spot, and nine times out of ten the soft spot is softened by an idiotic desire to overreach the man that is about to overreach us. This is just the spot on which the Confidence man works.

As early as 1860, police captains in New York estimated that close to one in ten professional criminals in their city was a confidence man. With just that one sentence—"Have you confidence in me to trust me with your watch until to-morrow?"—Williams had conceived an entire industry.

The Confidence Man did not, of course, invent confidence artistry; he merely perfected a particularly efficient and viral adaptation of it. Williams's thievery had such an instantaneous impact because it crystallized a set of anxieties that had plagued Americans since before they were Americans. In the seventeenth and eighteenth centuries, as the colonists argued and fought their way to nationhood, a central question that threaded through their debates was: What is the right and proper investment of confidence? Virtually all colonial enterprises—education, judicial courts, taxation, self-defense, currency, churches—required an element of trust, because the colonists had rejected the tradition, class structure, and institutional memory to bolster them. Just as merchants extended credit to grease the engine of trade, so did citizens extend confidence to the strangers who visited their distant towns and the authority figures who ruled them from afar.

And so genuine confidence men, those who betrayed the trust placed in them, captured the public imagination as symbols of the nation-building project. The colonists understood them not as outlaws, or as exceptions to the rules that governed democratic society, but as the logical extension of those rules. Con men differ from later American frontier heroes such as cowboys and private eyes, men who placed themselves beyond the edge of civilization and exercised their freedom by fighting lawlessness. Con men work firmly within the structures of American democratic capitalism, exploiting uncharted territory inside the system itself. They are the innovators and entrepreneurs of such a society, no less than was Benjamin Franklin, their closest forebear. Even in their day, the stories of early American swindlers laid bare a terrible truth. Their country needed them. The new nation would never have prospered without imposture, speculation, and counterfeiting, because America was, from its inception, a confidence trick.

~

In 1739, Benjamin Franklin, then a printer, invited into his home a school-master named William Lloyd, who impressed him with his excellent manners and learning. Lloyd knew Latin and Greek, which Franklin found humbling because he was struggling to teach himself Latin on the side. After the school-master had departed, Franklin saw with dismay that he'd helped himself to a "fine . . . ruffled" shirt and a handkerchief "mark'd with an F in red silk." His guest was no schoolmaster, and his name was not Lloyd. Franklin had been duped, almost certainly by Tom Bell, the most notorious impostor of the American colonies.

Like Franklin, Bell was the son of an upwardly mobile family in Boston. Like Franklin, he had attended the Boston Latin School and obtained an excel-lent education, advancing even further than Franklin, who was forced to leave at age ten when his father could no longer afford the tuition. Bell's diploma gained him entry to Harvard, but in 1729, the year before he matriculated, his sea captain father unexpectedly died, throwing the rest of the family on hard times. His mother sold off some property, and Bell entered college as planned, but it was an uneasy fit. He lacked the resources to consort with his prominent classmates, and he lacked the discipline to apply himself to his studies. A few weeks into his first year, he earned a reprimand from the faculty for "Saucy behavior," and the next two years were peppered with punishments for steal-ing letters, wine, and, most egregiously, a chocolate cake. The latter finally got him expelled in his junior year.

Like Franklin, he began adulthood without money, reputation, a trade, or a patron. And so he faked it. He ordered a silk jacket and hose on credit (and later lost the lawsuit the tailor brought against him for failing to pay), then steadily acquired the rest of a wardrobe in lieu of a résumé. By adopting the dress of a minister, a schoolteacher, or a gentleman, he talked his way into households like Franklin's and passed himself off as a man of worth, earning free room and board while the deception lasted and often upgrading to a new suit of clothes or a new mount on his way out the door. He forged letters of introduction to ingratiate himself with wealthy families and to obtain business loans from them. His travels took him from Massachusetts to Barbados, with stops at the penitentiary in between. The farther he traveled and the more frequently his deceptions were unmasked, the wider grew his notoriety as a mumper—someone who cheats as well as begs. It was hard to attain celeb-rity in the mid-eighteenth century when it took weeks for news to travel by horseback. Yet before long, articles about Bell referred to him as "a famous impostor" or "the famous, or rather infamous Tom Bell," and the mumper's artistry became increasingly difficult to practice as he began to be recognized. He was almost as renowned in his time as Franklin himself.

Even beyond the striking similarities of their early lives, the two men could be described in nearly identical terms. Both were self-made men who found opportunity in the undefined crevices between social classes. Both exhibited the self-reliant individualism by which colonists characterized themselves in opposition to the Crown. Perhaps most crucially, both manipulated appearances to cultivate impressions among their peers. In perhaps the most frequently quoted passage of his autobiography, Franklin says, "In order to secure my Credit and Character as a Tradesman, I took care not only to be in *Reality* Industrious & frugal, but to avoid all *Appearances* of the Contrary. . . . [T]o show that I was not above my Business, I sometimes brought home the Paper I purchas'd at the Stores, thro' the Streets on a Wheelbarrow." Franklin performed his hard work as a printer for his neighbors. It is passages like this that have led some historians to place Franklin somewhere on the slippery continuum between huckster and con man. Franklin was, in John Updike's estimation, "an inveterate impersonator." His personality was constructed of sheathed layers, "one emerging from another like those brightly painted Russian dolls which, ever smaller, disclose yet one more, until a last wooden homunculus, a little smooth nugget like a soul, is reached."

The trouble was, Bell's pretenses revealed as hollow that which he imitated. Bell's education not only gave him rudimentary Greek and Latin; it also schooled him in the manners of the elite, so that when he passed himself off as a refined gentleman, he gave a letter-perfect performance. He knew how to tie a cravat, knew the family trees of New England's dynasties, knew how to pronounce the names of distant places, knew how to conduct a fluent conversation ranging amusingly on literature, philosophy, and current events. His travels only added to this storehouse of competencies, because in the mid-eighteenth century only ministers and peddlers were as well traveled as swindlers, and people looked to such men for news from faraway colonies. Bell knew, in other words, how to manipulate the social markers by which the elite identified themselves. Bell's exploits revealed gentility as a covertly political project. Politeness was supposed to be synonymous with moral authority, granting its bearer a natural power over lower, coarser citizens. Colonial elites used the conventions of gentility to retain hierarchies in a democratizing society, a way to define who should naturally rule over the masses. Bell implicitly demonstrated how easily these conventions could be counterfeited, thus reopening the question of how a purportedly classless society should be organized.

In January 1792, a letter reached William Duer at his stone and brick mansion in the Hudson River valley. Duer was the master of Philipse Manor Hall, the former county seat of Frederick Philipse, a wealthy Dutch trader and the founder of the town of Yonkers. Philipse had been an unrepentant Loyalist, and when war broke out, he was arrested and his fine house confiscated by the State of New York. Not only did Duer purchase it at auction for a sliver of its value; he also paid for it with money earned from veterans' pay notes that he'd bought at a discount from desperate soldiers and then redeemed at face value from the government. He lived like a baron as he presided over the estate, attended by liveried footmen under the rococo ceiling. So the letter that reached him from a stranger in a debtor's prison in Baltimore that January had little impact on him. "From ill-placed Confidence I have been steeped in Poverty to the very lips," the letter began. "I have borne the proud Man's Contumely, and the oppressor's wrong; I have felt scorn, and Contempt; and even Insult with Impunity. In this State Poverty is one of the Greatest of Crimes, and of that offense I have been convicted Seven long years." The letter writer had heard of Duer's financial success and wrote about his own experiences with debt in order to caution Duer against continuing in his present course. "I sincerely wish, that you would set limits to your Desires. If you had drank deep, as I have done, of the bitter Cup of adversity, you would never Risk Independence again. May the voice of friendship take the liberty to intreat you to stop in time; and sit down, with so ample an Independance [sic], in peace of Mind, and Body!"

Duer did not stop in time. Two months later, he moved from Philipse Manor Hall to the third floor of the New Gaol in lower Manhattan to begin his own seven-year term for insolvency—not, like his Baltimore correspondent, because he'd misplaced his confidence, but because he'd stolen confidence from so many others. He would spend the next seven years mustering all of his resources to obtain an early release, to no avail. He died there at the end of his term in 1799, the scourge of the thousands who had invested with him and who became paupers and debtors themselves when his insolvency triggered the first financial crash in the nation's young history.

William Duer was born in England, educated at Eton, and schooled in market relations at his father's prosperous West Indies plantations. He left Antigua for New York in 1768 with a "handsome pecuniary legacy," which he eventually supplemented with his marriage to the wealthy Catherine Alexander, daughter of Major General William Alexander, Lord Stirling. Duer came to the thirteen colonies to fulfill a contract to supply the British navy with masts and spars formed of New World wood, but as the war approached and the British let his contract expire, he smoothly shifted to provisioning New York's Fort Miller with wood for barracks and frigates, eventually expanding to alcohol, horses, ammunition, and cattle. By October 1776 he was profiting more than $1,000 a month at a time when other citizens were being asked to weather hardships on behalf of the war effort.

Even had he played by the rules, Duer's position as a middleman between farmers and army provisioners would have opened him to patriotic wrath, because it was in his interest to underpay civilian merchants and overcharge the government. But Duer played dirty. He manipulated the price differences by hoarding goods, which led to shortages and higher prices; he paid himself before he paid his suppliers; he paid his suppliers in depreciated Continental currency while hoarding the more valuable specie; he obtained commodities from the enemy and paid for them with American agricultural products, for which he faked customs clearances and bribed officials at foreign ports; and he used public money to speculate in bills of exchange, keeping the profits for himself.

William Duer was America's first high-flying speculator at a time when speculation was a sin and bankruptcy a crime. When the British colonists moved in, they had no capital other than their own future productivity, but they disdained speculation as antithetical both to the Puritan values of thrift and industry and to the Whig values of self-reliance and civic participation. To eighteenth-century clergymen, artisans, and yeoman farmers, the merchant capitalism that the Dutch brought with them from Flanders and Antwerp was far more treacherous than the simple, steady accumulation of wealth that in Protestant theology bespoke God's will for the chosen. The speculator made money by exchanging paper, and he built fortunes out of airy nothings. Colonists feared that profit untethered from labor, whether speculation or gambling, would encourage dissolute lifestyles untethered from morality. Cotton Mather warned that "gains of money or estate, by games, be the games what they will, are a sinful violation of the law of *honesty* and *industry*, which God has given us."

In pre-Revolutionary days, the rhetoric invoked a more secular hell, the threat of enslavement. Benjamin Franklin, in *Poor Richard's Almanack*, warned against allowing one's paper wealth to outstrip one's resources, in such now-familiar maxims as "He that goes a borrowing goes a sorrowing," "When you run in Debt, You give to another Power over your Liberty," "The Borrower is a Slave to the Lender, and the Debtor to the Creditor," and "Rather go to Bed supperless than rise in Debt." Thomas Jefferson was deeply suspicious of the effects of capital derived from sources other than direct labor and trading. As secretary of state, he led the opposition to a federal bank and the government-backed financial instruments that would entice and enable speculators. He thrust on President Washington his belief "that all the capital employed in paper speculation is barren and useless, producing, like that on a gaming table, no accession to itself, and is withdrawn from commerce and agriculture, where it would have produced addition to the common mass: that it nourishes in our citizens habits of vice and idleness, instead of industry and morality." Government, in Jefferson's opinion, had as little business in the fiscal arena as it did in the religious, and citizens should be free to create their own local networks of trade without the seduction of government-backed bonds and securities.

But the republican ideology of public virtue and self-restraint was insufficient to the demands of the times. The Revolutionary War hammered on the moral opposition to speculation until it began to give way in the exigencies of the fight. Many of the private merchants who supplied the troops speculated with the bills of exchange that they received as payment, as did Duer.

Duer went much further. His privileged social position enabled him to help shape the government's fiscal policies in his own interests. He was elected to the Continental Congress in 1777, appointed secretary of the Treasury Board in 1786, and appointed assistant secretary of the Treasury in 1789 under Alexander Hamilton (whose wife was a cousin of Duer's wife).

In the 1780s, Americans found themselves in a changed economic landscape, and the plentiful opportunities for money made purely from money led to a "spirit of speculation." In 1780, Congress depreciated its national currency, giving investors the opportunity to exploit the difference between face value and trading value. When soldiers were discharged, they were paid with settlement certificates that themselves became a kind of currency, traded at ten or fifteen cents on the dollar. Indeed, each new form of government issue, from land warrants to debt certificates, turned ordinary citizens into speculators. Duer's friend Hamilton conceived a bold plan to fund the war retroactively while stimulating the new nation's economic growth: he proposed that the federal government purchase the Continental Congress's securities at face value in return for interest-bearing bonds in the new national government. True, Hamilton's plan would create a moneyed elite among the merchants and bankers who held the government securities, but it would also free capital to water the parched nation, and Hamilton defined capital broadly. "Every thing that has value is capital—an acre of ground, a horse, or a cow, or a public or private obligation, which may, with different degrees of convenience, be applied to industrious enterprise," he wrote in answer to his critics, namely Jefferson and James Madison, who thought that speculation deadened industrious enterprise. Hamilton wanted to make debt productive for the new nation.

Duer, of course, was one of those elites in a position to gain from Hamilton's plan, and he endorsed it in his official capacity as assistant secretary, but he also benefited from insider knowledge of it. It was strictly illegal for him to profit from his foreknowledge of Hamilton's national funding scheme, but the lure was too great, and he began "talking outdoors" to speculator friends, who invested his money in government securities using their names.

Even this most advantageous government position proved too constraining for Duer's speculative lust, and he voluntarily left his post at the Treasury after only six months to return to the financial industry. He then launched the project that would send him plummeting into debtor's prison. Together with Alexander Macomb, a fellow wealthy New Yorker and former war supplier, he spread rumors that he was about to charter a new bank, called the Million Bank. Hamilton reacted exactly as Duer expected: he opposed the new bank on the grounds that speculators would withdraw capital from the recently formed Bank of New York and the soon-to-be-established New York branch of the Bank of the United States, weakening both with the loss of specie and reputation. The next stage of the script called for Bank of New York stock prices to fall, at which point Duer and Macomb would corner the market and gain a controlling interest in the bank. The final, astonishingly audacious stage called for leveraging their capital to do the same to shares of the Bank of the United States—at which point a single investor would be in charge of one of the federal government's most powerful financial institutions. But news of Duer's intentions on the Bank of New York leaked, and he had to act faster than he'd planned to raise enough capital. He sold one of his estates and "borrowed" money from his other concerns, and then he frantically started to borrow money from everyone who trusted him, promising them fantastic returns.

The unraveling came quickly. Other wealthy investors thwarted Duer's designs on the Bank of New York, in part by withdrawing gold and silver from their accounts, which forced banks to call in loans, drove up interest rates, and made it ruinously expensive for Duer to borrow money. At the same time, Duer was suddenly summoned to Philadelphia to answer nettlesome questions about a $240,000 gap in the Treasury books from the time of his tenure there. And then his debts fell due. Duer was arrested for insolvency the very day after the Bank of the United States, the bank he hoped to control, opened for business. He owed an astonishing $475,000 to his associate Walter Livingston, or about $11 million in today's currency. And he owed far smaller amounts to dozens and dozens of New Yorkers. One contemporary calculated his total indebtedness at $3 million, or $70 million in today's currency. The losses rippled out from there. Livingston, of course, declared bankruptcy, as did Macomb and about twenty-three other speculators. Soon the effects of Duer's overreach spread beyond New York's financial elite to the rest of the market. Real estate prices dropped, credit seized up, and about $5 million in shareholder value simply evaporated. Thomas Jefferson, for one, felt delicious vindication that the speculators had finally gotten their just due. He was confident that now people would return to "plain unsophisticated common sense." Madison, too, believed the crash to be gratifyingly fatal: "The gambling system . . . is beginning to exhibit its explosions."

Jefferson's vindication, though, was a deceptive one. Like Bell, Duer was not an exception to the rule of post-Revolutionary market relations. His career utterly exemplified early capitalism. In fact, Duer's leveraged trading and subsequent bankruptcy, which represented the worst in eighteenth-century financial transgressions, would simply be considered ordinary business today, when bankruptcy is no longer a crime and business failure has lost much of its stigma. The panic Duer incited was sensational but shallow, and it prompted speculators not to reform their gambling impulses but to normalize them by founding the New York Stock Exchange.

One way to describe the evolution of American capitalism in the nineteenth century is the steady domestication of gambling. By the end of the century, gaming had been outlawed, but speculation had been entirely institutionalized, codified, and tamed. It began just a few decades after Duer's calamity, when New York State was hugely successful at raising capital to dig the Erie Canal from Albany to Buffalo, beginning with the Canal Act of 1817. The state paid for the construction through bonds sold not to the merchant elite, who scorned the project, but to ordinary savings bank clients in New York City, who realized fabulous returns when the canal opened in 1825, two years ahead of schedule. Wall Street princes took note, and when western land and railroad companies adopted the Erie Canal strategy, the money poured in. There was no turning back the stock ticker. America in the nineteenth century was speculating its way westward.

In Melville's *Confidence-Man*, an old man sits at a marble table as white as his own snowy hair. By the light of the single lamp in the gentleman's cabin on the Mississippi steamboat, with the confidence man bending over his shoulder, the old man takes out two bills from his vest pocket and proceeds to compare them against the *Counterfeit Detector*, a guide to each of the denominations of currency printed by each of the hundreds of banks in existence by the mid-nineteenth century. The old man learns from the *Detector* that if his $3 bill from the Vicksburg Trust and Insurance Banking Company is legitimate, "it must have, thickened here and there into the substance of the paper, little wavy spots of red; and it says that they must have a kind of silky feel, being made by the lint of a red silk handkerchief stirred up in the paper-maker's vat." The confidence man asks him if his bill passes muster. "Stay," says the old man, as he continues to read and scrutinize, "that sign is not always to be relied on; for some good bills get so worn, the red marks get rubbed out. And that's the case with my bill here—see how old it is—or else it's a counterfeit, or else—I don't see right—or else—dear, dear me—I don't know what else to think." And so he tries again. "It says that, if the bill is good, it must have in one corner, mixed in with the vignette, the figure of a goose, very small, indeed, all but microscopic; and, for added precaution, like the figure of Napoleon outlined by the tree, not observable, even if magnified, unless the attention is directed to it." The old man cries despairingly, "Now, pore over it as I will, I can't see this goose." The confidence man urges him to give up "a wild-goose-chase," throw the *Detector* away, and simply spend the money as if it were good.

"As if": in those two small words lies much of the basis for market relations in the late eighteenth and early nineteenth centuries. Speculators like Duer frightened more conservative investors because their heedless stock manipulations laid bare the groundless nature of the growing economy that rose from nothing more than borrowing and leveraging. But the even more alarming truth was that it wasn't only the "stock-jobbers," "plungers," and "jackals" who risked everything in the chase for future profits. Every last person who participated in the market was a speculator, simply by his use of paper currency. It wasn't until surprisingly late in American history, with the passage of the

National Bank Acts of 1863 and 1864, that the country had a national system of banking and a standardized national currency backed by U.S. Treasury securities. Before then, state-chartered banks purportedly guaranteed their notes with specie—metal money in the form of gold and silver resting undisturbed in their vaults—but most banks issued far more notes than they could back if every one of them were redeemed. Banknotes were thus speculative bills of exchange. One commentator in 1839 called them *"credit*-money, or *confidence*-money,"* deriving their value solely from the *"promise to pay,* which, by universal understanding, is meant to signify a promise to pay *on condition of not being required to do so."* And so it was up to the bearer or receiver to decide whether or not to extend confidence to the bank behind it. If, as frequently happened, the bank's reputation softened or collapsed, all of its bills in wallets and cash registers would instantly depreciate. Most of the bills in circulation did not trade at their face value, and so newspapers published rates of exchange between different local and regional currencies. Buying goods required the discernment of an art historian and the numerical nimbleness of a mathematician. Sometimes it was easier—and more profitable—to turn off one's doubts and simply pass money *as if* it were real.

Paper money, for all its glaring flaws, was an absolute economic necessity. Before the discovery of native silver and gold mines, North America consistently found itself on the short end of a trade imbalance in specie with other nations, as the metal money flowed overseas to pay for the finished goods that could not yet be made in America. Colonists experimented with various mediums of exchange, such as wampum in New England, tobacco in the South, and playing cards in Canada. But as networks of trade expanded and thickened, especially at the ports, merchants needed something fungible across local regions to clear the path for their commodities. By the mid-nineteenth century, each of the colonies had issued its own paper currency. Pennsylvania, for instance, had issued about 45,000 pounds' worth of currency in 1723 and 1724, backed not by specie but by the land assets of those who borrowed the currency from the government and by the future taxes that could be paid with the currency. But, like most such issuances, Pennsylvania's currency was set to expire and be withdrawn from circulation in 1731. One of the most ardent supporters of continuing the paper money project was Benjamin Franklin.

Though *Poor Richard's Almanack* relentlessly warned against the enslavement of personal debt, Franklin also fervently believed that a tradesman's good credit was essential to building his strong reputation, and that dependence was a necessary first step to independence. When he looked around at the stagnant state economy, dousing it with an influx of paper money seemed to him solid fiscal policy. In 1729, just twenty-three years old, he published an anonymous pamphlet titled *A Modest Enquiry into the Nature and Necessity of a Paper Currency.* He argued that a greater amount of currency in circulation would drive down interest rates and encourage spending and building. He admitted that this policy would not be popular with moneylenders, land speculators, and the lawyers who profited from debt disputes, but surely all of the "Lovers of Trade" could see the benefits of inexpensive debt. Franklin's view prevailed. In his *Autobiography,* he recalled that though the pamphlet did not bear his name, "My Friends there [at the Pennsylvania statehouse], who conceiv'd I had been of some Service, thought fit to reward me, by employing me in printing the Money, a very profitable Job, and a great Help to me." Franklin would continue printing millions of dollars' worth of currency for Pennsylvania, Delaware, and New Jersey until 1764. He implored his fellow citizens to have confidence in the state, then profited mightily from their investment.

Franklin designed as well as printed currency, inventing his own method of "nature printing" to transfer the imprint of a sage leaf to the paper bill via a copperplate press in order to guarantee the bill's authenticity. Each of the banks that issued currency devised its own markers of validity, but the result was a disorienting array of denominations and designs—a situation practically calculated to encourage counterfeiting. It was up to the bearer to decipher the signs and ascertain the legitimacy of the notes in his or her wallet, or up to the shopkeeper to determine whether he or she would accept the note proffered across the counter. Purchases in dry goods stores and taverns often began with the same matchup between bill and *Counterfeit Detector* that engrossed Melville's old man.

Yet there were precisely as many ways to pass fake currency as there were ways to detect it, for each method devised to identify a counterfeit bill spawned a twin method for ensuring its smooth passage. For instance, pamphlets like the *Counterfeit Detector* reproduced the signatures of bank presidents and cashiers so that storekeepers could verify the signatures on banknotes. But those same pamphlets acted as primers for counterfeiters to practice their handwriting. Or counterfeiters would game the pamphlets: they would issue false notes with a noticeable flaw; then, after the next pamphlet had been published which mentioned the flaw, they'd correct that single detail for a new issue of notes, which would then pass scrutiny because that detail would be the only aspect that bearers would check. Best of all, counterfeiters could simply counterfeit counterfeit detectors, and substitute them in shops with sleight of hand. As Melville's confidence man points out to the disquieted old man, the tools for increasing confidence in the money supply have exactly the opposite effect: "Proves what I've always thought, that much of the want of confidence, in these days, is owing to these Counterfeit Detectors you see on every desk and counter. Puts people up to suspecting good bills. Throw it away, I beg, if only because of the trouble it breeds you."

One counterfeiter in the late eighteenth century used the confusion around paper currency to justify his art. "Money, of itself," he argued, "is of no consequence, only as we, by mutual agreement, annex it to a nominal value, as the representation of property. Anything else might answer the same purpose, equally with silver and gold, should mankind only agree to consider it as such, and carry that agreement into execution in their dealings with each other." Value is not inherent in money because of the intrinsic worth of its materials. It is the product of a contract between bearer and receiver. In the hustle and bustle of the marketplace, it mattered little how full a given bank's coffers were; what mattered was the interaction at the moment of exchange: Could the bill pass? The counterfeiter urbanely concluded that this rendered a false bill no less valuable than a real one. "Therefore, we find the only thing necessary to make a matter valuable, is to induce the world to deem it so."

The counterfeiter was Stephen Burroughs, a man who knew much about confidence and how to manipulate it, for he was an impostor cut from the same die as Tom Bell. He too was born to a respectable family in 1765—his father was a clergyman in Hanover, New Hampshire—and he too had a classical education at Dartmouth that ended in an early departure for youthful high jinks like stealing a watermelon and attending class without shoes. With boyish romanticism, he conceived the idea of setting off to sea, so he pretended to have medical training and set sail on a privateer as the ship's physician. On the journey home, the captain locked him in irons for stealing wine, and he once again found himself in New England, thrust back upon his own resources. Stealing a page from Bell's playbook, Burroughs boosted ten of his father's sermons, acquired some ministerial garb from another clergyman, and descended upon Pelham, Massachusetts, in 1784 to give the weekly sermon, which was so successful the townspeople hired him as their preacher. Upon discovering his deception, the Pelhamites ran him out of town, but hardly had he gotten out of earshot of their invectives than he was caught passing counterfeit coin and sentenced to three years in "the Castle," a jail on Castle Island in Boston Harbor. After his release, Burroughs tried his hand at respectable living, starting a family and a business, but he discovered his true genius only after moving to lower Canada, where he began forging American coins and bills with such skill that his reputation seeped back over the border and he became a kind of mythic outlaw hero. In the early nineteenth century, every instance of counterfeit immediately invoked Burroughs as its putative source.

For Burroughs, the turn from imposture to counterfeiting was entirely natural. In fact, he might have said that the two practices are different sides of the same coin: both entail passing into circulation untrue representations whose authenticity is explicitly in question. For both, the success of the endeavor is determined at the moment of exchange. Unlike magicians and swindlers working the big con, Burroughs could not make use of the one-ahead by preparing his deception in advance. Any moment of commerce in the late eighteenth and early nineteenth centuries was already framed as an occasion for suspicion and enhanced scrutiny.

And yet this structural parallel between imposture and counterfeit did not prevent early Americans from equating the face value of paper money with the public reputation of the men printing it. At the very close of his *Autobiography*, Franklin describes an instance when the Pennsylvania legislature came close to repealing 100,000 pounds of currency. Franklin was able to stop the repeal and buoy the value of all the currency in circulation by signing his name to a document promising the bearers that the new issuance would not detrimentally affect their investment. Franklin converted confidence in himself into confidence in the state, yet his signature was no less abstract than the state's promise to redeem the note for specie.

Magically, incredibly, the paper money handed from money belt to till to pocketbook around the colonies and states did what it was supposed to do. America between the Revolution and the Civil War experienced dramatic economic development as the frontier moved westward and the eastern cities commercialized. This development happened not *despite* but *because of* counterfeit. At a time when the appetite for development outstripped the available credit, the fake bills that inflated the money supply performed a public service, especially in the West. A Michigan citizen testified that "counterfeiting and issuing worthless 'bank notes' . . . was not looked upon as a felony, as it would be today. Of course it was taken for granted that it was a 'little crooked,' but the scarcity of real money, together with the necessity for a medium of exchange, made almost anything that looked like money answer the purpose."

The historian Stephen Mihm in *A Nation of Counterfeiters* argues that this dimension of nineteenth-century history should rewrite economic theory.

When the story of American capitalism is told from the perspective of imposture, speculation, and counterfeiting—from just below the surface of a vast
deception—it looks not like Max Weber's theory of the "plodding, methodical,
gradual pursuit of wealth" described in *The Protestant Ethic and the Spirit of
Capitalism*. Rather, it is "the get-rich-quick scheme, the confidence game, and
the mania for speculation" that drove our nation into the modern age. Against
a litany of reasons why it was foolish to do so, Americans simply decided to
have confidence.

Jill Lepore

"All About Erections":

From *The Mansion of Happiness: A History of Life and Death* (2012)

This is not a history of skyscrapers. Nor does it analyze the 1950 Bette Davis vehicle, *All About Eve*. Better, perhaps, to think of Jill Lepore's essay as a pack of conundrums.

It would be possible, of course, to write with great seriousness about the history of American attitudes toward sex, and about the rise of adolescence as a new, scientifically understood stage of human development, and about the facts-of-life guides marketed to the people now known as tweens starting in the early twentieth century. But Lepore, an academic historian who writes regularly for the *New Yorker,* is not one to miss out on the possibility of a masturbation joke. So instead of a clinical explanation of the "insanity" thought to be caused by excessive self-abuse, or a Foucauldian analysis of how American prudishness is a cover for a cultural obsession with sex, we get gnomic pronouncements about how adolescence over the years has seemed to grow "harder and harder," and descriptions of the moralist Sylvester Graham whipping himself into a froth while delivering lectures on the evils of overstimulation. (The crackers he invented were meant to tamp down desire; every s'more you eat causes him to writhe in his grave.)

Humor appears in academic history writing about as often as dream sequences. One could argue that it just doesn't belong, especially when it nudges readers toward an attitude of dismissiveness. Certainly, on epistemological grounds, we ought to be wary of mocking someone like Graham, since the goal is to understand him according to the norms of his own time rather than ours. Yet, as Lepore suggests, we can never escape our own historical context, and sometimes chuckling out loud instead of in our sleeve is the more honest approach. Sharing a laugh about Graham might even make for a more visceral understanding of just how strange his era was in its extreme embrace of temperance.

At one point in the essay, Lepore cites two earlier *New Yorker* writers, James Thurber and E. B. White, who asked themselves if sex was necessary, and answered, "Not strictly, no, but it beats raising begonias." Humor in history writing is not necessary, either, but it does provide some welcome stimulation.

It was in the living room. My father was reading the newspaper. I was reading Sir Arthur Conan Doyle.

> Sherlock Holmes sat up with a whistle. "By Jove, Peterson!" said he, "this is treasure trove indeed. I suppose you know what you have got?"
>
> "A diamond, sir? A precious stone. It cuts into glass as though it were putty."
>
> "It's more than a precious stone. It is *the* precious stone."
>
> "Not the Countess of Morcar's blue carbuncle!" I ejaculated.

I looked up from my book. "Hey, Dad."

"Hmm?"

"What does 'ejaculate' mean?"

He put down the newspaper. He sighed.

I never did find out who stole the Countess's blue carbuncle.

At the start of the twenty-first century, kids with questions had another option: they could read a whole slew of books, with illustrations. "You already know a lot about your penis," Karen Gravelle remarked in *What's Going on Down There? Answers to Questions Boys Find Hard to Ask*. But she knew more.[1] In *Sex, Puberty, and All That Stuff: A Guide to Growing Up*, Jacqui Bailey offered this: "Whether her hymen is holey or whole, a girl is always a virgin if she has not had sexual intercourse."[2] Lynda Madaras's *On Your Mark, Get Set, Grow!* included a section called "All About Erections," although the Bette Davis joke was likely lost on her readers; they were supposed to be in fourth grade.[3]

"Pads are also called sanitary napkins," Robie Harris explained in *It's Perfectly Normal: A Book About Changing Bodies, Growing Up, Sex, and Sexual Health*, for ages ten and up, and then she had the good sense to add, "*Sanitary* means *clean.*"[4] Harris's books, which include *It's So Amazing! A Book About Eggs, Sperm, Birth, Babies, and Families*, for ages seven and up, were genuinely sweet, in a genre where, for all its good intentions, there was a fairly despicable tendency to be edgy, brash, and cool, as if what kids put out must be what they want from grown-ups. She had a section called "What's Love?" and sensible, even existential answers ("Sometimes people just love each other"), along with a remarkably thoughtful discussion about love between men and men and between women and women. Harris's books also boasted by far the best illustrations, honest and tender drawings by Michael Emberly.[5] The worst? Robert Leighton's cartoons in Gravelle's books, which took their sensibility from *Mad* magazine—to wit, syphilis, gonorrhea, and chlamydia as bug-eyed, slimy monsters, and, for a mascot (most of these books have a mascot), a tiny, naked, bald homunculus who walks around with an erection. In an illustration for a discussion titled "How Much Does a Girl Bleed? Does She Have to Wear a Bandage?" that homunculus guy is taking a nap on a sanitary pad.[6]

Think of the genre as Kinsey for kids. The big hits in the 1970s were *Where Did I Come From? The Facts of Life Without Any Nonsense and with Illustrations* (1973) and *What's Happening to Me? The Answers to Some of the World's Most Embarrassing Questions* (1975), both written by Peter Mayle. If you put your mother and your father in a bathtub, Mayle suggested, you'd notice that they're different. "You've probably noticed that already," he granted, "but you notice it much more when you put them in the bath together." "Vagina" rhymes with "Carolina," Mayle explained, and an orgasm is like a sneeze.[7] Ah-choo?

While not the world's most embarrassing question, here's a good historical question: How did these books come to be? If the answers to life's secrets are to be found in books, why *these* books? Couldn't at least a few of life's secrets be discovered on a foggy day spent at the neighborhood branch of your local public library, even in the Children's Rooms started by Anne Carroll Moore, reading something else? What is love? Read a novel. Where did I come from? Philosophy, Religion. Dewey decimals 100–299. How are babies born? Librarians usually keep one or two well-illustrated anatomy textbooks near the reference desk. What does "ejaculate" mean? Dictionaries are *made* for this kind of thing. "E-jac-u-late, *v.* to eject semen." "Semen" gets you to "spermatozoa," which gets you to "ovum," and before you know it, you know it all. I once saw two cats go at it beneath a blackberry bush in a vacant lot after dark; later, one of those cats gave birth to a litter of kittens in our cellar and, although at first I thought they were three blind mice, that, *Webster's New Collegiate,* and *Gray's Anatomy* pretty well covered it, which was good, because the Holmes chat had left me wondering, "Dr. Watson did *what*?"

Books about sex, usually offering advice about how to do it better, have been around for a long time. The most popular manual, even into the twentieth century, was *Aristotle's Master-piece; Or, The Secrets of Generation,* which was

first published in English in 1684. It caused a stir in Northampton, Massachusetts, in 1744, when Jonathan Edwards discovered that a dozen young men in
his congregation had "read Aristotle," a "nasty book, about womenkind."[8] It
went through twenty-six American editions between 1766 and 1831 alone.[9] It
wasn't exactly a masterpiece, and it certainly wasn't written by Aristotle. No
one knows who wrote it; it's a hodgepodge. But it's got both handy anatomy
lessons ("The Clytoris . . . is the Seat of Venereal Pleasure") and useful tips:
"They that would be commended to their Wedlock actions, and be happy in
the fruit of their Labour, must observe to Copulate at distance of time not too
often, nor yet too seldom."[10]

Aristotle's Master-piece, though, wasn't a kids' book; it was written and published before kids' books existed. Books explaining the facts of life to kids have
been around only since the beginning of the twentieth century—the so-called
golden age of children's literature—which is also when adolescence as a stage
of life was invented. And, curiously, the books and the stage are tangled together, because adolescence, at least when it started, meant the time between
when you learn about sex and when you do it.

Aristotle (the actual Aristotle) wrote about three ages of man: youth, the
prime of life, and old age. In the seventeenth century, Boston's Puritan poet
Anne Bradstreet followed medieval writers, by describing four:

> Lo now! four other acts upon the stage,
> Childhood, and Youth, the Manly, and Old-age.[11]

In early America, "youth" could mean anyone up to the age of thirty. Jonathan
Edwards called the young men in his congregation who were reading Aristotle's Master-piece "boys"; their average age was twenty-four.[12]

The ages of man followed the order of the natural world—the days and the
seasons. Morning, noon, night. Spring, summer, fall, winter. "One man in his
time plays many parts, / His acts being seven ages." (There were seven plan-
ets.) Shakespeare's player goes straight from "the whining school-boy, with
his satchel" to "the lover, / Sighing like a furnace." John Wallis's New Game of
Human Life had seven ages, too. His character is a "boy" until twelve, when he
turns into a "youth"; he's not a "man" until he's twenty-four.[13]

Rousseau talked about l'adolescence in Émile in 1762, which is one route
by which the word, and the idea, entered the English vernacular.[14] He called
adolescence a second birth. "We are born, so to speak, twice over; born into
existence, and born into life." The time when a child "leaves childhood behind
him," Rousseau warned, will be a time of peril: "he is a lion in a fever." If childhood is a paradise, the best plan, Rousseau thought, is to prolong it by staving

off the onset of adulthood. This requires keeping the secrets of generation secret.

The problem is, the little pipsqueaks ask so many questions. "'Where do little children come from?' This is an embarrassing question," Rousseau admitted, "which occurs very naturally to children, one which foolishly or wisely answered may decide their health and their morals for life." He recommended dodging it:

> Should we enlighten children at an early period as to the objects of their curiosity, or is it better to put them off with decent shams? I think we need do neither. In the first place, this curiosity will not arise unless we give it a chance. We must therefore take care not to give it an opportunity. In the next place, questions one is not obliged to answer do not compel us to deceive those who ask them; it is better to bid the child hold his tongue than to tell him a lie. He will not be greatly surprised at this treatment if you have already accustomed him to it in matters of no importance. Lastly, if you decide to answer his questions, let it be with the greatest plainness, without mystery or confusion, without a smile. It is much less dangerous to satisfy a child's curiosity than to stimulate it.

That is, if you can't skirt these questions, better to be honest, early, before your child becomes a lion with a temperature of a hundred and three.[15]

The paradise of childhood was a product of the Enlightenment, but the storm of adolescence descended upon the United States with urbanization.[16] Children used to be able to see for themselves how animals mate, bear, and nurse their young. But when people left the farm and moved to the city to work in factories, the way Milton Bradley's father did, kids missed out on the chance to watch animals . . . sneezing.[17] And then, oddly enough, parents began solemnly informing their children that babies, swaddled in blankets, are dropped down the chimney by a tall bird with long legs and a heavy bill.

Storks, which are common in northern Europe, are known for taking particular care of their young. (Storks haven't always been associated with fertility; in fact, the reverse has just as often been the case. In eighteenth-century Philadelphia, syringes marketed as abortifacients were "ingenious things said to have been suggested by the stork." The stork feeds its young by inserting its bill down their throats, and a woman who thrust this syringe up her vagina and through her cervix could induce a miscarriage, or die trying.)[18] In the United States, the rise of the myth that babies come from storks dates to the publication in 1838 of "The Storks," a story by Hans Christian Andersen. In a nest on the roof of a house in a little village, a male stork guards a female and her hatchlings. Down below, a rascally boy sings:

> *Stork! stork! long-legged stork!*
> *Into thy nest I prithee walk;*
> *There sits thy mate,*
> *With her four children so great.*
> *The first we'll hang like a cat,*
> *The second we'll burn,*
> *The third on a spit we'll turn,*
> *The fourth drown dead as a rat!*

The baby storks tell their mother they would like to exact some vengeance on the boys below.

> "Shall not we fly down, and peck out their eyes?" said the young ones.
> "No, leave them alone!" said the mother.

Instead, she teaches them to fly.

> "Now we will have our revenge!" said they.
> "Very well!" said the mother; "I have been thinking what will be the best. I know where the pool is, in which all the little human children lie until the storks come and take them to their parents: the pretty little things sleep and dream so pleasantly as they will never dream again. All parents like to have a little child, and all children like to have a little brother or sister. We will fly to the pool and fetch one for each of the boys who has not sung that wicked song, nor made a jest of the storks; and the other naughty children shall have none."
> "But he who first sung those naughty rhymes! that great ugly fellow! what shall we do to him?" cried the young storks.
> "In the pool there lies a little child who has dreamed away his life; we will take it for him, and he will weep because he has only a little dead brother."[19]

And that is just what they do.

"The Storks" is as cruel as the darkest of the Grimms' tales, but it also explained, in one fell swoop, both birth and infant death. Andersen's fables were hugely popular in the United States.[20] Soon, the stork myth was everywhere: there were stork books, stork toys, stork baby bottles, and stork postcards. Nineteenth-century Americans, squeamish, but with eggs on their minds, grew all but obsessed with the idea that babies come not from women but from birds.

To all this, Sylvester Graham objected, strenuously. He was an anti-stork man. Graham was born in West Suffield, Connecticut, in 1794, the youngest of seventeen children. His grandfather, a Scottish emigrant, was a minister. His father, who died when Sylvester was a baby, had been a charismatic preacher during New England's Great Awakening, in the 1740s, when Jonathan Edwards was preaching—and banning *Aristotle's Master-piece*. After the death of her husband, Sylvester Graham's mother was deemed by the court to be "in a deranged state of mind" and unable to care for her children.[21] From the age of three, her youngest son was farmed out to neighbors and relatives; he never had much of a childhood. A wayward and melancholy youth, he once wrote an autobiographical poem about that uncomfortable, feverish age between childhood and manhood:

> *In gloom, in sadness, and in tears,*
> > *Through childhood's period then did'st languish;*
> *And up through manhood's early years,*
> > *Thy every pulse was beat in anguish.*[22]

In 1823, Graham began a course of study at Amherst. Then he had a breakdown. The next year, he married the daughter of a sea captain. And then he was born again. Like many young men of his day, Graham was swept away by what came to be known as the Second Great Awakening, a religious revival that aimed at a wholesale reformation in manners. Preachers shunned everything earthy, bawdy, and reckless in favor of everything refined, restrained, pious, and purposeful. In 1776, about one in six Americans belonged to a church; by 1850, that number had risen to one in three. In roughly the same period, the amount of alcohol Americans drank dropped from more than seven gallons per adult per year to less than two. Sobriety, orderliness, and punctuality: these were deemed essential traits for a people leaving farms and working, instead, in factories and in offices, striving to accumulate, achieve, invent, progress, and succeed.[23]

Although Graham was licensed to preach in 1826, he never established his own congregation, partly because he was plagued by ill health. He suffered from a series of vague ailments: dyspepsia, sciatica, rheumatism, and neuralgia. For a while, he made a living as a temperance reformer, warning of the dangers of drink. Then he began having visions of a coming apocalypse—an apocalypse of children. "Thousands and thousands of children are springing into existence, and rising up into civil and moral society, and becoming incorporated with the body politic of the nation, without receiving any regular moral culture of the heart," he preached in Philadelphia in 1829. A half-million children had already reached adulthood without having been given religious instruction, and some two and a half million children were in danger of following them into ruin. This river of children, he said, was more powerful than the Mississippi:

> The millions of children, which are now unseen and unfelt in our Country, with the thousands that are daily gushing into life,—if measures be not taken to qualify and direct their course, will inevitably, from their condition and circumstances, soon unite in one dark and mighty confluence of ignorance and immorality and crime, which will overflow the wholesome restraints of society, and sweep away the barriers of civil law, and sap the foundations of our Republican institutions.[24]

The more he considered the coming apocalypse, the more Graham came to believe that this wasn't so much a religious matter as a medical one. The problem at the heart of the body politic was a problem in the human body itself, and especially in the bodies of young men. They were overflowing; they were spurting: they were ejaculating.[25]

Graham didn't use the word "adolescence." He talked, instead, about "children" and, more often, about "youth." Still, the people he was worried about were between ten and twenty-four: growing up, but not yet married. He was more worried about boys than girls. He wasn't alone. In 1829, the Connecticut minister Joel Hawes remarked, in *Lectures to Young Men on the Formation of Character*, that on the voyage of life, the waters traveled between the ages of fourteen and twenty-one are the most perilous: "On this sea, my young friends, you are now embarking, with little knowledge of what is before you, and many of you, I fear, without line, or compass, or chart." Henry Ward Beecher warned, in his own *Lectures to Young Men*, that "a young man . . . feels in his bosom the various impulses, wild desires, restless cravings he can hardly tell for what." He is on a quest, "thirsting for happiness."[26]

All this worry about young men was by no means without cause. The period between childhood and adulthood was, at the time, getting longer. Puberty was beginning earlier (at least as measured by the age of menarche, which was declining), and young people were starting work and marrying later. Girls remained dependent even after getting married, but prolonged dependence was a particular problem for boys, who were trying to grow into men in a nation that had revolted from its parent country and that prized no value more than independence. There were a great many young people around; the average age of the population was seventeen. And many of those young people were living near factories, as Dorus Clarke, a Springfield, Massachusetts, minister, remarked in his *Lectures to Young People in Manufacturing Villages* in 1836. Clarke preached that the first generation of Americans to come of age during the age of machines faced dangers unknown to any prior generation: "Never before was the world in such an excitable, impressible state."[27]

Graham started delivering his own *Lecture to Young Men* in the 1830s. He wanted to warn them about excitement by telling them about sex, not storks. In one thing, he sided with Rousseau: "Through a fear of contaminating the minds of youth, it has long been considered the wisest measure to keep them in ignorance." This would be fine, except that "the natural inquisitiveness of the young mind has been met by misrepresentation and falsehood, on the part of those who would preserve their purity." This, Graham believed, was a disaster, because young people are as curious as cats—theirs is a "restless and prying curiosity"—and they'll find out about sex, by hook or by crook, "So that while parents have been resting securely in the idea of the ignorance and purity of their children, these have been clandestinely drinking in the most corrupt and depraving knowledge from mercenary and polluted hands."[28]

People often called him "Dr. Graham," but Sylvester Graham was not a physician. Still, the confusion is a good illustration of the era's shifting source of authority for how to steer your course through the voyage of life: rules for conduct once laid down by clergymen were, more and more, made by doctors. Graham's lectures were based in morality—his was a theory, finally, about virtue and vice—but he called it something else. He called it "the science of human life."

Graham believed that the human body had two functions, nutrition and reproduction, connected by the same bundle of nerves. Stimulation of either system was debilitating. The nineteenth century's combination of excitements—the processed food of the factory and the frenzy of city life—was responsible not only for specific diseases, including devastating outbreaks of cholera, but also for a general American malaise, caused by overstimulation. All those hordes of unmarried young people living in cities were eating, instead of fresh farm foods, tinned meat and canned vegetables and bread made with processed flour. Worse, old enough to know about sex but not old enough to marry, they were masturbating. "Self-pollution," he said, "is actually a very great and rapidly increasing evil in our country."[29] Young Americans were spilling their precious bodily fluids; the nation was at risk.

This was, for Graham, a matter of national political urgency. The new republic—Young America it was called—was not only full of young people, it was a young country, and it was also the world's first modern democracy. It was precarious, an excitable experiment. Graham put it this way: "Whether a national Government can permanently and beneficially exist, whose ultimate power is in the hands of the people, and whose form of existence and mode of operation depend on the popular will, is yet a matter of experiment, with us; not only for ourselves, but for the whole human family; and it may be, for ages or forever!" No government in the history of the world, he argued, had so entirely depended on the virtue of its people. The United States was "the political POLE-STAR of the world; by which the political philanthropists of every nation, are endeavoring to govern their course."[30] The health of the nation's youth would determine the future of the republic. If the American body politic spent its time masturbating, what then?

Haranguers, of course, had damned masturbation before. In the 1790s, before Parson Weems wrote his *Life of Washington,* he sold *Onania,* a treatise against masturbation. (Weems, an itinerant bookseller, also pocketed tidy sums peddling *The Lover's Almanac* and, in 1799, a book dedicated to George Washington called *The Philanthropist; Or, A Good Twelve Cents Worth of Political Love Powder, for the Fair Daughters and Patriotic Sons of Virginia.*)[31] But Graham went much further than moralists who damned only masturbation—he also damned intercourse. For Graham, it wasn't solitude that was the problem; it was ejaculation. Before Graham, sex within marriage, at least, hadn't been bad; usually, it was considered good for you. *Aristotle's Master-piece* described intercourse as a release: "It eases and lightens the body, clears the mind, comforts the head and senses, and expels melancholy." The best sex was "furious": "The act of coition should be performed with the greatest ardor and intenseness of desire imaginable, or else they may as well let it alone."[32] The Garden of Eden, after all, was a "Place of Pleasure"; Adam and Eve were together, "compleating their mutual Happiness" in "the Paradise of Paradise itself."[33]

With all this, Graham could hardly have disagreed more strenuously. "Sexual excess within the pale of wedlock" was, he argued, a national crisis. If a man was exceptionally robust, and terribly lucky, he might indulge in it once a month without too much ill effect. Much more, and he would grow old before his time, and die an early and miserable death.[34] Graham did not consider marital sex a mansion of happiness. Ejaculation was an injury; even the most innocent sexual release was debilitating. "There is a common error of opinion among young men, which is, perhaps, not wholly confined to the young,— that health requires an emission of semen at stated periods, and that frequent nocturnal emissions in sleep are not incompatible with health. . . . All this is wrong,—entirely, dangerously wrong!"

Graham's lectures were wildly popular, and no wonder. He was a stagy talker, famous for shouting and sweating himself into a state of froth and fury. Nothing was so violent an overstimulation to the human body, he insisted, as sexual excitement. He compared arousal to a natural disaster: "the body of man has become a living volcano." During the climax of one of his lectures, when he described orgasm—"the convulsive paroxysms attending venereal indulgence"—he could barely contain himself: "The brain, stomach, heart, lungs, liver, skin, and the other organs, feel it sweeping over them with the tremendous violence of a tornado." All this, he said with a shudder, is "succeeded by great exhaustion, relaxation, lassitude, and even prostration."[35] And then, he nearly collapsed.

Gesundheit.

Curiously, what Graham described as the consequences of masturbation sound like nothing so much as the ravages of old age: "The sight becomes feeble, obscure, cloudy, confused, and often is entirely lost—and utter blindness fills the rest of life with darkness and unavailing regret." Masturbators were sure to suffer not only from loss of sight but also from diseases of the heart, lungs, kidneys, and liver, and, in the worst cases, memory loss, brain damage, and death.[36] "The skin loses its healthy, clear and fresh appearance, and assumes a sickly, pale, shriveled, turbid and cadaverous aspect;—becoming exceedingly susceptible to the injurious effects of cold, heat, moisture, and other disturbing causes."[37] (Graham also believed masturbation caused insanity. Under the influence of Graham's ideas, "masturbatory insanity" was a leading cause of admission to the State Lunatic Hospital, in Worcester, Massachusetts, second only to intemperance. And those suffering from masturbatory insanity had, of all inmates, the poorest chance of recovery.)[38]

What would happen to the United States if young Americans didn't stop masturbating? They, and the republic, would grow as feeble and decrepit as the Old World. Still, there was hope, boundless hope. If eating the wrong kind of food and having too much sex is what causes disease, then disease can be avoided. And if disease is what causes aging, then aging can be avoided, too. "If mankind always lived precisely as they ought to live," Graham explained, "they would—as a general rule—most certainly pass through the several stages of life, from infancy to extreme old age, without sickness and distress, enjoying, through their long protracted years, health, and serenity, and peace, and individual and social happiness, and gradually wear out their vital energies, and finally lie down and fall asleep in death, without an agony—without a pain." Illness and decline were unnatural. "Disease and suffering are, in no degree, the legitimate and necessary results of the operations of our bodily organs," Graham maintained, "and by no means necessarily incident to human life."

The science of human life promised to cure all disease and relieve all pain. The rules were simple. For the digestive system, Graham recommended abstinence from meat and processed food and prescribed cold plain foods, whole grains, and the digestive crackers that still bear his name. (John Harvey Kellogg, who read Graham as a boy, later founded the Battle Creek Sanitarium, in Michigan, where he prescribed enemas and cold—and eponymous—breakfast cereal, to stifle desire.)[39] For the reproductive system, Graham recommended sexual abstinence, or close to it. And then, decades would pass, but you wouldn't feel the years. You couldn't live forever, but you could live for a very long time, disease-free.

Grahamism marked a turning point between a religious conception of the good life and a medical one. With Graham, the wages of sin became the stages of life. "For the wages of sin is death; but the gift of God is eternal life through Jesus Christ our Lord" (Romans 6:23). Graham believed in Christ, death, and eternal life; he just didn't believe in sex, sickness, or aging. They weren't necessary. No, he said: "God made you to be happy."[40]

This led Graham to a rather uncomfortable position: to be saved, children had to be taught the facts of life. But to advocate this position was to court more controversy than he could bear.[41] "When I commenced my public career, as a Lecturer on the Science of Human Life, it did not, in any degree, enter into my plan, to treat on this delicate subject," he insisted. (He had also been attacked by mobs: once by a posse of commercial bakers, once by angry butchers, and once for delivering an arousing lecture about chastity to young women.)[42] But, at least as he told it, he had been persuaded of its necessity because so many very young men had approached him, complaining of all manner of illness and having not the least notion that their suffering was the consequence of masturbation. Something had to be done.[43]

Crowds thronged by the thousands to see him speak, thrillingly, about volcanoes and tornadoes. And they scooped up copies of his book, too. *A Lecture to Young Men, on Chastity, Intended Also for the Serious Consideration of Parents and Guardians* went through ten editions in fifteen years. He always insisted that it wasn't really appropriate for children: "It may, perhaps, be said, that this work is better calculated for adults than for young boys. This is true."[44]

He never discounted the idea of writing a book about the science of human life for young men and women, rather than for their parents. One day, he thought, it may "be found expedient and desirable that a work should be produced on the subject, more peculiarly adapted to young minds."[45] He never wrote it. Despite a strict adherence to his regimen, his health declined. He abandoned lecturing. He abandoned writing. He got sick, and then he got sicker. As he languished, at the end of his life, at his home in Northampton, Massachusetts, he tried eating meat, and even drinking alcohol.[46] Nothing helped. He died in 1851, at the age of fifty-seven. A postmortem was conducted, but no one was quite sure what had killed him. He seemed, simply, to have wasted away.[47] Before his final illness, he had been at work on a new book. It was to be called *The Philosophy of History.*[48]

"Perchance the mantle of Graham may fall upon the shoulders of someone who, availing himself of all that Graham learned, and rejecting all his errors, shall carry on the work," observed one obituary writer.[49] The year Graham died, Granville Stanley Hall was seven years old and living on a farm in western Massachusetts, about twenty miles from Graham's house. Hall's father, a farmer, was also a temperance lecturer. He must have known Graham; he certainly knew of him. Young Stanley was said to have been "unusually inquisitive about the origin of babies." He asked a lot of questions, including whether God had ever been a baby. He read everything he could get his hands on. Very likely, he read Graham's *Lecture to Young Men*. Told that masturbation causes leprosy, he tied himself up at night, with bandages.[50]

When Hall grew up, he went to study in Germany, where he learned all about kindergartens; he helped bring them to the United States. In the 1890s, he founded the child-study movement, which is what led to children's rooms at public libraries. He earned the first PhD in psychology awarded at an American university. Psychology was Hall's science of human life. He founded the *American Journal of Psychology,* and he founded and served as first president of the American Psychological Association. But what G. Stanley Hall is best remembered for is what Anne Carroll Moore captured when she called him "the great explorer of adolescence."[51]

In *Adolescence: Its Psychology and Its Relation to Physiology, Anthropology, Sociology, Sex, Crime, Religion and Education*, an exhaustive, rambling, and at times downright bizarre two-volume study published in 1904 (and that sold more than twenty-five thousand copies), Hall finished what Graham had begun, stirring in much of Darwin and a great deal of Freud, insisting that the time between childhood and adulthood is a stage of life all its own.[52] It happens, he explained, between the ages of fourteen and twenty-four. It is marked by Sturm und Drang, storm and stress. On the voyage of life, adolescence is when you have to steer your ship through a hurricane.

This stage of life was, to Hall, living in an age of psychological explanations, mostly in your head. "The dawn of adolescence is marked by a special consciousness of sex," he wrote. Its dusk is the act itself. Hall condemned masturbation, but, unlike Graham, he didn't condemn intercourse. Instead, in language no less fevered and millennialist than Graham's, he celebrated sex as the birth of the adult. The crisis of adolescence, Hall argued, is solved by the integration of religious fervor and sexual passion. That integration is accomplished by the realization—earned by experience—that sex is sacred. Here is Hall on intercourse:

> In the most unitary of all acts, which is the epitome and pleroma of life, we have the most intense of all affirmations of the will to live and realize that the only true God is love, and the center of life is worship. Every part of the mind and body participates in a true pangenesis. This sacrament is the annunciation hour, with hosannas which the whole world reflects. Communion is fusion and beatitude. It is the supreme hedonic narcosis, a holy intoxication, the chief ecstasy, because the most intense of experiences; it is the very heart of psychology, and because it is the supreme pleasure of life it is the eternal basis and guarantee of optimism. It is this experience more than any other that opens to man the ideal world. Now the race is incarnated in the individual and remembers its lost paradise.

It was a mansion of happiness, regained.[53]

Books like *Where Did I Come From?* came from G. Stanley Hall. It was Hall's work on adolescence that led, at the beginning of the twentieth century, to facts-of-life books for "teenagers" (the word, an Americanism, was coined not long after *Adolescence* was published).[54] Adolescent boys, Hall reported, spend nine-tenths of their time thinking about sex, and they don't know what to think.[55] He therefore argued for sex education; adolescents could enter that mansion of happiness only if they were taught about sex. They needed help: they needed something to read.[56]

Under Hall's influence, books explaining sex to kids, directly, and not through their parents, began to proliferate during Anne Carroll Moore's golden age of children's literature, which also happened to be a time when there was a lot of talk about sex. "Sex O'Clock in America" is what one pundit called it, in 1913.[57] At the same time, venereal disease had come to be seen as the cause of all manner of social problems, including a perceived crisis in the American family, marked by a falling marriage rate, a rising divorce rate, and a declining fertility rate, at least within the middle class. Teaching "sexual hygiene," celebrating chastity and marriage, was to be the solution.

Early-twentieth-century Progressives, who could make a science of licking envelopes if they set their minds to it—which is why so many ideas about life and death hinge on this period—made a science of adolescence. Sex education in the public schools began in the 1910s; by 1922, the subject was taught in nearly half of all public schools in the United States.[58] The first sex books for kids were schoolbooks. About matters anatomical, they were candid. About the dangers of venereal disease, they were concerned. But as for that question Rousseau mentioned—"Where do little children come from?"—they were, as yet, coy.

"All live things start from eggs," wrote Winfield Scott Hall in 1912 in *Life's Beginnings: For Boys of Ten to Fourteen Years.* Hall, a professor of physiology at Northwestern University, and no relation to G. Stanley Hall, was, at the time, America's foremost sexologist.[59] The author of such classics as *From Youth into Manhood,* he wrote with a winning frankness ("Turning our attention now to the testicles . . .") and had been particularly commended for his forgiving attitude toward the nocturnal emission ("It is a perfectly natural experience that results in no loss of vitality, only a slight depletion of material").[60] His books about what he called "the great truths of life" included a twenty-five-cent pamphlet titled *Instead of "Wild Oats"* and a collaboration with his wife, Jeannette Winter Hall, *Girlhood and Its Problems: The Sex Life of Woman,* although he was perhaps best known for a 320-page manual, *Sexual Knowledge: In Plain and Simple Language,* published by the International Bible House in 1913 and available, for two dollars, bound in morocco.[61]

In *Life's Beginnings*, a twenty-five-cent primer published by the YMCA, Winfield Scott Hall aimed to explain the birds and the bees by way of the barnyard, as if every boy were William Harvey: "All boys are interested in live things, therefore all boys are interested in eggs. The best place to see all kinds of eggs is out on a farm."[62] Let's go out to the country, he told his readers, city boys all. In the henhouse, a "motherly old biddy" sits on a nest of eggs. Where do those eggs come from? Let's follow the farmer's wife into the kitchen, where she's butchering chickens for Sunday dinner. "When the farmer's wife opens the bodies of these hens to remove their internal organs, she finds in each an ovary or egg-sack, with many eggs in different stages of development," Hall explains. "If the egg is to develop into a chicken it must be fertilized. Every day the rooster deposits the fertilizing fluid in the pouch or *cloaca* of the hen."[63] Next he takes his readers down to the pond, to watch the frogs spawn. By chapter 3, he's moved on to kittens and puppies, colts and calves. Do these animals come from eggs, too? "Yes, all these animals begin as tiny little eggs. But they are so delicate that, if they were deposited in any nest outside of the body, they would surely be destroyed, so nature has provided that in all these animals the delicate eggs should be held within a sort of nest in the mother's body. This nest is called the *womb*." And then, somewhat abruptly, our tour comes to a close:

> You return to the city after three months on the farm, to be introduced to a baby sister, who came into your home two weeks ago. When you come into the house and see your little sister you find that she is in the act of taking her dinner from her mother's breast, and after the first rush of joy at the sight of them both—joy and surprise nearly smothering you—it all comes over you that little baby sister has come in the same way the little baby colts and calves and kittens and lambs came. "Mother," you ask, "was my sister formed from an egg and did she grow within your body?" Your mother will of course answer "Yes," and you will go away and think it over.[64]

That, it hardly needs to be said, leaves rather a lot to the imagination.

E. B. White was thirteen years old when Winfield Scott Hall published *Life's Beginnings: For Boys of Ten to Fourteen Years*. In 1929, the year he married Katharine Angell, White, with his officemate, James Thurber, published his first book, *Is Sex Necessary?* (Their answer: not strictly, no, but it beats raising begonias.) *Is Sex Necessary?* is a lampoon of the sex books that White had grown up with. It features fake Freudian sexologists (viz., the undersized Dr. Samuel D. Schmalhausen) and a chapter, written by White, addressing the child's perennial question: "What shall I tell my parents about sex?" The answer: "Tell them the truth. If the subject is approached in a tactful way, it should be no more embarrassing to teach a parent about sex than to teach him about personal pronouns. And it should be less discouraging."[65]

White's first children's book, *Stuart Little,* could easily have been titled *Is Childbirth Necessary?* (Not strictly, no, but it beats banning books.) Plenty of grown-ups got the joke about how the tale of the mouse was, among other things, a sly commentary on Progressive-era sex education. The *Washington Post* even ran a review that took the form of a loving imitation of *Is Sex Necessary?* right down to the idiotic Freudian sexologists, in this case, Dr. Hans Von Hornswoggle, who asserts that *Stuart Little* must be a hoax: "'Lacks verisimilitude from the very first line,' said Herr Von Hornswoggle. 'Man or mouse, homo sapiens or *Mus musculus*—no little rodent can sail a ship in Central Park lagoon while still teething. Much, much too Jung.'"[66] Kids, though, were too young to get that one.

"Have you ever thought about an egg, perhaps the one you know best, the chicken egg?" Books like *Window into an Egg: Seeing Life Begin,* which explained the story of life through pictures of a chicken egg with a piece of the shell missing, were still being published in 1969.[67] But that same year also saw the publication of *Everything You Always Wanted to Know About Sex (But Were Afraid to Ask),* which rather dramatically raised the stakes (and inspired a Woody Allen film). Sex left the farm.

The possibility that books explaining sex to kids could become far more explicit came into play after 1957, when, in *Roth v. United States,* the Supreme Court drew a distinction between sexual explicitness and obscenity, which meant that, if being explicit had a redeeming social value, you could be explicit.[68] By the 1960s, sex education had become a partisan battleground, especially after the founding of both the Sexuality Information and Education Council of the United States and a flock of local organizations, like the New York League for Sexual Freedom. Their reforms of the sex education curriculum in public schools—which consisted not only of greater explicitness but also of a rejection of the Progressives' chastity-and-marriage curriculum, the promotion of contraception, and the discussion of homosexuality—led to campaigns to regulate it by organizations including the John Birch Society, whose founder called sex education a "filthy communist plot."

Is the School House the Proper Place to Teach Raw Sex? was the title of a pamphlet published by the Christian Crusade in 1968.[69] In the 1970s, the battle over sex education got nastier, especially in the wake of *Roe v. Wade*.[70] Kids trying to figure out sex were caught in the middle. Then came AIDS. During all this time, a great deal remained as unspeakable as it had been in the days of Sylvester Graham's brimstone. In 1994, U.S. surgeon general Joycelyn Elders was asked, at an AIDS forum, whether it might not be a good idea to discuss masturbation with children. "I think that it is something that's part of human sexuality and it's part of something that perhaps should be taught," Elders said. "But we've not even taught our children the very basics. And I feel that we have tried ignorance for a very long time and it's time we try education." Within hours, Elders was asked to resign.[71]

Teaching sex became a political minefield. And facts-of-life books changed. They no longer involved going to a farm or studying other animals; this is not zoology class. We are not dissecting frogs; we are thinking about ourselves. Late twentieth-century books were full of anatomical drawings of the insides of kids' bodies, with cross sections of gonads on every page. That's partly because, outside a laboratory or a surgery, some of those things had only recently been photographed, Lennart Nilsson–style. But it's also because of the culture's inward looking. Eggs and sperm aren't to be found out there in the barnyard or on some farmer's wife's kitchen table: they are inside of *you*.

By the beginning of the twenty-first century, nothing was left to the imagination anymore: "1 sperm + 1 egg = 1 baby," Robie Harris explained, in *It's NOT the Stork! A Book About Girls, Boys, Babies, Bodies, Families, and Friends* (2006). "When grownups want to make a baby," she went on, "most often a woman and a man have a special kind of loving called 'making love'—'having sex'—or 'sex.' This kind of loving happens when the woman and the man get so close to each other that the man's penis goes inside the woman's vagina."[72] *Life's Beginnings* was for boys ten to fourteen; *It's NOT the Stork* was for kids as young as four.

Over the course of a century, where babies come from had become baby stuff. Books for kids older than about seven or eight covered that subject, but they were far more concerned with the perils of puberty. Adolescence seemed to be starting earlier and earlier and, somehow, to be getting harder and harder. Since the beginning of the nineteenth century, every generation of

Americans has found adolescence to be stormier than it had been, ever before. Meanwhile, the beginning of life, a mystery that evolved into a science, became yet another form of therapy, as if every kid needed Von Hornswoggle. The disorder it treated was growing up.

"It is much, *much* harder to be a teenage girl now than ever before," insisted the gynecologist Jennifer Ashton in 2009, in *The Body Scoop for Girls: A Straight-Talk Guide to a Healthy, Beautiful You.*[73] "Am I weird?" you wonder. *"No!"* Lynda Madaras insisted, in *Ready, Set, Grow!* "You are not weird. You are 100% NORMAL! You're just starting puberty." Madaras's book included a chapter called "B.O. and Zits."[74] You're 100 percent normal, but you stink, and if you would only be more careful about your grooming, you could look so much better. "If puberty is something that just happens, why do you need to read about it?" Louise Spilsbury asked in *Me, Myself and I: All About Sex and Puberty,* in 2009. Her answer: "Finding out more about puberty will also help you deal with the practical side of it, from shaving to sanitary pads."[75] And, to be sure, there was in that era's crop of well-intentioned books an abundance of practical information. *The Care & Keeping of You: The Body Book for Girls,* published in 1998 by the makers of the American Girl dolls, had this to say about underarm hair: "Whether you want to remove it or leave it there is a very personal decision."[76] No subject was too small. How to shave your legs, how to shave your face ("take special care when shaving around pimples"), how to insert a tampon, how to ask someone on a date, what to say on a date, what not to say ("Never Tell Your Boyfriend You're on the Pill," advised Ashton), how to spy on your vagina with a hand mirror, how to brush your hair ("use a wide-tooth comb to detangle small sections"), even how to brush your teeth. If you find that your clothes are suddenly too small for you, one author patiently explained, that's because you're *growing,* dear.[77]

For adults, there were, at the turn of the twenty-first century, a new generation of books offering guidance on how to talk to kids about sex, including *Ten Talks Parents Must Have with Their Children About Sex and Character,* in which Pepper Schwartz and Dominic Cappello provided scripts, line-by-line instruction. "I'm reading this chapter about sex and character," you were supposed to begin, holding the book in your hands. "I need to talk to you for five or ten minutes."[78] Ten minutes? How much more can a kid take?

It was in the kitchen. I was reading the newspaper. A small, bookish boy sat by my side.

"Hey," he said.

"Hmm?"

"Do you need a conundrum for oral sex?"

I put down my newspaper. I sighed. And then, carrying on an ancient and honorable family tradition, I whiffed the bejeezus out of that one.

NOTES

1. Karen Gravelle with Nick and Chava Castro, *What's Going on Down There? Answers to Questions Boys Find Hard to Ask* (New York: Walker, 1998), 5.

2. Jacqui Bailey, *Sex, Puberty, and All That Stuff: A Guide to Growing Up* (New York: Barron's, 2004), 47.

3. Lynda Madaras, *On Your Mark, Get Set, Grow!* (New York: Newmarket, 2008).

4. Robie H. Harris, *It's Perfectly Normal: A Book About Changing Bodies, Growing Up, Sex, and Sexual Health* (Cambridge, MA: Candlewick, 2009), 35.

5. Robie H. Harris, *It's So Amazing! A Book About Eggs, Sperm, Birth, Babies, and Families* (Cambridge, MA: Candlewick, 1999), 30.

6. Gravelle, *What's Going on Down There?*, 36, 39, 91, 60.

7. Peter Mayle, *Where Did I Come From? The Facts of Life Without Any Nonsense and with Illustrations* (Secaucus, NJ: Lyle Stuart, 1973), n.p.

8. One young man "sat 'till midnight reading one of them books"; another told a friend he could see it for ten shillings. An account of the "bad book" episode is contained within Ava Chamberlain, "The Immaculate Ovum: Jonathan Edwards and the Construction of the Female Body," *William and Mary Quarterly* 57 (2000): 289–322; see especially 313–18.

9. Stephen Nissenbaum, *Sex, Diet, and Debility in Jacksonian America: Sylvester Graham and Health Reform* (Westport, CT: Greenwood, 1980), 27. Otho T. Beall Jr., "*Aristotle's Master Piece* in America: A Landmark in the Folklore of Medicine," *William and Mary Quarterly* 20 (1963): 210.

10. *Aristotle's Master-piece; Or, The Secrets of Generation* (London, 1694), 99, 10. On this work in England and America, see Roy Porter and Lesley Hall, *The Facts of Life: The Creation of Sexual Knowledge in Britain, 1650–1950* (New Haven, CT: Yale University Press, 1995); Beall, "*Aristotle's Master Piece* in America," 207–22; Mary E. Fissell, "Hairy Women and Naked Truths: Gender and the Politics of Knowledge in *Aristotle's Masterpiece*," *William and Mary Quarterly* 60 (2003): 43–74; Janet Blackman, "Popular Theories of Generation: The Evolution of Aristotle's Works, the Study of an Anachronism," in *Health Care and Popular Medicine in Nineteenth Century England: Essays in the Social History of Medicine*, ed. John Woodward and David Richards (New York: Holmes and Meier, 1977), 56–88; and Vern L. Bullough, "An Early American Sex Manual; Or, Aristotle Who?," *Early American Literature* 7 (1973): 236–46.

11. Bradstreet, "The Four Ages of Man," in *Poems of Anne Bradstreet*, ed. Robert Hutchinson (New York: Dover, 1969).

12. Chamberlain, "Immaculate Ovum," 320. On the language of youth, see Joseph F. Kett, *Rites of Passage: Adolescence in America, 1790 to the Present* (New York: Basic Books, 1977), 11–14. Kett, in pointing out the vagueness of early modern language, uses, instead, the language of dependency, semidependency, and independence.

13. You can see this in Raleigh's *History of the World* (London, 1614):

> Our Infancie is compared to the *Moone,* in which wee seeme only to live and grow, as Plants; the second age to *Mercurie,* wherein we are taught and instructed; our third age to *Venus,* the dayes of love, desire, and vanitie; the fourth to the *Sunne,* the strong, flourishing, and beautifull age of mans life; the fifth to *Mars,* in which we seeke honour and victorie, and in which our thoughts travaile to ambitious ends; the sixth Age is ascribed to *Jupiter,* in which we begin to take accompt of our times, judge of our selves, and grow to the perfection of our understanding; the last and seventh to *Saturne,* wherein our dayes are sad and over-cast, and in which we find by deare and lamentable experience, and by the losse which can never be repayred, that of all our vaine passions and affections past, the sorrow only abideth" (book 1, chapter 2, section 5).

See also J. A. Burrow, *The Ages of Man: A Study in Medieval Writing and Thought* (Oxford: Clarendon, 1988); Deborah Youngs, *The Life Cycle in Western Europe, c. 1300–c. 1500* (Manchester, UK: Manchester University Press, 2006); Michael Kammen, *A Time to Every Purpose: The Four Seasons in American Culture* (Chapel Hill: University of North Carolina Press, 2004); Elizabeth Sears, *The Ages of Man: Medieval Interpretations of the Life Cycle* (Princeton, NJ: Princeton University Press, 1986). Behind all these works lies Philippe Ariès, *Centuries of Childhood: A Social History of Family Life* (New York: Vintage, 1962). "Until the eighteenth century," Ariès wrote, "adolescence was confused with childhood" (25). Shakesepare, *As You Like It,* act 2, scene 7. John Wallis, *The New Game of Human Life* (London, 1790).

14. Another: the purpose of Tristram Shandy's father's Tristra-paedia was "to form an INSTITUTE for the government of my childhood and adolescence." Laurence Sterne, *The Life and Opinions of Tristram Shandy,* volume 3, chapter 16.

15. Jean-Jacques Rousseau, *Émile,* trans. William Payne (New York: D. Appleton, 1909), book 4. "If you are not sure of keeping him in ignorance of the difference between the sexes till he is sixteen, take care you teach him before he is ten."

16. See Kett, *Rites of Passage;* Kent Baxter, *The Modern Age: Turn-of-the-Century American Culture and the Invention of Adolescence* (Tuscaloosa: University of Alabama Press, 2008); and Jon Savage, *Teenage: The Creation of Youth Culture* (New York: Viking, 2007).

17. "The birth of a mammal was once a closed book to me," E. B. White wrote ("A Shepherd's Life," in *One Man's Meat,* 126; the essay originally appeared in *Harper's* in April 1940). Histories of sexual education include Claudia Nelson and Michelle H. Martin, eds., *Sexual Pedagogies: Sex Education in Britain, Australia and America, 1879–*

2000 (New York: Palgrave Macmillan, 2004); M. E. Melody and Linda M. Peterson, *Teaching America About Sex: Marriage Guides and Sex Manuals from the Late Victorians to Dr. Ruth* (New York: New York University Press, 1999); Susan K. Freeman, *Sex Goes to School: Girls and Sex Education Before the 1960s* (Urbana: University of Illinois Press, 2008); Kristin Luker, *When Sex Goes to School: Warring Views on Sex—and Sex Education—Since the Sixties* (New York: Norton, 2006); Julian B. Carter, "Birds, Bees, and Venereal Disease: Toward an Intellectual History of Sex Education," *Journal of the History of Sexuality* 10 (April 2001): 213–49; Janice M. Irvine, *Talk About Sex: The Battles over Sex Education in the United States* (Berkeley: University of California Press, 2002); and Jeffrey P. Moran, *Teaching Sex: The Shaping of Adolescence in the Twentieth Century* (Cambridge, MA: Harvard University Press, 2000).

18. Susan E. Klepp, *Revolutionary Conceptions: Women, Fertility, and Family Limitation in America, 1760–1820* (Chapel Hill: University of North Carolina Press, 2009), 212.

19. Hans Christian Andersen, "The Storks" (1838), in *Danish Fairy Legends and Tales* (London: W. Pickering, 1846), 83–91.

20. On Andersen, see Jackie Wullschläger, *Hans Christian Andersen: The Life of a Storyteller* (New York: Knopf, 2001). And on his publishing history, see Helle Porsdam, ed., *Copyright and Other Fairy Tales: Hans Christian Andersen and the Commodification of Creativity* (Northampton, MA: Edward Elgar, 2006).

21. Jayme A. Sokolow, *Eros and Modernization: Sylvester Graham, Health Reform, and the Origins of Victorian Sexuality in America* (Rutherford, NJ: Fairleigh Dickinson University Press, 1983), 57.

22. R. T. Trall, "Biographical Sketch of Sylvester Graham," *Water-Cure Journal* (November 1851): 110.

23. Daniel Walker Howe, *What Hath God Wrought: The Transformation of America, 1815–1848* (New York: Oxford University Press, 2007), 186, 167–68.

24. Sylvester Graham, *Thy Kingdom Come: A Discourse on the Importance of Infant and Sunday Schools* (Philadelphia, 1831), 9, 17, 21–22. The lecture was delivered on December 18, 1829, at the Crown Street Church, Philadelphia. On Graham's life, see Nissenbaum, *Sex, Diet, and Debility,* and Sokolow, *Eros and Modernization.*

25. In 1832, Graham blamed a devastating cholera epidemic on "dietetic intemperance and lewdness." Sylvester Graham, *A Lecture on Epidemic Diseases Generally, and Particularly the Spasmodic Cholera* (New York, 1833), 40. See also Charles Rosenberg, *Cholera Years: The United States in 1832, 1849 and 1866* (Chicago: University of Chicago Press, 1962).

26. Joel Hawes, *Lectures to Young Men on the Formation of Character,* 3rd ed. (Hartford, CT: Cooke, 1829), 34. Henry Ward Beecher, *Lectures to Young Men on Various Important Subjects,* 2nd ed. (Salem, MA: John P. Jewett, 1846), 120–21. Beecher in John Demos and Virginia Demos, "Adolescence in Historical Perspective," *Journal of Marriage and the Family* 31 (1969): 634.

27. The best discussion is Kett, *Rites of Passage*, especially chapters 1 and 2. Dorus Clarke, *Lectures to Young People in Manufacturing Villages* (Boston: Perkins and Marvin, 1836), 31, 44. Emphasis in original. Campbell Gibson, *American Demographic History Chartbook: 1790 to 2000* (2010), chapter 5, figure 5–1, http://www.demographicchart book.com. Lindsey Howden and Julie Meyer, *Age and Sex Composition: 2010* (U.S. Census Bureau, May 2011), http://www.census.gov/prod/cen2010/briefs/c2010br-03.pdf.

28. Sylvester Graham, *A Lecture to Young Men, on Chastity, Intended Also for the Serious Consideration of Parents and Guardians* (Boston, 1839), 10. On its publishing history, see Nissenbaum, *Sex, Diet, and Debility*, 28.

29. Graham, *Lecture to Young Men*, 101–26, 20.

30. Graham, *Thy Kingdom Come*, 23.

31. Marcus Cunliffe, introduction to *The Life of Washington*, by M. L. Weems (Cambridge, MA: Belknap Press of Harvard University Press, 1962), xi, xii. Other eighteenth-century treatises on the subject include *Onania: Or, The Heinous Sin of Self-Pollution* (London, 1723); Samuel Auguste Tissot, *Onanism* (London, 1766); and William Farrer, *A Short Treatise on Onanism* (London, 1767).

32. *The Works of Aristotle the Famous Philosopher, in Four Parts* (New England, 1828), Part I. *His Complete Master-piece*, 239, 35.

33. *Aristotle's Compleat Master Piece* (London, 1749), 26.

34. Graham, *Lecture to Young Men*, 20, 85.

35. Ibid., 85, 35, 39, 49–50.

36. Ibid., 102–26.

37. Ibid., 111. The idea that masturbation leads to "immature old age" was not original with Graham; it appears, for instance, in J. H. Smyth, MD, *A New Treatise on the Venereal Disease*, 5th ed. (London, 1771), 52.

38. Massachusetts General Court, *Reports and Other Documents Relating to the State Lunatic Hospital at Worcester, Massachusetts* (Boston, 1837), 114, 161. See also Sokolow, *Eros and Modernization*, 88–89. On this subject, see also R. P. Neuman, "Masturbation, Madness, and the Modern Concepts of Childhood and Adolescence," *Journal of Social History* 8 (1975): 1–27.

39. Graham, *Lecture to Young Men*, 34–35. John D'Emilio and Estelle B. Freedman, *Intimate Matters: A History of Sexuality in America* (New York: Harper & Row, 1988), 68–69.

40. Graham, *Lecture to Young Men*, 35.

41. Ibid., 89–90.

42. Ibid., 12. Nissenbaum, *Sex, Diet, and Debility*, 14.

43. Graham, *Lecture to Young Men*, 12.

44. Ibid., 40. A preface appearing in this edition is dated 1834. On its publishing history, see Nissenbaum, *Sex, Diet, and Debility*, 28.

45. Graham, *Lecture to Young Men*, 14–15.

46. Nissenbaum, *Sex, Diet, and Debility*, 14–15. And, on Graham eating flesh in his final days, see also Trall, "Biographical Sketch of Sylvester Graham," 110.

47. "Death of Sylvester Graham," *Medical Examiner and Record of Medical Science*, November 1, 1851, 726.

48. "Death of Sylvester Graham," *Water-Cure Journal* (October 1851): 89.

49. "Sylvester Graham: The Father of Grahamites and the Godfather of Graham Bread," *Home Journal*, October 11, 1851, 1.

50. G. Stanley Hall, *Life and Confessions of a Psychologist* (New York: D. Appleton, 1923, 1927), 357–58, 131–32. Dorothy Ross, *G. Stanley Hall: The Psychologist as Prophet* (Chicago: University of Chicago Press, 1972), 3–6. Louis N. Wilson, *G. Stanley Hall: A Sketch* (New York: G. E. Stechert, 1914), 15–18.

51. Anne Carroll Moore, *My Roads to Childhood: Views and Reviews of Children's Books* (Boston: Horn Book, 1961), 305. The best discussion of Hall's work on adolescence is John Demos and Virginia Demos, "Adolescence in Historical Perspective," *Journal of Marriage and the Family* 31 (1969): 632–35, but see also Kent Baxter, *The Modern Age*, especially chapter 2, and Jon Savage, *Teenage*, chapter 5.

52. Ross, *GSH*, 336. See also Kett, *Rites of Passage*, chapter 8.

53. G. Stanley Hall, *Adolescence* (New York: D. Appleton, 1904), 2:97, 122–23. For Hall, as Gail Bederman argued, sex wasn't dirty; it was holy (*Manliness and Civilization: A Cultural History of Gender and Race in the United States, 1880–1917* [Chicago: University of Chicago Press, 1995], 104).

54. Baxter, *Modern Age*, 13. See also Steven Mintz, *Huck's Raft: A History of American Childhood* (Cambridge, MA: Belknap Press of Harvard University Press, 2004), 239.

55. G. Stanley Hall, *Adolescence*, 2:97.

56. Notably, Hall, more a Grahamist than a Freudian, was not remotely forgiving of the solitary vice. In a 1907 article he contributed to the *Ladies' Home Journal* called "How and When to Be Frank with Boys," Hall offered tips about how to keep boys' hands out of their pants—"The first trousers should bifurcate low down, be loose, not warm nor rough, and pocketless"—and suggested that, at about age ten, "the boy should be concisely told that there are always certain dirty boys who abuse their bodies, and of the evil effects of this habit, and exhorted to break all acquaintance with such companions." Hall, "How and When to Be Frank with Boys," *Ladies' Home Journal* 24 (September 1907), 26. G. Stanley Hall, *Life and Confessions*, 407–8. Ross, *GSH*, 384.

57. "Sex O'Clock in America" was announced by *Current Opinion* and is quoted in David M. Kennedy, *Birth Control in America: The Career of Margaret Sanger* (New Haven, CT: Yale University Press, 1970), 139.

58. Allan Brandt, *No Magic Bullet: A Social History of Venereal Disease in the United States Since 1880* (New York: Oxford University Press, 1987), 28–31.

59. Winfield S. Hall, *Life's Beginnings: For Boys of Ten to Fourteen Years* (New York: Young Men's Christian Association Press, 1912), 3.

60. Winfield S. Hall, *From Youth into Manhood,* 10th ed. (New York: Association Press, 1918), 34, 59. In an introduction, George J. Fisher writes of Hall: "His theory on the physiology of noctural seminal emissions . . . is most unique" (7).

61. Winfield S. Hall, *Instead of "Wild Oats": A Little Book for the Youth of Eighteen and Over* (New York: Fleming H. Revell, 1912); Winfield S. Hall and Jeannette Winter Hall, *Girlhood and Its Problems: The Sex Life of Woman* (Philadelphia: John C. Winston, 1919); and Winfield S. Hall and Jeannette Winter Hall, *Sexual Knowledge: In Plain and Simple Language* (Philadelphia: International Bible House, 1913), preface, 9.

62. Winfield S. Hall, *Life's Beginnings,* 3.

63. Ibid., 3–5.

64. Ibid., 18, 22–23.

65. James Thurber and E. B. White, *Is Sex Necessary? Or, Why You Feel the Way You Do* (New York: Harper & Brothers, 1929; New York: Perennial, 2004), 113. According to John Updike, White wrote the even-numbered chapters. This is chapter 6. See Updike's foreword, xv.

66. "Stuart Little," *Washington Post,* October 21, 1945. The review is unsigned. On the book's reception as a satire (for adults), note that, in some book pages, it was reviewed under "Humor," not "Juvenile."

67. Geraldine Lux Flanagan, *Window into an Egg: Seeing Life Begin* (New York: Young Scott Books, 1969), 9. Lynn Marie Morgan, in *Icons of Life: A Cultural History of Human Embryos* (Berkeley: University of California Press, 2009), writes, "Chick hatching conveys another important cultural message, which is that life unfolds in the interval between conception and birth. Birth marks the end of the gestational period and the culturally approved beginning of independent life" (38–41).

68. There is some discussion of this case in Irvine, *Talk About Sex,* 21.

69. Gordon Drake, *Is the School House the Proper Place to Teach Raw Sex?* (Tulsa: Christian Crusade, 1968).

70. This battle is best related in Irvine, *Talk About Sex.* She argues that "opposition to sex education was a bridge issue between the Old Right and the New Right" (9).

71. Elders is quoted in Irvine, *Talk About Sex,* 1. See also Paul Richter and Marlene Cimons, "Clinton Fires Surgeon General After New Flap," *Los Angeles Times,* December 10, 1994.

72. Robie H. Harris, *It's NOT the Stork! A Book About Girls, Boys, Babies, Bodies, Families, and Friends* (Cambridge, MA: Candlewick, 2009), 28.

73. Jennifer Ashton, *The Body Scoop for Girls: A Straight-Talk Guide to a Healthy, Beautiful You* (New York: Avery, 2009), 4, 21.

74. Lynda Madaras, *Ready, Set, Grow!* (New York: Newmarket, 2003), 14.

75. Louise Spilsbury, *Me, Myself and I: All About Sex and Puberty* (New York: Hodder Wayland Children's, 2009), 4.

76. Valorie Lee Schaefer, *The Care & Keeping of You: The Body Book for Girls* (Middletown, WI: Pleasant Company, 1998), 42.

77. Gravelle, *What's Going on Down There?*, 17; Ashton, *Body Scoop for Girls*, chapter 9; Schaefer, *Care & Keeping of You*, 17; Jacqui Bailey, *Hair, There, and Everywhere: A Book About Growing Up* (New York: Barron's, 2008), 20.

78. Pepper Schwartz and Dominic Cappello, *Ten Talks Parents Must Have with Their Children About Sex and Character* (New York: Hyperion, 2000), 31. G. Stanley Hall also said, in "How and When to Be Frank with Boys," that what boys need to know can be explained to them in "a ten-minute talk."

Jonathan Holloway

From *Jim Crow Wisdom:*
Memory and Identity in Black America Since 1940 (2013)

A historian walks into a museum. What are the odds he's going to like it?

Most history writing still takes the form of critique. We associate celebratory prose with advertisements and popular magazines. If a historian decides to analyze the ways in which memory and identity are enshrined in the tourism economy, it's a good bet that he will position himself as having a deeper, more authoritative understanding of history than whatever poor schmucks might have designed the hopelessly naïve shrines. You can expect a writerly voice that floats above it all, explaining how the curators and designers missed certain opportunities and failed to strike certain balances.

But Jonathan Holloway is as interested in embodied presence as he is in critical distance. He has actually visited the museums and heritage sites that he writes about, and he consistently places himself in his prose. We see him reacting, trying to make sense of the material as he takes it in, revealing his own blind spots and uncertainties. There are some exhibits he even seems to admire.

In Memphis, Holloway is taken with the "richly historical" approach of the National Civil Rights Museum, established in the hotel where Martin Luther King, Jr., was shot. He praises its careful design, which allows visitors to "receive a very thorough recounting of an expansive civil rights narrative and experience the emotional trauma of bearing witness." But his quiet appreciation is disrupted by the stubborn protests of a woman on the street, whose perspective Holloway might never have considered had he not actually traveled to the old Lorraine Hotel, from which, it turns out, this woman, Jacqueline Smith, was evicted in 1988. After its life as a hotel, the Lorraine became a low-income boardinghouse, and when the decision was made to convert the building into a museum, its residents were forced to leave. Ever since, Smith has been out on the street, insisting that Dr. King had been more interested in helping the poor than in commercial memorialization.

And Holloway leaves us with the sense that ever since he encountered Jacqueline Smith, he has been wrestling with his own perspective on the museum. He eschews the historian's easy, conclusive authority. His writing is an invitation to come along with him and share the conundrums he has encountered. After that, we might consider making the trip on our own.

~

MAKING A MUSEUM (MEMPHIS)

The sky was spotless as I made my way through what seemed to be a gentrifying arts district of Memphis. I wasn't far from my destination, but I was already finding it difficult to imagine a different era, since it was clear that so much had been cleaned up in the last handful of years. Even the trolley trundling past didn't look authentically old, since it was so clearly new. The place even verged on being antiseptic—the sidewalks seemed devoid of foot traffic. Granted, it was a midmorning weekday in late summer. It is likely the neighborhood's character changed in the evening when the bistros and restaurants began to fill up for happy hours and then again on the weekend when the city's farmer's market, located just around the corner, opened for business.

I wasn't there, however, to go on a pub crawl or to shop for local produce. Where was the museum? I should be close. And then, one block down, I saw it. Not the museum, but the hotel.

For anyone who studies the African American past and, likely, for most people who pay even the slightest attention during Black History Month or in their high school social studies units, you could not help but notice the sign. It seems silly to say, but it looked just like it did in the photographs. Granted, there wasn't a crowd of men, frozen on the balcony, pointing across the street to where James Earl Ray had fired his rifle, but they didn't need to be there to provide the effect of the moment.

I literally gasped, and my stomach dropped.

This was the Lorraine Hotel.

Of course, the museum was also the hotel, but the stagecraft of the museum was such that—even the vehicles parked immediately in front of the hotel were vintage cars similar to those in the parking lot when King was murdered—when you pulled up to the front of the museum, the only thing you could process was the fact that you were staring at the hotel where King spent his final moments, the hotel from all of the textbooks and documentaries, the hotel you knew even though you had never before stepped foot in the hotel, much less Memphis.

Opened in the 1920s as the Windsor Hotel, the building was purchased and renamed by Walter and Loree Bailey in 1945. The Lorraine Hotel became known for its high-profile guests who were performing a block away on Beale Street, the heart of Memphis's black community and the incubator of so many of the country's blues performers. After the shock of King's murder—and it literally was a shock, as co-owner Loree Bailey died of a heart attack after running out into the parking lot and seeing that King had been shot—the subsequent years of urban decline, and then a postsegregation renewal that meant that black visitors could stay in other, more modern facilities, the Lorraine faced foreclosure in 1982. It had become a long-term, low-income apartment complex when local activists and business leaders came together to purchase the space at auction with the intention of turning it into a civil rights museum. The museum opened to the public in September 1991.[1]

The museum is much more than a tribute to the civil rights movement's greatest leader: It aims to present a richly historical narrative of what historians now call the long civil rights movement. The museum's curators follow a straightforward chronological narrative, but they stretch the boundaries of the movement far beyond its typical start in the mid-1950s. By plotting great triumphs in the civil rights struggle along a 400-year timeline and by pointing out that slave revolts in the 1600s were nothing if not battles for civil rights, the exhibits force visitors to reimagine the familiar terrain of civil rights. The familiar is still there, however, as visitors see authentic Ku Klux Klan robes; sit in the kind of bus (and listen to the sneering remarks of an imagined bus driver played over hidden speakers) that black Montgomerians boycotted for over a year; and walk past a replica of the Birmingham jail where King penned one of the great documents in the American canon.

As they pass by other exhibits that share the history of other, less-well-known moments in modern civil rights history, visitors may be unaware that they are slowly but steadily moving up a gently sloping walkway. Until, that is, they turn a corner and are bathed in the natural light from the windows that overlook the second-floor balcony where King was shot. The museum effectively pulls you into that small space by having you walk between two hotel rooms restored to how they appeared in April 1968 when King was there. Tourists who originally saw the iconic hotel and then immersed themselves in the museum "experience" for over an hour are whipsawed back to the fact that they are in the hotel, mere feet from where King slept on April 3, mere feet in a different direction from where he collapsed on April 4.

It is a very quiet space even when it is crowded.

The final exhibit space in the museum is across the street and brings the visitor to the spot where James Earl Ray spied King through his rifle's sight and pulled the trigger. Although this exhibit is theatrical in its clear attempt to broker an emotional response, it is hard to find fault with the effectiveness of the curators' decision to re-create these scenes in this progression. Here, in the course of about two hours, visitors receive a very thorough recounting of an expansive civil rights narrative and experience the emotional trauma of bearing witness to a great tragedy. But the curators' efforts to re-create a scene of horror so that visitors could make a deeper, visceral connection to the site and to the history was not met with universal praise.

Jacqueline Smith, a longtime resident of the Lorraine after it became a low-income boardinghouse (in some accounts she is listed as a cleaning person who happened also to have a room at the facility), refused to leave the building when it was sold and being prepared for the renovation that would convert it into the National Civil Rights Museum. Smith stayed in her room after other residents had moved out, after a court order declared she needed to vacate, and after her water and heat were shut off. Finally, on March 2, 1988, two months into her illegal occupancy, four Shelby County deputies forced open the door to her room and carried her and her belongings out to the curb.

When she first announced in January that she would not leave despite the court order, Smith said that "Dr. King would have wanted me to stay here. He said he didn't want any memorial, but he wanted to help the poor." On the morning of her eviction, a sobbing Smith declared that she had no place to go: "This is wrong. You people are making a mistake."[2] Smith sat on the sidewalk among her belongings and refused to leave. More than two years later, Smith was in the same spot when another court order forced her to move. This time she was accused of trespassing on a construction site. After she ignored the order, her possessions were placed in the street, and she was moved, while sitting in her lawn chair, to the sidewalk opposite the museum. When asked by a reporter for the Associated Press why she was opposed to the museum, Smith reasserted her sense that King wanted to serve the poor—and that is exactly what the Lorraine was doing until it was closed and she was evicted. For Smith, the Lorraine—and King's legacy—were being desecrated: "This sacred ground is being exploited."[3]

More than twenty years have passed since this second forced move.

Jacqueline Smith is still there.

Smith maintains this protest vigil, urging visitors approaching the museum not to go inside. The museum, and the neighborhood gentrification that has accompanied it, she avers, has destroyed the area by making it unaffordable to longtime residents like herself. The whole neighborhood was now reserved for tourists; it was turning into Disneyland.[4] Even in Memphis's unrelenting late summer sun, Smith stands at her corner opposite the museum, behind two tables filled with copies of newspaper articles relating to her eviction. In front of one of the tables is a banner with a large counter tracking the years and days "since I began my personal protest to speak on behalf of the disadvantaged and displaced." Beneath this statement is a website where the tourist (who likely hadn't bargained on this part of the excursion) can go to learn more about Smith's efforts. Smith's website, fulfillthedream.net, presents a timeline of King's life but largely focuses on Smith's arrest and vigil and the museum's shortsightedness and crass devotion to the tourist dollar. The site does not mince words: "The National Civil Rights [Museum] has from day one, considered the ghoulish needs of the mass tourist market greater than the real need to educate and inform."[5]

In many places throughout the site, Smith invokes religious language and equates the museum's work as a "desecration" of a "sacred" space. Indeed, she faults the entire project for how it goes about the work of recording civil rights history, wondering aloud if this is the best use of a nation's memory:

> The National Civil Rights Museum exists to educate the public about the history of the Civil Rights Movement and to promote Civil Rights issues in a proactive and non-violent manner.
>
> Sadly, it fails to live up to these ideals. The truth is that the museum has become a Disney-style tourist attraction, which seems preoccupied with gaining financial success, rather than focussing on the real issues. Many people have criticized the "tone" with which information is portrayed—Do we really want our children to gaze upon exhibits from the Ku Klux Klan, do we need our children to experience mock verbal abuse as they enter a replica bus depicting the Montgomery bus boycott. Do we have so little imagination, that we need to spend thousands of taxpayers

dollars recreating a fake Birmingham jail, to understand that Dr. King was incarcerated?[6]

With one exception, the museum does not recognize Smith or her protest. It invests in the seriousness and integrity of its educational work and is equally determined to honor King and his legacy and to tell the larger story of civil and human rights struggles in the United States and beyond. The museum does acknowledge Smith's presence, however. On the "Frequently Asked Questions" page for the museum's website you will find the following at FAQ number eight (of twelve): "Who is the protestor outside? Her name is Jacqueline Smith and she has protested the museum since ground was broken in 1987—though she has never been inside the museum."[7]

Even though the museum recognizes Smith's protest, if only barely, her vigil tells us something valuable about the production of history, the sanctification of certain experiences over others, and the interplay between an individual and an institution. Here, a single person with a particular set of memories and a determination to remember a figure of such importance as King in a specific way finds herself facing an institution with a public commitment to remembrance that has become the individual's horror.

MAKING A MUSEUM (GREENSBORO)

There are no protesters outside the International Civil Rights Center and Museum. The building, located in the heart of downtown Greensboro, North Carolina, is the site of the former F. W. Woolworth Company. Unlike Memphis, Greensboro cannot be interpreted as a place where the civil rights movement died. In fact, the lunch counter sit-ins that began at Woolworth's on February 1, 1960, are generally understood as the seedbed for change, as they sparked a nationwide wave of similar protests against racism and segregation that ultimately led to the formation of the Student Nonviolent Coordinating Committee, one of the most influential national protest organizations for most of the decade. Locally, the sit-ins fostered, at least among black Greensboro citizens, a sense of a new beginning in that city's seemingly polite yet still complicated racial landscape.[8]

While it may seem that creating a memorial and perhaps even a museum on the site of King's assassination was an obvious step in the country's progress toward having more open and honest conversations about the horrors in its racial past, the determination to memorialize the Woolworth's lunch counter was a less certain affair. One of the significant differences between the sites is that the Lorraine was an independent operation and its owners lacked the capital to do much more than scratch out an existence. The Woolworth's in Greensboro, on the other hand, was part of one of the largest convenience store chains in the country. As such, the company had much greater flexibility in how it wanted to respond and recognize its own role in the civil rights struggle.

Clarence Lee "Curly" Harris, the local Woolworth's manager, acknowledged from the very beginning that the company's decision to integrate its lunch counter was as much a nod to a basic sense of decency as it was a recognition of the financial bottom line.[9] The store needed the money and could no longer afford the negative publicity. Indeed, with the passage of time, the Greensboro Woolworth's made a point of honoring the events of February 1. On the twentieth anniversary of the sit-ins, for example, Woolworth's vice president Aubrey Lewis served the four men who started the sit-in movement at the same lunch counter that denied them service when they were in college. That same day, a state historical marker was placed outside the building acknowledging the events that transpired in 1960.[10] On the thirtieth anniversary, a plaque with the four protesters' embossed footprints was placed in the sidewalk in front of the store, and the street beside the store was renamed February One Place.[11]

A moment of reckoning arrived in 1993 when the Greensboro Woolworth's closed and the national company announced plans to tear down the original building, which had been there since 1939. The company was financially imperiled, and the downtown Greensboro store was easy to slate for closing. Further, the city's downtown core had been in decline as the area's textile mills began to close and jobs and manufacturing moved out of the area and then overseas. But closing a site whose historical importance did not diminish with capital flight and corporate globalization made for a more complicated situation.

A local radio station organized a petition to save the site. It garnered immediate and widespread support. Emphasizing the fact that the Greensboro Woolworth's is hallowed ground for black Americans, only three days after the station's petition began—much less time than it took the protesters to integrate the lunch counter thirty-three years earlier—the Woolworth company announced that it would preserve the site while financing was arranged to purchase the building to turn it into a museum. Two local politicians, Melvin "Skip" Alston and Earl Jones, founded the Sit-In Movement, Inc., with a goal of buying the property and establishing a museum honoring the sit-in and that moment's role in the broader civil rights movement.[12] Years passed before the museum was able to open its doors.

I had been visiting my grandparents in Greensboro since they returned to their birthstate in the mid-1970s to retire. They lived in a quiet, integrated, upper middle-class neighborhood west of downtown. There isn't much to my memories of Greensboro beyond their house, my grandmother's gardens, the local K&W Cafeteria with its incredible bargains and endless sweet tea, and the Krispy Kremes store five minutes away on Battleground Avenue. There were a few occasions, however, when I was put into the car—probably bribed with the promise of stopping at Krispy Kremes on the way home—to go on an errand downtown. I recall virtually nothing about those trips beyond the unrelenting heat (we always seemed to visit the grandparents during summer heat waves), the sheer emptiness of the business district, and on one occasion, my grandmother pointing out the "famous Woolworth's." We weren't stopping in the five and dime, so as quickly as she mentioned this historic site, my mind was probably off on something else, likely wondering if the red light signaling hot, fresh doughnuts was going to be on at Krispy Kremes when we got there.

My first adult memory of the Woolworth's building came decades later when I took my daughter downtown to visit the city's impressive children's museum. I could not quite recall where I needed to turn—I had left the map at my grandmother's home—so I was approaching each street slowly in order to read the street signs. Spring, Edgeworth, Eugene, Greene, Commerce, Washington—all perfectly unremarkable street names that did little beyond giving me a measure of confidence that I was getting close. Then I crossed February One Place. February One?

Only when I made a series of lefts to correct for a wrong turn did I find myself at February One Place again and, thankfully, waiting at a stoplight. And there it was: the future home of the International Civil Rights Center and Museum. By sheer coincidence I had returned to the intersection where my grandmother had pointed out the famous Woolworth's at least twenty years earlier. The long sign on the marquee above the street was still there, but it had faded so much that you didn't notice it. However, the collection of historical markers—there were at least three at the intersection then; there are more now—as well as the signs in the window indicating future plans for the museum made it clear where I was.

When the museum finally opened, fifty years to the day after the sit-ins began, it was clear that the curators and architects were determined to do more than narrate the triumph of the sit-in movement. To be sure, they did not miss the opportunity to point out the heroic past, but they didn't shy away from the horrors that motivated the students to protest in the first place.

In most museums, the informal, self-guided tour of the building and its exhibits is common practice. In Greensboro, however, the museum's curators were unable to find a way to allow such a casual visitation with the past. Due to some extreme subject matter and a determination that museum visitors not misinterpret curatorial intent, guests could only enter the exhibit spaces on guided tours.[13]

Excluding passageways such as the Hall of Courage that are lined with narratives of excellence in the long history of civil rights, the museum consists of six main spaces: a gathering room where a video puts the struggle for full civil rights into a larger context of American exceptionalism, a small theater where one watches a reenactment of the decision-making process that led to the Woolworth's sit-in, the actual lunch counter where the sit-in was held, a series of rooms filled with artifacts that narrate the injustices of racial discrimination, and a final space that turns the visitors' attention to the fact that the domestic battle for civil rights was part of a much larger and ongoing global struggle for full human rights. These spaces are informative, performative, captivating, and even inspirational. These also happen to be the spaces that everyone can visit. There is a sixth space, however, that is so challenging that a separate, circumventing passage is provided for children under the age of twelve. This is the Hall of Shame, and it immediately follows the contextualizing video that welcomes visitors to the exhibition space.

A pitch-black room that feels simultaneously cool and claustrophobic, the Hall of Shame shows iconic images from the civil rights movement in light boxes that seem to turn on and off randomly. But these are not images of iconic moments of triumph. They are, in fact, quite the opposite: the burned-out bus that the freedom riders had to flee in order to save their lives; southerners in Klan robes; victims of mob violence—those who survived and those who were staked and then burned or lynched; the unrecognizable Emmett Till in his coffin. Further, the light boxes are not neatly ordered rectangles, each containing its own image, but jagged, angular boxes with single images spread across three or four screens that cumulatively invoke the shattered windows so typical of moments of extreme race hatred when bullets, bricks, and bombs flew into living rooms and bedrooms.

It is an overwhelming and wrenching space whose effects are only mildly mitigated by the tour guide, who calmly offers a very nuanced and historically rich interpretation of the images and the contradictions embedded in the fabric of the triumphalist narrative of American exceptionalism. It is also a space that without this narration leaves itself open to being little more than a site of horror that runs counter to what is ultimately the museum's message of triumph in the face of ongoing challenges. It is for this reason, and seemingly this reason alone, that visitors must be accompanied by a tour guide. The narrative of horror, then, is very present, but one is led to it and then away from it.

Indeed, after exiting the Hall of Shame, museumgoers find themselves turning a corner, seeing a re-creation of the students' dorm room at the North Carolina Agricultural and Technical State University, and then watching a gauzy reenactment of the students' decision to march to Woolworth's the next morning. Since the visitors know that this story becomes heroic and that the students were not physically harmed, the brutality of the images in the preceding room begins to fade. This effect is magnified in the passageway from the dorm room and video that heads to the lunch counter. That passageway is titled the Hall of Courage, and in very traditional curatorial fashion (large, two-dimensional head shots of famous individuals, with narratives describing their accomplishments) reminds visitors of the great, constructive work that has defined so much of the struggle for civil rights in the United States. In their own very intimate way, the experience in the Hall of Shame and then the exit from it into the subsequent spaces figuratively amount to a process of truth and reconciliation.

Just as in so many southern cities that were sites of famous civil rights struggles, issues of truth and reconciliation were never so clear in Greensboro. Even though the city long prided itself as being a beacon of progress in the history of race relations, according to some local activists the city has never come to terms with a spectacular moment of violence and seeming racial horror that happened as the city approached the twenty-year anniversary of the sit-in triumphs.

On November 3, 1979, the Communist Worker's Party (CWP), a group made up primarily of activists from outside Greensboro, organized a Death to the Klan rally and invited members of the Ku Klux Klan to attend and respond to the CWP's critique. The Klan, joined by members of the Nazi Party, took up the CWP's challenge and, after an altercation with CWP marchers, opened fire on the activists. Five protesters were killed in the shootout, and many more were injured. Most Greensboro citizens were horrified, and their dismay only increased when nine months later an all-white jury acquitted the defendants despite overwhelming evidence that the accused had killed the marchers.[14]

In the heat of the moment, city leaders declared that the violence was co-incidental to Greensboro itself, since virtually none of the individuals involved were from the greater Greensboro area. The CWP knew it could garner attention for its struggles to organize workers in the local textile industry while addressing what it viewed as the linked problems of racial and economic injustice by invoking Klan racism. In this way, CWP activists understood that race continued to be a live wire in the post–civil rights South. Although they certainly did not seek out the violence that resulted, the labor organizers knew it would be easy to goad the Klan into some sort of confrontation. So much of the South was built on these kinds of horrors.

Twenty years after the November clash, a coalition of progressive Greensboro activists called for a truth and reconciliation commission—the first in the United States—in order to answer the questions, "What if America's cities—especially Southern cities—stopped ignoring the skeletons in their closets? What if they were inspired by the potential of the truth & reconciliation model as demonstrated in South Africa, Peru, and elsewhere, to help them seek life-affirming restorative justice and constructively deal with past incidents of injustice?"[15] Although the subsequently formed Greensboro Truth and Reconciliation Commission (GTRC) had no subpoena power and could not redistribute resources or reallocate justice, the GTRC believed it important to address the festering pain of the shooting, the subsequent trial, and more fundamentally, the long-term silence in the community about racial, economic, and social injustice that led up to and then followed the violence.

The commission clearly believed its work was productive, even if in the process old wounds reopened. When it published its final report in May 2006, the GTRC used the words of legal scholar Martha Minow as the lead epigraph: "Failure to remember, collectively, triumphs and accomplishments diminishes us. But failure to remember, collectively, injustice and cruelty is an ethical breach. It implies no responsibilities and no commitment to prevent inhumanity in the future. Even worse, failures of collective memory stoke fires of resentment and revenge."[16] The GTRC recognized that the scale of atrocities that called other truth commissions into being was different from what even the most skeptical and hardened activist would claim in Greensboro, but the GTRC hoped that its work remained a timely reminder "of the importance of facing shameful events honestly and acknowledging the brutal consequences of political spin, calculated blindness, and passive ignorance."[17]

Although the efficacy of the GTRC report is unclear—some local business and civic leaders still think the violence in 1979 did not reflect Greensboro's social interactions and core values, and they also feel that the GTRC only stirred up trouble for the sake of stirring up trouble[18]—it appears that the spirit of the report is at least figuratively found in the International Civil Rights Museum's Hall of Shame. That room, with its jagged and searing reminders of the ugliness in our recent past, and the Hall of Courage that follows soon after remind us that the fight for a just and better world cannot happen without a sincere and thorough engagement with the past.

While the museum still wishes it enjoyed greater foot traffic, it has played a pivotal role in the redevelopment of the downtown business district. The blocks of empty streets and stores integral to my memory of downtown Greensboro have been reenergized, and there is a growing nightlife in the city. Local bars and clubs anchor the southern end of the development district, while more family-oriented facilities—the Greensboro Children's Museum, active green spaces and parks, the first-rate downtown branch of the city library system, and an intimate minor-league baseball stadium that is home to the Greensboro Grasshoppers—define the northern boundary. The museum is in the geographic center. In this regard, it has fulfilled at least one of the goals of its founding leadership. In a June 2001 press release that announced a staffing reorganization and offered an update on the planning process for the museum, David Hoard, the newly appointed chief executive officer of the museum project, declared, "This is a unique opportunity for all involved. We are working together to open a Civil Rights Center & Museum that will document some of America's greatest victories. The International Civil Rights Center & Museum will highlight history and will positively affect economic development downtown as a tourist attraction."[19]

Greensboro leaders saw the development of the International Civil Rights Center as at least in part an investment in the city's tourist economy. In this regard, these leaders are no different from those in other southern cities and towns who viewed their complicated racial histories as present-day opportunities to attract and inspire African American visitors.[20] Without a doubt, this modern faith in the commerce of memory has plenty of antecedents. The perfect manifestation of this phenomenon would surely have been realized if the Walt Disney Corporation had been able to build its theme park, Disney's America, adjacent to Civil War battlefields in Manassas, Virginia. Disney's plan ignited a firestorm of protest from historians and preservationists for a variety of reasons, chief among them being that Disney would simplify and sanitize American history, and that Disney's crass commercialism was an offense to the adjacent grounds where thousands of Union and Confederate soldiers died. As Disney discovered, there are limits to the commercialization of the sacred.[21]

MAKING MUSEUMS (WILLIAMSBURG)

Colonial Williamsburg occupies a curious place in this continuum. Conceived in 1926 by local Episcopal rector W. A. R. Goodwin and oil tycoon John D. Rockefeller Jr. as a "shrine to the spirit and values of the American Revolution," Colonial Williamsburg still imagines itself a "patriotic institution charged with conveying fundamental American values."[22] In the wake of the turn toward social history in the early 1970s, the private battles historians always have about how to interpret the past became very public at Colonial Williamsburg as the institution's curators increasingly advocated an approach to history that recognized the past as a site of contestation and not merely celebration. Put another way, Colonial Williamsburg's internal debates concerning how to represent the past turned into a very public struggle about the very history and memory it was selling.

My sole visit to Colonial Williamsburg preceded these public debates, but the challenges of sharing a history that wasn't part of my literal and figurative family's memory was apparent even to my fourth-grade eyes. For me, the moment of clarity came when I saw a door to a pew.

It was 1976 or 1977, and my class was heading south on a three-day field trip to Williamsburg and Yorktown, Virginia. It was an era of national celebration: Two hundred years of freedom! Two hundred years of the perfection of liberty! Two hundred years of independence!

Beyond using my brand-new Kodak Instamatic camera with a rotating flash cube on top to take tons of pictures—many, it would turn out, were pictures of my friends taking pictures of me, and many would prominently feature the tip of my finger in the frame—I mostly remember two things about that trip: the walking tour of Williamsburg and the church pew.

The visuals from my walk in Colonial Williamsburg still spring to mind clearly: the crushed, tan gravel under my feet; the old buildings with rippled glass windows; and the craftsmen who showed us how our ancestors made paper, shaped candles, or smithed iron. I would be lying if I said that I began to think that something wasn't quite right about the day's narrative while I posed, smiling, standing in the stockade outside the legislative chambers. No, I'm sure the idea didn't sneak into my brain then. The stockade photo opportunity was too cool, after all. But I do know that at some point between the blacksmith and the stockade I noticed that there weren't any black people working at Williamsburg—anywhere.

Williamsburg had yet to wrestle publicly with the issue of how to portray the enslaved past to the tourists who flocked to its manicured grounds. The curators of this fascinating outdoor museum had not yet resolved how to tell a story about a broader narrative of what it might mean to talk about "our" ancestors in a new way. The whitewashing of our nation's past—in a year of celebration, no less—didn't strike me then as a deliberate attempt to fashion a script of who belonged to the American narrative. But something in me stirred while standing on that stage, something that spoke to a different past.

Soon after, and by freakish coincidence, my hope was answered, but not in a way that I could ever have imagined.

At our last stop on our field trip, the tour guide directed us into a church. I can't tell you much about the building except that it was a gorgeous colonial affair—all brick and white outside and row after row of white pews inside. I recall the guide going on about how the wealthiest people paid for church pews and, in recognition, had their names carved into the doors by a skilled craftsman. There is a lot of history to be found in those doors, she said. We can tell a lot about who lived in Williamsburg just by looking at those pew doors.

I was bored and was leaning into my mother (a trip chaperone), wondering how much more we had to endure before we could get on the bus and go home. And then, at the moment when all interest had flagged, a classmate poked me in the ribs. His eyes were wide as he pointed toward the pew door. It took me a moment to process what I was reading. I mean, I knew the words immediately, but the significance took a few more beats. I leaned into my mother with a true purpose now and pointed to the door. I can't begin to calculate the odds, but we were seated in a pew that had been paid for by none other than John Holloway.

Given how well-documented *some* of our ancestors are, I am confident I could easily find that church today, find that pew, and find out more about John Holloway. But if I did, what more would I know about myself, my family, or my past?

My people were from North Carolina—that's what I had always known. In time, I learned that there are a lot of Holloways in Virginia Beach and southern Virginia, in general. So, perhaps the odds weren't as long as I imagined them to be.

But what is worth knowing about this memory is the way I remember how my body tensed up when I saw my name—even though it was spelled differently—on that pew.

Those doors told us a lot about who made Williamsburg. They told us about our ancestors; they told us about our home; they told us about who belonged in one of our national monuments to freedom, to independence, to liberty. And yes, they told us something else about who belonged. Something else entirely.

The tension in my body was telling me something also. I look back and recognize that my visceral knowledge—my tension—was the physical manifestation of an absence that could only have been constructed by a systemic attempt to deny me (and my people) a knowledge of my memories and history.

Granted, the great majority of the visitors to Colonial Williamsburg wouldn't find anything physically unsettling or even noticeable about the narratives that presented themselves to my fourth-grade mind—even before I encountered that pew door that set my brain spinning. But historians and museum curators were increasingly unhappy with the very gentle portrayal of the colonial past that hewed too faithfully to Goodwin and Rockefeller's wish for a patriotic accounting of American history. While even in the mid-1970s a visitor could find the occasional black reenactor walking the grounds in Williamsburg, that same visitor likely left the site not knowing that over half of Colonial Williamsburg's population was black and enslaved.

In the late 1970s—a few years after my visit—the Colonial Williamsburg Foundation began the process of addressing this lapse in earnest. It established a Department of African American Interpretations and Presentations. The department set about collecting and reinterpreting artifacts found in the various archaeological sites at Williamsburg, and in so doing debunked the longtime curatorial consensus that the slave experience could not be reconstituted because insufficient physical material related to slavery survived.[23]

By the early 1990s, curators felt that they had enough evidence and that they knew enough about the slave experience in Williamsburg that they could make a bold statement about the colonial past. In 1994, they decided to hold a slave auction. This decision was a reflection of the department's dual commitment to be as historically accurate in its work as possible and to encourage visitors to reflect upon the meaning found in the horrors of slavery. This sensibility is embodied in the department's mission statement: "To preserve, recreate, and interpret the community and lives of Virginia's 18th-century Africans and African Americans; to engage and inform our audiences about the diverse

Africans who endured the horrors of slavery and formed new kinships and networks for survival; and to compel (encourage) people to examine their perceptions of the African-American past, the legacies of slavery, and understand the significance and contributions of Africans to the American character."[24]

There is little doubt that slave auctions were a regular part of Williamsburg's past, but it was far from clear that visitors—tourists, really—had any desire to learn any more about Colonial Williamsburg than I had in fourth grade. For example, prominent black betterment organizations were desperately anxious about the plan, and leaders of the local branches of the NAACP and the Southern Christian Leadership Conference showed up on the day of the auction to protest it, although they did not try to stop the auction from proceeding. Even for those who did not protest, there was no racial consensus on the event. One African American mother brought her daughter to the auction to show her that "black people had nothing of which to be ashamed," while a local editor of a black newspaper, the *New Journal and Guide*, argued that the auction trivialized the "African holocaust in America."[25]

However, if one were to believe R. Emmett Tyrell Jr., conservative journalist and editor of the *American Spectator*, one would think that the auction was a desecration of the tourists' right to an experience that offered wholesome portrayals of the past. When Tyrell heard about the plans for the auction, he wrote a blistering editorial that ran in the *Washington Times*:

> Unpack my bags! The family's summer excursion to Colonial Williamsburg is canceled! The politically correct uplifters have just brought their gruesome hallucination of American history down on once-charming Williamsburg. No longer is it a fit place for family outings. Perhaps if one's family is composed of neurotics and hysterics, Williamsburg is worth a visit. But cheerful, discerning families had best pursue more intelligent recreation.
>
> Not long ago mom and dad could pack the children into the family gas guzzler and drive off to Williamsburg for a pleasant—albeit idealized—immersion into a facsimile of America's 18th Century Colonial life. Standing on nearly 178 acres are nearly one hundred reproductions of Colonial homes and shops. Jolly women in bonnets and hoop skirts trundled along tidy streets. Friendly men in vests and calf-high stockings worked the blacksmith shop and other buildings. Whites appeared with blacks, some blacks being freemen, others being slaves. Visiting families could purchase Colonial fare in the shops and very good restaurants.

After an entreating and mildly educational day, family members could return home, their imaginations aglow with visions of the American past. Doubtless those of a skeptical temperament entertained normal questions: What of disease, of poverty, of slavery and the generalized harshness of the Colonials' more severe mentality? The politically correct uplifters may find it difficult to believe, but intelligent Americans visiting Williamsburg have over the years thought about such things.

Yet now the heavy hoof of the uplifter has transformed this pleasant family tourist stop. Today's visiting family returns home having been put through an emotional wringer during which many of man's meaner passions have been dramatically displayed. Skits put on by Williamsburg actors depict cruelty, racial bigotry and slavery, at their worst, right before the family's eyes.

Tyrell then sadly imagines a car ride home in which shocked tourists, traumatized by their visit, try to make sense of this new national story. He continues:

All this is the baleful consequence of new skits obtusely referred to as "Enslaving Virginia." One Harvey Bakari, development manager of Williamsburg's African-American program, explains that such distressing skits as a slave auction, the harassment of a pathetic black pedestrian by a "slave patrol" and a discussion by slaves about joining forces with King George's Red Coats are attempts to get tourists "to confront the reality of racial discrimination." But is a family tourist venue the appropriate place for confronting reality in all its grimness?

. . . Frankly, this is not the way I want to spend my vacation. . . . Most Americans rather like America, which is why as the years go on Williamsburg will attract fewer normal Americans and more lunatics.[26]

Christy Matthews (then Coleman) was the director of the Department of African American Interpretations and Presentations when Tyrell wrote his screed against the curators' decision to stage a slave auction. Indeed, Matthews was the driving force behind the auction and participated in it herself, portraying a crying woman, begging (but failing) to be sold to the same man who purchased her husband. Whether Matthews saw Tyrell's rant or not, she knew at the most personal level how upset many people were with her decision.[27] In the moments leading up to the start of the auction and in the controversy that ensued, Matthews was emotionally wrecked. However, her professional judgment told her that she was doing the right thing.

Recognizing that the past is filled with all manner of horrors, Matthews observed,

> In many cases, what propels the opposition is a belief that interpreting slavery or other tragedies of the American past somehow devalues our accomplishments. Nothing could be further from the truth. It could be argued that when an informed populace understands and accepts this nation's shortcomings and the sacrifices made to aspire to an ideal, a greater sense of empowerment often emerges. By delving into these harsher areas, we become more cognizant of the challenges that lie ahead and better prepared to find the solutions to problems that continue to plague us.[28]

As reasonable and rational as Matthews's observations may be, how does one reconcile that with Tyrell's argument, once you remove its excessive venom? How does one achieve a balance between a record of the past that is digestible to the greatest number of people and a record of the past that is unafraid to speak to the challenges that gave the past its true texture? These are the questions with which museums, public historians, and curators constantly wrestle. When it comes to heritage tourism, however, the institutional and professional standards that amount to a type of quality control in a museum setting are less consistently applied. Indeed, a key motivating factor behind much of the heritage tourism industry—dollars—complicates the work for those individuals who manage these sites and want to make them historically nuanced and educational. Sites of true horror—places where physical violence, cultural depravity, or moral failure made themselves known—are difficult to market, especially when visitors to these sites may view themselves as inheritors of the horror itself.

NOTES

1. National Civil Rights Museum at the Lorraine Motel, http://www.civilrights museum.org/?page_id=92.

2. William Green, "Woman Won't Vacate Motel Where Rev. King Was Slain," *USA Today*, Jan. 14, 1988, A3; Thelma Balfour, "Woman Evicted from Site of King Slaying," *USA Today*, March 3, 1988, A3.

3. "Protestor Is Removed from King Motel Site," *New York Times*, July 17, 1990: http://www.nytimes.com/1990/07/17/us/protestor-is-removed-from-king-motel-site .html.

4. Smith interview with author.

5. http://www.fulfillthedream.net/pages/mlk.boycott3.html.

6. "Why Boycott the Civil Rights Museum": http://www.fulfillthedream.net/pages/mlk.boycott1.html.

7. http://www.civilrightsmuseum.org/?page_id=484.

8. William Chafe writes that many white Greensboro citizens were deeply proud of their city's and even the state's reputation for progressive policies on racial matters. Black Greensboro citizens felt something else entirely about race relations in their city and state. See Chafe, *Civilities and Civil Rights: Greensboro, North Carolina, and the Black Struggle for Freedom* (New York: Oxford University Press, 1980), 98–101.

9. Karen Plunkett-Powell, *Remembering Woolworth's: A Nostalgic History of the World's Most Famous Five and Dime* (New York: St. Martin's Press, 2011), 159–61.

10. http://www.sitins.com/timeline.shtml.

11. Jim Schlosser, *Remembering Greensboro* (Charleston: History Press, 2009), 43.

12. Otis Hairston, Jr., *Greensboro, North Carolina—Black America Series* (Charleston: Arcadia Publishing, 2003), 80.

13. When this book went to press, the curators were still struggling with this issue and were working on a plan that would allow visitors to walk themselves through the exhibits.

14. William Chafe, *Civil Rights and Civil Liberties* (New York: Oxford University Press, 1981), 251–52; "Sequence of Events on November 3rd 1979," *Greensboro Truth and Reconciliation Commission Final Report* (May 2006), 170–89.

15. From the Greensboro Truth and Reconciliation Report website, accessed March 26, 2013, through http://web.archive.org/web/20070210222841/http://www.gtcrp.org/.

16. From Martha Minow, "Memory and Hate," Greensboro Truth and Reconciliation Commission Final Report, 9.

17. Introduction to Greensboro Truth and Reconciliation Commission Final Report, 15.

18. Author's interview with Methany, Greensboro City Council member at large.

19. "New Collaboration between Sit-In Movement, Inc., and North Carolina Agricultural and Technical State University," press release (June 26, 2001): http://www.ncat.edu/Sit-In_News.pdf.

20. Speaking specifically about Montgomery, Alabama, but clearly referencing the broader phenomenon, historian Glenn T. Eskew is critical of this impulse to mix a historical narrative with a municipal impulse to raise money. He writes, "What began as veterans of the struggle gathering to remember past events at sites of memory has become a civil rights industry that manufactures an ahistorical interpretation of the social movement as a means of promoting a new American civic religion of tolerance. Now sensing the profits to be made, Rotarians and other municipal leaders in Montgomery hustle a tourism package that embraces the Cradle of the Confederacy's dual

legacy as the birthplace of the modern civil rights movement": Eskew, "Selling the Civil Rights Movement: Montgomery, Alabama, since the 1960s," in Anthony J. Stanonis, ed., *Dixie Emporium: Tourism, Foodways, and Consumer Culture in the American South* (Athens, Georgia: University of Georgia Press, 2008), 196.

21. For more on this controversy, see Bruce Craig, "Historical Advocacy: The Past, Present, and Future," *Public Historian* 22 (Spring 2000), 71–74; Stacy Warren, "Saying No to Disney: Disney's Demise in Four American Cities," in Mike Budd and Max H. Kirsch, eds., *Rethinking Disney: Private Control, Public Dimensions* (Middletown, Conn.: Wesleyan University Press, 2005), 231–60; Charles W. Bailey, "How Washington Insiders Ambushed Mickey Mouse—Fight Against the Building of a Theme Park in Virginia by Walt Disney Co.," *Washington Monthly* 26 (December 1994), 10–14; and Noah Silberman, "The Battle That Disney Should Have Won," *Lingua Franca* 5 (No. 1, 1994), 24–28.

22. Eric Gable, Richard Handler, and Anna Lawson, "On the Uses of Relativism: Fact, Conjecture, and Black and White Histories at Colonial Williamsburg," *American Ethnologist* 19 (Nov. 1992), 793.

23. Christy S. Matthews, "Where Do We Go from Here? Researching and Interpreting the African-American Experience," *Historical Archaeology* (1997), 108–9.

24. Ibid., 110.

25. Robert L. Harris, Jr., "We Can Best Honor the Past . . . by Facing It Squarely, Honestly, and Above All, Openly," *Journal of African American History* 94 (Summer 2009), 394–95.

26. R. Emmett Tyrell, "Stinging Portrait of Slavery," *Washington Times*, July 10, 1999.

27. Cary Carson, "Colonial Williamsburg and the Practice of Interpretive Planning in American History Museums," *Public Historian* 20 (Summer 1998), 30.

28. Matthews, "Where Do We Go from Here," 107.

PART II
THEORY: MAKING THE
CASE FOR ARTFUL HISTORY

James Goodman

"For the Love of Stories":
From *Reviews in American History* (1998)

Narrative has proved to be a wonderfully—sometimes maddeningly—elastic term. In the following essay James Goodman explores its variant usage and complexity. How exactly does narrative relate to analysis? What is its bearing on the details—all the mechanics—of literary form? Does it require its own kind of relationship to evidence? These questions were slowly emerging when Goodman, as a graduate student, began to imagine himself as a narrative historian. (His subsequent book *Stories of Scottsboro* was shortlisted for the Pulitzer Prize.) In the years since, debate about historians as narrators—as tellers of stories—has spanned a wide continuum (Goodman's preferred word). His essay attempts to bring some order to this sprawl, to establish boundaries and inner coherence, even while leaving space for experimentation. In fact, narrative and experiment have long proceeded hand in hand. And the "revival of narrative" has produced a burst of reflection on the very foundations of historical study, including such matters as subjectivity, voice, and the roles of imagination and empathy. All through, Goodman is coy about defining narrative. But about "stories" themselves he is clear: he confesses simply to "loving" them. This in itself is something to ponder: how and where does "love" enter the work of historians?

He rarely admitted it, and when he did, only to a close friend or colleague, someone he trusted and thought might understand. Sitting in a coffee shop or walking along a city street, lulled by conversation into confession, he looked around, and then said it, softly, so that no one but his friend would hear.

To everyone else he said that there was no better way to understand the past. No better way to understand other people. No better way to try to reach broader audiences, to write some of the history that does its work in the world. Progressive historians could least afford to underestimate the social power of stories. He said that for the problems he was interested in, the questions he was asking, a story could show readers things about the past that traditional social analysis and cultural interpretation could not.

And all that was true.

Sometime after he settled upon a thesis topic but before he started writing, he had lunch with his thesis adviser. He had proposed to write a history of an event, the Scottsboro Case, from many different points of view. He imagined a modest experiment in historical form, a narrative in which he would answer the question "What happened?" with a story about the conflict among people with different ideas about what happened, the conflict among people with different stories of Scottsboro.

He talked about the research he had done, and then about the shape he thought the thesis would take. But he didn't have a good sense of the shape; he hadn't started writing.

"What book do you have in mind as a model?" his adviser asked.

Years later, after he had written the thesis and taken a teaching job, he asked his students some version of that question every time he asked for a term paper or thesis proposal. "What book or essay that we've read this term, or that you've read in another class, will your essay—the form of your essay, its shape, perspective, tone—remind us of? In what way? Why?"

He came to love the question. But at lunch that day he didn't have a good answer. He had taken the title of his dissertation proposal, "Thirteen Ways of Looking at Scottsboro," and many good ideas about perspective from Wallace Stevens. But he wasn't going to write his dissertation in verse. He had read many narrative histories, old and new, since he started graduate school. A few of them were experiments in historical writing. But he did not know of a historian who had written a narrative history from multiple points of view.[1]

"I don't have a model in history," he said. "But there are novelists who have done what I would like to do. Faulkner, for one, in the *The Sound and the Fury* and *As I Lay Dying*."

Thinking back on that lunch years later, he was grateful his adviser had not advised him to find another adviser.[2]

He did not have a model, but he did have the latest round of the debate, among working historians, about narrative. Lawrence Stone started it in 1979. A mere half-century after historians, en masse, had rejected narrative history for scientific history, Stone detected a strong undercurrent sucking many prominent historians back. He defined narrative (it is organized chronologically; it is focused on a single coherent story; it is descriptive rather than analytical; it is concerned with man not circumstances; and it deals with the particular and specific rather than the collective and statistical) and three forms of scientific history. He discussed four causes of the revival of narrative, two kinds of new, new history, five differences between the old narrative and the new, and four potential problems with narrative. "More and more of the 'new historians' are now trying to discover what was going on inside people's heads in the past, and what it was like to live in the past, questions which inevitably lead back to the use of narrative."[3]

Bernard Bailyn did not read Stone's essay until after he had drafted his 1981 American Historical Association presidential address, and so different was his address in emphasis and outlook that but for a single footnote in the published version readers would not have known for sure that he had read it at all. Bailyn began with a sweeping critique of modern historiography for its shapelessness, its emphasis on technical problem solving, its failure to see the forest for the trees. If Bailyn saw signs of a revival of narrative, he did not let on. But at every critical turn in his talk he made clear he wanted one: "The great proliferation of historical writing," he wrote, "has served not to illuminate the central themes of Western history but to obscure them." The challenge now was to "incorporate the mass of technical findings and the analytical studies that dominate modern research into historical narratives that explain how the world—or some large segment of it—evolved in the way it did."[4]

A few months later, C. Vann Woodward had his say. The editors of the *New York Times Book Review* had asked him to mark the occasion of the publication of the first volume of *The Oxford History of the United States* with "a short history of American history." Woodward described history's long literary tradition, noting that the nineteenth-century giants—Parkman, Prescott, and Bancroft—had been men of letters at a time when history was a popular branch of literature. Only in this century, Woodward wrote, had historians come to think of themselves not as writers but as scholars, even scientists, writing primarily for one another. Yet Woodward thought it the "duty and privilege of historians . . . to present the results of the guild's researches, or at least their significance, to the layman in readable, unspecialized prose he can understand and enjoy." The writing of popular history could not be left to the amateurs; there was too much they did not know. It had to be the professionals who were "able and happy to revive some very old traditions of the craft, including those of the storyteller."[5]

An academic debate is like a paragraph. It rarely recovers from a bad first line. The problem was not that Stone was mistaken. He argued that historians were turning from macro to micro, from economics and sociology to psychology and culture, from structures and processes to meanings and *mentalité*. The problem, as Stone himself hinted at the end of his essay, was that narrative was the wrong word for the changes in approach and method he had shrewdly identified and tried to explain.[6]

For a budding narrative historian, Bailyn's address was no more satisfying than Stone's. His true concerns were organizing principles, interpretative frameworks, and synthesis, all of which could be realized in analysis as easily as in narrative. Bailyn did not define narrative, and though he discussed in detail three historiographical developments that he thought would influence all future narratives—the fusion of latent and manifest events; the depiction of large scale spheres and systems; and the description of internal states of mind—he was vague about the form that those narratives would take. He imagined storytelling "with a complexity and an analytic dimension never envisioned before," but he left readers without a clue about what, when it came to form, that storytelling might be like.[7]

Woodward, like Bailyn, was much more precise about what he did not like (fragmentation, subdisciplines for every group of Americans and every approach, overspecialization, jargon) than what, besides clear, accessible writing, he liked; he was much clearer about history's history than its future. Woodward wanted historians to be writers again—literary craftsmen, inspired, as he himself had been, by poets and novelists. But he left would-be narrativists wondering what forms a history inspired by late-twentieth-century literature might take.[8]

Historians, of all people, ought to be wary of claims that the latest is the greatest and that the new has never been done before. But they are not, and in the 1980s, as in the 1970s, the name of every leading brand of history was fortified with the word "new." It was probably never in the cards that talk of a revival of a two-thousand-year-old tradition would be warmly received.

It didn't help that Stone claimed that what he called the revival of narrative followed not just from the disappointment with quantification (cliometrics sometimes "combined the vices of unreadability and triviality"; the "macro-economic model" was a pipe-dream; "scientific history," a myth) but also from the disillusionment with economic determinism and the decline of political commitment among intellectuals. He thereby managed to alienate social historians in every conceivable (and often hostile) camp. Bailyn was kinder to the cliometricians; he considered quantification fundamental to two of the trends remaking modern historiography and insisted that no future historian could be "innocent" of statistics. Yet Bailyn was perceived, by many, to be an enemy of the new history in his field, and Woodward, though the intellectual father and grandfather of scores of new historians, had, in the course of promoting narrative, accused the new historians not just of provincialism and incestuousness but also disarray and decay. "History was once called a habitation of many mansions," Woodward wrote, "but it has been more recently described as scattered suburbs, trailer camps and a deteriorating central city."[9]

In no time, if not from the start, many new historians concluded that the call for narrative was simply an attempt by traditionalists to stem the historiographical (and historical) tide of the 1960s and 1970s. "There is a conservative effort underway," Joan Scott said, "to undercut the power of the political analysis" provided by recent social history. The effort took a number of forms, but "above all," Scott said, it took "the form of a call for a 'return to narrative,' by which is meant telling stories 'as they happened' and with no obvious analytic stance." Eric Monkkonen defended specialization and technical vocabularies and expressed the sentiments of many historians when he suggested that those advocating narrative history were the historian's auxiliary of Reaganism and the right. The demand for narrative, Monkkonen wrote, was "an anti-intellectual demand for a return to simpler times and simpler tales, for a world no longer mired in complexity and opacity." Eric Hobsbawm urged radical historians to "resist this return to the historical stone age."[10]

The aspiring narrative historian could forgive the opponents of narrative the dichotomies between narrative and analysis, between description and interpretation, between accessible history and sophisticated history. As any child might have said, not without justice: Stone and Woodward used those dichotomies first. He could almost forgive the argument that narrative history was, by nature, conservative history. The calls for narrative were so muddled, the criticism of social history in those calls so clear, that radical social historians did not have to be paranoid to think that the old guard was out to get them.[11]

What he could not forgive, on all sides of the debate, was the association of all narrative history with traditional narrative, particularly traditional political narrative. The possibility that narrative historians might strike out in different directions somehow did not occur to the historians who entered the narrative debate, including many theoretically sophisticated historians. Consider, for example, Gordon Wood. Reviewing the first volume of the Oxford History to appear, Robert Middlekauff's *The Glorious Cause* (1982), Wood noted the calls for narrative, and he described both the contributions the social sciences had made to the discipline and the problems they had created. Wood, too, worried that the costs outweighed the benefits. Yet unlike those who looked to narrative to save the discipline from "self-destruction," Wood had kept abreast of the "intellectual fashions" of the late twentieth century, particularly the continental critiques of narrative of Jean-Paul Sartre, Fernand Braudel, Roland Barthes, and François Furet. Wood didn't think there was any going back to traditional narrative, and Middlekauff's history of the American Revolution struck him as just that. Its proportions, its idiosyncrasies, its selectiveness, its constructed nature, and its teleology made history an easy target for those, like Hayden White and E. L. Doctorow, who thought that there was no difference between history and fiction.[12]

Traditional narrative, Wood wrote, "depends on historians remaining mentally in the nineteenth century." Wood might have gone on to say that contemporary narrative historians, while avoiding epistemological extremes, might write narratives based on contemporary thinking about the relation between experience and perceptions, past and present, cause and effect, context and contingency, even history and fiction. They might move the genre from realism and naturalism to modernism and perhaps beyond. Instead Wood concluded that "narrative form, as a representation of past reality, particularly as Middlekauff has used it, may not bear much looking into."[13]

The historians had managed to have a debate about narrative that was not a debate about rhetoric, form, or literary method, a debate about narrative that was not about writing stories, which is what narrative historians do. There were only two exceptions. One was a 1983 essay by Mark Phillips, who labored to push the debate beyond its narrow definition of narrative, its simple-minded dichotomy between narrative and analysis, and its baffling avoidance of questions of form. (Stone's very definition, Phillips noted, drifted "away from narrative itself towards the question of its use or content.") Phillips suggested a number of directions in which new narrative historians might go: "Like the modern novelist, the historian may need to find a voice capable of acknowledging its own subjectivity. Like the medieval chronicler, he will need a more loose-jointed style of story-telling that makes the most of what he knows and is more tolerant than classical, linear narratives of shifts, gaps, and uncertainties." The particulars, Phillips thought, were best left to practice. But, like J. H. Hexter a decade and a half earlier, Phillips implored historians to pay more attention to the structure of history, to become practical critics of their own literature.[14]

Phillips wanted to save the debate. James Davidson seemed inclined to scrap it and start anew. In a gem of an essay, published in 1984, Davidson showed how all the talk of narrative had so far been talk of narrative as a means to analytical ends, as if stories had been created simply to lend support to sociological generalizations. What about narrative means to literary ends? What about narrative as imaginative writing? Instead of talking vaguely about "writing well," historians needed to "think concretely about the literary values affirmed by writers of fiction, as well as about the techniques these writers employ to achieve their ends." Davidson then went on, in a discussion of specificity, point of view, and indirection, to practice what he preached.[15]

He found it easier to knock the historians debating narrative for their definitions and dichotomies than to define narrative history himself. The dictionary said a narrative was a story, and a story was an account of an incident or event. He was tempted to say that he recognized narrative when he read it.

He was also tempted to say, as some of the theorists said, that there was nothing but narrative. Who, for example, told grander stories—with vast casts of characters, magnificent plots, unforgettable metaphors, and universal themes—than the great social theorists, Smith, Marx, and Freud. But as a practicing historian, and a teacher of historical writing, he didn't find the "everything is narrative" approach particularly useful. There were elements of narrative in every analysis and argument (and *vice versa*), but that did not mean that all history was narrative history.

He preferred to think of the rhetoric of history as a continuum, running from accounts of events, moments, periods, places, and lives (that appear to be devoid of explicit analysis of causes, contexts, and meanings) to explicit interpretations of processes, institutions, structures, and systems (that appear to be devoid of individuals, specific places and events, and sometimes even small units—hours, days, weeks, months—of time).[16]

"The earthquake struck T'an-ch'eng on July 25, 1668. It was evening, the moon just rising. There was no warning, save for a frightening roar that seemed to come from somewhere to the northwest. The buildings in the city began to shake and the trees took up a rhythmical swaying, tossing ever more wildly back and forth until their tips almost touched the ground." That is narrative. "To say that Puritans were capitalists—even of the communal variety—is, of course, to engage in a form of anachronism. The term 'capitalism' entered into social analysis primarily as a reaction to the nineteenth-century Industrial Revolution. And, as a consequence of the social depredations brought by that process, the term entered into scholarly discourse primarily by way of hostile critics." That is analysis. Most historical writing lies somewhere between the extremes, and many of the interesting questions about the rhetoric of history are questions about the kinds of narrative and analysis, and the proportions of narrative and analysis, and the manner in which (and the art with which) narrative and analysis are combined.[17]

Frustrated with the historians, he occasionally turned to the theorists—analytical philosophers, literary critics, and meta-historians—who had been debating narrative for many years. What might be lost in plain prose was gained in critical sophistication, and despite the hostility of some theorists to narrative as a form of historical knowledge, he took comfort in Hayden White's call for historians to use the techniques of modern art, in David Carr's insistence upon the continuity between the structure of narrative and the structure of human experience, and in Allan Megill's defense of description.[18]

Yet, like the historians, the theorists offered the narrative historian little practical advice, and the thought of one of them "reading" or "deconstructing" whatever narrative strategy he came up with on his own was terrifying. Mainstream historians called the theorists, particularly the postmodern theorists, relativists, and accused them of denying the possibility of truly and objectively representing the past. He thought otherwise. In their endless elaboration and critique of the fictions employed in every historical narrative; in their unmasking of the political and philosophical foundations of every representation; in their detection and naming of every silence, slippage, and attribution of difference, the meta-historians had become the profession's positivists. They were unrelenting in their search for representations that were true to the real world. They would not be easy to please.[19]

He went ahead and wrote the dissertation. After he completed it, he immediately began to rewrite it, to write the book. Years passed, years of writing and teaching, years in which he had time to read only the books he assigned to his students. When the manuscript was finally out of his hands, he turned eagerly to the history he had missed.[20]

Outside the academy, narrative history (written by journalists, novelists, biographers, and self-proclaimed practitioners of "literary non-fiction" and the "literature of fact") was thriving. And here and there people still talked of a revival of narrative among academic historians. But he didn't see the signs. What academic revivalists worthy of the name would fail to establish a journal? Or fail to ensure that at every major meeting numerous sessions were devoted to the practice of narrative? Or fail to hold meetings of their own in the hope of converting graduate students (and other untenured historians), the future of the profession, to the faith?[21]

What were those who still talked of a revival thinking? Some mistook a few narratives written by a few well-known historians for a revival of narrative. Others mistook the great wave of historical analyses of "stories," "storytelling," and "cultural narratives" for a revival of narrative, which was a little bit like mistaking the historical analysis of witchcraft for a revival of witchcraft.[22]

Happily, historians committed to narrative do not need a mass movement, not even graduate student historians. All they need is the desire and a cooperative adviser, and if they are fortunate, a few others around with narrative history on their minds. And there are historians around with narrative on their minds. Even in the heyday of scientific history, some professional historians wrote narrative history. Some still do, and a number of them are not just writing it but experimenting with its form, struggling to find the best way of telling the stories they want to tell.[23]

He found that a few of the historians writing narrative had written it, as he had, from multiple points of view. In *Chicago 1968* (1988) David Farber joined chapters of analysis with chapters of narrative, narrative written from the perspective (and sometimes in the vernacular) of three of the groups that clashed at the Democratic National Convention. Richard Price wrote *Alabi's World* (1990), a history of eighteenth-century Suriname, from four points of view, each of them set in its own typeface, three of them (all but Price's) drawn entirely from primary sources. Farber and Price both tried to show, empathetically, from the inside (as he himself tried to show, in fifty-four short chapters, each of them written from the limited third-person point of view of one or another Scottsboro participant or observer) how and why particular people came to see, understand, and explain the world in the ways that they did.[24]

Simon Schama's *Dead Certainties* (1991) is also rich with voices, including that of a common British soldier, a cultural historian, a biographer, a Massachusetts governor, a Harvard professor accused of murder, a Harvard janitor, and a playful post-modern novelist. But Schama is less interested in perspectives, worldviews, and social contexts than in historical possibilities and probabilities, the shadows historians are forever chasing, all the might-have-beens in the lives and deaths of General Wolfe and George Parkman, the "teasing gap separating a lived event and its subsequent narration."[25]

For all Farber's and Price's (and his own) play with perspectives, and Schama's play with uncertainty, they are all traditional narrators in one way. Like magicians doing the scarf trick, they take bits and pieces of evidence, much of it frayed at the edges, and transform it into long, smooth, seamless sentences, paragraphs, and scenes. In fact they take the magicians (who never reveal their tricks) one step further. They do not even reveal that they are doing a trick. Schama's lay readers understand that there will always be some mystery surrounding the murder of George Parkman. But they read page after vivid page without ever realizing just how great the distance is between the documents Schama uses and the interior worlds he so vividly manages to evoke, or just how difficult it is (and just how much imagination it takes) to create scenes, like Schama's scenes of nineteenth-century Boston, that readers can see and hear.

Others had given up on that kind of magic. In *Celia, A Slave* (1991), Melton McLaurin shows not just what the historical record reveals about Celia's murder of her master, but also what it conceals. In some places he does that quietly, dropping adverbs of uncertainty and probability—perhaps, probably, maybe, unlikely, and most likely—into key sentences. In other places, he bluntly confesses that there are things, important things, we cannot know: "The emotional response of the master and his slave to this violent act [rape] lie outside the methods of historical inquiry." Then he goes on to try to know them: "Nevertheless the historical record can be used to draw some reasonable conclusions."[26]

In *A Midwife's Tale* (1990), Laurel Ulrich introduces problems of evidence and interpretation by including portions of Martha Ballard's diary, without which, she writes, "Martha Ballard's biography would be little more than a succession of dates." Ulrich thereby provides a view of both the raw material her history is made of and the distance between that material—with its "dailiness," opacity, gaps, and incredible economy of expression (all of which led earlier historians to call it trivial)—and her own thick description and analysis. Had Ulrich decided not to include the diary excerpts, the main lines of her story and her interpretation would be much the same. What would be different is her readers' sense of the historian's craft, particularly their sense of just how much rule-bound interpreting, contextualizing, and imagining historians do.[27]

Winthrop Jordan goes even further, making the relationship between historical record and history a central theme of *Tumult and Silence at Second Creek* (1993), his history of an alleged slave conspiracy in Adams County, Mississippi, in 1861. Jordan found the silences at Second Creek as pronounced as the tumult; the only evidence of a conspiracy, for example, comes from coerced confessions and other equally problematic sources. He fills the silences with interpretations, discussions of what we know and what we do not know, chapter length explications of historical contexts ("Of Water, Land, and Work," "Of the Planting Classes," "Of One Kind of Politics," "Of Women White and Black"). Then, at the end, he reprints "all the documents" he found that "bear directly on the conspiracy." They take up nearly a quarter of the book.[28]

Robert Rosenstone had voluminous diaries, notebooks, manuscripts, and correspondence with which to write *The Mirror in the Shrine* (1988), a book about four American encounters with Meiji Japan. Yet he wanted to explore and call attention to the difficulties and limits of historical knowledge under the best of evidentiary circumstances, to break the spell of traditional narrative by making readers aware of the constructed nature of historical texts and the inextricable links between present and past, between historian and historical evidence, and between author, characters, and readers. He writes in the present tense; uses different voices; employs the cinematographer's "montages, moving camera and quick takes"; reflects explicitly upon problems of interpretation and narration; and directly addresses his readers, his characters, and himself. Much of Rosenstone's book reads like a detailed, quiet, carefully-crafted yet colorful journal, his subject's journal in some places, in other places, his own.[29]

In *The Natures of John and William Bartram* (1996), a book about the inner lives of (and complicated relationship between) two eighteenth-century naturalists, Thomas Slaughter grapples with both the historical and literary problems caused by a dearth of evidence and the historical and literary possibilities presented by an author's identification with his subject. To fill the gaps in the biographical and emotional record, Slaughter asks questions that take us places that evidence alone would not allow us to go. He suggests possibilities that he can't "prove." And he boldly imagines, in clearly identified imagining, thoughts and feelings that most historians leave to novelists. To suggest how closely his "life, consciousness, and nature" are "entwined" with his interpretation of the Bartrams, Slaughter uses first-person paraphrasing throughout the book.[30]

Rosenstone appears in his story as "the author" or "the "historian." Slaughter appears as the Bartrams. Other historians were beginning to appear as "I," crossing the boundary between front and back matter (the prefaces, introductions, afterwords, and autobiographical acknowledgements, where historians had appeared, in the first-person singular, with varying degrees of self-consciousness, self-reflexiveness, and self-disclosure, for many years) and the text itself. William Cronon opens *Nature's Metropolis* (1991) with a description of Chicago as it appeared to him as a small boy, approaching the city in the family station wagon. Cronon recalls his early dislike and distrust of the city and the sharp distinction he made between its nature and the nature of the country, where he lived. Then he ducks backstage for 350 pages, returning in the epilogue to pick up the themes of connection and disconnection, city and hinterland, Chicago and the great West, as he now understands them, from an autobiographical as well as a historical point of view. Nell Painter wrote herself into the final pages of *Sojourner Truth, A Life, A Symbol* (1996) to demonstrate the power of the symbol of Truth, its seeming immunity to scholarship. She does that by telling stories about her own (mostly futile) attempts to persuade students and colleagues that the symbol and the life are not one and the same. William McFeely is a character in *Sapelo's People* (1994) from first page to last, a character who turns a history of an island and its people into a story—part observation, part meditation, part history—about a historian's encounter, past and present, with an island and its people.[31]

Critics have not always been kind to the historians who, in one way or another, have made themselves characters in their histories. What is often lost in the criticism is that historians are always in their histories. The question is how, and that question is what makes John Demos' *The Unredeemed Captive* (1994), a history of the Deerfield massacre and the captivity of Eunice Williams, so instructive an experiment in narrative. Reading the opening pages, he thought that Demos had written his story from a single, straightforward, third-person point of view, enlivening that point of view with the present tense, with many sudden, cinematographic shifts in scene; and with tight, terse, teasing prose.

But as he read on, he realized that Demos had actually written his story from two perspectives, or at least in two voices. The second voice speaks most often (but not only) in countless parenthetical phrases, parentheses that grammar does not demand. The second voice may add information, qualify facts and interpretations, ask questions, identify sources, or distinguish between contemporary evidence (what might have been known at the time) and subsequent evidence (what could only have been known later). The second voice gently but persistently—ingenuously, he thought—reminds readers that this is not the past but a story about the past, a history, with a historian always at work.[32]

Demos, like Slaughter, struggles to make persistent speculation—adverbs of probability, questions (some simple, some elaborate), and whole passages that drip with narrative and interpretative possibility—a form of art. In a few clearly marked passages, Demos goes farther. In one, Demos imagines Eunice Williams' response to a visit from a trader hoping to persuade her to return to her family; in another, Demos imagines the substance of a short meeting, many years later, between Williams and her brother.[33]

He had learned an enormous amount about the past, about history, and about stories from fiction, and he did not have any qualms about historians trying to write it. Every now and then, in the privacy of his study, he tried to write it himself. Nor did he have any qualms about historians trying to enrich their history with fiction, so long as they let readers know what they were up to.[34] Yet so far, he found the history and historical understanding produced by historians' fiction less satisfying than the history produced by the same historians' non-fiction, by their efforts to push, with all the available evidence and imagination, at the outer limits of fact. Demos' description of the captives' march through snowy woods from Deerfield to Montreal (which an endnote shows to be partly based on "the author's personal knowledge of wintertime travel in the New England woodlands") is more powerful than Demos' imagining of Eunice Williams' thoughts at a moment when she quite consciously refused to speak and when her impenetrable silence may have been more telling than any sounds or thoughts could be. Similarly, *Dead Certainties* is most evocative (and instructive to other narrative historians) not in the passages that Schama describes as "pure inventions" but in passages where he takes standard historical evidence—letters to the governor of Massachusetts, for example, some urging clemency for John Webster, others urging execution ("sober petitions; wild looping scribbles on coarse paper; tiny, sinister script that looked as though a bug had tracked a pin across the page; blue sheets with newsprint cuttings pasted to them and a threatening, single, prophetic name—'Miriam' or 'Nehemiah'—signed at the foot")—and makes of them an unforgettable scene: the tormented governor, at his desk, trying to decide what to do.[35]

His reading reminded him that not every narrative was an experiment. In *The Kingdom of Mathias* (1994), Paul Johnson and Sean Wilentz wrote a lively linear narrative (from a single, omniscient, third-person point of view) about some untraditional subjects, including the prophet and his followers and "the contest over family life, sexuality, and social class that accompanied the rise of market society." In *Paul Revere's Ride* (1994), David Hackett Fisher wrote a lively and similarly straightforward narrative about a traditional subject.[36]

Not every narrative was an experiment, and not every experiment was a narrative. He could imagine all kinds of experiments with interpretative forms, and when he was in the mood for splitting hairs, as he often was, he thought it possible to say that many of the books he had read, including Ulrich's, Rosenstone's, and Slaughter's, were pathbreaking experiments in interpretation—compelling combinations of interpretative social history, cultural history, and biography—as much as they were experiments in storytelling.

He wondered if even narrative historians remained reluctant to fall fully into storytelling. "Most of all," Demos writes, "I wanted to write a story." By and large Demos does write a story, a brilliant, affecting story. Yet in places the narrator of *The Unredeemed Captive* sounds less like a self-conscious storyteller than a self-conscious analyst, a literary critic (reading John Williams' writings) in one chapter, an ethnographer (reading accounts of Kahnawake) in another. Critics and ethnographers can be storytellers too. But in those chapters, Demos decided not to translate his analysis into the main lines of the plot that flows, and grabs hold of readers, from the book's first pages. Without that translation, the movement from chapter to chapter sometimes seems like a movement from one form of historical writing to another.[37]

"This book is a story," Winthrop Jordan writes in the first line of *Tumult and Silence*, "but at the same time it is not." It is not a story, he says, because the gaps in the record, the silences, do not allow him to say what happened when. Yet countless stories are driven by uncertainty about what happened when. It is not the silences that forestall a story, but Jordan's strategy for filling them, his decision to interpret the tumult and silence explicitly for pages at a time rather than trying to transform the ingredients of his interpretations (background, history, context) into plot, character, and scene. Considering Jordan's strong sense that a conspiracy did take place, his story might have been a relatively straightforward tale of conspiracy, discovery, inquiry, trials, and punish-ment—all enriched by Jordan's remarkable knowledge of the place and time. Or, considering the real possibility that the slave conspiracy was a figment of slave owners' imaginations, he might have designed a plot with room for both the imagined conspiracy and the actual absence of one. Instead he chose to write an inquiry. That was a perfectly reasonable choice, but it was a choice, not a rhetorical inevitability.[38]

Perhaps his definition of narrative was too narrow. Perhaps narrative histori-ans were pushing the boundaries of the form beyond the limits of his imagi-nation. Edward Ayers had used the phrase "open narratives" to character-ize a wide range of experiments in Southern history, including Ayers' own combination of "open" and "fixed" narratives in The Promise of the New South (1992). Some open narrativists, Ayers wrote, "openly grapple with problematic sources and presentation." Others "fold" analysis and argument into their sto-ries, using them as a means to narrative ends. The latter "may intentionally leave ambiguities unresolved or seek tension and resolution less in profes-sional debate than in evidence, characters, and situations."[39]

He thought Ayers was absolutely right about the rhetorical strategies that particular historians employed. Yet he also thought it was important to distin-guish between historians who openly and explicitly interpret their sources and evidence (or who explicitly grapple with the nature and limits of interpreta-tion in any other way) and historians who fold their interpretation into their stories. There may even be a tension between the two, a tension between the desire to share all the secrets, struggles, mysteries, and tricks of the trade and the call and character of stories.[40]

Narrative historians might relieve some of that tension with innovative nar-rative strategies and styles, finding ways to embed historical quests in their stories as subtly as some embed historical interpretations. But they probably cannot relieve it all. That's because storytellers shape stories by saying some things indirectly, and by not saying other things at all, by consciously creating the silences that interpretive historians struggle to fill. Truth in narrative history, like truth in poetry and fiction, will sometimes issue from what is not said as well as what is, and professionally trained narrative historians may need to teach themselves to resist the urge to tell and show all that they know.

When historians experiment, post-modernism often takes the heat. But nar-rative historians acknowledged debts to imaginative writers more often than to post-modern literary critics, meta-historians, or philosophers. Rosenstone evokes, in epigraphs, two theorists, Hayden White and Paul Ricouer, and then goes on to compare his innovations to those of filmmakers and novelists. Schama evokes Robert Lowell and Henry James and dedicates *Dead Certainties* to John Clive, "for whom history was literature." Slaughter, in addition to numerous professional historians, acknowledges the influence of Julia Blackburn, Richard Holmes, Norman Maclean, Cormac McCarthy, N. Scott Momaday, and Wallace Stegner. Edward Ayers expresses his admiration for the open styles of John Dos Passos and James Agee.[41]

He thought the future of narrative would be made, as the history of narrative had been made, by historians, thinking of themselves as writers, learning from writers, and writing, taking the same care as poets and novelists with their words and designs, perhaps also taking some of the same risks. It would sometimes be made by writers who could keep secrets as well as tell them, satisfying readers by stringing them along. It would always be made by writers who trusted, and who could figure out how to fall into, and lose themselves in, stories.

Good criticism would also nourish narrative, and it could not be taken for granted. Historians are not trained to read for language and design. He himself did not really know where to begin. Once again he was tempted to say simply that he knew good criticism when he read it. Those who wrote it took language, structure, writing, and stories seriously, and they discussed a book's flaws with an understanding of the difficulty of the undertaking and an appreciation of the writer's literary intentions and aspirations.[42]

He was certain that narrative historians trying to write like John Dos Passos, Toni Morrison, or William Faulkner would often stumble and sometimes fall. Yet they were likely to write better history than they would have written if they had tried only to write well. So there's nothing lost, and much to be gained, by their trying.

But there was more to it.

"Between you and me," he said, "I do it for pleasure, and for love."

For the pleasure of meanings and explanations that leapt out, or had to be teased out, of plot, characters, points of view, and language. For the love of those few words, the short description, the bit of dialogue, sometimes just the simple, single verb, that made it possible to hear an abstraction—a social or cultural structure perhaps, a process, or a system. For the pleasure and love, always mixed with equal or greater parts of agony and sweat, of trying to do what he knew he could never do, write what he liked to read: a phrase that remained on the tip of his tongue for days; a turn of events that made him feel as if he were in an airplane that had suddenly dropped two hundred feet; pages that, whatever else he was doing, he could not wait to return to.

He knew what the theory people said. Stories impose a false sense of order on a disorderly world. But he believed that a good story left the world as messy as it found it. What a story did was stop the world for a few moments, long enough for him to get a look at it, to ask questions of it, to get lost in it. Stories allowed him to contemplate fear, pain, and sorrow, instead of simply being overwhelmed by them. To contemplate also fleeting possibilities.

Now and then he needed to stop the world. So he tried to write stories, for the same reason he read stories. It felt good. He had to. He loved to.

NOTES

I am grateful to Jan Lewis and Louis Masur for their good criticism, and to Kathleen Feeley for her good copyediting.

1. That lunch took place sometime between the spring of 1985 and the summer of 1986, most likely in the spring of 1986. Among the older narrative histories he had read were C. Vann Woodward, *Tom Watson: Agrarian Rebel* (New York, 1938); Arthur M. Schlesinger, Jr., *The Age of Jackson* (Boston, 1945); Edmund S. Morgan, *Puritan Dilemma: The Story of John Winthrop* (Boston, 1958); Morgan and Helen M. Morgan, *The Stamp Act Crisis: Prologue to Revolution* (New York, 1963); and David M. Potter, *The Impending Crisis, 1848–1861*, edited and completed by Don E. Fehrenbacher (New York, 1976). Among the newer narratives were Willie Lee Rose, *Rehearsal for Reconstruction: The Port Royal Experiment* (New York, 1976); Jonathan D. Spence, *The Death of Woman Wang* (New York, 1978) and Spence, *The Memory Palace of Matteo Ricci* (New York, 1984); Leon F. Litwack, *Been in the Storm So Long: The Aftermath of Slavery* (New York, 1979); Carlo Ginzburg, *The Cheese and the Worms: The Cosmos of a Sixteenth-Century Miller* (Baltimore, 1980); and Natalie Z. Davis, *The Return of Martin Guerre* (Cambridge, Mass., 1983). Four major narrative syntheses were in the works: Bernard Bailyn, *Voyagers to the West* (New York, 1986); James M. McPherson, *Battle Cry of Freedom: The Civil War Era* (New York, 1988); Eric Foner, *Reconstruction: America's Unfinished Revolution, 1863–1877* (New York, 1988); and Richard White, *It's Your Misfortune and None of My Own: A History of the American West* (Norman, Okla., 1991).

2. Asked the same question a year later, after he had had a chance to read it, he might have mentioned J. Anthony Lukas, *Common Ground: A Turbulent Decade in the Lives of Three American Families* (New York, 1985). Asked the same question in the middle of the 1990s, he would have mentioned the work of Anna Deavere Smith. See

Smith, *Fires in the Mirror: Crown Heights, Brooklyn and Other Identities* (New York, 1993) and *Twilight: Los Angeles, 1992* (New York, 1994).

3. Lawrence Stone, "The Revival of Narrative: Reflections on a New Old History," *Past and Present* 85 (1979): 13.

4. Bernard Bailyn, "The Challenge of Modern Historiography," *American Historical Review* 87 (1982): 8, 3, 7.

5. Woodward is the general editor of the *Oxford History*; the first volume published was the second in the series. C. Vann Woodward, "A Short History of American History," *New York Times Book Review*, Aug. 8, 1982, pp. 3, 14.

6. Perhaps the only major turn that Stone missed was the linguistic. Stone, *The Revival of Narrative*, 23–24. See also Stone, "A Life of Learning," *American Council of Learned Societies Newsletter* 36 (Winter–Spring 1985): 18–19. Good or great first lines do not ensure a great debate. J. H. Hexter's classic essays on the rhetoric of history, published in the late 1960s and early 1970s, though widely cited and sometimes even read, did not spark a debate about the writing of history in the discipline's mainstream. See especially "The Rhetoric of History" and "Doing History," both of which are reprinted in Hexter, *Doing History* (Bloomington, Ind., 1971), 15–76, 135–56. See also Peter Gay, *Style in History* (New York, 1974) and John Clive, *Not by Fact Alone: Essays on the Writing and Reading of History* (New York, 1989).

7. Bailyn, "The Challenge of Modern Historiography," 24.

8. Woodward, "A Short History of American History," 3, 14.

9. Stone, "The Revival of Narrative," 8–15; Bailyn, "The Challenge of Modern Historiography," 9–18, 24; Woodward, "A Short History of American History," 14.

10. Joan Wallach Scott, "Comment," in "Agendas for Radical History," *Radical History Review* 36 (1986): 43; Eric Monkkonen, letter to the *New York Times Book Review*, Sept. 5, 1982, p. 21; Eric Hobsbawm, "Agendas for Radical History," *Radical History Review* 36 (1986): 28. See also Hobsbawm, "The Revival of Narrative: Some Comments," *Past and Present* 86 (February 1980): 3–8; J. Morgan Kousser, "The Revivalism of Narrative," *Social Science History* 8 (Spring 1984): 133–49. A few years later, when Thomas Bender, who was much less interested in a revival of narrative than a revival of synthesis (which might come in analytical as well as narrative forms), proposed that historians of the U.S. use ideas about "the making of public culture" to "turn a vast supply of fine studies of parts . . . into a sense of the whole," he too was accused of trying to turn back the clock. See Bender, "Wholes and Parts: The Need for Synthesis in American History," *Journal of American History* 73 (June 1986): 120–36; Eric Monkkonen, "The Dangers of Synthesis," *American Historical Review* 91 (December 1986): 1146–57; "A Round Table: Synthesis in American History," *Journal of American History* 74 (June 1987): 107–30. Peter Novick sets the early 1980s debate about narrative in the context of the debate about objectivity in *That Noble Dream: The "Objectivity Question" and the American Historical Profession* (New York, 1988): 623–25.

11. In the form in which it came, the political argument against narrative was more reflex than thought. Monkkonen, for one, later backed off, admitting that there was no inherent reason narrative synthesis could not be radical history. See Monkkonen, "The Dangers of Synthesis," 1154. Monkkonen might also have noted that a number of radical historians were among the first to call for narrative synthesis. See, for example, Herbert G. Gutman, "The Missing Synthesis: Whatever Happened to History," *Nation*, Nov. 21, 1981, pp. 521, 553–54 and Eric Foner, "History in Crisis," *Commonweal*, Dec. 18, 1981, pp. 723–26. There are of course sophisticated theoretical arguments about the inherent conservatism of narrative in general and historical narrative in particular. For a summary of some of them, and many useful citations, see Hayden White, "The Question of Narrative in Contemporary Historical Theory," *History and Theory* 23 (1984): 1–33. See also C. Lévi-Strauss, *The Savage Mind* (London, 1966); Roland Barthes, "The Discourse of History," in *Rhetoric and History: Comparative Criticism Yearbook*, ed. Elinor Shaffer and trans. Stephen Bann (Cambridge, Eng., 1981) and Barthes, *Mythologies* (New York, 1972).

12. Gordon S. Wood, "Star-Spangled History," *New York Review of Books* 29 (Aug. 12, 1982): 3–9.

13. Wood, "Star-Spangled History," 8, 9. Those inclined to stress Wood's qualifying phrase, "particularly as Middlekauff has used it," should consider Wood's response to the radically different way that Simon Schama used narrative a decade later. See Wood, "Novel History," *New York Review of Books* 38 (June 27, 1991): 12, 14–16. Joan Scott was another extremely sophisticated historian who did not seem to consider the possibility that a revival of narrative might not be a revival of traditional political history. Scott's criticism of narrative came, ironically, in an appeal to "radical historians" to pay more attention to "symbols" and "texts" and the methods that (modern and post-modern) cultural anthropologists and literary critics used to analyze them. See Scott, "Comment," 43.

14. Mark Phillips, "The Revival of Narrative: Thoughts on a Current Historiographical Debate," *University of Toronto Quarterly* 53 (Winter 1983–1984): 150, 153. For J. H. Hexter, see Hexter, *Doing History*.

15. James West Davidson, "The New Narrative History: How New? How Narrative?" *Reviews in American History* 12 (September 1984): 322–34. That was the state of the debate in the middle of the 1980s. In the early 1990s, in another admirable effort to move beyond simple-minded oppositions between events and structures, historical narrative and structural analysis, storytellers and interpreters, Peter Burke explored numerous new directions in narrative history (including "micro-narrative, backward narrative, and stories which move back and forth between public and private worlds or present the same events from multiple points of view"). See Burke, "History of Events and the Revival of Narrative," in *New Perspectives on Historical Writing* (University Park, Pa., 1992): 233–48. Around the same time, in the face of the skepticism and doubts of so

many critical theorists, William Cronon struggled eloquently to find a place for stories in history. See Cronon, "A Place for Stories: Nature, History, and Narrative," *Journal of American History* 78 (March 1992): 1347–76.

16. For closely related views, see Burke, "History of Events and the Revival of Narrative," and Phillips, "The Revival of Narrative." See also Edward L. Ayers, "Narrating the New South," *Journal of Southern History* 61 (August 1995): 555–56.

17. Spence, *The Death of Woman Wang*, 1; Stephen Innes, *Creating the Commonwealth: The Economic Culture of Puritan New England* (New York, 1995), 39.

18. Hayden White, "The Burden of History," in *Tropics of Discourse: Essays in Cultural Criticism* (Baltimore, 1978): 27–50; David Carr, "Narrative and the Real World: An Argument for Continuity," *History and Theory* 25 (November 1986): 117–31; Allan Megill, "Recounting the Past: 'Description,' Explanation, and Narrative in Historiography," *American Historical Review* 94 (June 1989): 627–53.

19. The theoretical literature is voluminous, and runs across numerous disciplines. He had started with essay collections, including William H. Dray, ed., *Philosophical Analysis and History* (New York, 1966); R. H. Canary and H. Kozicki, eds., *The Writing of History* (Madison, 1978); White, *Tropics of Discourse* and White, *The Content of the Form: Narrative Discourse and Historical Representation* (Baltimore, 1987); W.J.T. Mitchell, ed., *On Narrative* (Chicago, 1981); and Lionel Gossman, *Between History and Literature* (Cambridge, Mass., 1990). For extended analyses, see Arthur Danto, *Analytical Philosophy of History* (Cambridge, Eng., 1965); Danto, *Narration and Knowledge* (New York, 1985); Robert Scholes and Robert Kellogg, *The Nature of Narrative* (New York, 1966); Hayden White, *Metahistory: The Historical Imagination in Nineteenth-Century Europe* (Baltimore, 1973); Maurice Mandelbaum, *The Anatomy of Historical Knowledge* (Baltimore, 1977); and Paul Ricoeur, *Time and Narrative*, trans. Kathleen Blarney and David Pellauer, 3 vols. (Chicago, 1984–1988). See also Nancy F. Partner, "Making Up Lost Time: Writing on the Writing of History," *Speculum* 61 (1986): 90–117 and Paul A. Roth, "Narrative Explanations: The Case of History," *History and Theory* 27 (1988): 1–13. For a discussion of narrative in the law, see Peter Brooks and Paul Gewirtz, eds., *Law's Stories: Narrative and Rhetoric in the Law* (New Haven, 1996). Numerous psychologists and psychoanalysts have also had their say. See Donald P. Spence, *Narrative Truth and Historical Truth: Meaning and Interpretation in Psychoanalysis* (New York, 1982); Jerome Bruner, *Actual Minds, Possible Worlds* (Cambridge, Mass., 1986) and Bruner, *Acts of Meaning* (Cambridge, Mass., 1990) and Bruner, "The Narrative Construction of Reality," *Critical Inquiry* 18 (Autumn 1991): 1–21; and Robert Coles, *The Call of Stories* (Boston, 1989).

20. James Goodman, "Stories of Scottsboro" (Ph.D. diss., Princeton University, 1990); and Goodman, *Stories of Scottsboro* (New York, 1994).

21. Among the countless works of narrative written outside the academy were Shelby Foote, *The Civil War: A Narrative*, 3 vols. (New York, 1958–1974); David Halberstam, *The*

Best and the Brightest (New York, 1972); Lukas, *Common Ground*; Norman Mailer, *The Executioner's Song* (Boston, 1979); Richard Holmes, *Footsteps: Adventures of a Romantic Biographer* (London, 1985) and Holmes, *Dr. Johnson and Mr. Savage* (London, 1993); Art Spiegelman, *Maus: A Survivor's Tale* (New York, 1986) and Spiegelman, *Maus II: A Survivor's Tale: And Here My Troubles Began* (New York, 1991); Taylor Branch, *Parting the Waters: America in the King Years, 1954–1963* (New York, 1988); Philip Roth, *The Facts: A Novelist's Autobiography* (New York, 1988) and Roth, *Patrimony* (New York, 1991); Neil Sheehan, *A Bright Shining Lie: John Paul Vann and America in Vietnam* (New York, 1988); Julia Blackburn, *The Emperor's Last Island: A Journey to St. Helena* (New York, 1991) and Blackburn, *Daisy Bates in the Desert* (New York, 1994); Melissa Fay Greene, *Praying for Sheetrock: A Work of Non-Fiction* (Reading, Mass., 1991); Doris Kearns Goodwin, *No Ordinary Time* (New York, 1994); and Jonathan Harr, *A Civil Action* (New York, 1995). See also two new books, John M. Barry, *Rising Tide: The Great Mississippi Flood of 1927 and How It Changed America* (New York, 1997); and J. Anthony Lukas, *Big Trouble: A Murder in a Small Western Town Sets Off a Struggle for the Soul of America* (New York, 1997). The one or two sessions devoted to narrative at each year's annual meetings are usually devoted to theory. In the last few years, there have been a couple of fairly well publicized meetings devoted to experiments in historical writing, but no regular meetings and no permanent organization. Robert Rosenstone, one of the organizers of "Narrating Histories: A Workshop," a lively meeting held at California Institute of Technology in the spring of 1994, is one of two editors of a new journal, *Rethinking History*, which Rosenstone promises will devote some of its pages to experiments in historical writing.

22. See, for example, David Samuels, "The Call of Stories," *Lingua Franca* 6 (May/ June 1995): 35–43; Sarah Maza, "Stories in History: Cultural Narratives in Recent Works in European History," *American Historical Review* 101 (December 1996): 1493– 515. See also Bill Buford, "The Seductions of Storytelling," *New Yorker*, June 24 & July 1, 1996, p. 12.

23. What follows is more of a sampling of histories, most of them American histories, than a survey of all the recent works of narrative and of experiments in narrative form. Among the books he does not discuss but might well have are Theodore Rosengarten, *Tombee: Portrait of a Cotton Planter* (New York, 1986); Inga Clendinnen, *Ambivalent Conquests: Maya and Spaniard in Yucatan, 1517–1570* (New York, 1987); Jonathan Spence, *The Question of Hu* (New York, 1988); Charles Royster, *The Destructive War: William Tecumseh Sherman, Stonewall Jackson, and the Americans* (New York, 1991); Greg Dening, *Mr. Bligh's Bad Language: Passion, Power, and Theatre on the Bounty* (New York, 1992) and Dening, *The Death of William Gooch: A History's Anthropology* (Honolulu, 1995); Martin B. Duberman, *Stonewall* (New York, 1993); Richard White, *The Organic Machine* (New York, 1995); David M. Oshinsky, *Worse Than Slavery: Parchman Farm and the Ordeal of Jim Crow Justice* (New York, 1996); Michael Grossberg, *A Judgment for*

Solomon: The d'Hauteville Case and Legal Experience in Antebellum America (New York, 1996); Stephen B. Oates, *The Approaching Fury: Voices of the Storm, 1820–1861* (New York, 1997), as well as the recent works of narrative synthesis, from McPherson, *Battle Cry of Freedom* to James T. Patterson, *Grand Expectations: Postwar America, 1945–1974* (New York, 1996).

24. David R. Farber, *Chicago '68* (Chicago, 1988). For a critique of Farber, particularly his use of the vernacular, see Maurice Isserman, "The Not-So-Dark and Bloody Ground," *American Historical Review* 94 (October 1989): 1004–5. Richard Price, *Alabi's World* (Baltimore, 1990); Goodman, *Stories of Scottsboro*. See also Oates, *The Approaching Fury*, another history written from multiple perspectives, and another example of how difficult it is for historians to put words in their subjects' mouths.

25. Simon Schama, *Dead Certainties (Unwarranted Speculations)* (New York, 1991), 320.

26. Melton A. McLaurin, *Celia: A Slave* (Athens, Georgia, 1991), 20–21. For additional examples, see 27–28, 35–36, 39–40, 51.

27. Laurel Thatcher Ulrich, *A Midwife's Tale: The Life of Martha Ballard Based on Her Diary, 1785–1812* (New York, 1990). Another work in which a historian has embedded a lengthy primary source in the heart of his text is Allen Tullos, *Habits of Industry: White Culture and the Transformation of the Carolina Piedmont* (Chapel Hill, 1989).

28. Winthrop D. Jordan, *Tumult and Silence at Second Creek: An Inquiry into a Civil War Slave Conspiracy* (Baton Rouge, 1993), 265. See also Rosengarten, *Tombee*, which is a biography and a diary in one volume.

29. Robert A. Rosenstone, *Mirror in the Shrine: American Encounters in Meiji Japan* (Cambridge, Mass., 1988), xii–xiv.

30. Thomas P. Slaughter, *The Natures of John and William Bartram* (New York, 1996), xix.

31. William Cronon, *Nature's Metropolis: Chicago and the Great West* (New York, 1991); Nell Irvin Painter, *Sojourner Truth, A Life, A Symbol* (New York, 1996); William S. McFeely, *Sapelo's People* (New York, 1994). For an innovative use of the first person singular in a historical essay, see Patricia Nelson Limerick, "Turnerians All: The Dream of a Helpful History in an Intelligible World," *American Historical Review* 100 (June 1995): 697–716. Numerous New Journalists, literary critics, anthropologists, feminist theorists and biographers, and critical legal theorists led the way across this boundary. See, for example, *Writing Culture: The Poetics and Politics of Ethnography*, ed. James Clifford and George E. Marcus (Berkeley, Calif., 1986); Clifford, *The Predicament of Culture: Twentieth Century Ethnography, Literature, and Art* (Cambridge, Mass., 1988); Patricia J. Williams, *The Alchemy of Race and Rights* (Cambridge, Mass., 1991); Williams, *The Rooster's Egg* (Cambridge, Mass., 1995); or more recently Janice Radway, *A Feeling for Books: The Book-of-the-Month Club, Literary Taste, and Middle-Class Desire* (Chapel Hill, 1997). For elegant evidence that historical writing in the first person singular is

not a post-modern invention (and is not a form that only a postmodernist could like) see John Clive, "The Most Disgusting of Pronouns," in *Not by Fact Alone*, 25–33.

32. John Demos, *The Unredeemed Captive: A Family Story from Early America* (New York, 1994). For criticism of historians who have made themselves characters in their own histories, see for example, Peter A. Coclanis, "Urbs in Horto," *Reviews in American History* 20 (March 1992): 14–20; Michael P. Johnson, "Twisted Truth," *New Republic* 215 (Nov. 4, 1996): 37–41; and Alan Taylor, "The Voyage In," *New Republic* 215 (Dec. 9, 1996): 42–45. The criticism in these reviews was not limited to the author's place in the text; each reviewer had other interpretive and methodological objections. Yet he suspected that irritation with the author's place in the text had something to do with both the caustic tone of each of these reviews and the *ad hominem* (or *ad feminam*) criticism in each of them. It may be that the reviewers concluded that personal history invited personal criticism. In the spring of 1997, the *Journal of American History* generated a storm of criticism and controversy by publishing a highly personal historical and historiographical essay written by Joel Williamson (as well as the referees' reports on Williamson's essay). Most of the criticism was aimed at the substance of the essay (as opposed to its unusual form) and the editor's decision to print it in the first place. Still he feared that the publication of so rough and so weak a personal historical essay would give its form a bad name. See "What We See and Can't See in the Past: A Round Table," *Journal of American History* 83 (March 1997): 1217–72; and "What We See and Can't See in the Past: Responses," *Journal of American History* 84 (September 1997): 748–65. For a collection of brief personal historical essays, focused on the experience and history of World War II, published, without great fanfare, a few years earlier, see "A Round Table: The Living and Reliving of World War II," *Journal of American History* 77 (September 1990): 553–93.

33. Demos, *Unredeemed Captive*, 108–9, 189–90.

34. He could write an entire essay on the works of fiction, far too many to name, that had shaped his view of the past, of history, and of stories. Among the novels he regularly taught, and therefore returned to most often, were William Faulkner, *Absalom Absalom!* (New York, 1936); Robert Penn Warren, *All the King's Men* (New York, 1946); Ralph Ellison, *Invisible Man* (New York, 1952); Toni Morrison, *Beloved* (New York, 1987) and Morrison, *Jazz* (New York, 1992); Don DeLillo, *Libra* (New York, 1988); and Tim O'Brien, *The Things They Carried* (Boston, 1990). For a less sanguine view of historians' writing fiction (or mingling history and fiction), see Gordon S. Wood's review of Schama, *Dead Certainties*, in Wood, "Novel History." Cf. Louis P. Masur, "On Parkman's Trail," *William and Mary Quarterly*, 3d Ser., 49 (January 1992): 120–32; and Cushing Strout, "Border Crossings: History, Fiction, and *Dead Certainties*," *History and Theory* 31 (1992): 153–62.

35. Demos, *Unredeemed Captive*, 27–28, 108–9; Schama, *Dead Certainties*, 75–76. The latter is part of an unforgettable scene that a gifted graduate student might write

and, with a few footnotes, no dissertation committee could complain about, at least not on methodological grounds.

36. Paul Johnson and Sean Wilentz, *The Kingdom of Mathias* (New York, 1994); David Hackett Fischer, *Paul Revere's Ride* (New York, 1994).

37. Demos, *Unredeemed Captive,* xi, 55–76, 140–66. Considering that Demos structured *Entertaining Satan* (New York, 1982) around the movement from one form of social analysis to another, it is entirely possible that the shift from one historical form to another in his latest book was completely intentional.

38. Jordan, *Tumult and Silence,* 1.

39. Ayers, "Narrating the New South," 556. Edward L. Ayers, *The Promise of the New South: Life After Reconstruction* (New York, 1992). For another look at the writing of recent Southern history, see Joseph P. Reidy, "Calliope and Clio: The Style and Substance of Recent Historical Writing on the South," *Southern Review* 32 (Spring 1996): 373–89.

40. Perhaps the distinction was as simple as "open narratives" and "open interpretations."

41. For an example of a critic pointing his finger at post-modernism for a historian's experiment, see Howard N. Rabinowitz, "The Origins of a Poststructural New South: A Review of Edward L. Ayers' *The Promise of the New South: Life After Reconstruction,*" *Journal of Southern History* 59 (August 1993): 505–15.

42. See, for example, Wood, "Star-Spangled History"; Masur, "On Parkman's Trail"; Drew Gilpin Faust, "Inquisition in Mississippi," *New York Times Book Review* (May 9, 1993), 29; C. Andrew Gerstle, review of *Mirror in the Shrine, Journal of Asian Studies* 48 (November 1989): 876–77; Dan McLeod, review of *Mirror in the Shrine, New England Quarterly* 62 (December 1989): 594–98; Janet Buell Rogers, review of *Unredeemed Captive, New England Quarterly* 68 (September 1995): 483–87; Richard White, "Family Ties," *New Republic* 210 (June 13, 1994): 48–52; Edward L. Ayers, "Prisms and Prisons," *New Republic* 211 (July 11, 1994): 36–38; Robert P. Ingalls, review of *Stories of Scottsboro, American Historical Review* 100 (October 1995): 1322; Brook Thomas, "Ineluctable Though Uneven: On Experimental Historical Narrative," *Common Knowledge* 5 (Winter 1996): 163–88; and James Goodman, "Stealing Sheetrock," *Georgia Historical Quarterly* 76 (Winter 1992): 862–75. There are, thankfully, numerous other examples. He also recognized bad criticism when he read it, including simpleminded or confused tirades against experimentation. Assuming that other readers recognized bad criticism too, he saw no reason to name names.

Louis P. Masur

"What It Will Take to Turn Historians into Writers": From the *Chronicle of Higher Education* (2001)

Lou Masur is one of our most pithy historians. And writers.

His half dozen books of about 200 pages each qualified him to write *The Civil War: A Concise History*, which clocks in at 136 pages. The undeniably eloquent Shelby Foote needed 2,976 pages (in three volumes) to cover the same subject.

Sometimes, reading Masur, you might find yourself wanting more. You might start scribbling injunctions in the margins: "Develop this point!" "Elaborate!"

But then you might start hearing Masur's voice talking back to you as you do your own writing. "Do you really need that word? That sentence? That paragraph?"

No. Probably not.

I once read a review by Arthur M. Schlesinger Jr., at the end of which he described himself, or was described by the editors, as "an historian and a writer." The dual characterization struck me. Aren't all historians writers? Although neither Schlesinger nor the editors intended it, they had identified a meaningful difference.

An understanding of how academic historians differ from writers of history begins in the graduate reading seminar, where doctoral students are bombarded with professional narratives. Week after week, they are assigned lengthy books of historical argument and analysis. These are not intended to enlighten and move readers, but are aimed mainly at other scholars and focused largely on engaging what other professionals have already said.

Invariably, research is far more important than writing to academic historians. Their books are not so much designed to be read as to be skimmed. The guiding question is, "What does the author argue?" Books have to appear to say something new, to contribute to "the literature." Successful works become part of the historiography of a field and continue to be cited by other historians. The longer the better, since historians equate length with significance. The historiography game generates mountains of monographic work and rich academic rewards for those who play it well. But it rarely gives rise to works in which the art and craft of story-telling matter.

I came to graduate school in 1979 with a double major in history and English, and I never embraced the idea that contributing to historiography was the point of historical writing. To be sure, I learned the rules of the game, and I eventually passed my general examinations, where I had to recite the begats of various historiographic traditions. But those dense books never appealed to me. I wanted to be enveloped by primary sources—by the enduring voices and recorded actions of the past. Instead, my professors inundated me with secondary sources—the shout of academics making abstract arguments divorced from past experience and meaning. Graduate training may not always have been this way; but, with the deepening professionalization of academic life and the proliferation of books in the 1960's and 1970's, scholars turned historiography into a fetish. As if fearful of being contaminated by literature and creative-writing programs, they identified themselves as social scientists and migrated away from the humanities.

The effects of professionalization on any sense of history as a literary art have been catastrophic. Most academic historians publish books that are bloated with names, theses, and notes. They concentrate on explaining rather than showing, theorizing rather than describing. They think of themselves as historians working on problems, never as writers struggling every day to find the right words, voice, and structure.

Compared to academic historians, writers care about telling stories that illuminate the human experience. They use form to convey meaning, and seek to discover the truths of history through literary means. They write for themselves and hope, in so doing, to say something of value to others. In a letter to Walker Percy, Shelby Foote summarized the endeavor this way: "Most people think mistakenly that writers are people who have something to tell them. Nothing I think could be wronger. If I knew what I wanted to say I wouldn't write at all. What for? Why do it, if you already know the answers? Writing is the search for the answers, and the answer is in the form, the method of telling, the exploration of self, which is our only clew to reality."

Readers, like writers, need to search for answers. Part of the joy of literature is being surprised, but academic historians leave little to the imagination. The perniciousness of the historiographic turn became fully evident to me when I started teaching. Historians require undergraduates to read scholarly monographs that sap the vitality of history; they visit on students what was visited on them in graduate school. They assign books with formulaic arguments that transform history into an abstract debate that would have been unfathomable to those who lived in the past. Aimed so squarely at the head, such books cannot stimulate students who yearn to connect to history emotionally as well as intellectually.

I prefer that my students read histories that are crafted by writers—journalists, essayists, and those who work in a genre known as creative nonfiction. I'm thinking of people like John Barry, Melissa Fay Greene, John McPhee, Caryl Phillips, Luc Sante, Rebecca Solnit, and Lawrence Weschler. I also encourage my students to read novelists who use fiction as a means of contemplating historical truth: Julian Barnes, E. L. Doctorow, Toni Morrison, Tim O'Brien, or Philip Roth, for example. Such works complement the primary sources I assign, because they have the power to move readers with a turn of phrase, a dramatic scene, an angle of vision.

In the past decade, some academic historians have begun to rediscover stories. It has even become something of a fad within the profession. This year, the American Historical Association chose as the theme for its annual conference some putative connection to writing: "Practices of Historical Narrative." Predictably, historians responded by adding the word "narrative" to their titles and presenting papers at sessions on "Transnational Narratives of Race and Color," "Oral History and the Narrative of Class Identity," and "Meaning and Time: The Problem of Historical Narrative." But it was still historiography, intended only for other academics. At meetings of historians, we encounter very few writers talking about how they write, or reading from their work, or moving audiences to smiles, chills, or tears.

That is not to say that there are not dozens of academic historians who write well, offer valuable insights, and reach a general audience interested in nonfiction. Compared with scholarly writing in other disciplines, historians sometimes seem almost lyrical. Over the years, the *New York Times* best-seller list has included books by such scholars as Stephen E. Ambrose and James M. McPherson, writers adept at storytelling.

Far fewer in number, however, are those historians who write not only for an audience outside the academy, but also in self-consciously literary and artistic ways. Simon Schama's *Dead Certainties: Unwarranted Speculations* provides an example. It begins, "'Twas the darkness that did the trick, black as tar, that and the silence, though how the men contriv'd to clamber their way up the cliff with their musket and seventy round on their backs, I'm sure I don't know even though I saw it with my own eyes and did it myself before very long." Jonathan D. Spence's *The Death of Woman Wang* starts, "The earthquake struck T'an-ch'eng on July 25, 1668. It was evening, the moon just rising. There was no warning, save for a frightening roar that seemed to come from somewhere to the northwest. The buildings in the city began to shake and the trees took up a rhythmical swaying, tossing ever more wildly back and forth until their tips almost touched the ground."

There are signs as well that a younger generation of historians is willing to experiment with nonfiction that aspires to literary art. But, until the profession encourages and rewards those efforts, until more scholars start taking chances, academic historians will not become writers.

It is too soon to tell whether contemporary literary experiments, scattered as they are, will galvanize others. In 1990, I received a letter from Wallace Stegner, whose nonfiction works are as evocative as his fiction. He found the attitude of historians toward literary art puzzling. The interest in writing good history, he declared, "represents a tendency among historians that is always threatening to burst into bloom and produce some really splendid historical literature, but that habitually gets squashed down by the historical establishment. . . . It does so delight me when history as an art comes bulging through the covering tarpaulins that I wish it happened more often."

At various points throughout the 20th century, academics have denounced "dry-as-dust" writing (a favorite phrase of Columbia's Allan Nevins in the 1930's), and just as quickly the profession has staked off its academic ground more firmly. Without question, there is wide interest in history among a general audience: Best-seller lists and history programming on television suggest that this is a propitious moment for scholars to incorporate their skills in researching and reading texts with writing creative works of nonfiction.

To do so, they will have to stop thinking in terms of thesis and analysis. Instead, they will have to link themselves in a common endeavor with other writers. That will mean learning new ways to evaluate whether a story succeeds. That will mean trying to express the poetry that is the past. That will mean acknowledging the truth of Annie Dillard's dictum, dispensed in *The*

Writing Life, "It is no less difficult to write sentences in a recipe than sentences in *Moby-Dick.* So you might as well write *Moby-Dick.*"

In his recent autobiography, *A Life in the Twentieth Century,* Schlesinger talks about his career as a writer. It is not just that he has written some 15 books, countless essays and reviews, and numerous speeches as a ghostwriter for several presidents (in itself an act of ventriloquism that requires considerable skill). Schlesinger has also, throughout his life, done what most writers do—he has maintained a journal and forced himself to write every day. His father, a distinguished historian, once told him, "There is always a little thrill one gets from saying things well." For more than 70 years, Schlesinger informs us, that line "has lingered in my mind." Historians who strive to say things well—those are the ones on their way to becoming writers.

Aaron Sachs

"Letters to a Tenured Historian:
History as Creative Nonfiction—or Maybe Even Poetry"
From *Rethinking History* (2010)

Sometimes we historians, in explaining ourselves to the uninitiated, might note that our job entails reading other people's mail. Usually we're referring to primary sources.

This series of (fake) missives takes up the politics of writing artfully within the intensely hierarchical academy. Over the course of their short life, these letters have wound up offending some readers (usually older) and bolstering others (usually younger). Any offense was unintentional; it's the bolstering that matters.

After the most recent round of earthquakes, mudslides, and fires, when Southern California was finally abandoned, many of the collections of the Huntington Library were brought to the ever-expanding Capital Archive here in Winnipeg. A friend in the Manuscripts Division called our attention to a particular file labeled 'Historiography: Correspondence'—donated anonymously but compiled, we think, by a professional historian of an earlier time (textual evidence dates the materials to 2008 or 2009, just before the end of the paper era). The strange thing about one set of 'letters' in the file is that they are printed continuously, on plain paper (rather than letterhead), as if meant to be taken together and read like an essay. We here at the Journal, as we flipped through these moldering leaves, felt somewhat frustrated at not being able to see the other half of the dialogue—if the letters are anything, they are one-sided, as it were, though whoever printed them used double-sided printing—but then we realized that there probably never was a real correspondent.

Who would write such fake epistles, and footnote them, to boot? And was it the author himself who printed and filed them, or some friend or acquaintance who received them on email, or perhaps a curious stranger who downloaded them from a blog? We can't even venture a guess. Nor do we embrace the letters' 'argument,' which seems to us divided between a familiar critique of academic writing and a loose-minded complaint about academic hierarchy. Yet we have chosen to publish them here as telling historical curiosities. We presume that our readership will agree that these letters at the very least present us with a snapshot of academic culture in the early twenty-first century, a time of important transitions, filled with its share of turmoil. As the letters remind us, it was an era of small, radical journals—like *Rethinking History*, whose full paper run we actually have here at our offices; perhaps these old issues might prove to be grist for a valuable dissertation?

Winnipeg, September 2049

Try to love *the questions themselves*.
(Rainier Maria Rilke, *Letters to a Young Poet*)[1]

LETTER 1

Dear Sir or Madam,

Thank you for your application to be my mentor in the writing of history. The response to my job posting was overwhelming—especially given how little I was offering in the way of remuneration. There were hundreds of qualified applicants. I am heartened to know that you, and so many of our colleagues, share my interest in the problem of how to be both a historian and a writer at the same time.

Unfortunately, while I found all the applications quite impressive by every traditional academic standard, I was not actually *moved* by any of them. A publisher might say that the proposals just didn't fit with the house's current agenda. In any case, much to my regret, I have, for the moment, decided to leave the position unfilled.

Again, I am grateful for your interest in the job, and for the time and energy you put into the rigorous application process. Your desire to serve as a mentor is one I admire and appreciate. I wish you the best of luck in fulfilling it.

Sincerely,
Your Junior Colleague

LETTER 2

Dear Senior Colleague,

Thank you for writing back. Of course, I can't agree with you that my letter was 'mean-spirited,' let alone 'smarmy,' but clearly the joke went awry. Forgive me. I did not intend to set unrealistic standards for the writing of history nor to express scorn for the entire body of historical scholarship produced in the last 40 years.

In all honesty, the letter was a rhetorical device. I was hoping it would suggest the inadequacy of formulaic writing. I'm sorry to have made the point seemingly at your expense. What I am lamenting, ultimately, is that so many professional histories seem to be produced like form letters, and especially that graduate students are so often taught to be fearful of any deviation from the formula.

I fully realize that there are many sympathetic scholars out there, so in that sense my letter was disingenuous: I can think of several I would hire instantly. (If you'd like a listing, just ask—assuming you're willing to write to me again. I hope you are.) But I've already approached many of the sympathetic ones, and even they tend to take the pragmatic attitude that people like me should simply 'wait until tenure' to write the way we want to. Pay our dues, play it safe, produce the first monograph according to the formula—and then get creative. That in many ways is solid advice, meant to protect our long-term interests. But it is also crushing, in the same way that it's crushing to receive a formulaic rejection. I am deeply grateful to those sympathetic professors, but why couldn't they, after warning us of the dangers, nevertheless support us in our desire to write against the formula, now, at the start of our careers? As the literary critic Marjorie Garber recently asked, 'Why can't scholars write their second books first?'[2] If we have our wings tied for six years as grad students, and then six to ten more as post-docs, adjuncts, and assistant professors, how many of us are suddenly going to be able to soar once we get tenure?

I want to acknowledge right away that, thanks to people like Professor Garber and my own advisers, I got to write the book I wanted to write. (Thanks also, probably, to my academic experience at certain kinds of schools; I, too, have benefited from The System—though I also think I benefited from spending a few years outside The System, developing my voice as a writer.) There are clearly openings in the history profession for scholars trying to write creatively. But there are also strong pressures still driving young historians toward established conventions, pressures that go beyond personal opinions to the deep structures of the profession and the discipline. Every single graduate student I have ever spoken to has acknowledged that he or she feels compelled to write according to a particular formula; some are perfectly at peace with that state of affairs, and others chafe against it. I want more space for young historians to be true to their personal vision of history—which also, I think, will mean the production of more professional history writing that could touch the lives of a broader range of readers.[3]

I almost dropped out of graduate school myself, because the books were killing me. Sometimes, they had impressive arguments, and the jack-hammer prose, even if somewhat predictable, fit well with the author's approach. Lumped together, though, those works of history produced a picture of a discipline that seemed mechanistic in its structural and tonal uniformity. There was clearly a template—and, in my courses, the template was being celebrated. Here: follow this set of rules. The more precisely you follow them, with regard to both writing *and* reading, the more successful you will be in this profession. Everything can be boiled down. Wake up, eat your breakfast, pick up a book, mine it for an hour or two, and complete your 500-word review by lunchtime.

I had gone to the academy seeking an alternative to the rat race, and I found myself getting trained according to a Taylorist model of industrial production (and consumption). I did learn a great deal of history. And I gradually began to understand the system. Maybe all the authors *expected* to get skimmed. Some of them clearly warmed to the template, and templates may well be necessary for the maintenance of a discipline. Moreover, given the proliferation of scholarship, the fetishization of clarity, especially in a book's Introduction, made a certain sense. Indeed, a bold, sweeping, clearly articulated argument right at the beginning of a book can be quite exhilarating. I even came to respect the intellectual labor of 'covering' a field, of dipping into as many books as possible and figuring out how to put them in conversation with one another. Yet I constantly found myself yearning, in the midst of all this breadth, for some complementary depth. Even more, I missed the pleasure of reading, really reading, becoming immersed in the flow of a book.

The emphasis on clearly stated arguments often results in schematic writing, based on social science models. There is no hope of immersion when you're reading an Introduction in which each of the book's chapters is outlined in a paragraph. Most 'signposts' seem to be open invitations to skim. Of course, it has lately become almost fashionable to embrace skimming as a justifiable and even creative act. We skim in order to have at least a passing familiarity with everything in our field, rather than risk the distraction of getting wrapped up in the particulars of just a few books. Skimming is democratic! Maybe skimming becomes necessary sometimes, in the context of both research and teaching. But it makes for a rather superficial intellectual culture—don't you think?[4]

Anyway, I knew myself well enough to realize that I would never, as an author, be happy to get skimmed. I read every word on every page when I started grad school because I felt I owed it to the author and because I thought of books as works of art, and I eventually wanted to write artful history, history that was broadly relevant and humanistic. But I was being trained to follow a narrow, scholastic formula—and to lie about what I had 'read.'

I must admit that I started to feel a tinge of resentment toward certain Tenured Historians. If they liked the template, I could live with that, but did so many people in the discipline really have to follow it so precisely? Did it have to be imposed in every seminar, at every conference panel, in every dissertation defense, in every peer review? Artists need to learn skills and disciplines, too, but they are encouraged to innovate from a relatively early stage; scholars of history get taught to adhere for years to *de facto* formal models developed by the loose 'community' of academic historians. I wanted to write a dissertation that conformed to my own vision, wanted license to stretch conventions. I tried to bow my head and think of myself as an apprentice, a trainee—but I couldn't. I wanted mentors, not masters.[5]

I was lucky to find them. Perhaps you could have been one, too? Or perhaps not. I hope you won't be offended if I propose the unlikelihood of our compatibility. You have, after all, gone on record insisting that history and art are incommensurable. Listen: I would not be writing you this letter if I didn't care about your opinion. The question is whether I can explain my critique without provoking indignation.

My goal is to express myself forcefully yet without appearing so polemical as to seem unreasonable. Such a writing challenge, in my view, is not ultimately so different from the challenge of writing fresh history. Theoretically, I think we all want history that is both grounded and provocative. But our professional guild—for all its industrial-style production, it is still a guild—tends to err on the side of groundedness.

Despite our dedication to critical rigor, we often have simple knee-jerk reactions to books written in styles that are not immediately recognizable as academic: they rub our sensibilities the wrong way. If the argument seems too political or the narrative too lively, we almost automatically start to wonder if the author might be either unreliable or unserious.[6] We depend on formulas. It's hard to imagine many graduate advisers proposing that a student try to write a journal article that did not conform to the classic journal article template.[7]

Meanwhile, I am clearly 'off formula.' I hope that you're still reading this letter, but I fear you may already have decided that my tone is far too precious. I have probably tried your patience. All I can say is that what may seem precious to you may be necessary for me. Can I ask you to trust me, for now, that I have solid reasons for writing in this style, and in this form?

Respectfully,

Your Junior Colleague

LETTER 3

Dear Senior Colleague,

Fair enough: I haven't yet earned your trust. I fell back on another rhetorical device at the end of my last letter. I just wanted to be sure you'd write again. You call it a cop-out; I call it arousal.

I don't believe that refusals and silences are necessarily deficiencies. Uncertainty can create an instructive tension. A more indirect, poetic mode of writing can force readers to question their deepest assumptions.

I'm thinking, in particular, of the distinction drawn by Giacomo Leopardi between words (parole) and terms (termini). As the scholar of Italian literature Robert Pogue Harrison has explained, himself using an intriguing mixture of words and terms, parole 'preserve their metaphorical and sensory prehistory, conveying in their etymons and phonemes a host of accessory images, indefinite connotations, and tropological associations'; termini 'are abstract, univocal, often scientific locutions that have no such recessive draw.' Poets tend to be attracted to words, while scholars often prefer terms. That preference perhaps helps scholars to delineate more precisely what their discipline is seeking to accomplish. With the same goal in mind, they are more likely to tell than to show, to define than to suggest, to fill in than to leave out. But this approach entails a significant sacrifice—one I'm not sure scholars, and especially historians, should be so willing to make. 'For all their referential precision,' Harrison says, 'termini lack the parola's genetic bond between word, world, memory, and time. They denote but do not, as it were, arouse.'[8]

Of course, in a sense, you're right: my last letter was meant to be provocative, and now I owe you some grounding. Arousal is not sufficient; indeed, it can sometimes block understanding. So let me marshal my evidence. Let me also note at the outset, however, that I have no expectation of definitively proving any point. I worry that you will disapprove of my sample size, my selection criteria, my collation of the data, my failure to define my terms, and, not least, my interpretations. Well, I don't believe simply that I'm right and you're wrong, nor do I wish to convert you. All I ask is that you continue to withhold your verdict—that you accept some slight discomfort—that you open the door to doubt.

Forthwith, three raw data sets, each comprising three quotations, with explanations to follow, though not before you have a chance to formulate your own interpretive framework.

Category 1

1. This book has developed from a study that was first undertaken a number of years ago, when Howard Mumford Jones, then Editor-in-Chief of the John Harvard Library, invited me to prepare a collection of pamphlets of the American Revolution for publication in that series.

2. The question of nationality—of 'identity'—has stalked Afro-American history from its colonial beginnings, when the expression 'a nation within a nation' was already being heard . . . In this book I refer to the 'black nation' and argue that the slaves, as an objective social class, laid the foundations for a separate black national culture while enormously enriching American culture as a whole.

3. Popular folklore of the Great Depression often celebrates how Americans, as individuals, coped with the greatest economic calamity in the nation's history, how they delayed planned marriages, sustained themselves with home gardens, and perhaps most notoriously, sold apples on street corners. But all too often these tales overlook the more political and collective responses many people made.

Category 2

4. On July 2, 1946, Medgar Wylie Evers celebrated his twenty-first birthday by leading a group of World War II veterans, including his brother Charles, through the nearly abandoned streets of Decatur, Mississippi.

5. At 7:00 p.m. EWT (Eastern War Time) on August 14, 1945, President Harry Truman announced to a packed press conference that World War II had ended.

6. October 2, 1904, Night. North Clifton, Arizona. When the posse arrived at Margarita Chacon's house at 11 p.m. on this rainy night, George Frazer, superintendent of the copper smelter, banged on the door with the butt of his Winchester.

Category 3

7. This book was undertaken for a selfish and private reason: I wanted to see the plains again.
8. Eight months of the year Hallowell, Maine, was a seaport.
9. In March northern Florida is blessed with azure skies, shirt-sleeve-warm days, and best of all, the transporting perfume of orange blossoms wafted upon gentle breezes.

So: what do you make of my data?

Categorically,
Your Junior Colleague

LETTER 4

Dear Senior Colleague,

I understand your desire to withhold comment for now. But you're of course correct that the quotations come from the beginnings of nine different history books. Those books do have one thing in common, besides being the work of professional historians: they all happen to have won the annual Bancroft Prize, awarded by Columbia University for excellence in American history, sometime in the last 40 years.[9]

Which immediately—and productively, I hope—raises the question: how do we historians define 'excellence'?

I do not intend, by analyzing Bancroft winners, to further the academic fetishization of prizes, awards, and other distinctions. Our profession is already too hierarchical. Nor am I plotting simply to undermine the value of the Bancroft Prize by wagging my finger and claiming that even these alleged examples of excellence leave much to be desired. On the contrary, I value all of them as rich, path-breaking histories. Specifically because I think almost all professional historians would be inclined to agree on the merits of the *research* in these particular books, I'm hoping it will be that much easier to focus on how the books are *written*.

Still, if it is clearly unfair to judge a book by its cover, is it any fairer to judge a book by its opening lines? No, unequivocally. But I am not proposing to judge these books individually; my interest is in patterns. If the opening lines cannot be said to be representative of the way the whole book is written, they may at least suggest what the author wanted our first substantive impression to be. Opening lines matter, palpably, both to authors and to readers. So: what might they reveal, when grouped together in various classes?

I think they often tell us, directly or indirectly, how to think about the author's relationship to her material. My 'Category 1' quotations, for instance, all serve to frame research questions, thereby signaling the authors' desire, in my interpretation, to have their readers understand these books principally in terms of their contribution to a certain scholarly field. I trust you still have my previous letter? Well, then you can see that the Category 1 authors are at pains, from the outset, to delineate what their books are, and what they are not; what lacunae they fill; what kinds of method and data they are built on; where they stand in relation to other well-known works. These works are meant to be judged primarily as worthy research projects. After all, that ultimately seems to be the principal way in which academics define excellence and evaluate their peers—the quality of the research determines promotions—and so it comes as no surprise that the vast majority of Bancroft-winning books fall within this grouping. It was easy to find works that started this way: there were multiple examples from each of the last four decades. According to my evaluation of the data, then, the three quotations in Category 1 represent what the history profession values most: clear, precise demarcations of how you're chipping in, definitions of your research terms.

The quotations in Category 2, though, represent a different trend in recent historical writing. They are the equivalent of 'Once upon a time.' Since they are all written by professional scholars, you can be sure that there are important research questions to be addressed in them, that they will eventually get around to revealing a key historiographical contribution. Meanwhile, though, the first impression they give is that you are meant to be stirred in more than just rational ways. Their authors would like you to get swept up in a story.

This kind of opening was not nearly so easy to find as the Category 1 type, but I did have a number to choose from. In the end, I took all of my examples from the last 15 years, the period that clearly had the greatest concentration of narrative-oriented Bancroft winners. This trend would seem to bode well for the history profession, from the perspective of anyone who cares about writing. Indeed, these openers reveal authors working actively to depart from the safe template of academic prose, and innovation in form is always welcome. The sentences have been constructed with great care: these three writers clearly value rhythm, drive, resonance, and a richness of detail, and they have taught themselves how to achieve these effects. Of course, this kind of approach to history is not exactly new, but I think it does mark a shift in the profession away from the dominant social-science model of the New Social History, especially as practiced in the 1960s and 70s. Or, it could mark a shift away from the jargon-filled prose of the 'linguistic turn' in history that developed in the 80s and early 90s. In any case, a new market seemed to develop in the 90s for a kind of history that could appeal both to scholars, forever enamored of arguments, and to the broader reading audience of well-educated story-lovers.[10]

When I consider the three openers in Category 2 individually, I quite like them—don't you? As a group, though—as a trend—they seem somewhat disappointing, despite the freshness they evoke in comparison to the more traditional Category 1 openers.[11] I realize I have stacked the deck with my selections, but I think it's quite representative of this new historiographical tendency that these openers' themes verge on the melodramatic: we're dealing, in Category 2, with racial confrontations, war, peace, and the threat of violence. In addition, each of these works starts off by locating an event, with a straightforward declarative sentence, on a specific date in the past, possibly lending readers the comforting feeling that history really does spin out in a simple, linear fashion, from one significant occurrence to the next.[12] Most of the literary devices employed in these sentences are strictly conventional, if not old-fashioned: they create an obvious narrative tension—the streets are eerily empty, the posse enraged—that calls to mind the novels of Dickens or Bronte or Kipling rather than of Woolf or Faulkner or Rushdie. As long ago as the late 1970s, some observers were finding evidence of a 'new narrative' thrust in the writing of history, but if this narrative form seems 'new,' then we need more studies of the history of the writing of history.[13] To my twenty-first-century eye, the 150-year-old narrative histories of Romantics such as Francis Parkman, George Bancroft (*not* the Bancroft of the Bancroft Prize), and Jacob Burckhardt all seem in many ways to display more authorial self-consciousness about method than many of the 'straight' narratives being produced today.[14]

Fortunately for us, we have Category 3. I don't mean that my Category 3 examples are inherently better than those in the other categories. Indeed, Categories 1 and 2 both serve crucial purposes. In my ideal intellectual world, every discipline would manage to celebrate a great diversity of approaches to knowledge and understanding. But what I see in these Category 3 openers—about the plains, Maine, and northern Florida—is evidence that serious, epistemologically self-conscious history can take on the qualities of art. And that is a beautiful thing. Let me be clear from the beginning of this argument: I am not suggesting that all history should be written this way. I just want to open up the possibility that *more* history *could* be, if professional historians made more of an effort to appreciate and then to teach this approach, instead of throwing up the barricades and defining 'legitimate' history in increasingly narrow ways. 'Humanist, quantifier, what you will,' wrote the geographer O.H.K. Spate, 'it is never wrong to plug your own line; it is almost always wrong to write off others.'[15]

(An aside: It is of course difficult to find the kind of negative evidence necessary to prove that creative approaches to history are being squashed, but I think any professor who speaks regularly and openly with graduate students will have heard them remark upon the homogenizing pressures of the profession. Much of the appropriate evidence may also be hidden within the insidious framework of 'peer review,' where historians regularly feel free to take anonymous potshots at any scholar who doesn't seem to accept what they see as the [always ill-defined] Professional Code of Conduct. If I had more space [and perhaps the help of a social-science historian], I would embark on a systematic rhetorical analysis of the book reviews published in our more esteemed journals, attempting to show that the language of evaluation we use implicitly circumscribes the range of 'good history.' [One immediate measure might be simply to ban adjectives like 'definitive,' 'comprehensive,' and 'authoritative.'] Anyway, as Dominick LaCapra has put it, we generally still award 'the greatest prestige . . . to the historian who revises standard accounts on the basis of massive archival research'.)[16]

A Francophile such as LaCapra would say that we should return to our sheep, but sheep is precisely what the historians in Category 3 are not. The author of the first Category 3 opener gleefully commits a cardinal sin, not only by employing what Gibbon called 'the most disgusting of pronouns' but also by offering a motivation not intellectual and pure but 'selfish' and 'private.'[17] This historian is not simply attempting to put forward truth claims on behalf of the past. Rather, he is making a disclosure about his relationship to his topic, and the somewhat poetic longing he expresses gives such a shock of incongruity—this book, remember, is written by an academic, a professional, an expert—that I find myself more drawn in than I often am by even the most compelling narrative openers.

In the Maine quotation, the author makes an observation that becomes more and more intriguing: it is a simple declarative sentence, yet it suggests much more than it actually says. It spurs the reader to think about seasons, geography, weather, commerce. While a traditional narrative hook certainly makes you curious to hear more, this kind of tantalization literally transforms you into a participant in an intellectual discussion. It simultaneously tells a story and makes analytical assertions.[18]

My last choice for Category 3, taken from a very recent book (one of the 2007 prizewinners), actually enacts the kind of relationship with a place that is only alluded to in the opener about the plains. This author is in love with Northern Florida. The sensual, emotional, opinionated prose ('best of all' is a phrase most 'disinterested' historians would shy away from) personalizes the writer and welcomes the reader to a party. There is a joy here that is not to be found in most history books. And while I can't praise every decision this author made (I assume I am not alone in having had enough of perfumes wafting on gentle breezes), I find the phrase 'shirt-sleeve-warm days' to be absolutely entrancing. Some books feel like work; this one feels like spring break.

It was not easy to find these three openers, and I'd be hard pressed to extract even one more that I'd want to put in this category. But, for me, they are powerful evidence of a potential affinity between historical and writerly impulses. I find all three to be surprising and stimulating, and these are the qualities in writing that always make me want to read on. What I think their authors have in common, besides an interest in history, is a commitment to adopt the concerns and techniques of twentieth-century fiction—or, perhaps more appropriately, to write in the genre of what in the last 15 years or so has come to be called creative nonfiction. There's no easy way to define this genre, but, for starters, it's a fluid mode that sometimes seems to blur the boundary between fiction and fact and yet ultimately has a profound respect for truthtelling. Here's how it's described by the editor of the pioneering journal (*Creative Nonfiction*, founded in 1993) that solidified the genre's name:

> Dramatic, true stories using scenes, dialogue, close, detailed descriptions and other techniques usually employed by poets and fiction writers about important subjects—from politics, to economics, to sports, to the arts and sciences, to racial relations, and family relations.

> Creative Nonfiction heightens the whole concept and idea of essay writing. It allows a writer to employ the diligence of a reporter, the shifting voices and viewpoints of a novelist, the refined wordplay of a poet and the analytical modes of the essayist.

> We want the essays we publish in *Creative Nonfiction* to have purpose and meaning beyond the experiences related by the writers. Good essays embrace a larger audience. They strike a universal chord.[19]

I guess the fundamental question is whether such a genre is compatible with the academic discipline of history. Can history be art? Would we even want it to be? I know how you've responded to the first question in the past; is that your final answer?

Rhetorically,
Your Junior Colleague

LETTER 5

Dear Senior Colleague,

I'm not surprised by your insistence, and I agree with you that you are probably in the majority (at least in professional circles). Yet I still don't understand precisely *why* it seems to you so crucial to distinguish between history and art. I worry about the danger of claiming that there is only one kind of good history (the authoritative account of what happened in the past) and that artfulness is nothing but relativism—especially without working definitions of 'authoritative' and 'relative.' As one historical epistemologist has recently commented, 'historians are among the most untheoretical of scholars, and so the rules [of the discipline] are often not articulated in an explicit way.' We say we know good history when we see it and then excuse ourselves to go back to the archives. Indeed, a number of our colleagues simply refer to a kind of positivism as their default methodological philosophy: they 'still cling to logical empiricist dicta of many decades ago and trot them out whenever they want to appear rigorous and methodological.'[20] Some of them even take the next step of applying those dicta in order to dismiss whichever works of history strike them as too artistic and therefore relativistic.

But why? One might perhaps explain this trend in three different ways: historically, sociologically, and epistemologically. The first two categories are closely connected and can, I think, be dispensed with relatively quickly.

In the late nineteenth-century rush toward professionalization, 'new' historians in the United States had to distinguish themselves from the Romantic men of letters who dominated the field. Most of the freshly minted professionals, therefore, inspired by Leopold von Ranke, defined history as a science. While all Romantic historians came to be seen as self-indulgent and ideology-driven aesthetes, scientific historians claimed to sacrifice everything to the god of Objectivity, an abstract disciplinary ideal that, in practice, conflated empiricism, neutrality, rationalism, universalism, and Whiggishness—not to mention a disavowal of anything that smacked of 'style.' Substance made the man.[21]

For the first half of the twentieth century, 'substance' entailed both disciplinary method and convergence in research topics: all serious historians were supposed to examine the record from a god's-eye view with no preconceived agenda, and yet the only questions they ultimately seemed to comment on were how and why white males of European descent had created such progressive, liberal societies. Occasionally, a skeptical voice—like Carl Becker's, declaring 'everyman his own historian' in 1932[22]–challenged various aspects of Objectivity, but as the profession exploded demographically in the post-World-War-II era, its American practitioners clearly established themselves as rigorous, scientific-minded leaders in the public discourse of consensus. Of course, that demographic explosion then became a key force driving the 1960s trend toward fragmentation in professional research agendas. Conflict began to replace consensus as scholars legitimated a wide array of new subjects— women, slaves, workers, immigrants—in their attempt to write history 'from the bottom up.' But if the new breed of historians repudiated their forefathers' belief in a single, universal History, they actually glorified Ranke's generation when it came to methodological doctrine. Perhaps anxious to shore up their own authority to explore areas and perspectives that had long been considered marginal, or perhaps just enamored of the quantitative potential of the ascendant social sciences, they tended to frame their books primarily as presentations of carefully collected evidence or data sets—and to demonize the prose of leading consensus historians like Perry Miller and Richard Hofstadter as being far too smooth. In the classroom, they were politically engaged, but in their scholarship they evinced a disinterested focus on the simple, choppy realities of the past. Now it was method alone that defined the true historian. As the always-diplomatic Christopher Lasch put it, 'radical historians,' struggling to be taken seriously as 'partners in the scholarly enterprise,' eagerly demonstrated 'their willingness to observe the prevailing conventions and to write books that were just as narrow, tedious, and predictable as the books written by their ideological opponents.'[23] Actually, many of the old consensus histories were quite broad, lively, and surprising compared to much of the new social history.

Of course, the more recent rise of the new *cultural* history has brought with it further shifts in professional self-positioning,[24] but the sociological pressures on academic historians have remained fairly constant over the last four decades. If a young scholar wants to succeed in this business, he can't look anything like the Romantic historians of the 1850s (too literary and therefore too hegemonic) or the consensus historians of the 1950s (too hegemonic and therefore too literary). Sadly, dear colleague, I feel obliged to point out that you and your cohort, while eager to criticize hegemony in history, have often failed to confront hegemonic patterns within the historical profession. You've taught several waves of graduate students to be extremely conservative in their research methods and their writing, and when any of these young scholars have chafed against such limitations, you've tended to dismiss them as 'soft' and to ask them, 'Well, what book do you have in mind as a model?'[25]—and by 'book' you've always meant 'book written by an authoritative academic historian in the last 40 years.' In short, as Foucault might suggest, I worry that your insistence on the sharp distinction between history and art might ultimately represent an effort to Discipline your junior colleagues. While it is to be expected that some professional historians will continue to embrace positivism and to define themselves as social scientists rather than humanists, it would be tragic if the legitimacy of those choices continued closing off other legitimate approaches to history.

So much for history and sociology—but there remains the very serious question of epistemology. Is it possible that art and history simply have too different an orientation toward knowledge and truth to be compatible? Is the aesthetic model inherently irresponsible, self-indulgent?

Consider that the epistemologists themselves did away with positivism decades ago; that, according to a good 30 years of postmodernist theory, to define one's terms is merely to offer an idealized (or fictive) construction of an uncontainably messy reality; that philosophers of history from Michel de Certeau to Hayden White to Dominick LaCapra have all agreed on the need to acknowledge that a massive portion of the past is simply unknowable, that most of the gaps on the maps will never be filled in, that history will always involve a tension between the struggle to represent the truth and the truth of absence and darkness.[26] One reason for our abiding interest in the foreign country that is the past, as White puts it, is that 'historicality itself is both reality and mystery.'[27] We are enraptured by the problem of trying to recapture what may or may not be lost in the press of time. 'Saying *true* things about the past is easy,' writes F. R. Ankersmit; '—anybody can do that.'[28] What makes for compelling history, though, is a dogged effort to explore the border of the unknowable territory.[29]

All of which makes history seem a lot like art. In a recent book called *A field guide to getting lost,* the writer Rebecca Solnit, who has identified herself variously as a historian, an art critic, and simply an essayist, asserts that 'it is the job of artists to invite in prophesies, the unknown, the unfamiliar.'[30]

In doing such a job, an artist cannot afford to be formulaic. The novelist—and historian—Wallace Stegner once tried to explain his approach to art by distinguishing himself from a highly successful but somewhat robotic short-story writer whom he encountered when he was young. This author

> had nothing *but* method. He wrote from an unvarying blueprint . . . There was no fire in his belly, no passion or vision or doubt in his mind, no penetration or challenge in what he wrote. He illuminated nothing, opened no windows, left no worm of wonder working in his readers' heads.[31]

Would we expect Stegner to have adopted an unvarying blueprint when he turned, as he often did, from fiction to nonfiction? I recently read what is sometimes referred to as his autobiography, *Wolf Willow*.[32] In fact, the book is a conscientious blend of memoir, history, and fiction about life on the north-western plains (where Stegner spent part of his childhood) in the early twentieth century. He starts off with memory and all its gaps and questions, then moves to a fairly traditional form of history, though he himself never quite disappears from the narrative, and though he substitutes the fictional name 'Whitemud' for the actual name of the town he grew up in, Eastend; and then, 138 pages in, he says that 'if we want to know what it was like on the Whitemud River range during that winter when the hopes of a cattle empire died, we had better see it through the eyes of some tenderfoot, perhaps someone fresh from the old country, a boy without the wonder rubbed off him and with something to prove about himself'—at which point Stegner proceeds to launch a novella about the disillusionment of a cowboy, who is a stand-in for himself, and, perhaps, for the entire mythicized story of western settlement.

In a brief postscript, Stegner admits the possibility that in *Wolf Willow* he has 'occasionally warped fact a little in order to reach for the fictional or poetic truth that I would rank a little above history.' But I'm not sure that says exactly what he meant. Even if there are sections of the book that are more clearly history or fiction, the entire thing was based on loads of primary-source evidence—and was also filtered through the creative imagination of a writer reaching for significance beyond those documents. It's not so much a matter of making sharp distinctions between historical and poetic truth and ranking one higher than the other. Rather, the book itself suggests to me a belief that no traditional, narrowly defined discipline or genre is ever sufficient, that, in fact, if history sometimes looked a little more like poetry, no one would ever be tempted to diminish its stature. *Wolf Willow,* then, stands as a testament to the fundamental human need to wrestle with the past—and powerfully suggests the value of experimenting with different grips and holds.[33]

Inconclusively,
Your Junior Colleague

LETTER 6

Dear Senior Colleague,

You honestly can't see past Stegner's 'errors of fact and interpretation'? But *why,* exactly? What's at stake here? Even the most fact-based history gets re-written by every subsequent generation.

If we're going to close our profession to people like Stegner, we had better know precisely what we're defending. What's the opposite of 'errors'?

While wrestling with you in these letters, I have also been grappling with a brand-new book by Allan Megill, called *Historical knowledge, historical error: A contemporary guide to practice.* It represents a welcome invitation to all historians to come to grips with what is most crucial, epistemologically speaking, about our discipline. Why are disciplinary boundaries necessary?

I find it notable that Megill leaves room in professional history for description, narrative, presentism, political bias, speculation, and mystery—especially mystery. I should also emphasize Megill's insistence that history has no single authorized method, and that we should always question our own theoretical assumptions, confront the inevitable fictionality of our work, and look outside the discipline for alternative approaches.[34] Yet his book is infused with a conviction that the discipline itself is still necessary, because, if I read him correctly, it is an effective spur to epistemological responsibility, a check on personal excess, a reminder that if you're not struggling with unknowability, then you're verging on hubris. Megill's refrain is a plea to put a record of that struggle into your history, to be clear about the constant necessary process of assessing evidence, of constructing and dismantling arguments—to prove, in effect, that you have acknowledged your own personal commitments or biases and then worked to achieve some measure of distance from them.[35]

In this light, the narratives in *Wolf Willow* do begin to seem too easy and smooth, so Megill might well agree with you, and suggest that they 'are better seen as subjective encounters with the past than as history.' But I think it's also possible that he would give Stegner credit for being more honest than most historians about his uncertainty, for having 'a greater humility and reflexiveness with regard to the interpretation of the past.'[36] While *Wolf Willow* may suffer from its lack of footnotes, it does effectively convey the reality of an author trying absolutely everything he can think of to make sense of a particular time and place, from as many different perspectives as possible. He knows his memory is flawed; he knows the documents are limited in scope and reliability. It's just that most of Stegner's struggle with the material of the past is implied rather than explicitly explained. You have to read the entire book, word by word, with a vigilant commitment to interpretation, if you want to get the point. You can't just skim the Introduction.

That may sound harsh, and if so I apologize, but I was trying to hint at a very real problem plaguing this whole debate. Megill's epistemological responsibility seems to me to have more to do with research and the conceptualization of arguments than with the actual form of the writing. Isn't it possible to establish the same sense of responsibility through suggestion as through declaration? While many historians worry that messing with the disciplinary formula would send us spiraling into relativism, the epistemologists seem to be saying that formal experiments could actually serve to strengthen the discipline's validity. The problem is that many historians are used to reading books only on a surface level, to treating them only as containers of information. Engaging with subtlety and suggestiveness takes a lot of time and energy, not to mention a different set of skills, and for that reason alone it could be seen as incompatible with professional history, since we professionals already have a lot of legitimate demands on our time and energy.

'Art,' as Albert Camus once noted, 'has impulses of discretion. It cannot say things directly.' Historians, meanwhile, tend to place the highest value on a clear, straightforward presentation. As Susan Sontag put it, though, 'there is no neutral, absolutely transparent style. . . . What Roland Barthes calls "the zero degree of writing" is, precisely by being anti-metaphorical and dehumanized, as selective and artificial as any [other kind of prose].'[37]

Not every history book should be a *Wolf Willow*. But what someone like Stegner does for us, when he is included in the ranks of historians, is force us to think explicitly about writing as a problem rather than a given, and especially to think about finding a form that is appropriate to our content. He suggests to us that form itself can convey meaning. Poetry can be lyric, epic, even narrative; why should there be only one kind of history writing? If you'd like to stick to the templates of Categories 1 and 2, those options are clearly available, but someone like Stegner pushes us into the surprising, mysterious, and experimental zone of Category 3. He reminds us that the effective combination of content and form, as practiced by poets for millennia, has the power to leave readers not just intellectually impressed but also aroused, moved, transformed.

Hopefully,
Your Junior Colleague

LETTER 7

Dear Senior Colleague,

I appreciate your objections. You're right: most historians simply aren't poets. The two groups usually do have different talents and inclinations these days. But not always. I'd wager that there are even a number of historians who have written poems. Have you? I have. I realize that most of mine deserve to stay buried in my most private boxes and drawers: I'm not saying that historians will ever have an *easy* time writing poetically.[38] Nor am I suggesting that we should abandon the groundedness of our discipline—not entirely, anyway.[39] What I do believe is that poetry and history—or art and science, or emotion and reason—are not as far apart as we tend to think.

Many of us turn to poetry in times of need, when haunted by death or war or depression, or at moments marked by joy and hope. Why should such concerns be so far outside the realm of history writing?[40] When the historian Jules Michelet was composing the end of a chapter about how villages in France celebrated the first Bastille Day, he admitted—inserting himself directly into the historical narrative—that his own spirits had been rising dramatically as he'd been writing, but that now, as he reached the moment when the parties were dying down, he found himself in despair: 'I leave here an irreparable moment of my life, a part of myself, which, I plainly feel, will remain here and accompany me no more: I seem to depart poor and needy.'[41] The thing is, no such emotional investment in history, on the part of either writer or reader, is ever possible when history is addressed only to analytic and explicatory concerns, and only to experts in the field.

Robert Pinsky, poet laureate of the United States during the late 1990s, once wrote a book of creative nonfiction called *Poetry and the world*, in which he agonized over the competing claims of aesthetics and social engagement. The conflict is a difficult one: much overtly political literature is also didactic, or, in Camus's terms, indiscreet. It doesn't fire the imagination. But Pinsky is determined to forge a reconciliation between poetry and the world—or, for our purposes, between poetry and history. At one point he asks, rhetorically: 'Is my desire to make something capable of giving surprise, or giving a sensation of elegance, or a feeling of attraction—my desire to make something *pleasing*—simply a petty or irresponsible aspect of my strivings?'[42] Of course not: it is also, after all, a desire to give, a generous impulse to make readers feel a new sense of connectedness, and it is in many ways parallel to the historian's desire to share relics of the past, even to be true to the past on its own terms. Rebecca Solnit has commented that nonfiction—or history, we would say—might be thought of as 'photographic; it poses the same challenges of finding form and pattern in the stuff already out there and the same ethical obligations to the subject.'[43] Aesthetic demands might well shake your camera, but it's still possible to get a clean shot, to deliver an image that could be meaningful and valuable both to artists and to archivists. A good photograph, like a good poem or a good history, could, in Pinsky's phrase, become 'a bridge or space between the worldly and the spiritual' without corrupting either realm.[44]

Perhaps this whole debate boils down to the infamous 'audience question.' The historian Bernard Bailyn once commented that 'there is no systematic reason why good history can't be popular, but it seldom is, simply because . . . it is so difficult to maintain the historian's discipline and at the same time make the story compelling and broadly accessible.' What I like about that assertion is the 'no systematic reason' part; what I find rather outrageous is the knee-jerk reification and essentialization of both disciplinary and popular history. Does either kind of history actually make firm, specific demands about the *form* of the written product? For Bailyn, 'good' history means 'accurate' history, and 'accurate' means 'balanced and nuanced' and 'based on technical details.'[45] But the market is flooded right now with the works of journalists and essayists and 'amateur' historians who write 'balanced and nuanced' prose that is 'based on technical details'—writers such as John McPhee, Michael Pollan, Stella Tillyard, Oliver Sacks, John Barry, Adam Hochschild, Lawrence Weschler, and Rebecca Solnit. Admittedly, 'creative nonfiction' as a named genre has exploded in the years since Bailyn made his proclamation. But it had already existed for decades.[46] To suggest that one needs a Ph.D. in history to adhere to Bailyn's standards is merely to express the status anxiety of our profession.[47]

It is equally fallacious, in my opinion, to suggest that the general reading public will pick up only history that has a 'compelling story' and a simple, 'accessible' prose style. Trade publishers regularly offer up 'quality' fiction and nonfiction books that they expect to be popular *enough* but that don't ever come close to the bestseller lists and certainly don't comfort readers with smooth, easy-to-follow narrative trajectories.[48] Indeed, most of the books reviewed in newspapers and magazines fall into this category. In other words, there seems to me to be a substantial amount of real and potential overlap between disciplinary and popular history, and the two could clearly learn from each other. I would never argue that all historians should try to reach that coveted 'broader audience'—just that those who wish to should be encouraged in the endeavor, and that their works should be taken just as seriously by academics as those works that are written in a more academic style. It would be wrong to suggest that becoming a public intellectual is an easy or straightforward goal, but it is perhaps even more misleading to call it an impossible one. One can point out the risks—oversimplification, sloppy argumentation, redundancy—without dismissing an aim that has the potential to enrich our culture quite drastically (indeed, many popular scholarly writers have done just that). Ultimately, why shouldn't each historian be free to imagine her own ideal audience, however large or small, rather than being disciplined into submission?[49]

Of course, it must be admitted that different audiences do sometimes make different demands, and that writers would be foolish to ignore those differences completely. Many authors trying to bridge audiences wind up writing in layers: perhaps, in some cases, parts of the text will be directed primarily to amateurs, while many of the footnotes will principally address professionals. In my ideal world, though, it would be incumbent on the professionals to learn different ways of reading, so that hybrid works could be better appreciated on their own terms. Historians would perhaps first of all have to adjust professional expectations so that they had time actually to read rather than just skim. Given the vast overproduction of scholarly tomes, shouldn't we all make the humble admission that we'll always be ignorant of many of the 'important' books in our field? Could we possibly agree to value depth as much as breadth? I'd also like to see more historians value reading as a journey rather than an effort to extract a single kernel of truth that can be summed up in a single sentence. And, in addition, historians would have to learn how to tease out arguments that are made through suggestion, how to appreciate careful uses of language that go well beyond the goal of clarity, how to analyze structure and metaphor and pacing and tone and character development and perspective and texture—how to read for sense *and* sensibility.

The insistence on the separation of content and form, combined with what Sontag called 'the well-intentioned move which makes content essential and form accessory,' point to the modern desire for ultimate knowability. The scholarly historian yearns to throw back the curtain with an aggressive flourish, to say, 'What *really* happened is X,' to destroy all 'manifest content' in his excavation of 'latent content': in Sontag's phrase, this kind of interpretation represents 'the revenge of the intellect upon the world.' The problem is that the world, or the past, exists as much *in* the curtain as behind it; what we may need, more than assertive acts of exposure, are subtle acts of provocation and engagement, historians with patient hands who stop to feel the fabric as they gently fold back corners, making cracks through which we can all witness something filtered and fleeting. Sontag's 40-year-old polemic against the violent interpretation of artworks can today be applied to historical scholarship: 'In place of a hermeneutics we need an erotics' of history.[50]

One of the great things about creative nonfiction is that its audience is amorphous—so no potentially tyrannical group of professionals can establish a set of rules about how it should be written. There's a built-in understanding that different people will have different sets of expectations and different levels of background knowledge, and that's OK—how could any author possibly please everyone? Moreover, the genre has a flexibility that could work beautifully in the context of history writing. While we seem to cling to an almost Aristotelian notion of formal unity, practitioners of creative nonfiction have, to exhilarating effect, combined memoir, narrative, art criticism, scholarly debate, oral history, and even policy recommendations, all in the same piece of writing. Shouldn't we, in a history book, have the freedom to zoom in for a close-up, set a scene, tell a joke, spin an anecdote, sing a song, speculate about the human condition? Such shifts represent risks, to be sure. They will almost always leave some readers feeling shaken, not stirred.[51] But I think many students of history would enjoy a good shaking every now and then.

Thankfully, I have begun to feel less and less alone in these concerns. I still worry, in particular, about how the older generation of historians disciplines the younger one, but I have also seen a number of signs that many historians of all ages are ready for scholarly history that's written in a greater variety of ways. A number of recent books by academics have struck me as both creative and captivating, have, in John Clive's words, 'cast that spell that lingers in the memory and is conducive not just to reading, but to rereading.' (That reminds me: several letters back, you asked for a list of professional historians I'd be willing to have as mentors; well, some of them are listed below. OK, I admit that footnoted letters can be cumbersome. But I've been hoping you'd see my notes as signals of solidarity.)[52]

Articles continue to appear with titles like 'The rebirth of narrative' and 'Style is not a luxury option' and 'What it will take to turn historians into writers.'[53] Graduate students in at least a couple of programs that I know intimately are banding together to do the analyses of storytelling and form and rhythm that never seem to come up in their official seminars. The founding of the journal *Rethinking History,* meanwhile, in 1997, has given such students hope that their own experimental writing might find a sanctioned scholarly outlet. And out at the Huntington Library, about 20 California-based historians and writers, together with some of the Huntington's visiting researchers, have organized themselves into a group called Past Tense, with the goal of slowing down, relaxing (ah, California!), and really *reading,* so as to have genuine conversations about *writing*—about, as one participant put it, 'voice, authorial presence, lexical choice, and especially the triangulation of author, subject, and reader.'[54] When I had the opportunity to speak with these admirable, sun-drenched scholars, I asked them their opinion about why Joseph Conrad might have used the words 'brooding' and 'gloom' five times each in the first seven paragraphs of *Heart of darkness* (obviously, I live in a much less sunny region of the country). As we tried out various ideas about the music of those words and how their repetition affected us and how they fit with the themes of the story, I think we all felt—well I did, anyway—as though we were wrestling with giant worms. But I've always enjoyed such slippery and inconclusive struggles.

I have never wished you pinned, dear colleague, let alone wriggling—but I hope you are feeling sufficiently triangulated.

Amateurishly,
Your Junior Colleague

LETTER 8

Dear Senior Colleague,

Please accept my warmest thanks. I was stunned to open your latest and find the envelope stuffed with your poems. I am honored that you would share such exquisite bits of yourself with me. If I have to agree with you that it would be wise to keep your day job, I will say, nevertheless, with Rilke, that the poems 'do have silent and hidden beginnings of something personal.'[55]

It strikes me, here, that what I perhaps find most lacking in professional history writing is that hint of the personal element. The discipline of history seems to train us to repudiate ourselves: somehow we can't be true to the past unless we empty ourselves of content, become transparent vessels. And so we hide in the third-person omniscient, and, when forced to make an appearance, turn to the ridiculously royal-sounding 'we' or the awkward, self-deluding formality of 'the author.' We sacrifice any attempt at style to the gods of apparent neutrality. Good luck to us. What's worse, though, is that we also sacrifice our voices. The discipline's unwritten writing rules constitute a recipe for conformity, homogenization, conventionalism. 'Perhaps,' as Rilke suggests, 'all professions are like that, filled with demands, filled with hostility toward the individual.'[56] I realize that many of our colleagues will say they read history not for voice but for information about what happened in the past. But haven't you ever been carried away into a different world on the strength of a new voice?[57]

Margaret Atwood once asked as many creative writers as she could find to explain why they wrote. A few sounded almost like scholars: 'To serve History,' one said; 'To speak for the dead'; 'To give back something of what has been given to me.' Noble aims, all. But the vast majority said something to the effect of: 'To express myself.'[58] Is this simply another difference between poets and historians? They are associated with voices, we merely with subjects?[59] Is it really so greedy to want both?

As always, dangers abound. I don't buy the epistemological ones; in fact, it seems to me that examining one's subjectivity in the middle of one's history-making may be the best way of establishing a truly meaningful objectivity.[60] And even if you see history as a science and not an art, you'd have to follow Heisenberg in recognizing that the role of the investigator must always be accounted for.[61] More serious concerns might involve irrelevance, the overvaluing of experience or identity, self-indulgence, even narcissism—but these are concerns that autobiographers have been negotiating for centuries, and so far not even the most self-denying scholars have seen fit to discredit the entire genre of autobiography.[62]

I have always been quickest to trust those nonfiction writers who fully inhabit their prose. This is not to say that every historian must analyze every aspect of his subject-position in everything he writes. But I think it is more honest to undergo a self-conscious search for a voice than simply to plug one's research into a pre-packaged template. Shelby Foote once commented that 'writing is the search for the answers, and the answer is in the form, the method of telling, the exploration of self, which is our only clew to reality.'[63]

Voices can be more or less subtle, more or less personal. In every case, though, they both reflect and inspire empathy. A good history will reinscribe the pastness of the past, will leave us awed by the gulf between us and our ancestors, but it must also at least hint at the author's desire to bridge that gulf, must give us glimpses of continuity and connection. I want a history I can use, and I can use it more easily if you show me the passion of your own investment in it. If you present it 'for its own sake,' as if you didn't care, then it dies again on the page.

When I dropped out of college for a year, feeling crushed by the demands of the academic rat race, I was able to sustain my commitment to history by remembering the words of one of my teachers, the professor who had, without realizing it, gotten me through my sophomore year. During an informal talk with a group of about fifteen undergraduates, John Clive had explained that he had become a historian not to answer some abstract scholarly question (not that there's anything wrong with such questions) but simply to indulge his burning curiosity about the human character.

Midway through my year off, I got the news that Clive had passed away. I didn't really want to return for my junior year, but I did, to find that I had been assigned a new adviser, Lou Masur, who made a point of getting to know me quite well. After a few months he gave me a present: John Clive's last book, *Not by fact alone: Essays on the writing and reading of history*. It turned out to be one of the most meaningful gifts I have ever received. I dove into the book immediately, and my immersion continued until I reached page 32, when I suddenly felt I could hear Clive's voice speaking aloud:

> Michelet would have shaken his head in wonderment at our current discussions as to whether the past is or is not 'usable.' As far as he was concerned, the whole point of writing history was to re-create a past that not only could, but must, be used—eventually by the historian's readers, but in the first place by the historian himself—to satisfy his own psychic and spiritual needs, and to inspire him both to bear witness to past virtues and to do his share in the rooting out of present evils. For Michelet, writing history is tantamount to self-expression, to total commitment at the most personal level.[64]

I felt intensely grateful for Lou Masur, John Clive, and Jules Michelet. Here was eloquent re-confirmation that my favorite discipline was not just intellectual and analytical but also spiritual and personal, and the personal was political, and the historian's voice could be as inspirational, perhaps, as the poet's.

In my senior year, I wrote a history thesis, trying my hand for the first time at artful scholarship. It was reasonably well received, but one randomly selected reader railed against me for essentially ripping up and trampling the (unwritten) Code of Conduct for Academic History Writing. My sins were many, but the one that this particular scholar simply could not abide was my use of the first person. 'On page after page,' said the report, 'the author intrudes himself.' (Yes, I still have the report.) The thesis, by the way, was 139 pages. I'd used the first-person singular exactly four times.

I missed John Clive. But I had enough energy left, during those last few weeks of college, for one final academic act: I nominated Lou Masur for the first-ever John Clive Teaching Prize. At the end-of-the year ceremony for my department, a professor I knew well, Jan Thaddeus, stood up to distribute all the honors. I had taken a poetry-writing seminar with her as a freshman, and as a senior I did an independent study with her on the writing of personal essays. She seemed to look straight at me. And then she was reading something out loud, and I recognized my own prose: it was the nomination letter I had written for Lou. I started to cry.

At that moment, I think I realized I might want to be a professor—and maybe even a historian. But I admit it: I had always wanted to be a writer.

Reflexively,

Your Junior Colleague

LETTER 9

Thank you, dear colleague, for responding with such generosity to a story that was not easy to tell.

I sense that you've begun to appreciate my dilemma. I always come back to Stegner, who once suggested that in 'the guts' of every serious piece of writing is 'an anguished question.'[65] Ideally, the question resonates, and it spurs further questions, pushing limits, overturning assumptions. Sometimes that process can be wrenching. But I think it is the anguish, in a sense, that keeps us honest. Margaret Atwood called her book about writing *Negotiating with the dead*, because she believes that every act of writing of any kind represents a struggle to connect with what is gone.[66] Every writer is a historian; and every historian is also a writer, whether he likes it or not.

In another book about confronting loss, *The dominion of the dead*, Robert Pogue Harrison suggests that our 'ultimate imperative—to keep the story going, however absurd or unredeemed it may be—comes to us from the giant family of the dead, who live on only as long as the story continues.' Meanwhile, Harrison himself, channeling the voices of those with whom he has negotiated, continues the story—and consistently urges that we should, too. 'Before turning this book over to its audience,' he says, at the end of his Preface,

> I would like to state that it is above all a reader's book. Some books are writers' books, in that their authors undertake the largest share of the labor, do most of the thinking, circumscribe (as much as possible) the horizon of reference, and draw the final conclusions. *The dominion of the dead* is different. It is more like a net than a cloth. Its articulation is full of empty spaces for the reader to enter and wander about in. It calls on its interlocutor not only to think along with the author but to establish independent connections, leap over abysses, pursue his or her own paths of inquiry, bring to bear adventitious considerations, and, through the tracings offered here, discover the topic for him- or herself . . . The result is a book that only the reader can finish writing.[67]

Most works of creative nonfiction lack such an injunction, because it is simply implied. Harrison had to make his explicit because he is an academic, and his fellow academics are not used to reading so actively. Almost every work of scholarly history I have ever read has been a writer's book. We earn reputations—we earn tenure—by narrowly circumscribing the meaning of our arguments. But what if some of us, gradually, from our earliest days in graduate school, started remembering our drive to express ourselves, and started learning how to compose reader's books?

Inquisitively,
Your Junior Colleague

LETTER 10

Dear Senior Colleague,

Thank you so much for your kind words and honest assessment. I feel as though we've finally begun to understand each other, as though there's been a small forest fire and we are both creeping out from the tangled underbrush into some newly cleared common ground. (I know, I know: too many metaphors. Forgive me.)

I have just one last anguished question. Would you be willing to write me a letter of recommendation?

Seriously,
Your Junior Colleague

NOTES

1. Rilke (1987, 34), emphasis in the original.

2. Garber 2005; she has my eternal gratitude.

3. Or, to adapt Robert Rosenstone's phrase, from another essay for which I am deeply grateful, I want 'Space for the bird to fly' (in Jenkins, Morgan, and Munslow 2007, 11–18). Of course, some personal visions could result in histories so poetic that they sell only as well as poetry—and that's fine, too, especially since such works would still be broadening the range of history.

4. But I suppose I sound like a hopelessly idealistic crank—at least, to a cheery skimmer like Pierre Bayard, whose recent book (2007) actually became a bestseller in France, lending a certain post-structuralist *je ne sais quoi*, a certain *caché*, you might say, to superficiality. OK, I admit it, Professor Bayard: you win. I only skimmed your book.

5. I owe the 'mentors/masters' distinction to Heather Furnas, for which much thanks.

6. These snap judgments, in my opinion, have gotten even snappier in the wake of recent scholarly scandals (see Hoffer 2007).

7. Usually, the rules and templates are simply implied or understood, but occasionally some of them do get written down, especially in guides meant primarily for students working on term papers, theses, or dissertations (Rampolla 2006; Marius and Page 2006).

8. Harrison (2003, 73). If you're an avid reader of Rilke, you'll remember that his correspondent in *Letters to a Young Poet* composed a poem called 'To Leopardi,' which Rilke judged to be 'lovely' (4–5).

9. *Category 1*: Bailyn (1967, v); Genovese (1976, xv); Cohen (1990, 2). *Category 2*: Dittmer (1994, 1); Patterson (1996, 3); Gordon (1999, 1). *Category 3*: Worster (1979, vii); Ulrich (1990, 3); Kirby (2006, 1).

10. Hoffer (2007, 1–10, 62–139); Megill (2007, 1–14).

11. The 'new historicist' literary scholar Stephen Greenblatt, in a recent meditation on his own writing (2007), notes that he developed a habit of launching his essays in a very similar way—'which became a bit too familiar . . . so I had to stop.' The first sentence was always a straightforward bit of factual reportage, and it always had a date in it. Indeed, many scholarly writers might be well served to follow Greenblatt's example of self-assessment and shake themselves out of their tired writing habits.

12. For a sustained analysis of the function of narrative in history writing and of the ways in which it both mirrors and distorts our experience of the past, see the work of Hayden White (1973, 1978, 1987).

13. This need provided one of the key spurs to my conceptualization of these letters. I am attempting to respond to a 30-year-old debate in the journal literature that started most obviously with Lawrence Stone's essay (1979), 'The revival of narrative: Reflections on a new old history,' and that has been continued, most productively for my purposes, in Phillips (1983); Davidson (1984); Norman (1991); Cronon (1992); Ross (1995); and especially Goodman (1998). Also crucial to me were a number of articles by John Demos (1998, 2002, for example).

14. I would also include the following on my list of impressive Romantic stylists: Henry Adams, Thomas Carlyle, Edward Gibbon, Thomas Babington Macaulay, Jules Michelet, and William Prescott. Simply to dismiss these men on epistemological or political grounds (as many do) is to miss seeing the great literary potential of history writing. For good explorations of nineteenth-century history, see Levin (1959), Gay (1988), and Clive (1989, 1–145). See Hoffer (2007, 17–31 and 52) for a typical dismissal of the Romantics and for the mistaken notion that the Bancroft Prize is named for George Bancroft; in fact, it is named for the early twentieth-century historian Frederic Bancroft. (I apologize, dear colleague, for the obvious debunking spirit here, but I am especially sensitive when it comes to nineteenth-century historians.)

15. Spate (1966, 181).

16. LaCapra, 'Writing history, writing trauma,' in Monroe (2002, 151). For a theoretical defense of peer review, despite certain reservations about current practices, see Fink (2007).

17. See the thoughtful and witty essay on using the first person in history writing by John Clive, 'The most disgusting of pronouns' (1989, 25–33), and note Clive's own use of the first person in 'The use of the past' (1989, 3–12).

18. I certainly don't mean to imply that narrative should be seen solely as instrumental—that is, as a means to delivering analysis. As James West Davidson has argued (1984), it's crucial to recognize what narrative has to offer on its own terms, the satisfactions it can deliver better than any other form. But I do have the feeling that historians tend to under-appreciate the potential of the storytelling mode to succeed *simultaneously* in narrativistic and analytical terms. A good example demonstrating the way in which historians still separate 'text' and 'context,' as it were, is Linda Gordon's already-cited Bancroft-winning book (1999), which actually alternates between chapters of narrative and chapters of traditional historical argumentation and analysis.

19. See the *Creative Nonfiction* website, http://www.creativenonfiction.org/the journal/whatiscnf.htm, from which I took this quotation on 19 October 2007.

20. Megill (2007, 13, 83). Alas, as Megill notes here and as I tried to suggest indirectly in my form letter rejecting your application to be my writing mentor, we academics seem to fear that we have nothing going for us but the appearance of rigor. Also see

Megill (2007, 233–34), where he more matter-of-factly cites a study from the late 1980s arguing 'that an "informal positivism" remained prevalent at that time among historians.' Given how well academic culture replicates itself, and, frankly, how long-lived academics tend to be, I consider it not unlikely that this default position is still held by many historians today. Dominick LaCapra offered a corroborating viewpoint in 2002, asserting that 'a documentary or self-sufficient research model . . . has to a significant extent persisted in professional historiography.' See 'Writing history, writing trauma,' in Monroe (2002, 148).

21. See, for instance, Hoffer (2007, 28–43), Novick (1988, 21–108), and Breisach (1983, 215–90).

22. Becker (1932).

23. Lasch (1989, 458). On the history of history writing in the twentieth century, see Novick (1988, 111–629), Hoffer (2007, 39–92), Kelley (2006), Iggers (2005), and Fitzpatrick (2002).

24. Note the general defense of the methods of the new social history of the 1960s and 70s against the cultural or linguistic turn in Appleby, Hunt, and Jacob (1994) and in Windschuttle (1996); contrast those perspectives with the embrace of certain aspects of the linguistic turn (at least in the context of method) in Harlan (1997); and also see the attempt at compromise between a rigorous historicism and postmodern skepticism in Berkhofer, Jr. (1995).

25. Goodman (1998, 255).

26. Dear colleague: might it not be liberating to give up the presumption to expertise and omniscience? See Megill (2007, 38, 56, 213, and passim); also note Lyotard (1984), Breisach (2003), and Clark (2003).

27. White (1987, 53).

28. Ankersmit, 'Reply to Professor Zagorin,' in Fay, Pomper, and Vann (1998, 209).

29. Greg Dening makes a similar argument, with great eloquence, in 'Writing, rewriting the Beach,' in Munslow and Rosenstone (2004, esp. 31–32, 51–52).

30. Solnit (2005, 5).

31. Stegner, 'The law of nature and the dream of man: Ruminations on the art of fiction,' in Stegner (1992, 216).

32. I am deeply indebted to Daegan Miller for founding the Historians Are Writers working group at Cornell University in fall 2007 and for choosing *Wolf Willow* as the first text to be discussed. I'm also grateful to Daegan, Heather Furnas, Rebecca Macmillan, and Katie Proctor for their contributions to the discussion about Stegner.

33. Stegner (2000, 138 and 307). Stegner's son Page notes in his introduction to the 2000 Penguin edition that the book's subtitle was the creation of Viking Press, the original publisher, and that it 'satisfied nobody, including its author, because the formulation—*A history, a story, and a memory of the last plains frontier*—suggests a kind of tidy tripartite package that the work itself doesn't entirely support' (xi). Note that Beth LaDow has written a work of creative nonfiction (2002) that makes use of

Wolf Willow in ways that I'm guessing would meet with approval from both Wallace and Page Stegner. And also see Simon Schama's book *Dead certainties: Unwarranted speculations* (1991) for a wonderful attempt by an academic historian at a Stegner-like melange of different approaches to the writing of history, including historical fiction. Schama's experimentation was attacked, in perhaps predictable ways, by Gordon Wood (1991) but defended by Louis P. Masur (1992).

34. Megill (2007, 182–87).

35. Ibid., passim. For a somewhat more traditional justification of disciplinary boundaries, see Evans (1999). Both Megill and Evans (and many of the other recent authors I've been citing here on historiographic issues) see themselves as continuing the debates launched in certain classic works, especially Collingwood (1946), Bloch (1953), Carr (1962), Elton (1968), and Fischer (1970).

36. Megill 2007, 108 and 186.

37. Camus (1965, 81). Sontag, 'On style,' in Sontag (1996, 16–17).

38. I agree completely with James Goodman (1998), who admitted being 'certain that narrative historians trying to write like John Dos Passos, Toni Morrison, or William Faulkner would often stumble and sometimes fall. Yet they were likely to write better history than they would have written if they had tried only to write well. So there's nothing lost, and much to be gained, by their trying' (269).

39. Ultimately, I can see Megill's point about the epistemological value of maintaining history as a discipline. Yet I also have some sympathy with David Harlan's polemical position, which posits that the emphasis on method and the ideal of doing 'history for its own sake' competes detrimentally with the more important project of developing a fertile relationship between present and past. Harlan wants 'a history concerned not with dead authors but with living books, not with returning earlier writers to their historical contexts but with reading historical works in new and unexpected contexts, not with reconstructing the past but with providing the critical medium in which valuable works from the past might *survive* their past—might survive their past in order to tell us about our present.' To achieve such a history, Harlan argues, 'historians should simply drop the question of what counts as legitimate history and accept the fact that, like every other discipline in the humanities, they do not have, and are not likely to have, a formalized, widely accepted set of research procedures' (Harlan 1997, 31).

40. John Demos eloquently suggests the possibility that historians, without sacrificing epistemological responsibility, might easily 'take a larger view of our own efforts' and engage with the kind of 'generically significant experience' that seems 'to transcend historically delimited time and place'—might actually 'confront those parts of all lives (including our own) which can be lumped together as (how else to say it?) simply, and quintessentially, "human."' See his essay 'Real lives and other fictions: Reconsidering Wallace Stegner's *Angle of repose*,' in Carnes (2001, 142–43).

41. Clive (1989, 32).

42. Pinsky (1988, 31).

43. Solnit (2005, 144).

44. Pinsky (1988, 3).

45. Bailyn (1994, 70 and 69).

46. Besides the authors listed above, consider the historical writing of nonfiction artists such as Evan S. Connell, Bernard DeVoto, Samuel Freedman, Stephen Jay Gould, J. Anthony Lukas, Carey McWilliams, Wallace Stegner, and Deborah Tall—not to mention (more recently) Timothy Egan, Louis Menand, Jennifer Price, Carlo Rotella, and Dava Sobel.

47. De Botton (2004).

48. For more on narrative, see Megill (2007, 63–103) and especially Goodman (1998). As Goodman says, a 'good story' will leave the world 'as messy as it found it' (269).

49. I believe there are productive ways of engaging with market forces: paying attention to certain 'popular' trends can earn a scholarly author more relevance and more readers. See Greenberg (2005) and Benton (2006). On the other hand, I don't agree with authors like Rachel Toor (2007) who basically seem to advocate an attitude of pandering to what seems to me a caricature of 'the general reader.' A good counterpoint to Toor's perspective is Robert Johnston's important reminder (2003) that 'citizen-readers' surely deserve 'access to scholarly debates, so many of which are of critical importance and do not need to be dumbed down, or locked away in secret vaults' (xiii).

50. Sontag, 'Against interpretation,' in Sontag (1996, 4, 7, and 14). Also see LaCapra (1985, 15–44). On the explicit need for historians to learn how to read in new ways, see Goodman (1998, 268). And on the problem of the pace of professional life, see Waters (2007).

51. For a good example of this kind of reaction, typical, I think, of historians who resist the flexible, boundary-breaking form of creative nonfiction, see Cushing Strout's response to Schama (1992).

52. I'm thinking, for instance, of John Demos, Greg Dening, Timothy Gilfoyle, James Goodman, Saidiya Hartman, Martha Hodes, Jane Kamensky, Suzanne Lebsock, Jill Lepore, Peter Mancall, Louis Masur, William McFeely, Scott Reynolds Nelson, Robert Rosenstone, Simon Schama, and Timothy Tyson.

On experimenting, also note Hodes (2007) and Munslow and Rosenstone (2004). The quotation is from Clive (1989, xiv).

53. Strauss (2005), Muller (2006), and Masur (2001).

54. Mitchell (2007). I'm grateful to the Past Tense group—especially to Michelle Nickerson and Peter Mancall for the invitation to visit.

55. Rilke (1987, 4).

56. Rilke (1987, 57).

57. For helpful meditations on the tension between intellectual detachment and personal commitment in history writing, see Demos (2002) and (for numerous case studies) Kammen (1997, 3–71).

58. Atwood (2002, xx–xxii). Atwood also contributed to a stimulating forum on the border between history and fiction shortly after her historical novel *Alias Grace* came out (AHR 1998). Her contribution is followed by the responses of three historians— Lynn Hunt, Jonathan Spence, and John Demos.

59. We historians still insist on searching for new material to study. Virtually every other kind of scholar and writer has acknowledged that there's not much new under the sun, and is therefore focused on figuring out new ways to cover old subjects. Having a voice often helps in that kind of project. As Megill has commented (2007), 'in view of the vast, utterly unmanageable body of *primary* historiography that has been produced,' it may be time to push for a 'historiography more in the manner of meditation or commentary, which, in a Montaignean spirit and in the essay form, would comment on the significance of that body for us, now. In its meditative and reflective mode, [this] historiography would engage not in the dredging up of new facts—that is, would not engage in historical research as it is normally understood—but would instead engage in the philosophical task of reflecting on the significance of facts already in some sense "known"' (186–87). An 'essay,' literally, is nothing more than an attempt—its spirit scorns the very idea of a definitive or comprehensive study. Imagine a body of history writing as unpredictable and un-scholastic, as provocative and invigorating, as personal and engaging, as Montaigne's *Essays!*

60. Megill (2007, 87); but also note that 'full disclosure' must ultimately be taken as nothing more than another rhetorical device rather than anything approaching objective truth. See Berkhofer Jr. (1995, 138–69).

61. For a differing perspective on both history and Heisenberg, see Gaddis (2002).

62. The autobiographical mode is actually tailor-made for irony, humility, and flexibility, in my opinion, though I realize that some scholars will never be able to abide the first person no matter how useful it may seem. See the attack against it by Daphne Patai (1994), and the subsequent defense by Ruth Behar (1994). On the complicated issue of coming to grips with experience, see LaCapra (2004, 1–105), and LaCapra, 'Writing history, writing trauma,' in Monroe (2002, 176–80).

63. Quoted in Masur (2001).

64. Clive (1989, 32). It is perhaps also worth noting that Simon Schama dedicated his book *Dead certainties* to Clive, 'for whom history was literature.' And what a wonderful irony it is that, though their views on the writing of history were radically different, Clive and Bernard Bailyn were actually close friends—they even collaborated once on an article (Bailyn 1994, 80). Who knows—maybe that means it would be possible for the likes of you and me to collaborate?

65. Stegner, 'The law of nature and the dream of man,' in Stegner (1992, 220).

66. 'Not just some, but *all* writing of the narrative kind, and perhaps all writing, is motivated, deep down, by a fear of and a fascination with mortality—by a desire to make the risky trip to the Underworld, and to bring something or someone back from the dead' (Atwood 2002, 156).

67. Harrison (2003, 89 and xii). Atwood would approve: 'One of my university professors, who was also a poet, used to say that there was only one real question to be asked about any work, and that was—is it alive, or is it dead? I happen to agree, but in what does this aliveness or deadness consist? The biological definition would be that living things grow and change, and can have offspring, whereas dead things are inert. In what way can a text grow and change and have offspring? Only through its interaction with a reader, no matter how far away that reader may be in time and in space' (Atwood 2002, 140). All of which reminds me of a passage from Rebecca Solnit's book, *Hope in the dark: Untold histories, wild possibilities* (2004, 64–65): 'Writing is lonely. It's an intimate talk with the dead, with the unborn, with the absent, with strangers, with the readers who may never come to be and who, even if they do read you, will do so weeks, years, decades later. An essay, a book, is one statement in a long conversation you could call culture or history; you are answering something or questioning something that may have fallen still long ago, and the response to your words may come long after you're gone and never reach your ears—if anyone hears you in the first place. After all, this is how it's been for so many books that count, books that didn't shake the world when they first appeared but blossomed later. Writing is a model for how indirect effect can be, how delayed, how invisible; no one is more hopeful than a writer, no one is a bigger gambler.'

REFERENCES

AHR Forum. 1998. Histories and historical fictions. *American Historical Review* 103: 1502–29.

Appleby, J., L. Hunt, and M. Jacob. 1994. *Telling the truth about history.* New York: Norton.

Atwood, M. 2002. *Negotiating with the dead: A writer on writing.* New York: Anchor Books.

Bailyn, B. 1967. *The ideological origins of the American revolution.* Cambridge, Mass: Harvard University Press.

Bailyn, B. 1994. *On the teaching and writing of history.* Hanover, NH: University Press of New England.

Bayard, P. 2007. *How to talk about books you haven't read,* trans. J. Mehlman. New York: Bloomsbury.

Becker, C. 1932. Everyman his own historian. *American Historical Review* 37: 221–36.

Behar, R. 1994. 'Dare we say I?' Bringing the personal into scholarship. *Chronicle of Higher Education,* 29 June.

Benton, T. H. (pseudonym) 2006. Leaving the village: It's time for professors to abandon the genteel pose of being aloof from the sordid marketplace. *Chronicle of Higher Education,* 17 February.

Berkhofer, Jr, R. F. 1995. *Beyond the great story: History as text and discourse.* Cambridge, Mass: Harvard University Press.

Bloch, M. 1953. *The historian's craft.* New York: Knopf.

Breisach, E. 1983. *Historiography: Ancient, medieval, modern.* Chicago: University of Chicago Press.

Breisach, E. 2003. *On the future of history: The postmodernist challenge and its aftermath.* Chicago: University of Chicago Press.

Camus, A. 1965. *Notebooks 1942–51,* trans. J. O'Brien. New York: Harcourt Brace Jovanovich.

Carnes, M. C., ed. 2001. *Novel history: Historians and novelists confront America's past (and each other).* New York: Simon & Schuster.

Carr, E. H. 1962. *What is history?* New York: Knopf.

Clark, J.C.D. 2003. *Our shadowed present: Modernism, postmodernism and history.* London: Atlantic Books.

Clive, J. 1989. *Not by fact alone: Essays on the writing and reading of history.* Boston: Houghton Mifflin.

Cohen, L. 1990. *Making a new deal: Industrial workers in Chicago, 1919–1939.* New York: Cambridge University Press.

Collingwood, R. G. 1946. *The idea of history.* Oxford: Clarendon Press.

Cronon, W. 1992. A place for stories: Nature, history, and narrative. *Journal of American History* 78: 1347–76.

Davidson, J. W. 1984. The new narrative history: How new? How narrative? *Reviews in American History* 12: 322–34.

De Botton, A. 2004. *Status anxiety.* New York: Pantheon.

Demos, J. 1998. In search of reasons for historians to read novels. *American Historical Review* 103: 1526–29.

Demos, J. 2002. Using self, using history. *Journal of American History* 89: 37–42.

Dittmer, J. 1994. *Local people: The struggle for civil rights in Mississippi.* Urbana: University of Illinois Press.

Elton, G. R. 1968. *The practice of history.* New York: Crowell.

Evans, R. J. 1999. *In defense of history.* New York: Norton.

Fay, B., P. Pomper, and R. T. Vann, eds. 1998. *History and theory: Contemporary readings.* Oxford: Blackwell.

Fink, L. 2007. Unearthing a genre. *Chronicle Review* 53.

Fischer, D. H. 1970. *Historians' fallacies: Toward a logic of historical thought.* New York: Harper & Row.

Fitzpatrick, E. F. 2002. *History's memory: Writing America's past, 1880–1980.* Cambridge, Mass: Harvard University Press.

Gaddis, J. L. 2002. *The landscape of history: How historians map the past.* New York: Oxford University Press.

Garber, M. 2005. Why can't young scholars write their second books first? *Journal of Scholarly Publishing* 36: 129–32.

Gay, P. 1988. *Style in history: Gibbon, Ranke, Macaulay, Burckhardt.* New York: Norton.

Genovese, E. D. 1976. *Roll, Jordan, roll: The world the slaves made.* New York: Vintage.

Goodman, J. 1998. For the love of stories. *Reviews in American History* 26: 255–74.

Gordon, L. 1999. *The Great Arizona orphan abduction.* Cambridge, Mass: Harvard University Press.

Greenberg, D. 2005. That Barnes and Noble dream. *Slate,* 17 May. www.slate.com/id/2118854/entry/2118924/ (accessed 18 May 2006).

Greenblatt, S. 2007. Writing as performance: Revealing 'the calculation that underlies the appearance of effortlessness.' *Harvard Magazine,* September/October, http://harvardmagazine.com/2007/09/writing-as-performance.html (accessed 30 October 2007).

Harlan, D. 1997. *The degradation of American history.* Chicago: University of Chicago Press.

Harrison, R. 2003. *The dominion of the dead.* Chicago: University of Chicago Press.

Hodes, M. 2007. Experimental history in the classroom. *Perspectives* 45, May, http://www.historians.org/perspectives/issues/2007/0705/0705tea2.cfm (accessed 3 October 2007).

Hoffer, P. C. 2007. *Past imperfect: Facts, fictions, fraud—American history from Bancroft and Parkman to Ambrose, Bellesiles, Ellis, and Goodwin.* New York: Public Affairs.

Iggers, G. G. 2005. *Historiography in the twentieth century: From scientific objectivity to the postmodern challenge.* Middletown: Wesleyan University Press.

Jenkins, K., S. Morgan, and A. Munslow, eds. 2007. *Manifestos for history.* New York: Routledge.

Johnston, R. D. 2003. *The radical middle class: Populist democracy and the question of capitalism in progressive era Portland, Oregon.* Princeton: Princeton University Press.

Kelley, D. R. 2006. *Frontiers of history: Historical inquiry in the twentieth century.* New Haven: Yale University Press.

Kirby, J. T. 2006. *Mockingbird song: Ecological landscapes of the South.* Chapel Hill: University of North Carolina Press.

Kammen, M. 1997. *In the past lane: Historical perspectives on American culture.* New York: Oxford University Press.

LaCapra, D. 1985. *History and criticism.* Ithaca: Cornell University Press.

LaCapra, D. 2004. *History in transit: Experience, identity, critical theory.* Ithaca: Cornell University Press.

LaDow, B. 2002. *The medicine line: Life and death on a North American borderland.* New York: Routledge.

Lasch, C. 1989. Consensus: An academic question? *Journal of American History* 76: 457–59.

Levin, D. 1959. *History as romantic art: Bancroft, Prescott, Motley, and Parkman.* Stanford: Stanford University Press.

Lyotard, J.-F. 1984. *The postmodern condition: A report on knowledge,* trans. G. Bennington, and B. Massumi. Minneapolis: University of Minnesota Press.

Marius, R. A., and M. E. Page. 2006. *A short guide to writing about history,* 6th ed. New York: Longman.

Masur, L. P. 1992. On Parkman's trail. *William and Mary Quarterly, 3rd series,* 49: 120–32.

Masur, L. P. 2001. What it will take to turn historians into writers. *Chronicle of Higher Education,* 6 July.

Megill, A. 2007. *Historical knowledge and historical error: A contemporary guide to practice.* Chicago: University of Chicago Press.

Mitchell, L. J. 2007. 'Beyond tense': Encouraging historians to think hard about writing and reading. *Perspectives* 45, April: 31–32.

Monroe, J., ed. 2002. *Writing and revising the disciplines.* Ithaca: Cornell University Press.

Muller, J. Z. 2006. Style is not a luxury option: Reflections on the prose of the profs. *Perspectives* 44, March: 44–45.

Munslow, A., and R. A. Rosenstone, eds. 2004. *Experiments in rethinking history.* New York: Routledge.

Norman, A. P. 1991. Telling it like it was: Historical narratives on their own terms. *History and Theory* 30: 119–35.

Novick, P. 1988. *That noble dream: The 'objectivity question' and the American historical profession.* New York: Cambridge University Press.

Patai, D. 1994. Sick and tired of scholars' nouveau solipsism. *Chronicle of Higher Education,* 23 February.

Patterson, J. T. 1996. *Grand expectations: The United States, 1945–1974.* New York: Oxford University Press.

Phillips, M. 1983. The revival of narrative: Thoughts on a current historiographical debate. *University of Toronto Quarterly* 53: 149–65.

Pinsky, R. 1988. *Poetry and the world.* New York: Ecco Press.

Rampolla, M. L. 2006. *A pocket guide to writing in history,* 5th ed. New York: Bedford/St. Martin's.

Rilke, R. M. 1987. *Letters to a young poet,* trans. S. Mitchell. New York: Vintage.

Ross, D. 1995. Grand narrative in American historical writing: From romance to uncertainty. *American Historical Review* 100: 651–77.

Schama, S. 1991. *Dead certainties: Unwarranted speculations.* New York: Knopf.

Solnit,. R. 2004. *Hope in the dark: Untold histories, wild possibilities.* New York: Nation Books.

Solnit, R. 2005. *A field guide to getting lost.* New York: Viking.

Sontag, S. 1996. *Against interpretation and other essays.* New York: Picador.

Spate, O.H.K. 1966. *Let me enjoy: Essays, partly geographical*. London: Methuen.

Stegner, W. 1992. *Where the bluebird sings to the lemonade springs: Living and writing in the west*. New York: Penguin.

Stegner, W. 2000. *Wolf willow: A history, a story, and a memory of the last plains frontier*. New York: Penguin.

Stone, L. 1979. The revival of narrative: Reflections on a new old history. *Past and Present* 85: 3–24.

Strauss, B. 2005. The rebirth of narrative. *Historically Speaking* 6: 1–5.

Strout, C. 1992. Border crossings: History, fiction, and dead certainties. *History and Theory* 31: 153–62.

Toor, R. 2007. The care and feeding of the reader. *Chronicle of Higher Education* 14 September.

Ulrich, L. T. 1990. *A midwife's tale: The life of Martha Ballard, based on her diary, 1785–1812*. New York: Knopf.

Waters, L. 2007. Time for reading. *Chronicle of Higher Education* 9 February.

White, H. 1973. *Metahistory: The historical imagination in nineteenth-century Europe*. Baltimore: Johns Hopkins University Press.

White, H. 1978. *Tropics of discourse: Essays in cultural criticism*. Baltimore: Johns Hopkins University Press.

White, H. 1987. *The content of the form: Narrative discourse and historical representation*. Baltimore: Johns Hopkins University Press.

Windschuttle, K. 1996. *The killing of history: How literary critics and social theorists are murdering our past*. San Francisco: Encounter Books.

Wood, G. 1991. Novel history. *New York Review of Books* 38: 12 and 14–16.

Worster, D. 1979. *Dust bowl: The southern plains in the 1930s*. New York: Oxford University Press.

Jane Kamensky

"Novelties: A Historian's Field Notes from Fiction": From *Historically Speaking* (2011)

Just over a decade ago (2007–8), Jill Lepore and Jane Kamensky, two accomplished historians who were close friends and colleagues, began a joint effort of fiction writing. Planned initially as a kind of elaborate skit, what finally emerged was a lively and historically resonant novel entitled *Blindspot*. Set in Boston during the years just before the Revolution, the book traced the doings of a portraitist and his cross-dressing (female) apprentice/lover. Kamensky would subsequently draw on her experience with this project in a short but brilliantly artful essay directed to fellow historians. Her "Novelties" professes to be "field notes" but is actually quite a lot more. Verging at times on becoming a how-to manual—the subtitles take imperative form—it amounts also to a deep exploration of craft in *both* history and fiction writing. From its outset the essay presses upon historians a mode of engagement, a "fully operational sense of our subjects' present," rarely found in the world of academic scholarship.

Here in the twilight of the Enlightenment, academic historians have fallen in love with how little we can know. Over the last fifty years, people, events, even places in the past have grown more obscure to many of us. Compare a work of history written in 1960 to one published in 2010, and you might wonder whether the mists of time have somehow thickened.

Can aspects of the novelist's imagination help us to cut through the fog? Two years ago, the historian Jill Lepore and I published a novel we wrote together. Set in Boston in 1764, *Blindspot* started out as a lark, a gift for a friend. It grew into a project that felt important, even urgent, to us as scholars: a different way of knowing and telling the past. What follows are nine lessons learned in that effort to conjure a known and knowable world: a Then as real as Now, in our minds and on our pages.

1. FACE IT

Most historians suffer from prosopagnosia: face blindness. My co-author and I had written a goodly number of pages when it dawned on us that we had yet to tell our readers what our two first-person narrators looked like. In a novel that is, in large measure, about seeing, such description seemed a matter of duty. Our readers, not to mention our narrators themselves, needed to know how tall Fanny and Jamie stood, the color of their hair, the cut of their proverbial jibs.

How tough could such an accounting be? This was fiction, after all; we answered only to our characters. But confronted with this delectable task, we promptly choked. Their eyes, how they twinkled; their dimples, how merry: it seemed we had naught but rank cliché at our fingertips.

How do you take stock of a human face? Every time you walk in to a bus, a bar, or a classroom, you take people's mettle visually, instantly, almost without thinking. But the sheer narrative terror of that moment made me realize that, as historians, we seldom confront the embodied nature of past individuals. We're capable of writing the history of the self, or the history of the body, or even the history of sexuality, without crafting characters capable of staring back at us, as a good portrait does.

Writers of fiction give their characters faces and yea, even bodies, in a variety of ways. Consider this description, so thorough and meticulous that it bends in spots toward inventory:

> Thomas Cromwell is now a little over forty years old. He is a man of strong build, not tall. Various expressions are available to his face, and one is readable: an expression of stifled amusement. His hair is dark, heavy and waving, and his small eyes, which are of very strong sight, light up in conversation: so the Spanish ambassador will tell us, quite soon. It is said he knows by heart the entire New Testament in Latin, and so as a servant of the cardinal is apt—ready with a text if abbots flounder. . . . [H]e is at home in courtroom or waterfront, bishop's palace or inn yard. He can draft a contract, train a falcon, draw a map, stop a street fight, furnish a house and fix a jury. He will quote you a nice point in the

old authors, from Plato to Plautus and back again. He knows new poetry, and can say it in Italian. He works all hours, first up and last to bed. He makes money and he spends it. He will take a bet on anything.[1]

Cromwell, of course, is a character from history *and* from fiction, in this case Hilary Mantel's magnificent novel, *Wolf Hall*. Her description begins with a physical body, and a face, courtesy of Hans Holbein's 1533 portrait. But then she peers through the eyes to the soul, as if she *knows* the guy, and her reader should, too.

Can historians do anything quite so wonderful? We don't know the inner life of our subjects the way a novelist can know her characters. After all, a writer of fiction invents the soul whose windows the eyes become. Mantel's Cromwell isn't, can't, and shouldn't be history's Cromwell. Thomas Cromwell merely lived; Mantel's Cromwell soars. Yet almost every line in her description can be fully sourced: to the portrait, to Cromwell's letters, to contemporaneous descriptions of the man. At bottom, Mantel's path to knowing Cromwell isn't all that different from a scholar's. The magic comes in the author's moral confidence in what she's got—and then, of course, in the telling. Biographers, who live a long time with their subjects, offer readers hard-won, hard-working encapsulations of character all the time. Historians, trained to concentrate on the background at the expense of the figure in the portrait, do so less often than we might.

Of course, those who study remoter pasts and less celebrated people rarely even know what their subjects looked like. Yet no matter how obscure the actors, they had eyes and mouths, expressions and gestures that quickened the pulse of loved ones and triggered the loathing of enemies. Even when we cannot see the people we write about—perhaps especially then—we'd do well to remember that they weren't made of paper, and didn't pass their fleeting lives in acid-free boxes within temperature-controlled archives. They lived behind faces and within bodies, in heat and in cold, pleasure and pain, experiencing the present from the inside out. Their present became our past, and we're stuck working from the outside in, from the page to the person. That's no excuse for confusing the journey with the destination.

2. TASTE IT

The challenge of "facing" our subjects represents the merest tip of a vast and complex phenomenological iceberg. As a sometime novelist, I spent a lot of time presumptuously tasting, hearing, smelling, seeing, and feeling on my characters' behalf. Since *Blindspot* is set in the sweltering summer of 1764, that wasn't always pleasant.

The novelist is not alone here. In the last two decades the "history of the senses," pioneered by scholars including Michael Baxandall and John Berger (sight), Alain Corbin (smell), and Richard Rath and Mark Smith (sound), among others, has become a flourishing subfield.[2] I admire this work a great deal. But for all its sophistication, the history of the senses is as remote from sensorily rich history as the history of the body is from embodied history.

Because they create rather than discover a world, writers of fiction constantly index and mobilize the senses. Think of Proust's madeleine, surely the most famous cookie in literature, whose lime-scented crumbs set off a four-page-long reverie that begins in Swann's aunt's kitchen and spreads to encompass "the whole of Combray, and its surroundings, taking their proper shapes and growing solid . . . town and gardens alike, from my cup of tea."[3]

In nonfiction writing it can be no coincidence that some of the best sensory-laden storytelling comes from authors not burdened by Ph.D.s. Consider two examples, each describing the day-to-day operations of the print trades in the 18th century. The first comes from a superb work of academic history, Jeffrey L. Pasley's *The Tyranny of Printers:*

> Though printing had its cerebral and prestigious aspects, it was still a dirty, smelly, physically demanding job. One of the first chores that would be delegated to a young apprentice printer was preparing the sheepskin balls used to ink the type. The skins were soaked in urine, stamped on daily for added softness, and finally wrung out by hand. The work got harder from there, and only a little more pleasant. Supplies of ink were often scarce in America, so printers frequently had to make it on site, by boiling lampblack (soot) in varnish (linseed oil and rosin). If the printing-office staff survived the noxious fumes and fire hazards of making ink, their persons and equipment nevertheless spent much of the workday covered in the stuff.[4]

This is lucid, economical writing, pointed toward a set of important questions about the role of printers in the emergent public sphere of the early United States.

Now compare Pasley's to this description, by the journalist Adam Hochschild, of James Phillips's London print shop, hard by the Bank of England, where a crucial meeting of Granville Sharp's antislavery society took place in May, 1787:

> Type would be sitting in slanted wooden trays with compartments for the different letters; the compositors who lined it up into rows, letter by letter, would be working, as the day ended, by the light of tallow candles whose smoke, over the decades, would blacken the ceiling. . . . Around the sides of the room, stacks of dried sheets, the latest antislavery book or Quaker tract, would await folding and binding. And finally, the most distinctive thing about an eighteenth-century print shop was its smell. To ink the type as it sat on the bed of the press, printers used a wool-stuffed leather pad with a wooden handle. Because of its high ammonia content, the most convenient solvent to rinse off the ink residue that built up on these pads was printers' urine. The pads were soaked in buckets of this, then strewn on the slightly sloping floor, where printers stepped on them as they worked, to wring them out and let the liquid drain away.[5]

Though the two passages rely on some of the same sources, Hochschild's version owes as much to Dickens as to Pasley. It is specific and transporting rather than generic and distancing. Key differences reside in the sensory details: one paragraph, three senses. Sight: the blackened ceilings, the smoking tallow candles. Touch: compositors' fingers flying over cast-iron type, the heft and texture of the wooden-handled pads, the disequilibrium of standing on that sloping floor. And of course smell: the close shop on a warm spring night reeking of piss as well as Enlightenment ideals.

These sensory details give Hochschild's scene volume. But they do more than that. The sight, feel, and smell of the shop impart a *frisson* of opposites—these are "unlikely surroundings," as Hochschild puts it, for a key moment in the transformation of humanitarian thought. Then, quickly, we're on to the substance of that meeting, an intellectual history drawn from tract literature. Sensory does not mean sensational.

3 · PLACE IT

Historians have long argued for the importance of place. Francis Parkman's timeworn dictum, *go there*, marries well with the material-culture scholar's more recent mantra, *events take place*. Great nonfiction writing honors both commandments.

In the writing of *Blindspot,* I would like to believe that our historians' commitment to place served us well. We "went there," Parkman-style, tramping through the tangled streets of Boston's North End, and setting up camp in an early 18th-century house museum, whose cramped staircases and tiny rooms with walls out of plumb became home to the characters in the novel. We couldn't possibly have understood our characters—not just their sensory lives, but the proxemics of the 18th-century port town—had we not done that kind of homework.

But the place-based writing lesson I'm referring to here is slightly different, something closer to what the young Bill Bradley once told John McPhee: "When you have played basketball for a while, you don't need to look at the basket. . . . You develop a sense of where you are."[6] Fiction requires an author to possess a constant sense of where the characters are—where, that is, besides on the page.

If a scene started on the road to the Boston Neck, and then the action went someplace else, we had to know the route, whether it took us via Washington Street or via flashback. We got a copy of John Bonner's 1764 map and "walked" it constantly. If a conversation began in the parlor but ended in the painting room, we needed to get the speakers upstairs. But having a sense of where you are doesn't require you to describe it in painful detail. It's a question of trust. To feel secure in your hands, the reader needs to know that *you* know exactly where the action in your pages is taking place, even (or especially?) if that action unfolds in other pages.

Knowing where you are concerns not just place, but position. First-person narration is particularly unforgiving in this regard: if the narrator doesn't see it, think it, read it, or overhear it, neither she nor the reader can know it. But even a first-person narrator takes in the world at more than one focal length. Some narrative junctures demand close-ups, others, crowd shots. Since we were writing a novel of 18th-century art, we thought about shifts in scale and depth of field in those terms. Some scenes needed the intimacy of a portrait by Joshua Reynolds, while others called for the teeming distance of a Hogarth engraving. As 18th-century theorists of the picturesque pointed out, the eye likes variety. So, too, the mind's eye.

4. SMILE EVERY NOW AND AGAIN

Here in the late age of "human nature," we are loath to universalize. But I'm going to risk it. *Everybody laughs,* even under Stalin or the Taliban. In sickness and health, famine and feast, war and peace, the emotional lives of human beings are multidimensional and complex. We have highs and lows, often both at once. History deserves a broader emotional range than the tight-lipped expressionless stare of a newscaster.[7]

One of *Blindspot*'s narrators couldn't manage to laugh at her plight, even when it was funny; the other had little but laughter—sometimes misplaced—with which to meet the world's travails. The chiaroscuro of his lightness and her darkness created one kind of emotional variegation. Another came from History itself. At one key juncture in the novel, two characters cross into what an 18th-century writer would have called the bower of bliss, only to discover upon waking a handbill detailing draconian new restrictions visited upon the town's slave population. With the full freedom of fiction at our disposal, we wrestled with this unseemly juxtaposition. We thought about moving up the publication of the handbill, or postponing it, anything to give our lovers the chance to bask in a rosy glow a while longer. For a fleeting moment, we considered softening the laws, so our characters didn't have to face anything quite so dark as . . . history. And then we decided to allow the emotional contradiction of pleasure and pain in the past, just as we do in the present, every time we laugh at a funeral, or weep amid plenty.

5. TURN OFF THE METRONOME

Thinking in time is the historian's master skill; years are the vertebrae of our disciplinary spine. Mathematically speaking, each year is always and ever the same, a 365 and 1/4–day whirl through the seasons and round the sun.

Yet we experience time's relentless march differentially. August sprints; February crawls. When my children were toddlers, the days felt like years, the years, like days. Life romps and rushes, outwaits and outpaces us.

Novels revel in the unevenness of human time. Fiction allows some moments to be languorous, others hectic. Each can be enchanting. A slow-moving stream of time invites reverie. Nicholson Baker's haunting and strange first novel, *The Mezzanine*, a sort of *Ulysses* in miniature, begins, "At almost one o' clock I entered the lobby of the building where I worked and turned toward the escalators," and ends, 135 pages later, "[a]t the very end of the ride" up the moving staircase to the floor above.[8]

In mystery, by contrast, time habitually flies. The calculus of the page-turner is all first derivative; speed increases at an increasing rate. "I fear that events begin to outpace my pen," confesses *Blindspot*'s compulsively candid yet unreliable male narrator—more than once.[9]

Plot-time—for all its contrivance—in some ways approximates real time, at least as physics understands it. *Pace* Stephen Hawking: time bends. History too often trudges: left foot, right foot, cradle to grave. We would serve our readers better by moving, on occasion, by way of leaps and bounds, or baby steps, just as life does.[10]

6. PLAY IT FORWARD

Though life's pace—past and present—is uneven, time's arrow moves in one direction. The shattered cup doesn't pick itself up from the floor. We know this in our bones (or, Hawking says, we deceive ourselves into believing it). Yet historians too rarely cultivate a fully operational sense of our subjects' present, and, consequently, of the irreducible contingency of their future. Staring into the past, we flatten the horizon; it's all so *then* to us. Trained to value distance, we favor the retrospective half of Kierkegaard's famous maxim: "Life . . . can only be understood backwards." Writing a novel—a novel in the realist mode, at any rate—shifts attention to the other half of the aphorism: "But it must be lived forwards."[11]

Historians understand *Blindspot*'s temporal location—the waning months of 1764—as a passage in a deepening imperial crisis that, we know, would not resolve soon or peaceably. But *Blindspot*'s narrators don't understand their lives that way at all, any more than their neighbors John Hancock and Samuel Adams could have done. Our invented Stewart Jameson sees that summer and fall as a passage in the building of his competence and the deepening of his humanity. The rocky fortunes of Boston in the wake of the French and Indian War matter a great deal to him, but the squawks of townsfolk against the Sugar and Currency Acts (passed that year) and the Stamp Tax (already anticipated) amount to little more than background noise. Around our other narrator, the twenty-year-old Fanny Easton, the circle of the present contracts still further, by dint of her age and gender and poverty. Geopolitical time means little to her. Neither character knows even remotely how the story will end—and that's just *their* story (as we defined it), never mind The American Story. Even when they sensed that they lived in Historic Times, past actors—real ones, I mean—were no less mired in the noise of the now than we are.

Granted the advantages of hindsight, historians take it upon ourselves to lend the good people of the past a hand. We pit our bifocals against their uncorrected myopia, allowing them to see a little more clearly through our eyes. Our narration cleans out their attics, pruning and purging. Keeping only the important stuff, we make their lives rather more tidy than our own. That's our job. But we need to do it carefully, lest the tidiness of our analyses lose sight of the muddle of the middle in which our subjects lived.

7. WORK IT

One of my all-time favorite books is Richard Scarry's *What Do People Do All Day?* Published in 1968, when I was five, it's still a steady seller. Like all of Scarry's work, its brilliance lies in the visual clutter of everyday life. Every page is crammed with a tangle of characters and tools and tasks showing the dense web of exchange connecting Farmer Alfalfa, Blacksmith Fox, Grocer Cat, Stitches the Tailor, and even Mommy. Lowly Worm pops up unexpectedly and always with great brio. Scarry's young reader, just past small-object fascination, barely knows where to look. (It's like Hogarth that way, with the satire dialed down a notch.)

In Scarry's busy, busy world, "Everyone is a worker."[12] Certainly the illustrator foregrounded work because the choice gave him wonderful things to draw. But he also seems to sense what many artists—including writers—know rather better than most labor historians. Work fascinates. Work matters. Work makes us human. Scarry and Vermeer, Steinbeck and Dickens, Alice Munro and Edward P. Jones: great artists wring profound beauty and epic significance from the ordinary labors that consume most of the waking hours of most people, in every past and every present.

An example: Philip Roth's *American Pastoral* is a sprawling novel about many things, ranging from love and loss in the household of Seymour Irving "Swede" Levov, the "household Apollo of the Weequahic Jews," to the seismic shifts that shook the urban United States in the 1960s. Throughout Roth's pyrotechnic changes of key and register, Newark Maid, the glove business that Levov inherited from his father, sounds a *basso ostinato*. Despite its name, Newark Maid manufactures on the margins of the American empire, in Puerto Rico. Why? Because Newark, once "the city where they manufactured everything," has lately become "the car-theft capital of the world." The work and the workers and most of the customers are gone, and the people left behind "don't know a fourchette from a thumb," Levov complains. "What's a fourchette?" our narrator asks. The Swede explains:

The part of the glove between the fingers. Those small oblong pieces between the fingers, they're die-cut along with the thumbs—those are the fourchettes. Today you've got a lot of underqualified people, probably don't know half what I knew when I was five. . . . A guy buying deerskin, which can run up to maybe three dollars and fifty cents a foot for a garment grade, he's buying this fine garment-grade deerskin to cut a little palm patch to go on a pair of ski gloves. I talked to him just the other day. A novelty part, runs about five inches by one inch, and he pays three fifty a foot where he could have paid a dollar fifty a foot and come out a long, long way ahead. You multiply this over a large order, you're talking a hundred-thousand-dollar mistake.[13]

The historian, who tends to traffic in abstractions, might rewrite this passage to highlight important themes: white flight, deindustrialization, globalization. Operating far above the ground upon which steel-toed boots trudge or the worn linoleum upon which rubber-soled white nurses' shoes squeak, we bypass the doing of work and the making of things. We want our readers to think about capitalism and democracy.

The novelist wants you to ponder those things, too. But first, he wants you to smell the glove.

8. FEEL YOUR WAY

History is work, too: the work of scavenging tattered remnants of the past. After writing *Blindspot*, that labor felt different. Which is to say, it *felt*, full stop. Having imagined an early American life from the inside out, I found myself allowing Intuition to accompany me into the archives. Sometimes Empathy pulled up a chair in the reading room, forcing Detachment and Skepticism to scoot over a mite.

Thus hemmed in on every side of a long wooden table in the attic library of the Royal Academy of Arts, which sits just far enough off Piccadilly to mute the street noise of central London, I recently read Sir Joshua Reynolds's sitter books, twenty-six duodecimo volumes spanning the decades from 1757 to 1790. Among those who study 18th-century culture, they're a well-known source. Curators use them to document the provenance and prices of the grand-manner portraits that took Sir Joshua to the very pinnacle of the European art scene. Cultural historians have used the volumes to map Reynolds's social circle, which included Samuel Johnson, Hester Thrale, David Garrick, Joseph Banks, and others of equal glitter and distinction.

I read the Reynolds sitter books in the course of researching a new project on American artists in Georgian London. *Blindspot* was done, but I couldn't quite shake the consciousness of our characters, Jamie and Fanny, who had struggled to make a living of art in Boston in 1764. Reynolds—His Majesty's

Principal Painter in Ordinary, the founder and longtime president of the Royal Academy—wasn't struggling. The sitter books document the whirl of polite society: audiences with the greater gentry, afternoons in coffeehouses, evenings at the opera. Reynolds's self-portraits likewise fashion the artist as a visionary genius, all eyes and mind, clean hands.

But Reynolds's sitter books are the household accounts of a preindustrial artisan. Every year, he painted like a house afire in May and June. In December, his appointments petered out just after noon. Why? Because, as I learned in the two o'clock dusk of that London winter, the light began to fail. The great Reynolds, like everyone else of his place and time, was a slave to the harsh diurnal realities of northern Europe. Lords and ladies beseeched his services; King George and Queen Charlotte sat for him in 1779; Reynolds commanded the muses from great heights. But the sitter books show something quite different: a working man whose social elevation might be compared, at many junctures, to the status of a servant in livery. He waited on ladies and gentlemen. He booked appointments with their children and even their pets, as he did in the fall of 1788, when he attended "2 dog[s] of Mr. Maclin."[14]

The sitter books also contain many entries, a handful every year, that read simply, "Infant." No parents, no servants, no family name, just "infant." Who were these babies? Art historians offer one answer: they were the subjects not of portraits—portraits have patrons, and patrons, even child-patrons, have surnames—but of Reynolds's "fancy pictures," little genre paintings like *Cupid as a Link Boy* (1774) and the kitschy allegory, *The Infant Academy* (1782). I'm as curious about fancy pictures and their buyers as the next scholar of the period. But the sometime novelist wanted to know something quite different: *Dear God, who were these babies?*

A different collection in the Royal Academy, the letters of Reynolds's apprentice and later biographer James Northcote, offers a tantalizing clue. "[C]oncerning drawing from naked women [it] is really true," he told his brother, "this is much disapproved of by some good folks."

> miss Reynolds says it is a great pitty that it should be a necessary part in the education of a painter but she draws all her figures cloath'd except infants which she often paints from life[,] some begger womans child[,] which is laid naked on a pillow or in the mothers arms.[15]

"Miss Reynolds" was Sir Joshua's younger sister, a forty-two year old spinster at the time of this exchange with Northcote. An ambitious painter in her own right, Fanny Reynolds could have been Shakespeare's sister, in Virginia Woolf's terms. That is, her gender defined the expression of her talents. Women couldn't study life drawing, which severely hampered their training in anatomy, and thus their chances at commercial success. Hers is a poignant story, versions of which feminist art historians have told.[16]

I have never read a line about the babies. *"Some begger womans child . . . laid naked on a pillow or in the mothers arms."* What might the pious, well-fed Miss Reynolds have offered a beggar woman to induce her to step inside the Reynolds's Leicester Square manse in the icy December of 1771? Was a farthing a fair price, or a cup of broth, or did the mother make the trade for warmth alone? These are, perhaps, a novelist's questions. But they deserve a historian's answers, answers leading to a richer, more nuanced portrait of the complex economy of culture.

9. ONLY CONNECT

"Only connect!" runs E. M. Forster's famous epigraph in *Howard's End*. The novel elaborates: "Only connect the prose and the passion, and both will be exalted, and human love will be seen at its height. Live in fragments no longer."[17]

For decades, scholars have generally followed the opposite impulse: only distinguish, only divide. Forster is out; L. P. Hartley is in—at least in the form of one remembered line from this forgotten author's forgotten novel, *The Go-Between:* "The past is a foreign country: they do things differently there."[18] We have honed our skepticism of broad claims about the so-called human condition on the whetstone of poststructuralism and its descendants. Tired of wholeness, we like the cutting edge; we ask our students to live and work along it. And to be sure, it has its virtues. Newly sensitive to the social construction of elements of life once considered fundamental to our species (when they were considered at all), we have discovered the impress of history and culture upon the emotions, the mind, the body, the self itself.

Trained at the very height of the poststructuralist moment, I cast my lot with the skeptics. I wouldn't, couldn't have it any other way. Yet the recovering novelist in me worries that we've thrown out the humanistic baby—that beggar woman's baby, posed naked on a pillow by Sir Joshua Reynolds's fireside—with the Enlightenment bathwater. Whither the sympathy in our science?

The past is a foreign country, yes, and we who study the paltry remains of various days are but curious travelers along its broadest byways. Yet like all good tourists, we would do well to remember that the past is not just a place where we pause to gawk while loading up on souvenirs. Real people lived there, people who resembled us in some ways, if not in others.

History is not a séance. Groping like drunks in the dark, we're doomed to get people wrong, as that great 20th-century American historian Philip Roth laments: "You get them wrong before you meet them, while you're anticipating meeting them; you get them wrong while you're with them; and then you go home to tell somebody else about the meeting and get them all wrong again." But what's the alternative? Precisely "what are we to do about this terribly significant business of *other people?*"[19]

The writer, the painter, the scholar: all of us make a living pressing that terribly significant business into two dimensions. My season as an accidental novelist reawakened the futile, insatiable hunger for a third.

NOTES

1. Hilary Mantel, *Wolf Hall* (Henry Holt, 2009), 25.

2. The *Journal of American History* recently published a lively round table on "The Senses in American History." See *JAH* 95 (2008): 378–451. On the return to phenomenology in historical scholarship more broadly, see Geoff Eley, *A Crooked Line: From Cultural History to the History of Society* (University of Michigan Press, 2005).

3. Marcel Proust, *Swann's Way* [1913] (Dover Thrift Edition, 2002), 37–40.

4. Jeffrey L. Pasley, *"The Tyranny of Printers": Newspaper Politics in the Early American Republic* (University Press of Virginia, 2001), 25.

5. Adam Hochschild, *Bury the Chains: Prophets and Rebels in the Fight to Free an Empire's Slaves* (Houghton Mifflin, 2005), 96.

6. John McPhee, *A Sense of Where You Are* (Farrar, Strauss & Giroux, 1965), 22.

7. Of course, the discourse and expression of emotions, too, are historical; see, e.g., Sarah A. Knott, *Sensibility and the American Revolution* (University of North Carolina Press, 2008); Nicole Eustace, *Passion Is the Gale: Emotion, Power, and the Coming of the American Revolution* (University of North Carolina Press, 2008); and too many volumes by Peter N. Stearns.

8. Nicholson Baker, *The Mezzanine* (Grove Press, 1988), 3, 135, 130.

9. *Blindspot*, 139, 411.

10. A young David Hackett Fischer labeled our tendency toward "misplaced temporal literalism" the "chronic fallacy." I like to think this is a double entendre. See Fischer, *Historians' Fallacies* (Harper & Row, 1970), 152–54.

11. Kierkegaard's diary, quoted in Michael J. Strawser, *Both/And: Reading Kierkegaard—From Irony to Edification* (Fordham University Press, 1996), 17.

12. Richard Scarry, *What Do People Do All Day?* (Random House, 1968), 6.

13. Philip Roth, *American Pastoral* (Houghton Mifflin, 1997), 4, 24, 27.

14. Reynolds sitter books, Royal Academy, London. REY 1/25 (1788), entry for 9/29.

15. James Northcote to Samuel Northcote, 21 December 1771, Northcote Papers, Item 7, Royal Academy, London.

16. See, e.g., Angela Rosenthal, "She's Got the Look! Eighteenth-Century Female Portrait Painters and the Psychology of a Potentially 'Dangerous Employment,'" in Joanna Woodall, ed., *Portraiture: Facing the Subject* (Manchester University Press, 1997), 147–66.

17. E. M. Forster, *Howard's End* (Knopf, 1921), 214.

18. L. P. Hartley, *The Go-Between* [1953] (NYRB Classics, 2002), 17. Cultural historian David Lowenthal took Hartley's line as the title to his powerful book about the historical construction of history and memory. See Lowenthal, *The Past Is a Foreign Country* (Cambridge University Press, 1986).

19. Roth, *American Pastoral*, 35.

John Demos

"History in the Head, History from the Heart: A Personal Minifesto"
(2016, previously unpublished)

First, in the 1960s, there was "the new social history." The point was to
shift quite drastically from what till then had served as the scholarly mainstream. No more of the old, essentially reportorial, form; instead, hard-
headed analysis and interpretation. No more wishy-washy "impression-
ism"; instead, systematic inquiry. No more Great Men doing Great Deeds;
instead, ordinary people and everyday life. And no more holding history
apart as its own sacred academic space; instead, beg, borrow, or steal
from other disciplines. It was heady stuff in more than one sense: brain
work, highly cerebral, dispassionate, "objective." But as all this rose high
during the next twenty years, doubts began to emerge. People—all the
living, breathing realities of past experience—had seemed to fade from
view. Moreover, the writing of history had become formalized, sometimes
technical—not to say, as general readers often did, unduly dry. Eventually,
the pendulum swung in a different direction. The latest "new" became
narrative, including a strong concern with literary form. Historical study
has long been seen as combining art with science. Science had a good
run; now it's time for art to take a turn.

What makes history—the writing of history—artful? The question has
dogged me for a long time. I knew from an early age (twelve?), that I wanted to
be a writer, and, insofar as possible, an "artful" one. My first adventures in putting pen to paper—no word processors way back then, even typewriters seemed
daunting—went toward fiction. Like so many other young wannabes, I aimed
for a truth that might come from inside my gut and from personal experience.

It didn't happen as hoped. For one thing, writing *dialogue* seemed maddeningly hard; my efforts that way sounded awfully tinny. And making good *plots* was equally difficult; how does one ever create a fresh, out-of-whole-cloth story? I just couldn't do it. Eventually, while falling back from these challenges, I settled on history. No call there for invented dialogue; quoting from the sources can be a kind of substitute. Moreover, in history the plots come ready-made.

But I have to admit that—to the present day—history stands at the bottom (fourth) in my rank-order of writing modes. Just above it comes what some call "creative nonfiction." (Perhaps we could define that as nonfiction that isn't about the past.) Second is fiction-writing, novels and short stories. And first is poetry, the highest and clearly the most sublime of all.

Still, we can do well enough with history. It has some parts—and presents certain opportunities—that converge with the other three. Foremost is simply this: the (re)creation of an unseen world. Each of the four works by the same kind of invisible magic—searching, picturing, molding, embellishing, finishing—history no less than the others.

In practice, history writing divides within itself, as the others do not. Think of two poles, placed as opposites. One we can call history-in-the-head, the other history-from-the heart. To be sure, there is a broad spectrum stretching between them, including many mixed positions. But the poles are worth examining in their "essential" state. Taken together, they frame our enterprise; no single work escapes them entirely. Head History is the product of mentation—of cognition—of intellect going full throttle. Whereas Heart History runs, first and last, on emotion—empathy—intuition—imagination.

The point of reference, in either case, is two-sided: reader as well as writer. Heart History will appeal chiefly to heart-centered readers, Head History to head-minded ones. No doubt some reversals are possible; for example, it could be that much cognitive effort (in the head) is needed to create a work whose effects fall largely on the emotional side. But these are second-order questions. It's the first order—the nature, and usefulness, of the distinction itself—that especially invites attention.

I have a list of nine differences between Head and Heart history, nine ways of setting them in contrast. It's not systematic—it's more like a grocery list, a little of this and a little of that. The list has grown over the years, in response to my own shifting priorities. I'm tempted to say that my head led me toward the act of history-making, while my heart, following behind and feeling a bit resentful, made sure that the history I wrote didn't wind up seeming too categorical and definitive. Then, as time went along, my heart claimed a larger and larger place.

The first of the differences is operational style. For Head History, this is *argument,* in a simple and straightforward sense of the term. There's a question that provides the starting point. Evidence is then arranged around it, typically as a line of progression, so as to yield a conclusion. The actual process of arrangement is crucial here; it involves what we call logic—and induction—and verification—even "proof." The most rigorously scientific versions of Head History include matters like hypothesis-testing, replication, and counterfactuals. Indeed, some (not all) Head History mimics science, or—to say it more strongly—aims at *becoming* science.

By contrast, the operational style of Heart History stresses *evocation.* This, too, is a summary term; what it means is a sustained effort to summon feeling states. All of us have a repertoire of these, liable to shape our experience as both creators and recipients of history writing. And they are key to Heart History. Their circuits go (metaphorically speaking) around the brain—or, maybe it's more accurate to say, are deep inside the cortex, and not part of any gray matter at all. They lean heavily on memory, and thus on previous personal experience. They also depend on empathy, on the ability to put oneself in the shoes (and the heart) of another. (This, too, does not seem to be a matter of brainpower.)

The second difference involves subject matter: what I'd like to call *structure,* on one hand, and *texture,* on the other. Head History, at least as practiced for the past forty years, is preeminently concerned with structural questions—how things are put together, how they work—power relationships, hegemonies, roles and functions, all manner of causes and effects. In the social sciences this is called a "systems" approach. Practically speaking, "system" means structure.

Texture, on the other hand, involves how things feel—how they look, and taste, and yield to touch (or not). Texture is, almost by definition, closer to the stuff of experience than structure. It's less abstract, more tangible; it evokes what people actually go through in their very own lives. It's more on the surface than structure; and it's more concerned with outcomes than with underlying motives and causes. It includes the whole time-travel excitement of reimagining the past: what it was like to be alive in 1400 or 1750, in ancient Greece or medieval China or pre-Columbian America. It is, therefore, no accident that many exemplary works of Heart History—especially the most fully narrative ones—pay close attention to all sorts of experiential details: the weather at particular moments, landscapes, material realities of every sort—in short, all that together adds up to life on-the-ground. To say it again: the whole textural dimension of being in the world of the past.

This leads quite directly to a third point of difference—in the matter of sources. Evidence about the past comes to us in two forms: texts (written words) and objects (what we call material culture). Texts belong, first and foremost, to the realm of Head History. The recorded words of historical actors express ideas and attitudes; these, in turn, prompt ideas and attitudes—and still more words—in the minds of historians. It's brain work—cognitive activity—on both sides.

Objects, by contrast, speak to us in unmediated, and visceral, ways. The musty ambience of an old farmhouse; the stately form of a pre-modern armchair; the stark lines of an early folk portrait; the forbidding heft of ancient hearthware: the process of confronting such things—in all their "thingness"—is of another sort entirely. The heart skips a little, the throat clutches; the brain, for its part, may temporarily recoil.

Certain manuscript documents present both sides—the textual and the material—together. Consider: A New England townsman, writing in his diary early in the eighteenth century, notes his wife's passing in this fashion: "my Dear Wife Died about half an hour before Sunrise." That's all: ten words, a spare recording of information, nothing more. One might wonder about the strength of the feelings involved. To be sure, the modifier "Dear" seems an emotional touch, but could also be read as formulaic. However, to *see* the same in the original manuscript leaves a different impression. The words enlarge and sprawl across the page; moreover, they are framed by a thin pen line. And there are stains that might well—who knows?—be tears. In short, the material aspects of the document—the paper, the ink, and especially the lettering—express the diarist's heart, and are experienced as such by a reader. Whereas the words themselves come from, and move toward, the head.

A fourth difference involves nothing less than fundamental goals and purposes—the why-we-do-it, the what-is-History-good-for, range of questions. I have suggested elsewhere that all historical inquiry represents—at least as potential, if not achieved, result—some combination of three quite distinct epistemological levels. The first, and most immediately recognizable, is the level of the *particular*—in short, things specific to a single time and place, with a clearly identified group of actors and events. The Peloponnesian War; the Black Death; the evolution of the Monroe Doctrine; the Cherokee trail of tears;

the love-life of Thomas Jefferson and Sally Hemings: it can be anything at all, as long as it's "particular." No doubt there is much to be said for this type of closely focused study; sometimes we undersell it. But most of us probably feel that it's not finally enough, in and of itself. So we push on and try to extract something else from it—something broader and deeper, something that looks more like a conclusion, or a generalization—which is why this second level can reasonably be called the *general*. We aim here not just at the specifics of the Monroe Doctrine, but how national diplomacy worked in the era of the Early Republic; not simply the details of Jefferson and Hemings, but race relations in the world around them.

I think a good many historians might be inclined to stop there. You take quite a lot of the "particular" and throw in some of the "general"—and that's the basic package, the sum of our hopes and aspirations. That was my own attitude, too, for a good many years. Yet, lurking somewhere in the background, I could sense (just barely) a third level—of issues and meanings that transcend any given historical period or group, and embrace the entire "human condition." In short: not just the "general," but the truly *generic*. Again, for a long time I assumed that historians stop with the "general," and perforce leave the "generic" to poets, novelists, philosophers, theologians, and their ilk. But now it all seems quite different. I've come to think that we, too, should claim a piece of that action—that infinitely broad, and ineffably deep, action—no less than any others.

This change was closely tied to the process of writing my book *The Unredeemed Captive*, with research begun in 1985 and publication in 1994. The subtitle of the book is *A Family Story from Early America*. And, on the level of the "particular," it seems to be exactly that: the story of a single family—the Williams family of eighteenth-century Massachusetts, with a branch in the Kahnawake Mohawk community in Canada. But I hoped, from the start, that it could serve a much wider purpose, could offer useful perspectives on Puritan family life (and, to a lesser extent, Native American family life) writ large. Moreover, as the project went along, I felt—seemingly in my blood and bones I felt—something else starting to happen. The project was touching me personally, in a way that I hadn't before experienced so directly. One thing led to another, and I could see more and more "generic" connections, although these didn't come fully clear until after the book was finished and in print. While sitting one evening in my living room, and reading a heart-breaking *New Yorker* article about the kidnapping of a young girl in California, I came across this passage:

There is something about kidnapping that retains a unique horror. It is, of course, the ultimate horror for parents, for it accomplishes in a single hour a realization that, under normal circumstances, is the work of years and years: the realization that *our children have a fate that is different from our own.* [emphasis added]

I read that, and broke into tears. There it was in a nutshell, the "generic" meaning of my own book, for sure: separation, within families, and across generations. Some readers and reviewers had gotten the point already. I recall a time when a very perceptive graduate student stopped me in the hallway to say a nice word or two about the book, and then commented, "It's a Dad's book, isn't it?" She was spot-on; my children were just then at the point of going through college, and working out their "different fates"—and I was feeling the change very acutely.

This last, about the three different "levels," is a digression from my theme of Head versus Heart History. So now to reconnect: Although any given project has the potential to include all three, in practice one of them may be powerfully emphasized, while the others are downplayed (or even excluded altogether). On the whole, Head History tilts strongly toward the "general"— toward underlying trends and tendencies in one or another place and period. Whereas Heart History offers especially strong opportunities to invoke the "generic": that's the chief point in my digressing. There is something intrinsic to emotion-driven work that carries it beyond specific locations. Emotion is, after all, a unifying element in all human experience. Put differently (and in the words of a leading theorist): "Affects are the primary motives of man." People in all venues and historical eras draw on the same limited, biologically rooted, affective repertoire. A smile is a smile everywhere. Tears are tears everywhere. Joy is joy everywhere. Nothing, in short, is more universal—more truly generic. No wonder, then, that Heart History opens the door to this broadest of human domains.

A fifth difference is nothing more, or less, than prose expression. Head History can be—as general readers often attest—awfully dry. In some cases, it is not only that, but inaccessible, too. A prime example is what used to be called "the new social history." This line of work, highly fashionable in the 1970s and '80s, was in many respects a major advance on more traditional scholarship. However, the prose it fostered has been justly faulted for various shortcomings: jargon, excessive abstraction, and, at least sometimes, sheer literary ineptitude (right down to the level of awkwardly constructed sentences, poorly chosen words, and the like). In truth, there is no necessary linkage here; quite a few works of Head History avoid jargon and make their case in at least relatively graceful form. Some are even better than that; one can think of examples to which the word "elegant" could certainly be applied. But, by and large, the predominant aim in the writing of Head History is *effective communication* of research findings. Writing becomes a way to get your point across; it's a vehicle, a conveyance, a means to some further end. It should never get in the way of the point; it's secondary, and subordinate, to the point. You do want to be clear, you do want to be accurate, you do want to be incisive—all this, as I say, to facilitate communication. Maybe you can be eloquent, too—but just as a flourish (if it happens at all). This, I submit, is the limit of what many historians have in mind when they speak of "good writing."

With Heart History the situation is very different. Here writing becomes vitally important—central—even primary. Nothing matters more than the way the words fall on the page, from one line to the next. Simply put, the goal is artful writing, "literary" writing—which involves quite a bit more than straightforward communication. A historian trying to operate in this way—or, for that matter, any writer trying to operate in this way—pays a lot of attention to issues of plotting and framing, to pacing and cadence, to pitch and tone. He or she tries to devise images, as a way to create an ambience, a mood, a "scene." Typically, this means creating visual, and auditory, and other sensory effects (alongside the primarily cognitive ones).

These five points of comparison—operational style, subject matter, evidence, basic purpose, and prose expression—capture much of the difference between Head and Heart History. But several additional contrasts seem worth at least a mention.

One is what might be called the method of knowing that each type embeds. For Head History this would be *induction*—unfolding a chain of discrete parts, each one of them linked directly to its immediate neighbors before and behind. For Heart History it is *insight*—responding to flashes of connection and understanding that may have a stand-alone quality.

A further, and related, point involves the style of reasoning. With Head History it's basically *linear*. The constituent parts proceed consistently forward, although not necessarily straight ahead. There can be zigs and zags, but no loose ends or unresolved forks. With Heart History, things can move in a *conditional* way; an "if . . . then" sequence may organize the whole. Indeed, the predominant mood may be interrogative, with content presented largely by way of questions, or the posing of alternatives.

Yet another contrast goes toward the experience of readers. In the case of Head History, the *destination* is key (that is, the point at which one ultimately arrives); without some form of conclusion, a project risks failure. In Heart History, it's the *journey* that matters as much as, or even more than, the endpoint. Put differently, the views en route provide their own justification, quite apart from the matter of reaching a terminus.

A final point involves dimension and direction. Historical projects can be either "vertical," with change over time at the center, or "horizontal," where the focus is a single moment. (In this regard a "moment" may span years or even decades, so long as change does *not* appear as a main feature.) Put differently: the first type is "motion picture" history, the second its "snapshot" counterpart—or, more informally, "from-to" versus "age of." Head History inclines (though not always) to the former, with change as its chief concern. Whereas Heart History shows definite leanings toward the latter. To be sure, these are tendencies, no more. The difference appears clearly enough in actual practice, but isn't based on any inherent logic.

I considered two other possible distinctions, but ultimately found that they didn't map onto Head and Heart History. For one, there is no clear linkage to interpretation versus description. To be sure, Head History seems to favor interpretation, but it can—and sometimes does—simply describe things. Heart History revels in describing, but may also aim for interpreting—albeit by its own, rather special route. Second, there is also no analysis-versus-narrative opposition here. I'd like especially to argue that Heart History doesn't always take a narrative form. It does so quite often, but, again, there is no intrinsic connection.

So what do Head and Heart History look like at their best? Let me offer a couple of examples, my personal favorites. Both come from early American history (my own specialty); both are well known, even famous. As a prime instance of Head History, I nominate *Salem Possessed: The Social Origins of Witchcraft*, by Paul Boyer and Stephen Nissenbaum, a book that is now four decades old but remains a classic. To be sure, it's had critics, including some who regard it as fundamentally mistaken about its subject (the Salem witch hunt of 1692). But that's not the issue here. What has most impressed me about the book, through several readings over many years, is its architecture, its mode of reasoning, the way the pieces unfold and are made to fit together. It starts with description—a kind of opening panorama—but then quickly turns to interpretation. From the entire Salem community, it moves toward particular families, then particular individuals, then the inner workings of a single individual at the center of the story. And it's an *argument* book, through and through. Carefully framed questions organize it at every point, and drive it toward a strong and arresting conclusion.

My prime example of Heart History is Laurel Ulrich's *A Midwife's Tale*, a book that isn't basically narrative but does, I think, meet all the criteria I've included on that side of my list. First and foremost, it's a work of great depth and dimensionality. It didn't become widely admired because a lot of readers cared greatly about midwifery in the era of the early republic. Rather, its fame (including a Pulitzer and other prizes) is for the way it presents the life struggles of a singular character, the Maine midwife Martha Ballard. "Singular" Ballard was, but at the same time "generic"—in the sense that we can all relate to the challenges she faced, the difficulties she endured (as Ulrich brilliantly presents them). It's a book about integrity, courage, the refusal of despair—what might even be called "virtue."

Finally, I'll mention a third book, somewhat more recent than the others: Linda Gordon's *The Great Arizona Orphan Abduction*. This one is interesting because it's a hybrid book; it tries, in a very out-front way, to combine Head and Heart History. (The basic principle is alternating chapters, first one kind, then the other.) I suspect this is a developing trend—experiments in different forms of "hybridization"—in short, trying to have it *both* ways.

Indeed, Gordon's book raises the question: why *not* value Head and Heart History equally, and try to write them both simultaneously? Another distinction I might have noticed earlier, perhaps an unfortunate one, is that Head History is tightly associated with the academy, while Heart History tends more toward the popular. These are bad raps. A compelling argument, passionately and eloquently delivered, can be exhilarating for any kind of reader, and even the eggheads of academe have some sort of emotional life (most do, at any rate). The distinctions I've laid out in no way make Head and Heart History incompatible. Pick up almost any work of creative nonfiction, and you're likely to find some passages that argue, and some that evoke, some that are structural and some that are textural, some that focus on information and some that set a mood. Why couldn't history writing be similarly limber?

If I were a fiction writer, I might end with an imagined dialogue between a Head Historian and a Heart Historian. (No chance.) If I were a Head Historian, then I'd offer a clear conclusion, which you could subsequently convey to others as the point of this essay. If I were exclusively a Heart Historian, then I'd perhaps end with a question, in the hope of provoking an emotional reaction as you consider what kind of writing you want to do next. At this stage of my career, though, I hope I've earned the right to live on the edge.

CONTRIBUTORS

JONATHAN SPENCE, Sterling Professor emeritus at Yale University, is the author of many books on the history of China.

ROBERT ROSENSTONE, professor of history emeritus at the California Institute of Technology, has written widely on American history, especially in relation to the visual arts.

SIMON SCHAMA, a University Professor at Columbia University, is a historian of Europe and the fine arts, and something of a television personality.

STELLA TILLYARD is an independent scholar, whose writings include cultural history, art history, and fiction.

SAIDIYA HARTMAN, a professor at Columbia University, writes on African-American history and culture and the practice of critical theory.

WENDY WARREN, a social historian with a focus on slavery and incarceration, teaches at Princeton University.

STEPHEN BERRY, professor of history at the University of Georgia, is the author or editor of several books on the antebellum and Civil War–era American South.

PAUL A. KRAMER, associate professor of history at Vanderbilt University, writes on modern American history, especially its transnational dimension.

CRAIG HARLINE, a professor at Brigham Young University, is the author of several books on religious history, especially in the era of the Protestant Reformation.

AMY READING, an independent scholar with a doctorate in American studies, writes creative nonfiction on topics in American cultural history.

JILL LEPORE, the David Woods Kemper '41 Professor of American History at Harvard University, is the author of twelve books (so far) and also writes regularly for the New Yorker.

JONATHAN HOLLOWAY, currently provost at Northwestern University, is a historian of African-American experience in the post-Emancipation era.

JAMES GOODMAN, editor of the journal *Rethinking History* and author of several works of history, teaches history and creative writing at Rutgers University–Newark.

LOUIS P. MASUR, Distinguished Professor at Rutgers University, has written histories of American politics, music, photography, and baseball.

AARON SACHS, a professor at Cornell University, writes about American cultural and environmental history, and teaches courses on those subjects as well as on historical writing.

JANE KAMENSKY, professor of history at Harvard University and director of the Schlesinger Library on the History of Women in America, is the author of books on American cultural history, gender history, and art history.

JOHN DEMOS, an emeritus professor at Yale University, is a social historian of early America, with a special interest in narrative.

CREDITS

Some of the selections are published here with all of their citations, but that wasn't possible in every case: sometimes the scholarly apparatus was just too involved for us to reproduce it efficiently. Additionally, we were unable to include any images, even though a few of our authors (Schama, Hartman, and Holloway) did make use of some powerful visual material. We hope that the affected authors will accept our apologies and ultimately agree that even though their work does not appear here in full, its spirit and its artfulness are certainly present. We also hope that readers will consult the originals for the full experience, especially where we have offered only an excerpt, and, indeed, that you will go beyond our selections and explore all the other writings of these worthy authors.

Books (UK) Canada, a division of Penguin Random House Canada Limited. All rights reserved.

"Prologue" from *Aristocrats: Caroline, Emily, Louisa, and Sarah Lennox, 1740–1832*, by Stella Tillyard. For the UK and Commonwealth countries: Reprinted by permission of The Random House Group Limited, © 1994, originally published by Chatto and Windus. For all other parts of the world: Reprinted by permission of Farrar, Straus and Giroux, copyright © 1994 by Stella Tillyard.

"Lose Your Mother" from *Lose Your Mother,* by Saidiya Hartman. Copyright © 2007 by Saidiya Hartman. Reprinted by permission of Farrar, Straus and Giroux. South Asian rights granted by Navayana Publishing Private Limited, New Delhi, India.

Wendy Warren, "'The Cause of Her Grief': The Rape of a Slave in Early New England," from the *Journal of American History,* published by the Organization of American Historians. Reproduced with permission of the Organization of American Historians via Copyright Clearance Center.

Stephen Berry, "The Historian as Death Investigator," from *Weirding the War: Stories from the Civil War's Ragged Edges,* edited by Stephen Berry, copyright © 2011 by the University of Georgia Press.

Paul A. Kramer, "The Importance of Being Turbaned," copyright © 2011 by the *Antioch Review,* Inc. First appeared in the *Antioch Review,* Vol. 69, No. 2 (Spring 2011), pp. 208–21. Reprinted by permission of the *Antioch Review.*

Excerpt from *Conversions: Two Family Stories from the Reformation and Modern America,* by Craig Harline, New Haven, Conn.: Yale University Press, copyright © 2011 by Craig Harline. Used by permission of Yale University Press.

"Chapter Two: Benjamin Franklin's Disciples" from *The Mark Inside: A Perfect Swindle, a Cunning Revenge, and a Small History of the Big Con,* by Amy Reading, copyright © 2012 by Amy Reading. Used by permission of Alfred A. Knopf, an imprint of the Knopf Doubleday Publishing Group, a division of Penguin Random House LLC. All rights reserved. Any third party use of this material, outside of this publication, is prohibited. Interested parties must apply directly to Penguin Random House LLC for permission. Used by permission of Writers House LLC acting as agent for the author.

"All About Erections" from *The Mansion of Happiness: A History of Life and Death,* by Jill Lepore, copyright © 2012 by Jill Lepore. Used by permission of Alfred A. Knopf, an imprint of the Knopf Doubleday Publishing Group, a division of Penguin Random House LLC. All rights reserved. Any third party use of this material, outside of this publication, is prohibited. Interested parties must apply directly to Penguin Random House LLC for permission. Used by permission of the author and her agency, Janklow and Nesbit Associates LLC.

Excerpt from *Jim Crow Wisdom: Memory and Identity in Black America Since 1940,* by Jonathan Scott Holloway. Copyright © 2013 by the University of North Carolina Press. Used by permission of the publisher, www.uncpress.org.